M000287739

Cathe Louis

Golf Course Irrigation

ENVIRONMENTAL DESIGN AND MANAGEMENT PRACTICES

James Barrett
Brian Vinchesi
Robert Dobson
Paul Roche
David Zoldoske

John Wiley & Sons, Inc.

This book is printed on acid-free paper. ∞

Copyright © 2003 by John Wiley & Sons, Inc. All rights reserved

Published by John Wiley & Sons, Inc., Hoboken, New Jersey
Published simultaneously in Canada

No part of this publication may be reproduced, stored in a retrieval system, or transmitted in any form or by any means, electronic, mechanical, photocopying, recording, scanning, or otherwise, except as permitted under Section 107 or 108 of the 1976 United States Copyright Act, without either the prior written permission of the Publisher, or authorization through payment of the appropriate per-copy fee to the Copyright Clearance Center, Inc., 222 Rosewood Drive, Danvers, MA 01923, (978) 750-8400, fax (978) 750-4470, or on the web at www.copyright.com. Requests to the Publisher for permission should be addressed to the Permissions Department, John Wiley & Sons, Inc., 111 River Street, Hoboken, NJ 07030, (201) 748-6011, fax (201) 748-6008, e-mail: permcoordinator@wiley.com.

Limit of Liability/Disclaimer of Warranty: While the publisher and author have used their best efforts in preparing this book, they make no representations or warranties with respect to the accuracy or completeness of the contents of this book and specifically disclaim any implied warranties of merchantability or fitness for a particular purpose. No warranty may be created or extended by sales representatives or written sales materials. The advice and strategies contained herein may not be suitable for your situation. You should consult with a professional where appropriate. Neither the publisher nor author shall be liable for any loss of profit or any other commercial damages, including but not limited to special, incidental, consequential, or other damages.

For general information on our other products and services or for technical support, please contact our Customer Care Department within the United States at (800) 762-2974, outside the United States at (317) 572-3993 or fax (317) 572-4002.

Wiley also publishes its books in a variety of electronic formats. Some content that appears in print may not be available in electronic books. For more information about Wiley products, visit our website at www.wiley.com.

Library of Congress Cataloging-in-Publication Data

Golf course irrigation : environmental design and management practices / James Barrett ... [et al.].
    p. cm.
Includes index.
  ISBN 0-471-14830-X (Cloth)
1. Golf courses—Irrigation. 2. Golf courses—Design and construction. I. Barrett, James, 1951–
  GV975 .G565 2003
  796.352'06'8—dc21   2002014439

Printed in the United States of America
10 9 8 7 6 5 4 3 2 1

Contents

6

Construction Management

7

Installation

8

Conservation   413

Glossary   419

Appendix: Tables and Charts   423

Standards   439

Index   441

Preface

There are approximately 17,000 golf courses in the United States alone; more than 300 new ones opened in each of the years from 1991 to 2001. According to the National Golf Foundation, more than 26,000,000 Americans play the game on a regular basis. U.S. golfers spend $22.2 billion per year in equipment purchases and fees.[1] U.S. golf courses spend $8.4 billion per year on maintenance.[2] Golf courses in the United States occupy 2500 square miles,[3] and irrigate approximately 1.3 million acres. U.S. golf courses consume more than 476 billion gallons of water annually.[4] Efficient irrigation is vital to the success of golf course operations. It is equally important to the national and international efforts to efficiently manage water and power.

Golf course irrigation systems range from simple hose outlets for portable sprinklers at greens to elaborate layouts with wall-to-wall coverage by pop-up heads, multiple pump stations, and highly sophisticated automatic control systems. The vast majority of existing systems in the United States are automatic, as are most of the new ones being installed. The cost of materials and installation for an 18-hole automatic system can range from $400,000 to more than $2,000,000.

Regardless of its scope or cost, an irrigation system is the single most important maintenance tool available to the golf course superintendent. The condition of the course has an obvious and direct effect on the success and bottom line of a golf facility, not to mention the effect it can have on the status of the superintendent's employment. The lack of a reliable and efficient irrigation system severely limits the superintendent's ability to produce playing conditions of the highest quality.

Competition among golf facilities to attract players is currently fueling a movement to improve all aspects of courses. In recent years there has also been an increasing demand by players for improved aesthetics and playing conditions on golf courses. This is probably due in large part to the fact that American golfers have been watching televised tournaments for nearly forty years. Tournament courses, particularly those used for the majors, are specially prepared for three years in advance. In the weeks immediately preceding a tournament, and during the event itself, extraordinary (and, some would say, outrageous) maintenance procedures are undertaken to ensure that the course looks and plays the best it possibly can.

Few, if any, courses can afford these extreme measures on a year-round basis, and turfgrass cannot survive for more than a few weeks under tournament conditions anyway. Nonetheless, golfers are demanding optimum conditions at the courses they play on a regular basis.

The endeavor to raise the quality of a course parallels a superintendent's ongoing efforts to be environmentally responsible and to conserve water and energy by all means possible. There is a finite supply of fresh water on the planet. Ninety-seven percent of the world's water is in the salt oceans. The remaining 3 percent is fresh water, but two-thirds of that is tied up in glaciers and polar ice caps. Therefore, only 1 percent of all water on the planet is available for all of humankind's use.

There are already shortages in many areas, and the mushrooming world population will continually increase pressure on the existing supply of fresh water. Although golf is not a big consumer of water in comparison with agriculture or manufacturing, it is still a significant user and a highly visible one. It is absolutely imperative that superintendents, equipment manufacturers, consultants, and system designers take all possible measures to eliminate the waste of water and optimize its use.

The same concerns apply to electric power. The application of unnecessary or excessive amounts of water and/or pressure results in a parallel waste of electric power at the pump station. Unnecessary use of power not only contributes to the frequent brownouts and outages experienced in summer months, but its generation also requires consumption of other natural resources, negatively impacting the environment.

In response to the demand for improved conditions, superintendents are employing more intensive maintenance practices, and one of the key ingredients is an efficient irrigation system. Such a system is also a necessary tool in conservation efforts. Manufacturers of irrigation equipment have responded with improvements to existing products and with the development of more efficient and reliable sprinkler heads, nozzles, sensors, valves, controllers, and pump stations.

Consultants and designers of golf course irrigation systems have risen to the challenge with innovative concepts intended to provide more precise and efficient irrigation without waste of water and power. Examples include low-pressure heads, individual head control, shorter-radius heads at closer spacing, part-circle perimeter heads around greens and other areas, and special treatment of areas such as south-facing slopes and the steep framing mounds often found around bunkers and greens. More sensors are being incorporated into designs and combined with "if/then" logic in the controls so that system operation can be automatically modified in response to changing conditions even during an irrigation cycle.

The resulting systems combine more uniform distribution with more accurate control and more precise timing. The key result on the golf course is more uniform playing conditions, with the ball landing and rolling the same speed on all fairways, on all approaches, and on all greens throughout the course. Turf in irrigated rough will also be more consistent, so that shots hit off-line will be uniformly penalized. Equally important, the improved accuracy and precision of properly designed systems helps in the effort to minimize the waste of water and power.

There are many differences between irrigation systems on golf courses and most of those intended for residential and commercial projects. These differences help to explain why golf course irrigation must be treated separately from other forms of turf and landscape irrigation. The components (pipe, fittings, sprinkler heads, valves, etc.) in golf systems are larger. System flow rates and operating pressures are substantially higher. With the higher operating pressures, designing to accommodate surge pressure or water hammer is more critical in golf systems. Typical golf course pump stations are complex and involve much higher voltage and amperage power. The hydraulic and electrical networks in golf systems are a great deal more elaborate and complex because of the nearly infinite flexibility of the control systems. The higher pressures and voltages in golf course systems make the safety of operating and maintenance personnel (and even players) a serious consideration. The potential for personal injury makes liability issues a real concern for manufacturers of irrigation equipment and for the designers, installers, owners, and operators of the systems.

Whereas most residential and commercial systems get their water from municipal potable distribution systems, golf course water sources can be wells, wastewater treatment plants, rivers, ponds, or lakes, and thus there can be significant water quality issues. And although most residential and commercial systems rely on the municipal system for operating pressure, nearly all golf systems require a dedicated pumping installation.

The end user (the golf course superintendent) is much more knowledgeable about irrigation and turfgrass management than most residential or commercial clients. He or she, therefore, has considerably higher expectations for system design, performance, and reliability.

The value of the turf on a golf course is generally much greater than that in a residential or commercial project. The potential for serious financial loss in the event of an irrigation system failure is also much higher for a golf course. Off-color or dead turf can result in very unhappy home owners or mall developers, but they usually do not lose money because of it. Inconsistent playing conditions or loss of turf on a golf course will definitely reduce the bottom line on the balance sheet and may cost one or more people their jobs.

This book is intended to be a practical tool for hands-on people involved in golf course irrigation rather than an in-depth explanation of the theoretical issues involved in the design and operation of irrigation systems and their components. The information it offers can prove valuable to golf course superintendents and irrigation technicians; golf course architects, irrigation consultants, and system designers; golf course developers, builders, and irrigation installers; and irrigation manufacturers and their distribution personnel. It can also be of value to instructors and students of irrigation, both in a college setting and in professional or vocational training programs such as those provided by the Irrigation Association and various local or state agencies and associations.

The construction of modern golf courses is expensive, as is the maintenance of the finished product. The irrigation system is a key tool in both the grow-in and long-term maintenance of the course. It is imperative that the system be designed, installed, operated, and maintained so that it will remain efficient and reliable for a long period of time.

Golfer demands for better playing conditions, growing pressure from regulatory authorities, new and ongoing environmental issues, and increasingly critical shortages in water and energy supplies all highlight the need for the most accurate, efficient, and reliable irrigation systems possible. Golf courses are highly visible users of our limited water supplies, so the design, installation, management, and maintenance of their systems must be of the highest quality to provide the best possible playing conditions, to avoid waste of water and energy, and to prevent adverse effects on the environment.

References

1. National Golf Foundation, Jupiter, FL. November 2, 2000. News release available on NGF website at www.ngf.org.
2. Aylward, Larry, ed. *Golfdom Magazine*. 2001 reader profile study.
3. Klein, Brad. *Golfweek Magazine*. 1996. The responsibility of challenge. Vol. 22 (November 22): 3.
4. Golf Course Superintendents Association of America. February 2001. Performance measurement survey 1999-2000: Preliminary results. Lawrence, KS. p. 3.

ACKNOWLEDGMENTS

The authors would like to thank the following individuals for their help in the preparation of the book: Lissa Barrett; Jeff Bowman; Bryan Campbell; Jack Christensen; Judy Dobson; Dave Goorahoo, PhD; Mike Harrington; Mike Hartley; Tom Haslinger; Charlie Krauter, PhD; Cory Metler; Chris Morin; Kimberly Morse; Vince Nolletti; Kate Norum; Joe Oliphant; John Riordan; Karen Roche; Ron Sneed, PhD; Bill Stinson; Tom Tanto; Dana Vinchesi; Ed Walsh; and Danaé Zoldoske.

Plant Irrigation Requirements

T his chapter introduces the relationships between the turfgrass plant, the host soil, and the irrigation water, which are key to proper irrigation design and management. It provides information on water movement through different soils and water uptake by plant roots. It discusses the concept of evapotranspiration (consumptive use) and its role in the calculation of water requirements. The chapter also includes information on various turfgrass types, their water requirements, and their relative drought tolerances.

SOIL-WATER-PLANT RELATIONSHIPS

Irrigation concerns the relationship between how a soil holds and stores water and how a plant uses water. Although you do not need to know a great deal about soil physics or plant physiology for proper irrigation, you do need to have a general knowledge of soils and to be familiar with how a plant, in this case turfgrass, uses water and uptakes it from the soil. There are a number of terms and concepts you should be familiar with in order to understand the soil-plant-water relationship.

Soils

A soil is made up of various amounts of sand, silt, clay, and organic material, as well as pore space. The pore space is filled with either air or water. The ideal mixture is 50 percent soil, 25 percent water, and 25 percent air. Under these conditions the turf expends a minimal amount of energy to uptake water and nutrients.

Texture is defined as the relative proportions of sand, silt, and clay in a soil. Texture cannot be changed or destroyed. Using an estimate of the percentage of each type, a soil can be classified in one of the 11 categories shown in the textural triangle in Figure 1.1. For example, as indicated in the textural triangle, a soil consisting of 50 percent sand, 30 percent clay, and 20 percent silt would be classified as a sandy clay loam.

The structure of a soil is defined by the arrangement of the various components that make up the soil texture. There are many types of soil structures, each with a specific name for its formation. In irrigation, a structure that allows for a high water-holding capacity is preferred. This structure is one that has medium-size pore spaces that

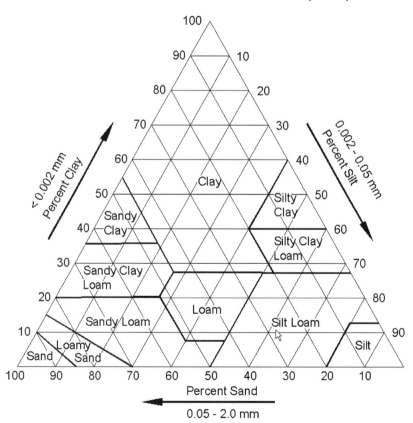

FIGURE 1.1
A textural triangle is used to generalize soils based on the percentages of silt, clay, and sand contained in the soil.
(Courtesy of the Irrigation Association.)

allows for some drainage but does not hold the water too tightly to the soil particles, such as clays. The structure of a soil can be easily changed with the use of various types of mechanical equipment such as rototillers, aerifiers, or bulldozers.

If you were to dig a deep hole in the ground with a backhoe and then jump into the hole, you could see how a soil consists of different layers. Each time the soil changes color, structure, texture, or other characteristics, there will be a distinct layer. These layers are called soil horizons. The makeup of all of the horizons in a soil create the soil profile. In a soil profile, the top layer, the soil growing the turf, is the first, or A, horizon. A small difference in the soil characteristics may make it the A1, A2, or A3 horizon. A significant change in the soil will change it to the B horizon. The C horizon is usually the parent material from which the upper horizons descended. In an undisturbed soil these horizons can be very old and quite consistent over large areas. On a golf course, significant grading has probably taken place as well as substantial amount of cutting and filling. As a result, the soil profile has been manipulated and the sequencing of the horizons disturbed. It is not uncommon to have the C horizon on top, with the original A horizon buried and the new A horizon probably brought in from another area of the site or imported onto the site. In dealing with a manipulated soil, it is important to figure out how the soil characteristics change with depth. On golf courses it is not uncommon to have a highly compacted impermeable layer of soil beneath the topsoil, or the A horizon, causing some irrigation and drainage problems.

Intake Rate

A soil's intake (infiltration) rate is a measure of how fast the soil will take in water, measured in inches per hour. In a dry, bare soil, the soil intake rate will initially be very high, but it slowly decreases to a point where it becomes consistent over time. Although the rate will be high at the beginning, in irrigation it is the leveled-off or basic intake rate that is of interest. Ideally, an irrigation system would never apply water at a rate greater than the intake rate of the particular soil being irrigated. On a United States Golf Association (USGA) regulation green, this ideal is easily obtainable, as the intake rate is significantly higher than the precipitation rate of the sprinklers. On a push-up green (constructed simply by shaping the existing soil—no drainage, gravel layer, or soil amendments are installed), however, the precipi-

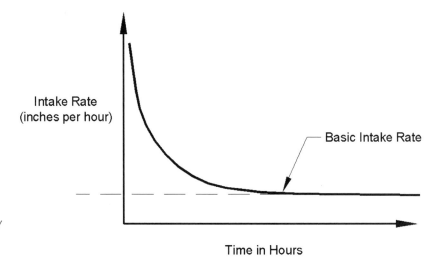

FIGURE 1.2
**Generalized soil intake graph,
intake rate versus time.** *(Courtesy
of the Irrigation Association.)*

tation rate may exceed the intake rate of the soil. To properly sched-ule irrigation and prevent runoff and puddles, the intake rate of the soil must be considered (Figure 1.2). If the precipitation rate of the irrigation system exceeds the soil intake rate, cycle and soak schedul-ing may be necessary to apply the required water efficiently.

Turf cover, compaction, and thatch all decrease the soil's intake rate. Compaction during construction, or even by the sprinklers oper-ating at a pressure that is too low, will influence the intake rate over time. Thatch buildup will decrease the intake rate, as may the long-term use of effluent water, depending on its quality. If you have iden-tified your soil type from the textural triangle, then a water intake rate can be estimated from information provided in a textbook on soils.

Soil Water Storage and Movement

The storage and movement of water in a soil is of great importance in scheduling irrigation efficiently and effectively. As the soil goes from wet to dry, the relationship of the water to the soil changes, as well as the type of movement and amount of storage (Figure 1.3). If you were to start with a dry soil and then irrigate it until it puddles or runoff occurs, the soil would have all its pore space filled with water and the soil would be saturated. If you stopped irrigating, the soil pore spaces would start to drain over the next 24 to 48 hours, and all of the water movement would be gravitational. At some point in time, the gravitational movement and drainage would slow to a very

Classes and Availability of Soil Water

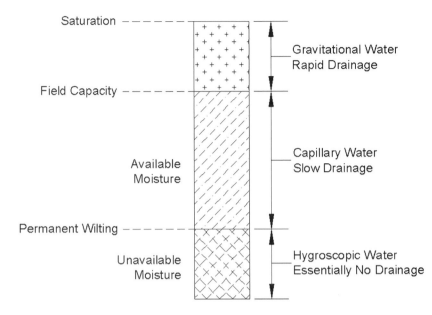

FIGURE 1.3
Soil moisture movement terms.
(Courtesy of the Irrigation Association.)

low rate. At this point the soil pore space would be approximately 25 percent water and 25 percent air. The soil particles would be holding the water to them with adhesive forces (soil to water), thus keeping the pore spaces from draining any further. At this point the soil is said to be at field capacity. Field capacity in regard to soil moisture can be defined as the point where water is most available to the plant. Because the turf consumes water between irrigation or rainfall events, the amount of water available to the plant continues to decrease. The movement of water at this stage is caused by capillary action. The cohesive (water-to-water) forces move the water from the soil pore spaces to the roots for uptake by the turf. This will occur for some time, with the turf having to exert more and more force to pull the remaining water away from the soil particles as the soil dries out. This process will continue until the soil reaches the permanent wilting point. At this point, the soil moisture will be severely depleted and the turf can no longer exert enough energy to pull the water away from the soil. At the permanent wilting point there is still water in the soil, but it is held so tightly by the soil that the plant cannot use it. The remaining moisture is hygroscopic water, which can be removed only by applying heat to force drying (i.e., "oven dried" soils).

Water-Holding Capacity

Between field capacity and permanent wilting point is the available water-holding capacity of the soil. Again, if you have generalized the type of soil from the textural triangle, a soils text or Internet site can provide information on the particulars of a soil's water-holding capacity in either inches of water per foot of soil or inches of water per inch of soil. For example, a sandy clay loam may hold 1.6 in. of water per ft of soil. Although this is the total amount of water held between field capacity and permanent wilting point, all this water may not be available to the plant. It is difficult for plants to obtain water below the root zone, so root zone depth is an important consideration in irrigation scheduling, as it severely limits water availability and thus dictates the irrigation interval.

By relating the root zone depth to the available water-holding capacity of the soil, the amount of water available to the turf can be determined. For example, if the turf has a 6 in. root zone and the sandy clay loam (mentioned earlier) has a capacity of 1.6 in. per ft, the available water-holding capacity would be 0.8 in. (1.6 in./ft × 0.5 ft). A 3 in. root zone would have half the available water-holding capacity of a 6 in. root zone, or 0.4 in. (1.6 in./ft × .25 ft).

Irrigation Interval

In scheduling irrigation frequency, it is best to replenish the available water supply before reaching the permanent wilting point. Target levels have been identified for different crop types, including turfgrass. A target level is referred to as management allowable depletion (MAD). It is a management decision as to how much of the available water should be depleted before the next irrigation occurs. For turfgrass, the MAD has been determined to be about 50 percent by most agronomists. For example, applying a MAD of 50 percent to 0.8 in. of available water at field capacity results in a target of 0.4 in. of water being extracted by the turfgrass (0.8 in. × 0.50) before the next irrigation event. The next irrigation will be a net water application of 0.4 in. to fully refill the root zone. The time (days) it takes the turfgrass to consume the target MAD of 0.4 in. of water is referred to as the irrigation interval.

EVAPOTRANSPIRATION

Water evaporates from soil and transpires from plant leaves. Together, these two phenomena are referred to as evapotranspiration (*ET*). There are several methods used to estimate the *ET* rate or value. For research purposes, a weighing lysimeter has been used to measure the loss of water from turfgrass plots. Typically, soil is placed in a box that is supported beneath by a weighing scale. Turfgrass is planted on the soil surface, well irrigated, and properly maintained. The surface area of the planted turfgrass and the change in weight due to evapotranspiration (water use) are measured. These two measurements form the water use requirements. These measurements are usually expressed in fractions of an inch of water consumed per day, or daily *ET* rate.

Lysimeters are too complex and expensive for normal water management, so weather conditions, such as wind speed, temperature, sunlight intensity, humidity, and other parameters are often measured to calculate the amount of *ET* or plant water use. Researchers, such as Penman (1948), developed formulas from their investigations to estimate potential crop water use based on changing weather conditions. A modified Penman equation is currently used by most publicly accessible weather stations in California to estimate crop water demand.

There are several variations of the *ET* definition or measurement that may be available. They all have slightly different meanings. ET_c or *ET* crop is the water use rate of the crop (turf) that is being scheduled or managed. ET_c is the amount of water that evaporates from the soil surface and transpires from the leaf surface to the atmosphere.

Calculating the *ET* of turf for an irrigation schedule usually begins with the acquisition of a reference *ET* value. Reference ET_o, as defined by Doorenbos and Pruitt (1975), denotes the "the rate of evaporation from an extensive surface of green grass cover, of uniform height, actively growing, completely shading the ground, and not short of water." This is the most common example of the use of the Penman equation to calculate evapotranspiration for a specific reference plant cover. Other examples often available are ET_p and sometimes ET_r. These are modifications of the Penman equation that calculate *ET*'s for reference crops other than turf. The Irrigation Association website includes an extensive list of *ET* sources for the United States.

Such calculations are widely used in the western United States by the U.S. Bureau of Reclamation to estimate agricultural crop water use requirements. This measurement is based on work developed by Jensen et al. (1970), in which ET_r "represents the upper limit or maximum evapotranspiration that occurs under given climatic conditions with a field having a well-watered agricultural crop with an aerodynamically rough surface, such as alfalfa with 12 in. to 18 in. of top growth." The *ET* of the plant cover being managed (*ET$_c$*) is related to the various *ET*'s (*ET$_o$*, *ET$_p$*, *ET$_r$*) by a value known as the crop coefficient (*K$_c$*). The mathematical relationship is defined as:

$$K_c = ET_c/ET_o \text{ or } ET_r$$

where:

K_c	= crop coefficient
ET_c	= evapotranspiration of the crop or turf being managed
ET_o	= evapotranspiration—grass-based
ET_p or ET_r	= evapotranspiration—alfalfa-based

However, because *ET$_o$* uses grass as a basis, versus *ET$_r$*, which uses alfalfa, the resultant crop coefficients can vary considerably. That is why it is critical to match the proper reference *ET* with the correct *K$_c$* adjustments. Using *ET$_o$*-based *K$_c$*'s with *ET$_r$* reference values, or vice versa, can result in significant errors in water use estimates.

Crop coefficients are seasonally adjusted values that take into account the crop type, stage of growth, and crop cover. For example, the difference in *K$_c$* between a Bermudagrass and a tall fescue grass could be substantial. The *K$_c$* developed during April for Bermudagrass is 0.72 or 72 percent of *ET$_o$*. For tall fescue during April, the *K$_c$* is 1.04 or 104 percent of *ET$_o$*. This is a potential difference of 30 percent for applied water. Other months vary to a lesser degree. Also note that the *K$_c$* values used in the preceding example apply to southern California geographic conditions. These values or coefficients are developed for specific regions, so be sure to select the appropriate references.

TURF TYPES

A key component in determining the plant water requirement is identification of the species and variety (cultivars) of the turfgrass. For new construction, the type of plant material must also be identified to estimate water requirements in the irrigation design phase.

Of the more than 1200 different turfgrass species available, only 20 to 25 are suitable for the golf industry. The reason is that most of these plants do not meet the requirements of heavy traffic, low cutting heights, disease tolerance, leaf texture, seedling vigor, and drought tolerance. There is a large ongoing effort to breed new turfgrasses that require less water, have deep root systems, and demonstrate improved salt tolerance.

Water has several key functions in a plant. It acts as a nutrient carrier within the plant; as a solution carrying nutrients in the soil to the roots; and, in the plant leaves, as a temperature regulator. Water is also required for absorption by seeds during germination. Of all the water consumed by a plant, only about 2 percent is used for metabolic purposes. The rest is used for cooling and respiration.

Excessive moisture levels can have detrimental effects on turfgrass, such as oxygen deficits and the unnecessary leaching of nutrients from the root zone. The available water must be managed in the root zone between the MAD and field capacity.

Generally, turfgrasses are grouped into two basic categories: warm-season grasses and cool-season grasses. The temperatures in which they thrive and length of growing season classify these two groups. Warm-season grasses are most active when temperatures are between 80°F and 90°F and will go dormant in cool winter months. Cool-season turfgrasses prefer 60°F to 75°F and will stay green year-round. In terms of plant water use, cool-season grasses tend to consume more water than warm-season grasses under similar weather conditions.

Although turfgrasses are classified into cool- and warm-season categories, each species and cultivar may have particular behavioral characteristics. Factors that influence behavior include soil type, shade conditions, air and soil temperatures, water quality, mowing heights, and other cultural practices.

The following guide can be used for estimating relative plant water use requirements:

Relative Drought Tolerance—Cool-Season Turfgrass

Bluegrass	Low to medium
Annual bluegrass	Low
Fescue	High
Ryegrass	Medium
Creeping bentgrass	Low

Relative Drought Tolerance—Warm-Season Turfgrass

Bermudagrass	High
Zoysia	High
Carpetgrass	Medium
St. Augustine grass	Medium
Buffalograss	High

Fescues tend to have the greatest tolerance for drought as cool-season grasses, primarily because of their rolled leaf structure, which protects the stomates from exposure during stress. The warm-season Bermudagrass tends to have an extensive, deep root system that aids it in extracting water from the soil.

Excellent sources for regional information on appropriate turfgrasses are local experiment stations and university programs. In addition, the National Turfgrass Evaluation Program (NTEP) can be contacted for information on regional turfgrass trial data at www.ntep.org.

Water Use Calculations

Reference *ET* values can be obtained from several sources. The most effective is a weather station located on or near the golf course. There are specific siting requirements for weather stations, but they generally include an unobstructed area around the station, irrigated and maintained turfgrass, and available power. Too many sites are located next to equipment yards where buildings interfere with wind measurements and heat is radiated from asphalt and concrete areas. Automated weather stations that read directly to a desktop computer are available with software that will calculate a reference *ET*. Be sure to get K_c values that match the particular reference *ET* calculated by your specific weather station.

Other sources of *ET* values are government-sponsored weather stations and local weather reporting. Some of these sources are available through the Internet. For example, WateRight.org provides *ET* values and matching crop coefficients and calculates irrigation requirements.

The procedure for estimating crop water requirements in "real time" is sometimes explained as the checkbook method. The analogy is that you start with a balance of money in your account; as you write checks and deduct the amounts from your balance, there is less money available in the account. From time to time money must be deposited back into your account or the account will become overdrawn. And just like you, a turfgrass will experience stress when the account (of water) is overdrawn.

In determining irrigation amounts and frequencies, the available water in the root zone should be considered as the bank account. Each day the grass extracts water (writes a check) from the available water account. The amount of water taken from the root zone (size of the check) is determined by the weather conditions (*ET*) and turf type

(K_c). The soil's water-holding capacity and depth of root zone determine the amount of water available (the size of the initial balance). The grass cannot withdraw more water than it has available, or it will die.

Calculating the size of the daily *ET* is the most difficult part of the process. Generally, water use calculations begin with a reference turf *ET* value for the local area. Next, the correct K_c value must be identified and used for the *ET* value (crop, period, and reference). *ET* values are usually expressed for a period of time (e.g., day, week, or month). Weekly *ET* values are normally sufficient to track seasonal changes in water use. There is typically enough water storage in the root zone to accommodate daily swings in *ET* during the week. However, using a monthly average may put the crop health in danger because of extended weather fluctuations.

The calculation is

$$K_c \times ET \text{ reference} = \text{crop water requirements for the calculated period of time.}$$

A more specific example is the use of a reference ET_o (grass-based) value of 1.8 in. per week for a week in May, say the first through the seventh. The calculated K_c value for Bermudagrass in May is 0.79 for a particular area. To estimate the crop water use for this first week in May, the following calculation is performed:

$$\text{Net water requirement expressed in inches for that week (1.42)} = K_c \,(0.79) \times ET_o \,(1.8) \text{ in./week}$$

where

K_c = crop factor for selected crop (Bermudagrass), time of year (May), and geographic region (Arizona)

ET_o = measured grass-based evapotranspiration for period of time (in./week)

The next week the weather could change and the ET_o could be higher or lower, but the calculation would be the same. If the calculation were performed for the last week in April instead, you would use a slightly lower K_c value, 0.72, to multiply by the estimated ET_o value for that week.

In summary, know your reference *ET* (grass- or alfalfa-based), identify the correct crop coefficients, time of year, and geographic region. The total calculated turf *ET*s since the last irrigation will be the amount to use when determining the total net water requirement for the next irrigation schedule.

Remember, the estimated crop water usage is not the amount of water you need to apply. System uniformity must also be accounted for in the total water application amount, along with any leaching fraction.

Leaching Fractions

Leaching fraction or requirement (Lr) is the amount of additional irrigation water required to move salts out of the root zone to maintain a healthy growing environment. The amount is dependent on numerous factors, including the salinity of the soil, soil type, water quality, rainfall, drainage, and crop tolerance. Probably the single most important factor is the quality of the water. This is especially true for golf courses that use effluent water supplies. The water quality sets the lower limit for the minimum salinity that can accommodate turfgrass growth. The water quality is usually expressed as the electrical conductivity (EC) of the water.

When plants extract water from the soil, salts are left to accumulate in the soil. Over time the level of salinity can build up to the point where it is toxic to the plant. Excess irrigation or rainfall will push the accumulated salts below the root zone, maintaining a healthy growing environment for the turfgrass.

In areas of limited summer rainfall, irrigation water is used to leach or "push" salts out of the root zone. With sufficient flushing, the EC of the soil will approach the EC of the water. The challenge is to determine exactly how much overirrigation to apply. The process starts with knowing the salt tolerance of the plant or turfgrass; this sets the minimum salinity level that can be used without damaging the turfgrass. Obviously, the EC of the irrigation water must be equal to or less than the tolerance limits of the crop.

In developing an irrigation schedule when salinity is a concern, it is important to make an estimate of the minimum quantity of water required to move excess salts out of the root zone. This quantity or leaching requirement may be estimated by using the salt balance equation developed by Hoffman and Van Genuchten (1983):

$$Lr = \frac{EC_I}{EC_D}$$

where

Lr = leaching requirement, the percentage of the irrigation that should pass through the root zone

EC_I = electrical conductivity of the irrigation water (dS/m) being applied

EC_D = electrical conductivity of drainage water above which turf damage occurs

In managing conditions of high salinity, the uniformity of the sprinkler system is extremely important. To meet the leaching requirement of the driest coverage areas (10 or 20 percent), a tremendous amount of water is wasted in the wetter areas in the form of overirrigation with nonuniform systems. Because the leaching requirement is only an estimate, periodic monitoring of the salinity in the root zone is highly recommended to maintain the appropriate salt balance.

Maintaining the appropriate salt balance is critical for several reasons. These include the health of the plant and the need to minimize the cost of water and energy wasted through overirrigation. But perhaps most important, when overirrigation occurs, it moves fertilizers and chemicals with the water toward underground aquifers. The intended efficacy of these materials is lost when they are moved below the root zone. Moreover, many of these underlying aquifers are close to cities and homes that use this water source for human consumption. If contaminants show up in public water supplies, and can be traced to mismanagement at the golf course, fines and/or litigation are likely to follow.

SOURCES

Doorenbos, J., and W.O. Pruitt. 1975. Guidelines for prediction of crop water requirements. *FAO Irrigation and Drainage Paper No. 24*. Rome, Italy: Food and Agriculture Organization of the United Nations.

Hoffman, G. J., and M. Th. Van Genuchten. 1983. "Soil properties and efficient water use: Water management for salinity control" in *Limitations to Efficient Water Use in Crop Production*, ed. by H. M. Taylor, W. Jordan, and T. Sinclair. American Society of Agronomy, pp. 73–85.

Jensen, M. E., D. C. N. Robb, and C. E. Franzoy. 1970. Scheduling irrigation using climate-crop-soil data. *Procedures of the American Society of Civil Engineering, Journal of Irrigation and Drainage, Division 96 (IT1)*, pp. 25–38.

Penman, H. L. 1948. Natural evaporation from open water, bare soil, and grass. *Proceedings of the Royal Society of London*. A193: 120–146.

2
Water Supply: Quantity and Quality

This chapter discusses the different types of water sources and the benefits and problems associated with each. Quality requirements for turf irrigation water are covered, as well as information on cross connection, the related health hazards, and backflow prevention procedures and devices.

SOURCES, WITHDRAWAL PERMITS, AND WATER RIGHTS

In the beginning stages of any irrigation system design it is essential to identify and, in most cases, obtain permits for an adequate water supply. The water supply must be large enough to provide the needed amount of water for the irrigation system; it must also supply water of acceptable quality throughout the irrigation season. Water is a finite resource, and there is increasing competition by all parties interested in using it. It is becoming more and more difficult to obtain water for golf course irrigation systems.

There are many ways a golf course can obtain water for its irrigation system. Some courses may have several different sources available, and an analysis of which will be best for a proposed irrigation system will be needed. Factors such as quantity, quality, location, elevation, and the availability of power must all be considered. Some courses may have only one available water source, and others may have to use a combination of sources to get adequate supplies. Sometimes a source will be obvious, and in other cases tens of thousands of dollars may be spent to locate and develop an adequate source of water.

Whatever the source of water, in most eastern states a water withdrawal or diversion permit is required of a party intending to use the water. Such permits can be difficult to obtain in some states or in areas where water supplies are under stress, and relatively easy in others. It will depend on the location of the course, what the competing uses are, how much water is being requested, and what type of water source is being proposed as the supply. In the western states, water rights can be a very large issue. The right to water is deeded to the user just like a piece of property. A water right is not necessarily attached to the property rights, so a developer can own a piece of property but have no right to the water on it or under it. Conversely, a person can own water rights without owning the property where the water is located. A right to use the water may have to be purchased, which usually entails a significant cost. Water right law is a booming business with the ever-increasing competition for water. A thorough investigation should be undertaken to determine whether there are rights to any water before a golf course irrigation project is initiated.

MUNICIPAL SOURCES

Municipal sources offer a consistent supply of water at the designated flow and a minimal pressure, for the most part, without interruption. Because the same system supplies drinking water to the populace, if there is a problem it will be rectified quickly. The water is there, 24 hours a day, 365 days per year. However, during a drought the situation can change significantly. If water restrictions are put in place, the use of municipal water may be curtailed. Under severe restrictions, golf courses may be limited to watering only the greens. With municipal sources, there is a fee for using the water. This fee varies with location and the amount of water used, ranging from a few thousand dollars to hundreds of thousands of dollars annually. The upside is that the water authority will be responsible for any diversion or withdrawal permits. The quality of water from a municipal source is generally very good, maybe too good in some instances, as it has to meet drinking water standards. There may be some residual chlorine, and the water should be tested or checked to see whether the chlorine, which is used as a disinfectant, is removed by the water purveyor following treatment. Municipal sources must be carefully sized to provide the required flow. Often, the adjacent pipelines are not large enough to provide adequate flow. Velocities through the service line into the golf course should not exceed 7.5 fps in steel pipe, or 5 fps if the line is polyvinyl chloride (PVC) pipe. A water meter and backflow preventer must be installed (Figure 2.1). The majority of municipally supplied golf course irrigation systems also require an automatic booster pump system to achieve the required operating pressure. Improperly sizing the supply line from the street or the booster pump station can lead to depriving the neighboring community of water or pressure when the golf course irrigation system is operating. This situation is not uncommon and can be very bad for a golf course's public relations. A qualified engineer should make sure that the irrigation system will not inhibit the municipality's ability to supply water to all of its customers.

FIGURE 2.1
Municipal supplies should include a backflow preventer and water meter such as shown here for a golf course practice area.

SURFACE WATER

Surface water, including lakes, ponds, rivers, and streams, is probably the most common source of irrigation water for golf courses. Although all these sources are surface waters, their size, flow, quality, and accessibility can vary considerably.

Ponds and lakes (Figure 2.2) are excellent water supply sources for golf course irrigation, providing they have a reliable source of recharge. Recharging may be provided by a stream, a canal, the water table, or underground sources such as springs. The size and depth of the pond or lake dictate how much water it stores and how much drawdown will occur during the irrigation cycle. The larger the surface area of the storage facility, the less the drawdown. With ponds, an important consideration is whether they are in or out of play. A pond that is being used for irrigation and is a part of the golf course architecture must stay relatively full or it will be an eyesore, detracting from the golf course when it is not full. For a pond in play a maximum drawdown of 12 in. is recommended. This prevents the look of an unsightly bank during play and deters the growth of unattractive vegetation. A pond out of play does not need this restriction, as it is there just for irrigation storage and the amount of drawdown may not be an aesthetic consideration. A pond or lake acts primarily as a storage facility, but also as a safety factor for the irrigation system. It can store enough water for a specific number of irrigation cycles. The number of cycles stored depends on the size of the pond or the lake and its ability to recharge after each cycle. With a large lake the number of cycles may be infinite, whereas with a small pond a cycle

FIGURE 2.2
Pond water supplies are excellent sources of irrigation water or for storage when supplemented by other sources.

may be only several days. If there is significant inflow, there may be a requirement to provide water to downstream users, which means that the lake or pond cannot impound all of the water flowing into it. Water use will be dependent on climatic conditions and the number of sprinklers, as outlined in Chapter 5. Water can be retrieved from a pond or lake by the use of a wet well, floating suction, or flooded suction, depending on the topography, the type of pumps, and the budget available. Water quality within ponds and lakes varies. The depth of these sources influences the growth of algae and other water plants (Figure 2.3). Ponds less than 5 ft deep are subject to sunlight penetration to the bottom and, as a result, algal blooms. Deeper ponds have fewer algal problems. All ponds, depending on their geometry and inflow, are subject to siltation over time and may need to be dredged every few decades. Other quality issues include pH, dissolved solids, and floating debris. Temperature may also be an issue. Shallow lakes and ponds have a tendency to heat up in the summer and may provide water that is detrimental to the turf. If this is the case, alternative sources may have to be developed.

Rivers and streams require an entirely different set of considerations than lakes and ponds. Often, the biggest problem with sources of this type is getting at the water. Rivers and streams (Figure 2.4) are subject to flooding, and it is important that the pump house not be

FIGURE 2.3
Shallow ponds are more susceptible to algae growth.

FIGURE 2.4
Rivers and streams can be used for irrigation supplies, but have to be available throughout the irrigation season.

flooded. In many situations pump houses are not allowed to be built in a floodplain. Some states have river protection acts that do not allow structures within hundreds of feet of a river. For rivers and streams considered to be navigable waters, no type of intake or structure is allowed in the water without an Army Corps of Engineers permit, which may or may not be obtainable, depending on the water course. The quality of water from these sources varies throughout the year, and low flows may be detrimental to the system. Frequently, a river or stream is so shallow that there is no way to get to the water without significant construction either in the water course or along the bank, which can be a significant permitting issue, taking a lot of time and costing large amounts of money. The consistency and availability of water within a moving body such as a stream or river must be carefully investigated to ensure adequate supplies in times of drought or during low flow periods (Figure 2.5). Minimum downstream flows may also have to be maintained. Ample water for fish and wildlife is a consideration. Analysis of the watershed above the golf course and research of historical flow records can help to determine whether a stream or river is a reliable source of water. Rivers and streams, because of their significant flows, especially during the spring, also have the ability to bring with them large

FIGURE 2.5
Changes in water depth can cause problems with intake lines.

FIGURE 2.6
Flooding is a concern on many golf courses and must be taken into consideration during the design process.

amounts of debris, including trees, limbs, rocks, and other large items. This type of movement can damage pump system intakes and pump houses. Just the force of water during a flood can cause significant damage (Figure 2.6). The intake system must be designed to withstand these problems.

Water quality in flowing water bodies changes on a daily basis, depending on the time of year, the weather, and what may be entering from upstream. Industrial plants, dairy barns, and municipalities discharging into the water body can all affect water quality.

GROUNDWATER

FIGURE 2.7
Groundwater sources can be pumped directly to the irrigation system or to a pond for storage.

Groundwater sources include shallow wells, deep wells, and artesian wells (Figure 2.7). The water supplied by these underground aquifers may be pumped into the irrigation system directly or into a storage facility of some type, such as a lake or pond. To pump directly into the irrigation system, a large well is needed, 800 gpm or more. With today's large flow requirements, several large-flow wells are usually needed. Large wells are typically found in sandy areas, such as along coastlines and in the midwestern United States. Bedrock wells yield smaller amounts of water and are usually used in combination with a storage facility. The diameter of the well depends on the amount of water that needs to be pumped and the size of the pump itself. The depth depends on the local hydrogeology. A hydrogeologist should be consulted when trying to locate large groundwater reserves. The type of well and how it is drilled will be based on local geography and standards. Groundwater exploration and well drilling can be expensive propositions, often coming up empty. Like drilling for oil, finding groundwater can be a risky proposition. An alternative is to employ a "dowser," although some think that dowsing is less science and more magic. A dowser locates water using a set of divining rods that react when they are over water. In many cases, dowsing has been successful in locating groundwater when other methods have failed. In supplying a golf course directly from groundwater, there is no safety factor. If the well deteriorates or the pump malfunctions, there will be no water. Pumping to a storage facility or from multiple wells is best, so as to protect the golf course from not having water during critical irrigation periods.

Groundwater is usually high-quality water, but in some locations it can contain problematic materials such as sulfur, manganese, or iron. The temperature of groundwater is usually near the average subsurface soil temperature and can help in keeping the turf cool in periods of high heat stress.

COMBINED SOURCES

Combined water sources may use one or several of the water sources discussed earlier. It is common for a golf course to have a pond that is supplied from another water source. The makeup water source can be groundwater, stream, municipal, or river flow or a transfer of water from a larger storage facility with its own makeup water capacity. Although irrigation can take place in less than an 8-hour period, the filling of the water source to its original level can take all day (24 hours). (As previously mentioned, this situation is not acceptable if the pond is visible to golfers.) With an 8-hour run time, the makeup water requirement would be one-third of the pump station capacity. With a 6-hour run time, one-fourth. For instance, a system that uses 1500 gpm over an 8-hour irrigation cycle will require a minimum makeup capacity of 500 gpm. Some courses may use a combination of several different sources to move water to a primary storage facility. For instance, a system may have two small wells that replenish a pond, backed up by a series of other storage ponds, which are then backed up by a river withdrawal. The sources are prioritized and come on line as stored amounts decrease, other sources are depleted, or more water is needed. A well-planned makeup water system should be automated to reduce the extent of management required.

ALTERNATIVE SOURCES

As the use of freshwater sources for irrigation is subject to increased pressure from competing uses such as development and the environment, alternative water supplies are becoming more important in investigating a source of irrigation water. Reclaimed, effluent, and gray water are all viable sources of irrigation water. Gray water in the quantities required would be difficult to obtain for a golf course system, but recycled water and, especially, effluent water are becoming increasingly popular as water sources for golf courses (Figure 2.8). Although not allowed in some states, effluent or recycled water offers advantages to both the water authority providing it and the golf course receiving it. The land application of effluent to the turf acts as another stage of treatment as the water flows through and enters the soil in which it is stored. Its application onto a golf course may preclude the need for a stream discharge permit for the effluent by the

FIGURE 2.8
Reclaimed water is becoming more popular as a water source for golf courses, and appropriate warnings must be posted when it is used.

water authority if the golf course is taking all of the effluent. Conversely, a golf course may face additional permitting considerations because of its use of effluent. The golf course benefits from what is usually high-quality water containing some level of nutrients, possibly reducing fertilization needs. A golf course in some cases may receive a fee for taking the effluent water or, conversely, may pay a fee, but one that is much lower than that charged for potable water. Often, cost sharing is involved, in which part or all of the irrigation system is paid for by the water authority that is producing the effluent water. There are disadvantages as well. In some cases, a golf course may be forced to take the effluent water whether it needs it or not, resulting in the turf's being overwatered or forcing the construction of large storage ponds. The quality of the effluent may be poor, containing high salt levels, heavy metals, or suspended solids. A stringent and ongoing testing procedure is needed to ensure that a consistent quality of effluent is being received. When effluent sources are used, there must be a source of fresh water that can be mixed with the effluent to reduce its concentration, to flush the system occasionally, and, most commonly, to water the greens. Many effluent or recycled water operations use a parallel piping and water supply system. Minimally, the operation has a piping system to water the greens that is separate from the effluent system. The fresh water system may also include the tees, and the effluent system waters the fairway and rough. The parallel system offers the superintendent more flexibility in the management and control of irrigation water. In designing any effluent or combination system for a golf course, a dual system should be considered. A clear understanding of environmental requirements is also needed, as in many cases a buffer may be required for the effluent, which in itself may dictate the need for a parallel system. In installing parallel or combination systems, regulations concerning backflow codes and environmental issues must be followed.

WATER QUALITY

Irrigation water quality analysis should be performed on a continuing basis, unless the water is coming from a reliable, clean, and consistent source. The quality of the water, whether surface, groundwater, or effluent, can change throughout the year. During high spring flows a stream may be muddy while a pond is crystal clear, whereas in the summer the stream may be running clear and the pond full of algae.

During a drought flows may be so low that the water quality deteriorates to unacceptable levels, for both effluent and stream water, as the concentration of contaminants increases with lower flows. In evaluating water for use as an irrigation supply, the following items may be of concern: chlorides, suspended solids, nitrogen, dissolved solids, manganese, pH, fecal coliform, and heavy metals (chromium, manganese, etc.). If the levels of any of these are high, they should be discussed with an agronomist to ensure that they will not be detrimental to the turf. Almost all water contaminants can be dealt with through filtration, injection, or proper management. For many water sources with poor quality, filters are used to remove suspended solids, floating debris, and other materials (Figure 2.9). Acid injection can be used to alter pH and other chemicals can be removed with the use of ion exchange technology. Storage water can be cleaned up by using aerators and sulfur burners (Figure 2.10). Some of these technologies are expensive, and an analysis should be made as to whether an easily obtainable source of poor-quality water that requires expensive treatment is as economical as a cleaner source that may be more difficult or expensive to obtain initially.

FIGURE 2.9
Poor-quality water may require that the irrigation water be filtered.

FIGURE 2.10
Water quality can be improved with equipment such as sulfur burners.

CROSS CONNECTION, BACKFLOW PREVENTION

Protecting the water supply is a requirement with any irrigation system. Water used for irrigation and water used for potable consumption must not be allowed to mix. There are many examples in which the health and safety of the public have been compromised when this has occurred. For instance, using a quick coupler connection on an irrigation lateral for a drinking water source has potential to cause significant illness. This situation would typically necessitate the design and installation of two separate water delivery systems.

Irrigation and potable water must always be separated. That is, the water sources cannot be commingled for either application without the proper form of backflow protection. It is usually acceptable for potable water supplies to be used as a source of irrigation water when the cross connection is properly protected with a backflow prevention device. However, it is never acceptable to use irrigation water as a supply for potable water needs, no matter what level of protection is provided.

The potential for back siphonage, or backflow, occurs primarily when the irrigation system is shut down. Water will flow by gravity to the lowest part of the piping system, which can be as simple as water falling back down a well. Water pumped uphill is also likely to return back toward the pump station or supply. The example of a fire truck pump drawing large amounts of water through a hydrant is often cited as potentially creating negative pressure in the supply side and drawing in contaminants from unprotected systems. Finally, any piping that has more than one source of water and pressure must include protection. An example is water pumped from a well into an irrigation system that also has a connection to a municipal supply. The well pumping system could easily provide more pressure than the municipal system, potentially sending well water and contaminants into an unprotected municipal water supply.

The highest form of protection against back siphonage is the air-gap. This is defined as a space (air-gap) separating, for example, the water supply pipe from the pond water level. The distance of the air-gap must be at least two diameters larger than the supply pipe, but in no case should it be less than 1 in. For example, an air-gap can be employed where a municipal backup is used to supply a pond. Most wells used for this purpose do not have a backflow device to protect against back siphonage, although they should.

The most common type of backflow protection is the "reduced pressure principle backflow prevention device," more commonly known as the RP device (Figure 2.1). The RP has the largest pressure loss across the valve as compared with other valve designs that provide lower levels of backflow protection. The RP device commonly requires 10 to 12 pounds of pressure loss to operate effectively. Designers must check the manufacturer's literature to determine the precise pressure loss at designed flow rates. It is also generally required that these devices, at a minimum, pass an annual operational inspection performed by a certified tester. This requires the installation of an isolation valve (usually a resilient seated gate valve) at each end of the backflow prevention device. Designers must check with the local water purveyor or health department for an approved list of manufacturers, types, and applications.

The RP device operates by maintaining a pressure differential between two check valves that are separated by a relief or dump valve. If the pressure in the reduced pressure zone between the two checks valves drops below the preset level, water is discharged to the atmosphere through the relief valve. This is a visual indication that a backflow condition exists and/or that the check valve is fouled. The situation should be corrected immediately.

Because the function of these valves is to discharge when a backflow condition does exist, they should not be installed indoors, in underground vaults, or in areas where the discharge water can create a hazard or cause damage to the immediate area. These devices are relatively long, and a common mistake is not to leave enough room for proper installation and maintenance. The backflow device should be placed in an area that is frequently inspected and easy to observe.

Chemigation, or injecting chemicals through the irrigation system, is often a practical and cost-effective method of application. This practice brings into focus the need for appropriate backflow devices and other safety equipment. For instance, all injection equipment should be interlocked with the pump power panel so that in the event of a pumping plant shutdown, the injection equipment will also be shut down. This reduces the hazard and likelihood of backflow contamination. Chemical storage tanks should be placed in secondary containment structures. Wells should be graded so that water runs away from, rather than toward, them. This will prevent chemicals from reaching the well in the event of tank rupture or flooding.

3

Pump Systems

The pump system is the heart of an irrigation system. It can be a complex combination of pumps, motors, valves and piping, sensors, electric switch gear, electronic control components, wiring, and software. This chapter describes various types of pump systems, the key material components, and their functions. It covers related subjects such as intake structures and discharge piping, filtration, fertigation and other injection systems, power requirements, remote monitoring, and efficiencies. The chapter also includes a discussion of spatial requirements and component layouts for pump system buildings.

PUMP TYPES

Many different types of pumps are manufactured for irrigation. The types of pumps used in golf course irrigation systems, however, are somewhat limited in number. The most common types are discussed in the following paragraphs. Every pump type used in golf course irrigation systems is a form of centrifugal pump. A centrifugal pump takes water in at its center and, using a rotating impeller, speeds up the water via centrifugal force and discharges it out of the pump volute at a specific flow and pressure. The action is much like swinging a rope with a weight at its end. Depending on the length of the rope (impeller diameter) and the speed of rotation (rpm), the weight will have more momentum and go farther when it is released (pressure).

End Suction Centrifugal

The most common type of centrifugal pump is the horizontal centrifugal (Figure 3.1). This pump has an end suction, and the discharge will be at 90 degrees to the inlet. The horizontal centrifugal is also frequently used for booster pump applications. The efficiency of a centrifugal pump is low (50 to 65 percent) in smaller sizes, but efficiency increases (60 to 75 percent) as the size of the pump increases. Most pumping problems (99 percent) with the use of centrifugal pumps in golf course applications occur on the suction (lift) side of a pump. There are strict theoretical rules regarding limitation of suction lifts on centrifugal pumps that must be adhered to. The pump must be as close to the water as possible to avoid high lift requirements on the suction side. Friction losses should be kept to a minimum on the suction side.

Another common application for a centrifugal pump is its use as a flooded suction centrifugal. In this situation, the center of the pump is below, rather than above, the water. Instead of necessitating a lift, this situation results in a positive pressure on the inlet side and eliminates the suction side problems caused by elevation, although high friction losses can still be a problem.

FIGURE 3.1
Centrifugal pumps are commonly used in golf course irrigation pump systems.

Vertical Centrifugal

In some instances a horizontal centrifugal pump is turned on its side and becomes a vertical centrifugal. This is common in booster pump applications. Some manufacturers include aids to help the suction side when the pump is installed vertically in a lift situation.

Submersible

Submersible pumps are centrifugal pumps with more than one impeller set in stages, much like a turbine. The more stages, the more pressure resulting from the discharge. Submersible pumps are most common in well applications to overcome the high lift from underground aquifers. Because the impellers are also located below the water surface, there are no suction side problems. All the lift that must be overcome is on the discharge side. The efficiencies of submersible pumps are lower than those of other pumps of comparable size. Submersible pumps are commonly used in golf course applications as pressure maintenance pumps, makeup water pumps, and transfer pumps from shallow water bodies. They are also used in smaller pump system applications, but are not a good choice for use in large horsepowers due to their lower efficiencies. At the larger horsepowers, services and repair costs are also higher because the motor and pump must be removed from the well for inspection or servicing.

Vertical Turbine

A turbine pump is a type of vertical centrifugal. The pump impellers are actually in the water, and the motor is out of the water, above grade (Figure 3.2). A stainless steel shaft connects through the center of the motor to the pump (impellers) stages and can be as long as necessary. Turbine pumps are preferred on golf courses because they are the most efficient type of irrigation pump, they require the least maintenance, and they seldom have suction problems. This type of pump is more expensive than others, however, as there are significant capital costs for purchasing and installing the required wet well, inlet piping, and screen. Permitting can also be more difficult with this type of installation, as the bank of the water source must be broken to install the inlet piping, which will be in the buffer zone of the water source.

FIGURE 3.2
Turbine pump systems have the pump in the water and the motor above ground.

PUMP SIZING

To select a pump, the required flow and pressure (head) must be calculated. The required flow is based on the needs of the irrigation system and the desired operating time. Suppose, for example, that an 18-hole golf course is using 3,650,000 gal per week during its peak demand season. The superintendent wants the capacity to water the golf course in 8 hours per night, 7 days a week. This provides 56 hours (water window) per week available to pump the 3,650,000 gal. Divide the water use by the water window and convert to minutes (3,650,000 gal a week divided by 56 hours per week = 65,179 gal per hour—divided by 60 minutes per hour = 1086 gal per minute). The 1086 gal would be required every minute of the 56 hours, so some flow should be added for the tail end of the schedule and as a safety factor. Consequently, a 1200 gal per minute (gpm) pump would be a good selection.

Table 3.1 indicates the various flows required for different water windows. As the amount of time available to water is decreased, the capacity of the pump system must become larger. Syringing time may also influence the pump system size, as many superintendents want the capacity to syringe the golf course very quickly when needed. In

TABLE 3.1
Flow Required Based on 3,650,000 Gallons per Week at Different Water Windows

Days per Week	Hours per Day	Minimum Flow	Design Flow
Seven	Six	1448 gpm	1600 gpm
Seven	Eight	1086 gpm	1200 gpm
Six	Six	1690 gpm	1800 gpm
Six	Eight	1267 gpm	1400 gpm

some cases the syringing requirement may dictate a pump system flow that is larger than the irrigation requirement. Leaching requirements can also increase the pump system flow requirement.

"Feet of head" is another measure of pressure, which is measured in feet instead of pounds per square inch (psi) (2.31 ft = 1 psi). In referring to pumps, pressure is always described in feet of head. The head required for a pump is a combination of three factors and is referred to as the total dynamic head (TDH). The three factors that make up TDH are elevation, friction loss, and sprinkler operating pressure. Elevation is the number of feet from the water surface to the highest point in the system; this can be either a positive or a negative number. Friction loss is the total pressure losses through the system from the water surface to the farthest sprinkler disregarding elevation. Operating pressure is the pressure needed at the base of the sprinkler according to the design, commonly 60, 65, 70, 80, or 100 psi. All of these values must be converted to feet in order to sum the required TDH. If an 18-hole golf course irrigation design requires 80 psi at the sprinkler, has 17.5 psi of friction loss in the worst case, and has an elevation change of 53 ft from the water source to the high point, the TDH is calculated as follows:

Elevation:	53.00 ft
Friction Loss:	17.5 psi × 2.31 ft/psi = 40.43 ft
Operating Pressure:	80 psi × 2.31 ft/psi = 184.80 ft
Total:	**278.23 ft (120.5 psi)**

In this case, we would want a pump system that discharges 1200 gpm at 279 ft (121 psi). If all the sprinklers were valve-in-head type and regulated to 80 psi, most manufacturers require an additional 10 psi for regulation, so the discharge would have to be 1200 gpm at 302 ft (131 psi).

Before selecting a pump, you must decide whether one or more pumps are required to achieve the desired flow and head requirements. Typically, a single 1200 gpm pump is not the solution unless, for example, the water source for the irrigation system is a single deep well and there is no storage pond and the 1200 gpm is pumped directly out of the well into the irrigation system. Most golf courses have multiple pumps—a situation that is more efficient, uses less electricity, and provides a backup in case one pump or motor fails. A typical system that pumps from a pond (or lake, river, etc.) may divide the demand to be more efficient and to ensure some backup in case there is a problem with one pump or motor. In a constant speed system there would be a pressure maintenance pump producing approximately 25 gpm, a jockey pump at approximately 200 gpm, and two 500 gpm main pumps, all providing the same head (Figure 3.3). Conventional systems in the past have utilized tanks in place of pressure maintenance pumps, but with the possibility of tanks failing or exploding, most manufacturers have elected to use more pumps in lieu of the tank.

FIGURE 3.3
Most golf course systems include multiple pumps—in this case a jockey and two mains.

In a variable frequency drive (VFD) system, the question is whether to have two or three main pumps. This system includes only a pressure maintenance pump and no jockey pump. The choice would be two 600 gpm or three 400 gpm pumps. The selection may be based on price or horsepower. There are two ways to determine the horsepower: from a pump curve or by calculations.

A pump curve indicates how a given pump will perform. This is a graph that shows flow in gpm (horizontally) versus head in feet (vertically) (Figures 3.4 and 3.5). A pump curve also provides the horsepower, efficiency (electrical energy to mechanical energy), and net positive suction head required (NPSHR) at various operating points. The most important thing to remember about a pump is that it will operate only along its performance curve, so selecting the proper pump is very important. There are thousands of pumps available.

Figure 3.4 shows a pump curve for a Cornell Model 2-1/2 YHB end suction centrifugal pump. There are actually four different curves represented, with each curve having a different impeller trim: 7, 8, 9, or 10 in. Once the pump is purchased with the chosen impeller, it will operate only along the curve for that impeller. In addition to the curves, Figure 3.4 shows that the pump is operating at 3600 rpm, has a single volute (one impeller), and uses a closed impeller. Closed impellers pass fewer solids than open impellers but are more efficient. The pump flows from 0 to 700 gpm at 0 to 500 ft of head. Notice that the pump is most efficient in the 450 to 650 gpm range. If we were to look at the previous 500 gpm at 279 ft requirement, we would find the curve (heavy line) at 500 gpm and go to the 279 ft mark. This point falls almost exactly on the curve for the 9 in. diameter impeller. At this point, the efficiency is approximately 73.3 percent (odd-shaped lines), interpolating between the 73 percent and 74 percent lines. The NPSHR is 17.5 ft, exactly in the middle of the 15 ft and 20 ft lines (almost vertical lines coming from the top down). The required horsepower is 60 hp, as it is just under the line (dashed lines labeled on the right as horsepower). Notice that if the gpm goes down, the head goes up. If the gpm goes up, the head goes down. Different pump designs change head at different rates, depending on the shape of the curve.

The curves show that as the flow changes, which is common during a cycle in a golf course irrigation system, the pressure changes. Therefore, the pressure must always be controlled, either through a pressure regulating valve or a VFD. The steeper the pump curve, the more important this becomes, as there are large changes in pressure

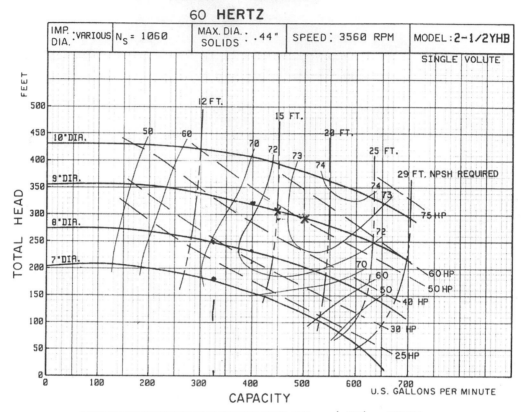

	MAXIMUM IMPELLER DIAMETER	
HP	FOR FULL MOTOR LOAD	FOR FULL MOTOR LOAD + 15% S.F.
75	A(10.00")	
60	B(9.06")	B+(9.94")
50	C(8.69")	C+(8.94")
40	D(8.12")	D+(8.56")
30	E(7.69")	E+(7.88")
25	F(7.12")	F+(7.44")

FT. × (.305) = METERS

GPM × (.227) = CUBIC METERS PER HOUR

Performances shown are for close-coupled electric configuration with packing. Other mounting styles may require horsepower and/or performance adjustments.

FIGURE 3.4.
Typical centrifugal pump curve. *(Courtesy of Cornell Pump Company.)*

with small changes in flow. Changing pressure with flow is also the reason that both mechanical and electronic high-pressure safeties must be included in pump systems. Imagine the problem if a valve or a whole section of a golf course irrigation system did not turn on when signaled to do so. The flow would be much lower and the pressure much higher than desired, potentially causing pressure damage to the system.

Figure 3.5 shows the performance of a Goulds Model 10RJMO vertical turbine pump. This graph shows three different curves, representing the performance of three impellers with diameters of 5.12, 5.87, and 6.62 in., respectively. Notice that these curves are much steeper. Changes in pressure due to changes in flow are much more significant. The Figure 3.5 shows that the pump is operating at 1760 rpm (1800 for practical purposes). The slower speed is typical of turbine applications, although 3600 rpm is also seen. Operating the pump at the slower speed causes less wear and therefore requires less maintenance, resulting in lower overall operating costs. However, it does increase the initial capital cost. This pump flows from 0 to 800 gpm at only 10 to 50 ft of head. The pressure is low because

FIGURE 3.5
Typical turbine pump curve.
(Courtesy of Goulds Pump.)

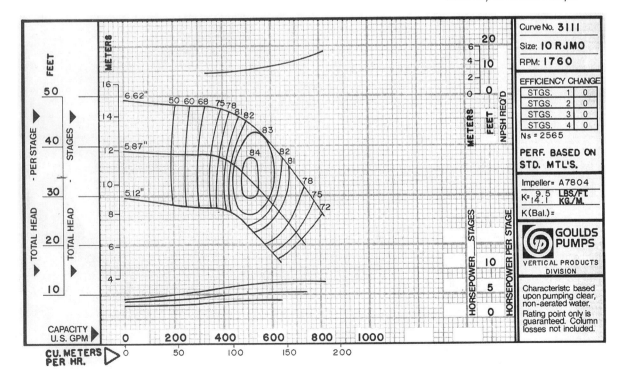

this curve represents the head for only a single stage. To obtain the desired pump head, many stages may be required. Notice that the pump is most efficient at about 500 gpm. If we were to look at the requirement of 500 gpm at 279 ft, we would divide the 279 ft requirement by the head per stage based on the impeller chosen. Follow the 500 gpm line to the 5.87 inch impeller curve. Then reading to the left (head), the axis would indicate approximately 34 ft of head; 279 ft divided by 34 ft is 8.2, or 9 stages required. Using the larger 6.62 in. impeller would yield 45 ft per stage, or 7 stages. With the smaller impeller, the efficiency is higher, more than 84 percent, so it is the better choice. The NPSHR, the single line at the top, at 500 gpm is 3 ft. Because this is a turbine, with the pump in the water, NPSHR can normally be ignored. The required horsepower is determined by looking at the bottom horizontal lines. Each line represents a different impeller. Note that at the middle line at 500 gpm, the requirement is almost exactly 5 hp per stage. With the 9 stages, that would be 45 hp, so a 50 hp motor would be needed.

Both of these pumps are in the 400 to 600 gpm range, to work with our 1200 gpm at 279 ft pump system. The turbine pumps require 10 hp less than the centrifugals because of their higher efficiency, which over time will add up to substantial electrical savings. With these savings, coupled with the lower maintenance costs, the long-term expense for this system is much less than that of the end suction system. Its capital costs, however, are much higher for purchase and installation. A thorough analysis of short- and long-term costs may be necessary to determine the type of system to be installed.

Horsepower is calculated using the following formula:

$$hp = \frac{gpm \times TDH}{3960 \times efficiency}$$

where

gpm   =   gallons per minute being pumped
TDH   =   total dynamic head required
3960   =   constant, for conversion of units
Efficiency   =   of the pump, from its curve

For a 500 gpm pump in the conventional system used previously with an efficiency of 72 percent:

$$hp = \frac{500 \text{ gpm} \times 279 \text{ ft}}{3960 \times 0.72} = 48.93 \text{ hp}$$

This pump requires a 50 hp motor. Notice that the theoretical horsepower is less than the 60 hp required by the curve. However, the curve horsepower would be the determining factor because it is based on actual pump tests, and the 60 hp motor would be needed.

For a 600 gpm pump in a turbine system:

$$hp = \frac{600 \text{ gpm} \times 279 \text{ ft}}{3960 \times 0.84} = 50.32$$

This pump requires a 60 hp motor, but if the designer is willing to give up a small amount of flow, a 50 hp pump can be used.

When a golf course irrigation pump system is designed, two types of pumping are possible, depending on the flow and pressure required. The pumps are configured either in parallel or in series. In parallel pumping (Figure 3.6), each pump has its own suction side (although they may share a common suction line) and the flow can vary from pump to pump. Because all of the pumps are pumping into a common discharge header, all of the discharge pressures must be the same, but the flows can vary. Parallel pumping is typical of a multiple-pump golf course system. For example, with three 400 gpm pumps in parallel discharging 120 psi, the pump system would discharge a total of 1200 gpm at 120 psi.

The use of pump systems in different locations on a golf course is a variation of parallel pumping. It is extremely important that the discharge pressures be the same (taking into account any elevation changes), as low pressure cannot be pumped into high pressure. If one of the pumps is not producing enough pressure, it will not be able to pump water into the higher pressure pipe system at the expected flow rate. The pump will move left on its curve until it can produce the required pressure. Otherwise, the pump impeller will

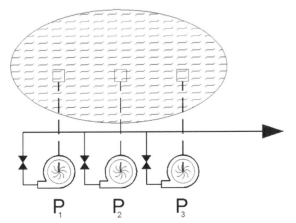

FIGURE 3.6
In parallel pumping, all pumps have access to the water source.

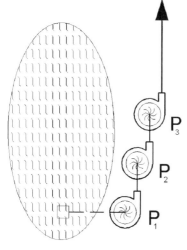

FIGURE 3.7

In series pumping, only some pumps have access to the water source.

just spin and move no water. It is a common problem in irrigation systems with multiple pump system locations to find that one pump is doing most of the work when it was thought they were all performing equally.

In series pumping the pump system may look the same, but not every pump has a suction in the water (Figure 3.7). Series pumping is most often seen on golf courses that have significant elevation changes, or separate high- and low-pressure discharges. In series pumping the flow stays the same from pump to pump, but the discharge pressures can vary. The pressure is boosted with each subsequent pump to a greater pressure. For example, if the three 400 gpm pumps discharging at 120 psi are installed in series, the discharge of the pump system is 400 gpm at 360 psi. Series pumping is typical of booster applications in which the booster pump is on the same skid as the main pumps or at a remote location.

Booster Pump Systems

Booster pumps increase the pressure of systems that are already under pressure (Figure 3.8). A booster pump is commonly used in municipally supplied systems, but may be used as a second pump system in an irrigation system with large elevation changes. The TDH for a booster pump is modified by subtracting the pressure or head that is already available at the flow required. If the system is using

FIGURE 3.8

Booster pumps increase water pressure, but not flow.

municipal water and the dynamic (residual) pressure at 600 gpm is 25 psi (57.75 ft), that value is subtracted from the system TDH of 279 ft, and the booster pump's TDH is then 221.25 ft. The required horsepower for a pump with a 72 percent efficiency is:

$$\text{hp} = \frac{600\ \text{gpm} \times 221.5\ \text{ft}}{3960 \times 0.72} = 46.56,\ \text{or } 50\ \text{hp}$$

Booster pumps increase only pressure; they do not increase flow.

MOTORS

Motors are matched to the specific pumps being used to provide the necessary horsepower. A good golf course pump system design has the operating point of the pump requiring less horsepower than required by the nameplate (attached to the motor), so that the motor is not overloaded. It is common practice with some companies to let the motor work within the service factor of the pump, which in most applications is 1.15. This means that the motor can be loaded at 15 percent more than the rated horsepower. For a 50 hp pump, the service factor will allow it to be used to 57.5 hp on an intermittent basis. This is a bad idea, however, as continued use of the motor at a horsepower greater than specified by its nameplate results in excess heat and increased maintenance requirements, thus reducing the useful life of the motor.

A motor's voltage, phase, hertz, and amperage must be matched to the incoming electrical supply. All of this information can be found on the motor's nameplate. Motors have different insulation class factors, which affect their price and durability. In irrigation systems, Class F, and, rarely, Class H insulation are commonly used.

Motor efficiency is also important. High- and premium-efficiency motors are more expensive, but usually pay for themselves in a three- to five-year period because of their 2 to 4 percent higher efficiency. The additional cost of high-efficiency motors may also be offset by utility companies in terms of a rebate. There are also motors specifically designed for use with VFD drives. These are more expensive than conventional motors because of special windings and insulation. They are popular in other industries, but rarely used in golf course pumping systems because of their high cost.

CONTROLS

A golf course pump system can be controlled in many different ways. The type of control depends on the size, budget, age, and type (VFD or conventional) of the pump system. The manufacturer's operation theory will also be a factor. If the system is small, such as including only a single pump, or an older multiple-pump system, it is most commonly controlled with pressure switches and a limit switch is installed on the pressure-regulating valve, if there is one. The limit switch sends a signal to the controls when the valve is opened or closed. The first pump, a jockey or pony pump, starts when there is a drop in pressure. The remaining larger pumps turn on and off based on various pressure points, and the system will shut off when there is no flow, which is sensed by the limit switch on the pressure-regulating valve or by an additional pressure switch. In some systems, the pressure-regulating valve may also switch the pumps, as this can be considered a measure of flow (how far open the valve is) (Figure 3.9). This setup is indicated by the presence of multiple limit switches on the top of the pressure-regulating valve. The signals from the pressure and limit switches are wired to relays, which then control the signals to turn the pumps on and off. The relays are usually a series of clear plastic cubes ("ice cube relays") plugged into the wiring system inside the control panel.

FIGURE 3.9
Use of a pressure-regulating valve is a common way to maintain a set pressure regardless of flow on a pump system.

Some technologies utilize automatic gear-operated butterfly valves installed on each pump's discharge. These valves regulate pressure in place of the pressure-regulating valve and do not require limit switches. This type of control provides a greater degree of accuracy and a quicker response for pressure regulation with less friction loss than a control valve.

A more modern type of control system utilizes a programmable logic controller (PLC) (Figure 3.10). A PLC takes input from pressure transducers and flow meters installed on the discharge manifold. These two inputs are wired into the logic controller. Using specialized software, the "logic" then decides what pumps should be on and off, or in the case of a VFD system, at what speed the pump should operate, and which pump should be controlled by the drive. The PLC also monitors all the pump system safety circuits and has built-in diagnostic capabilities. The logic controller also acts as the interface between the control panel and any monitoring software. In a VFD system, it signals the drive and may also monitor its safeties on a limited basis. The PLC also provides the user interface (display) with the information requested by the operator.

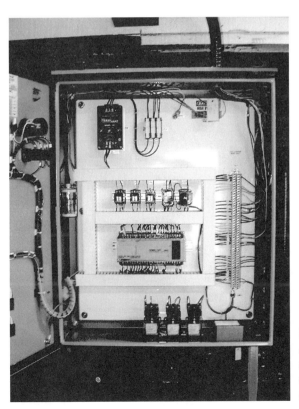

FIGURE 3.10
A programmable logic controller is a common component of a pump system control panel.

VARIABLE FREQUENCY DRIVES

Today almost all golf course irrigation pump systems utilize variable frequency drive (VFD) technology in one form or another (Figure 3.11). VFDs change the frequency of the electricity going to the pump motor, which in turn increases or decreases the speed of the motor (rpm). Increasing or decreasing the rpm allows the discharge pressure to remain constant with changes in flow, as opposed to a conventional system, which requires a pressure-regulating valve to control the pressure with changes in flow. Basically, the VFD allows the pump to operate on multiple curves. With the use of a VFD to change the frequency, the electrical requirements are less and the cost of electricity is lower. The motor uses only the electricity needed for the required flow, and not the full electrical requirement of the motor (nameplate horsepower) as in a conventional system. Moreover, a VFD system is much easier on the piping system than a conventional system. There are no surges resulting from pumps turning on and off, and most VFD control software has a slow fill mode that automatically fills the pipeline slowly whenever the system pressure has significantly dropped below the desired operating pressure.

A VFD also has its own set of safeties to protect the drive itself, included in its software. These are separate from the pump system safeties. The VFD safeties are numerous and include voltage, speed, and overload, among others. On some pump systems these safeties

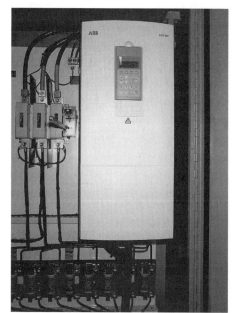

FIGURE 3.11
Use of a variable-frequency drive is a more energy efficient way to control pressure with changes in flow.

are interfaced with the control panel logic so they can be displayed, on a limited basis, on the pump control panel user interface.

PUMP SYSTEM SAFETY CIRCUITS

Because of the cost of today's pump systems, they need to be well protected against problems in the irrigation system operation and against malfunctions of their own components. There are standard safeties that must be installed for each type of system.

Phase

The incoming power should be monitored to make sure that the voltage is within proper limits so that the equipment will not be damaged, that all three phases are present, and that the motor is rotating in the proper direction. Newer motor starters may have built-in safeties, which include over- and undervoltage, phase reversal, and motor overload protection. Phase failure safeties may be installed on the incoming power or on each individual pump. It is also a good idea to install a voltage safety circuit on the low-voltage (120 V) control side.

High and Low Pressure

A low-pressure safety protects the system against problems in the field (such as a mainline break), which drastically lowers the pressure. The low-pressure safety shuts down the pump system if the low pressure condition occurs for a specified amount of time. Without this safety, the system would continue to pump water, flooding the golf course or creating more damage. The control system must be capable of overriding this safety so that filling of empty lines can still be accomplished after winterization or repairs. Conversely, a high-pressure safety protects the irrigation piping system from high pressures and possible breakage by shutting down the system after a specified time at an excessive pressure.

Low Water

A low-water safety is specific to wet well systems, usually turbines. The low-water-level safety turns off the pump system if the water level in the wet well drops below a predetermined point. Typically, the point is set about 3 ft above the bottom of a turbine pump or 18 in. above a screened inlet. This safety's primary purpose is to keep the pumps from running in a dry condition, which would damage the seals and other components. The safety includes a level sensor installed in the wet well. This safety can also be used in conjunction with an automatic makeup water system. A signal is sent to other water sources to turn on when the wet well has dropped below a specified level (meaning the pond needs recharge) and turn off when the level indicates a full condition.

Loss of Prime

A loss-of-prime safety protects a centrifugal pump from running dry. The safety senses that the pressure of the water on the suction side of the pump is too low and shuts the system down. On a booster pump installation this mechanism is called a low-inlet-pressure safety.

High Temperature

A high-temperature safety senses the temperature of the pump (Figure 3.12). When water is being pumped, the water cools the volute and maintains a low temperature. If water is not flowing

FIGURE 3.12

A high-temperature safety is an important component of a centrifugal pumping system.

through the pump, the temperature of the volute rises immediately because of the mechanical action that is taking place. This action generates heat, which activates the safety. This safety can also be used for loss-of-prime protection.

PRESSURE RELIEF VALVE

A pressure relief valve (Figure 3.13) is a mechanical safety (unlike the electronic high-pressure safety) that is designed to protect the piping system from damage. It senses the pressure in the pump system discharge and opens to relieve the excess pressure before it can damage components of the irrigation system. The opening pressure of the valve is set at some point above the desired operating pressure, typically 15 psi. The electronic high-pressure safety is then set about 10 psi above this point. The pressure relief valve for a VFD system should be sized for the full discharge capacity of the pump system so as to be effective in case the drive fails. However, in a conventional system, the relief valve can be smaller in size because it must lower the pressure only slightly, which can be accomplished by diverting a small percentage of the flow to the atmosphere.

FIGURE 3.13
A pressure-relief valve is a mechanical safety that protects the piping system from high pressure.

REMOTE MONITORING

Remote monitoring allows a golf course superintendent or other personnel to monitor the operation of the pump system without being in the pump house. Monitoring is usually accomplished with the use of modems linking the superintendent's office computer and the pump system control panel. Communication between the two modems can occur over telephone lines with dial up service, via hard-wired direct burial cables, or through radio. The advantage of using the telephone is that the system can be monitored from any location connecting directly to the control panel. The radio and hard wire can be on-line at all times, but monitoring from another location will require communicating with the office computer first, and then through it to the monitoring software.

Software of the past would allow monitoring of pump operation only. Factors such as flow, pressure, pump and alarm status, and so on, could be viewed from the software. With some software the pumps could be turned on or off and the total flow reset. The irrigation and pump systems were two separate systems, and the pump system would react only to the irrigation system's protecting itself from any problems with its many safeties. It was possible to monitor and manually react to such occurrences. Recently, more interactive systems have been developed by some manufacturers for communicating between the pump system software and the irrigation control software. The two software sets communicate directly with each other so that the pump system can be more reactive. For example, if the irrigation software thinks it is using 1000 gpm but the pump system says it is pumping only 850 gpm, the monitoring communication can have the irrigation control system turn on more sprinklers to utilize the 150 gpm still available from the pump system. This will allow the irrigation schedule to be completed faster, operating the pumps more efficiently and saving energy. Much of the interaction is based on an Internet protocol to allow monitoring and changes to the systems over the Internet in the future. These "smart systems" provide valuable information in terms of inputs and the ability to record and store large amounts of data.

POWER

Most irrigation pump systems are energized with the use of an electrical power supply. In areas where the proper amount of electricity is not available, engine-driven pumps are used. Diesel and liquid petroleum engines are most prevalent, and automated controls can be used to start and stop the pumps. Engine driven systems are usually avoided, however, as they are noisy, especially near a body of water that reflects the sound. Residential mufflers are a must. They also require containment for the fuel tank and have higher maintenance costs. Yet in some areas, the cost of establishing the proper electrical service may equal the costs of four or five engine-driven pumps. Although the pump is the same as with an electrical system, choosing the proper engine to drive it requires specific expertise and should be left to an experienced engine distributor or pump engineer.

In considering an electrical supply, phase, hertz, voltage, and amperage are all important factors. For motors with more than 10 hp (15 hp on submersible pumps), three-phase power is required.

Three-phase power can be difficult to obtain in some areas, and since the deregulation of electrical utilities it can be very expensive. Single-phase power can be converted to three-phase power with specialized equipment such as a roto-phase motor or VFD drives. These are expensive options from both a cost and an operating standpoint, but may be the only source available to power a pump system. They should be specified and designed only by experienced personnel.

Common voltages in the United States are 110/120, 208, 220/240, and 460/480. In Canada, 575 V supplies are common. It is important to have the correct voltage and phase, as the pump motors and control panel will work only at the voltage and phase for which they were designed. For example, 208 V power requires special motors and equipment, which are not stock items in most motor shops or electrical supply houses. Whenever possible a three-phase 460/480 V supply is the preferred choice for cost considerations as well as for availability of parts and service.

Amperage is a measure of the load being placed on an electrical supply. It is based on the horsepower and voltage of the pump motors and any other electrical demands that are being supplied from the same power source. The type of load (resistive, capacitive, inductive, or a combination of all three) determines the total impedance. Total impedance and load type determine amperage required. Voltage plays an important role in amperage calculations, as doubling the voltage halves the amperage. Inducing a third phase with a VFD or roto-phase will also require additional amperage as the voltages may be low. Moreover, most utilities allow the maximum electrical load to be only 75 or 80 percent of the service capacity. When a new pump system is to be installed, the power company will want to know what type of service is desired, including the amperage, normal and locked rotor, voltage, phase, type of start (across the line or reduced voltage), and how many pumps operate at a time. It will also want to know whether the service desired will be primary or secondary. Primary service puts the supply transformer in close proximity to the pump house (Figure 3.14), whereas a secondary service runs power wires from the transformers, usually pole mounted at the property line, to the pump house (Figure 3.15). Primary service is more direct, less troublesome, and requires little maintenance. However, the power company may require an easement and passable road along its total length.

FIGURE 3.14
Pad-mounted transformers are preferred for underground electrical supplies.

FIGURE 3.15
Pole-mounted transformers are normally used with overhead electrical supplies.

INTAKES AND DISCHARGES

Wet Wells and Intake Piping

For turbine type pump systems and some specialized centrifugal installations on surface water supplies, wet wells must be installed. A wet well is usually installed on the shore of the water source, and a pipe or intake flume is installed, reaching out into the water. This type of system is most common with surface water supplies such as ponds, lakes, and rivers. In some instances a wet well may be filled directly from another water source (well or city water), but these applications are rare. The size of the intake flume is determined by the amount of water being pumped, and the size of the wet well is determined by the amount of water being pumped and the size and number of pumps being installed in the wet well. The flume pipe should be installed with some type of screening at its end (Figure 3.16). This can be a self-cleaning rotating strainer if there is heavy debris, or a simple box screen to keep out fish and other large debris.

FIGURE 3.16
Inlets should be screened to prevent debris from entering the pumps.

It is desirable to have a shut-off device in the flume pipe to allow isolation of the wet well from the water supply for cleaning purposes, but these devices can be expensive.

The inlet piping should be designed so that the velocity of the water coming through it at the maximum pumping capacity is between 1.0 and 1.5 ft per second (fps). At these low velocities, most sand or other debris in suspension will settle out. For example, a 1200 gpm pump system would utilize an 18 in. inlet pipe for 1.5 fps and a 24 in. inlet pipe for less than 1.0 fps. The inlet pipe can be of a number of different materials, including SDR 35 PVC (because there is no pressure), HDPE, steel, corrugated steel, or drainage pipe. Plastic pipes last longer, but cost and availability are often the most important considerations in regard to the material chosen.

Suctions

It is important in a lift situation to have a flexible suction pipe that can bend or pivot with changes in water level. Suction piping can be made of several different materials, such as aluminum, HDPE, or steel. PVC is a poor choice, as it is vulnerable to degradation from ultraviolet light. A flotation device is needed to keep the end of the pipe off the bottom of the water source and at the proper depth to prevent vortexes (Figure 3.17). In shallow water a stand or support may also be included to keep the intake from getting too close to the bottom of the water source, where it can pull in debris. In a suction

FIGURE 3.17
Suction lift systems should utilize floats to allow for changes in water level.

situation, a foot valve is usually installed on the end of the suction pipe to keep it filled with water and maintain prime to the pump; alternately, some type of priming assistance system can be used. The foot valve is a specialized check valve that is used at the "foot" or intake of the suction pipe, usually in combination with a screen or strainer. A foot valve can be installed vertically or at an angle, in a swing check or positive (vertical) shut-off configuration. It opens when the pump turns on, as a result of water movement toward the pump.

During evaluation of the performance and requirements of a horizontal centrifugal pump in a lift situation, it is very important to consider pressure losses on the suction side. The values of net positive suction head "available" (NPSHA) and net positive suction head "required" (NPSHR) are needed. NPSHA is calculated based on the pump installation. NPSHR is a function of the pump and is obtained from a pump curve. It increases with pump capacity. A check valve and any other fittings on the suction side of the pump have friction losses, as does the suction piping itself. All of these friction losses, plus the elevation from the water source to the centerline of the pump, must be calculated to determine whether the pump will be able to take the required amount of water into its volute quickly enough. The temperature of the water and the velocity of water through the suction assembly must also be known, as they are all part of the NPSHA calculations. Because of the importance of minimizing losses on the suction side, the suction piping must be several sizes larger than the suction inlet on the pump. There should be no high points in the suction line, so that air does not accumulate. Eccentric reducers, located at the pump inlet, are used for this purpose. Atmospheric pressure at sea level is 14.7 psi or 34 ft and is reduced with increasing elevation. Theoretically, the suction lift of a pump cannot exceed the 34 ft. The elevation from the water source to the centerline of the inlet of the pump, friction losses through the suction assembly, including the foot valve, and the NPSHR from the pump curve all must add up to less than 34 ft so that the pump will not cavitate. Cavitation, in simple terms, means that a pump is discharging water faster than water is coming into the pump. It is easy to identify because a cavitating pump sounds as though it is pumping rocks.

For example, if, at sea level, a pump is installed 10 ft above the water source and there are 8 ft of friction losses (3.5 psi) in the suction assembly, a total of 18 ft is subtracted from the 34 ft, leaving 16 ft. The 16 ft is the NPSHA. NPSHA must always be greater than the NPSHR. So in this case, if a pump at the design operating point has a NPSHR of 16 ft or more, the pump will not operate properly. If NPSHR from the pump curve is less than 16 ft, it should not be a problem. Keep in mind that a pump moves along its curve. So if a pump is being operated at other points on the curve, NPSH must be checked for each operating point. The actual equation for NPSHA is:

$$\text{NPSHA} = H_a - H_s - H_f - H_{vp} - H_v$$

where

H_a = atmospheric pressure at the elevation of the water surface

H_s = static lift (vertical distance between the water surface and the centerline of the pump)

H_f = all suction assembly losses (entrance pipe, valves, fittings, foot valves, strainers, etc.)

H_{vp} = vapor pressure of liquid being pumped (in this case water)

H_v = velocity head ($V^2/2g$, where g is the acceleration due to gravity, 32.2 ft/s^2)

NPSHA/NPSHR is a hard concept to understand, and the selection of pumps when suction lifts are involved is best left to an experienced pump engineer.

It is also important to account for variations in lake level throughout the irrigation season.

FIGURE 3.18
Discharge piping should be steel in a zee or ell type configuration.

Discharge Piping

Discharge piping exiting a pump system is usually made of welded steel pipe or galvanized steel pipe and fittings. The use of PVC pipe and fittings is not recommended, as the velocities in the pump system are high and the added strength of steel and its heat dissipation characteristics are an advantage. In a golf course system, the discharge is usually routed through the wall of the pump house and then connected to the irrigation mainline below grade using a zee pipe (Figure 3.18). In some instances the discharge pipe may be routed through the pump house floor. However, if there is a problem with the discharge piping in the future, the floor will have to be taken up.

PUMP HOUSES

Size

The size of a pump house depends on a number of factors. The size of the pump system components or prefabricated skid will be important. Equally important, and frequently overlooked, is that the building must meet the requirements of the current edition of the National Electric Code (NEC). The NEC has been adopted in its entirety by most states and local jurisdictions in the United States. However, some cities and counties have modified portions, so it is important to thoroughly investigate all local code requirements before laying out a pump house. Local engineering firms and building inspectors are good sources of accurate code information. A pump house should be properly sized for the equipment installed, maintenance, and economic considerations. Turbine systems need crane access around the pump house for maintenance of the pumps. Over time, trees can grow up around the pump house and cause problems of access.

The NEC has very specific clearance requirements for electrical components. The basic requirement is 42 in. of clear space in front of any electrical panel of more than 150 V. This requirement not only includes the pump system control panel, which may be skid mounted or wall mounted, but also applies to all other panels, including the incoming power shutoff, the motor load control center, and any circuit breaker cabinets for the building. On the sides of the pump or skid without electrical panels, there should be at least 18 to 24 in. of clear space to allow access for maintenance and repair work.

Do not confuse the inside dimensions of the building with the outside dimensions, or you may calculate a space that is too small. The building may also have to house other equipment such as injectors for wetting agents, fertilizers, biological controls, and so forth. Fertigation systems essentially double the size of a pump house if the liquid fertilizer is to be stored inside. A pump house should be sized for the equipment to be installed when it is constructed and for any additional equipment that may be added in the future.

The reasons for constructing a building include protection against vandalism, security, equipment protection, aesthetics, and protection against liability. However, it is not always necessary to install a pump system in a building. Many systems are designed and built to be out in the elements. Some have only a fence for protection against vandalism; others have only a roof for protection against rain and sun.

A pump house can be constructed of many different materials. Most common is concrete block or concrete masonry unit (CMU) (Figure 3.19). Sometimes a decorative block is used to give the pump house a more attractive look. Other materials include wood and metal. Metal is less expensive, but the advantage of wood is that the finish can be quite varied, allowing it to match other buildings on the golf course or to blend in with its surroundings.

The slab and footing should be strong enough to support the building and carry the maximum load for the equipment being installed with the appropriate safety factor. In heavy frost areas, footings are installed below the frost line. Doors should be large enough to accommodate equipment and the fertigation tanks if they are stored inside the pump house. A double door usually works best. A window to allow view of the pump station control panel is a good idea. For a turbine system, a roof hatch is necessary to remove the

FIGURE 3.19
Pump houses are made of many different materials and should be sized for all necessary equipment.

pumps for maintenance. Often, the hatch is a skylight installed in the roof. The hatch should be sized to make the removal process as easy as possible. If the system injects chemicals, containment will be needed in the building around any storage tanks. There are various state laws (usually based on agricultural, rather than turf, issues) regarding how much containment is required, generally a certain percentage of the stored liquid. It is a good idea, however, to be able to contain the entire storage capacity in case of a problem. Containment usually consists of a wall around the storage area at a height and area large enough to hold the amount of liquid being stored (Figure 3.20). In a 24 × 24 building, about half the area would be contained and a 21- to 24-in.-high containment wall installed. It is important to extend the containment area under the injection ports, as that is where most of the leaks will occur or where a hose may blow off. It is useful to seal the inside of the containment wall with a concrete sealer to prevent the liquid from being absorbed into the material. In addition, all doors or wall penetrations into the building containment area must be above the minimum height of the containment wall. It is important that the building meet all national, state, and local building codes. Many pump houses will require a building permit. It is a good idea to have the pump house designed by an architect or engineer, although he or she will require knowledgeable assistance with the layout of the different pieces of equipment.

Ventilation

Cooling of the building is a necessary component of any pump system installation. As the system operates, the motors produce heat that must be dissipated to keep the motors operating efficiently and

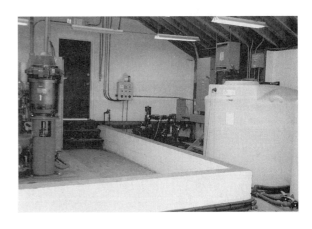

FIGURE 3.20
For fertigation, secondary containment, such as concrete walls as shown here, should be constructed.

to avoid shortening their useful life. There are two common ways to determine cooling requirements. One way is to base the requirement on the total horsepower in the building at a rate of 16 cfm per hp. For example, for a turbine VFD pump system consisting of three 60 hp pumps and a 3 hp submersible pressure maintenance pump, the cfm requirement would be 3 pumps × 60 hp × 16 cfm per hp, or 2880 cfm. The 3 hp pump need not be considered, as it is submerged in a wet well. A flooded suction system with three 60 hp pumps and a 3 hp pressure maintenance pump would require 3 pumps × 60 hp + 3 hp × 16 cfm per hp, or 2928 cfm. In both cases, a 3000 cfm exhaust fan would be installed. Any fertigation or injection pumps in the building must also be taken into consideration.

The second way of sizing the ventilation rate needed is to turn the building air over every five minutes. For example, if the building were 24 ft × 24 ft × 10 ft high, the cfm requirement would be 5760 cubic ft divided by 5 minutes, or 1152. A 1250 cfm fan would be required. VFD pump systems also require cooling of the control panel itself; this is accomplished with the use of a heat exchanger or small air conditioner installed directly on the side or back of the pump system control panel.

The pump house will have several different wires coming in through the walls and conduits must be installed for them. Wiring commonly includes communication wire between the pump control panel and the irrigation system computer, power for irrigation controllers, power supply for the building, pump system grounding, telephone, and other electrical devices such as fans, as well as aerators and fountains that may be out on the golf course but use the pump house for an electrical supply. Conduits installed through the floor or footing give the building a much neater appearance than conduits installed through the walls in many different locations. However, conduits cannot be installed through the containment wall, as this could cause problems with the containment area or wiring within the conduit.

INJECTION AND FILTRATION

The piping system of an irrigation system is intricate and detailed and provides a simple, existing means of applying materials to the turf and other areas of the golf course. In addition to water, an efficient irrigation system can be used to distribute various materials, such as fertilizer, acid, wetting agents, water conditioners, biological controls, and

FIGURE 3.21
Many different materials, including wetting agents, can be applied through the irrigation system.

other materials such as sulfur, gypsum, and molasses. It is important to do a detailed soil and water quality analysis to determine what materials, if any, will help with water or turf quality. Experience shows that each course responds differently to injection and that before spending large sums of money, due diligence must be performed. Many golf courses inject wetting agents into their irrigation water using simple to sophisticated equipment. Proper backflow prevention equipment must be installed when injecting into any irrigation system.

Fertigation

Fertigation systems are standard on new construction, as they reduce the amount of time that equipment must be taken out on the golf course while the course is being grown in. The amount of fertilizer needed may also be significantly reduced. In considering fertigation systems, rate and capacity are important details. Many inexpensive systems require a lot of water to be used in order to apply a small amount of fertilizer. The result is a flooded golf course with little fertilizer applied. Systems with capacities of 140 gal per hour or more seem to work best because they provide higher concentrations of nutrients without over-watering the golf course. A separate pump for mixing and transferring liquids between storage tanks makes the system more versatile. All such systems require space, either in or out of the pump house, and containment, as discussed earlier. In addition, they will require electrical power, conduits, and injection ports. Many have their own control panels that interface with the pump system flow meter, as a minimum, or with the logic controller itself in more sophisticated systems. Phase, voltage, and amperage must all be determined.

Filtration

Depending on the quality of the water source and the intake structure for the pump system, filtration may be needed. There are many different types of filtration devices available, ranging from simple wye strainers to large automatic self-cleaning screens (Figure 3.22). Any filter system needs to be sized for the full flow of the pump system and for the size of the material that has to be removed. In a well system, there may be no filtration required, or there may be iron or sulfur to remove. On a surface water system, primary filtration such

FIGURE 3.22
Filters are prevalent on pump systems where water quality is a concern.

as an intake screen is needed to keep out fish, debris, and other materials, and on the discharge side a secondary wye strainer can be installed to keep anything large from getting into the system if the primary screen fails. Sand, silt, algae, and other materials are more difficult to remove and require more sophisticated systems than screens and wye strainers. Sand filters, brush filters, screen filters, and sand separators are all commonly found on golf courses. They are designed to remove organics, inorganics, or both. Mesh sizes depend on what is to be removed. Zebra mussels require a greater level of filtration in the 25–40 micron range. Sand is best removed with a sand separator, but the separator will remove little else (Figure 3.23). Screen filters are good for removing inorganics, and sand media filters are best at removing organics. In situations where the water quality is very poor, both types may be needed. Again, before any equipment is selected, a detailed water quality analysis should be performed to make sure it will remove the intended materials throughout the irrigation season, even though there may be variations in water quality.

A filtration system, like an injection system, will require a larger pump house and will increase the electrical requirements of the overall system. It should be automated through the system logic controller so that it can be monitored and operated through the user interface. However, it may also have its own control panel. The backwash from

FIGURE 3.23
Larger particles, such as sand, can be removed with centrifugal separators such as shown here.

the filter system or wye strainer has to be piped out of the pump house in a secure and strong pipe (usually steel) back to the water source or a disposal area. When water is piped back to the water source, it should be discharged downstream of the inlet, or a minimum of 50 ft away, to keep the backwashed debris from returning through the inlet piping.

Pump components do wear, and they do wear out. When pressure and/or flow conditions change significantly, it may be advisable to have a pump test performed. The test will reveal if the pump is operating at design efficiency and will indicate whether repairs are necessary.

4 Materials

Many components of golf course irrigation systems have been borrowed or adapted from other applications. However, they all have two things in common: the ability to accommodate the high pressures and flow rates of golf course systems, and the strength to endure the harsh treatment of a golf course environment. The materials used in a golf course irrigation system are constantly evolving. This chapter discusses the materials and their compliance with codes and standards.

PIPE

Many types of piping materials have been used in golf course irrigation systems over the years. Galvanized steel, copper, brass, cast iron, ductile iron, and asbestos-cement have all played a part in the piping of earlier irrigation systems, with each material having some desirable characteristics. Since the late 1960s, in the United States and most other countries, thermoplastic piping materials have become the most common materials for golf course piping systems.

Thermoplastic piping materials used for golf course systems include polyvinyl chloride (PVC) and polyethylene (PE) pipe. Their desirable characteristics include resistance to corrosion and chemicals, high tensile strength, relatively light weight, long life expectancy, excellent insulating capability, high "C" factors (Hazen-Williams coefficient of flow, the smoothness of the inside wall of a pipe), and relative ease of installation. These materials are available in a wide range of sizes and pressure ratings, and a basic understanding of them can aid in their identification and application.

Because of the wide range of available thermoplastic piping materials, pipe standards have been developed to identify materials, dimensions, pressure ratings, installation, and fittings for the various piping materials. Such standards, however, are not consistent throughout the world.

Polyvinyl Chloride (PVC)

PVC pipe is generally available in sizes from ½ in. to 36 in. There is confusion because of the different PVC pipe pressure ratings. PVC is available as a schedule-rated pipe, in which the pressure rating decreases with larger diameters, or as a pressure-rated pipe, in which the wall thickness of the pipe varies between pipe sizes in order to keep a constant pressure rating. A pressure rating does not imply the safe operating pressure of the pipe material; it is used as a guide for the irrigation system designer, who will factor in potential surge pressures and a safety factor before a pipe material is selected.

- *Schedule-rated pipe*—The most common schedule-rated PVC pipe is known as Schedule 40. Schedules 80, 120, and 160 are also available. The higher the schedule number, the thicker the pipe wall. The outside diameter (OD) and wall thickness of a schedule-rated pipe is the same as that of the same sized schedule steel pipe. The pipe pressure rating decreases as the pipe size increases. For example a ½ in. Schedule 40 pipe made of standard PVC materials has a pressure rating of 600 psi; when the same Schedule 40 pipe size is increased to 6 in., its pressure rating is 180 psi.

- *Pressure-rated pipe*—Because of the undesirable variations in pressure ratings between the different pipe sizes, a pressure rating system based on a standard dimension ratio (SDR) or dimension ratio (DR) for piping materials is available. The dimension ratio is the ratio of the outside diameter of a pipe to the pipe's wall thickness. It ensures the same pipe pressure rating for all pipe sizes. This means that the pressure rating of a 2 in. SDR 21 PVC pipe is the same as the pressure rating of a

6 in. SDR 21 PVC pipe. The most common SDR ratings for golf course irrigation piping systems are SDR 13.5 (315 psi), SDR 21 (200 psi), and SDR 26 (160 psi).

SDR-rated pipe is typically used for golf course applications, although some designers prefer to use Schedule 40 pipe or SDR 13.5 for sizes of 2 in. and smaller, especially for use in rocky soils where the extra wall thickness may provide additional protection against abrasion or impact.

The outside dimensions of schedule-rated and SDR-rated PVC piping products are based on the equivalent outside diameters of standard iron pipe sizes (IPS), thereby allowing the use of the same fittings when using either piping material.

In larger pipe diameters (14 in. and greater) SDR series pipe is not always readily available. In such cases, C905 PVC pipe is often used. C905 pipe is produced to either IPS or cast or ductile iron outside diameters (CIOD) although the latter is more prevalent. C-905 pipe is available in IPS pipe sizes of 14 in. to 36 in. with a DR rating of 21, 26, 32.5, and 41 (200, 160, 125, and 100 psi). If a higher pressure rating is required, CIOD DR 18 (235 psi) is used for pipe sizes 14 in. to 24 in. For diameters less than 14 in., C900 PVC pipe is available, but only in CIOD dimensions. It is available in sizes 4 in. to 12 in., with a DR rating of 14, 18, and 25 (200, 150, and 100 psi).

PVC piping materials are available in 20 ft lengths with a gasket joint or solvent-weld bell end. Welded ends (glue joints) are common with smaller PVC pipe sizes, 2½ in. and less, on shorter pipe runs where the pipe can be snaked in the trench and the effects of thermal expansion and contraction are not as dramatic as they are with larger pipelines in which gasket joints are used.

The outside wall of a PVC pipe is marked, no less than every 5 ft, to aid the user in identifying the type of pipe. The information includes the following:

1. Manufacturer's name.

2. Pipe size.

3. PVC classification or code material: communicates type (impact strength), grade (chemical resistance), and hydrostatic design stress (in units of 100 psi)—for golf course irrigation systems type 1, grade 1, PVC with a hydrostatic design stress of 2000 psi is most common (PVC 1120).

4. Dimension ratio or standard dimension ratio at 23°C.

5. Product type, pressure class, or pressure rating.
6. American Society for Testing and Materials (ASTM) designation.
7. Production record code/date.
8. Seal of laboratory evaluating the pipe; for example, National Sanitation Foundation (NSF).

The determination of which PVC piping material to use is best left to an experienced irrigation system designer, as variables such as working pressure, soil conditions, surge pressure, and safety factors all affect the final selection the pipe.

Polyethylene (PE)

Polyethylene (PE) pipe has several unique physical characteristics that make it a desirable product for many golf course applications. PE displays a greater degree of flexibility than PVC pipe materials, which allows it to be snaked along a trench or the side of a bridge. It is more tolerant of the effects of freezing water, which is beneficial if a pipeline must remain in service during periods of freezing temperatures before it can be winterized. Its resistance to ultraviolet (UV) light allows it to be installed above grade. Lengths of PE pipe can be connected with the use of a special thermofusion welder or electrofusion coupling, eliminating the need for thrust blocks. This also permits it to be used in locations that allow only a limited amount of cover, where the pipeline can be installed without push-on gasket fittings. PE pipe cannot be connected with solvent-weld fittings. Instead, specially fabricated PE fittings (of the same material as the pipe) that require fuse welding, mechanical joint fittings, flanged fittings, and special saddles designed for use on PE piping materials should be used.

The coefficient of thermal expansion and contraction of PE pipe is three times as much as that of PVC piping materials. PE pipe can expand or contract up to 1 in. per 100 ft over a temperature change of 10°F. Design considerations in the selection of pipe fittings and potential temperature changes must be made when PE piping materials are used.

PE pipe is available in sizes from ½ in. to 63 in. There are different types of PE pipe, which relate to the density of the PE material. Lower- and medium-density PE pipe materials are the most flexible, and in smaller pipe diameters, up to 4 in., they are available in coils of 100, 200, 250, 300, 400, and 500 ft. The high-density product

(HDPE), which is less flexible, is available in 40 ft lengths. For golf course applications the high-density product is commonly used, as the lower-density products are more susceptible to stretching (creep) and have lower tensile strengths.

PE pipe is available in both inside diameter (ID) controlled dimensions, common to smaller-diameter PE pipe materials, and outside diameter (OD) controlled pipe dimensions. The ID controlled dimensions of PE pipe permit the use of internal, insert style, fittings. Both pipe styles are available in a schedule wall thickness rating and an SDR wall thickness rating, which varies according to pipe size while maintaining a constant pipe pressure rating. SDR ratings are available for PE pipe. However, the pressure ratings change, based on the type of PE material. The type of PE material is communicated on the side of the pipe with the material designation and a four-digit code that communicates density, high or slow crack growth resistance, and hydrostatic design stress at 73°F expressed as a two digit code in units of 100. Because of the different properties of PE pipe pressure ratings can vary. For example, 3408 HDPE is available with SDR ratings of: SDR 9 (200 psi), SDR 11 (160 psi), and SDR 17 (100 psi), whereas the same SDR ratings for 3406 HDPE are SDR 9 (160 psi), SDR 11 (125 psi), and SDR 17 (80 psi).

The current American National Standards Institute/American Society of Agricultural Engineers (ANSI/ASAE) Standard S376.2 (Jan98), titled "Design, Installation and Performance of Underground, Thermoplastic Irrigation Pipelines," describes important considerations for the use of PVC and PE piping materials as they apply to irrigation systems.

FITTINGS

Connections to pipelines are made with fittings. There are a wide variety of fittings available to provide a number of different connections, such as those used in connecting different piping materials, joining pipes of different sizes, joining different components to pipelines, changing the direction of a pipeline, and making system repairs. Just as the materials, pressure ratings, and specifications can vary dramatically between different piping materials, so too can the properties of pipe fittings. Fittings for new installations differ from the fittings used for repairs or additions (retrofitting) to the system, as do fittings for different pipe sizes and piping materials.

As with piping materials, acceptable fittings must be made to industry standards, and an understanding of the properties of the fittings and the standards to which they are made can help to ensure that the right fitting is used for the given application.

Fittings are generally referred to by the pipe material they are used for and the material they are made of. In the past there was a major difference between the heavier-duty fittings that were made for large-diameter pipelines, which were referred to as mainline fittings, and fittings for smaller pipe diameters, which were called lateral fittings. However, most manufacturers of the larger, heavy-duty fittings now make fittings with similar properties for pipe materials as small as 1½ in., and irrigation designers can select a fitting based on the durability of the product, the installation method, and the budget for the irrigation system.

The majority of fittings for golf course irrigation systems are included in one of the following categories: push-on fittings, mechanical joint fittings, solvent-weld and threaded fittings, threaded pipe, and saddles.

Push-on Fittings

Deep bell push-on gasket fittings are available in PVC or ductile iron for use with iron-pipe-size (IPS) PVC pipe materials. They allow quick and easy installation of tees, bends, reducers, plugs, and adapters for flanged and male threads.

DUCTILE IRON

Ductile iron fittings (Figure 4.1) have a tensile strength of 65,000 psi and are pressure rated for 350 psi. The deep bell, designed to be equal in depth to the bell of a PVC pipe, and the gasket joints provide room for pipe movement. These fittings are available with multiple reducers, which are mechanically restrained to prevent fitting separation and to provide a simple method of adapting to different pipe sizes. Deep bell ductile iron fittings are available in sizes ranging from 1½ in. to 12 in. and larger.

Service tees, also known as tapped couplings, are available to provide a means of connection to a threaded fitting. Depending on the size of the fitting, tapped outlets are available up to 3 in. with a

FIGURE 4.1
Ductile iron fitting.

female iron pipe thread (FIPT); on smaller service tees, 2 in. to 4 in., the threaded outlet is available with an ACME thread to accommodate ACME-threaded swing joints. ACME threads avoid the potentially damaging wedging effect of tapered threads.

PVC

Push-on PVC gasketed molded fittings rated for 200 psi are also available in sizes 1½ in. to 8 in. These fittings are significantly lighter than ductile iron fittings and are generally used in low-pressure systems or on smaller 1½ in. to 2 in. pipelines, where the potential for pressure surges due to water hammer is lower. Push-on PVC fittings are also available in multiple configurations, similar to those that are available in ductile iron.

Small-diameter, 1½ in. to 2½ in., service tees are available with a 315 psi pressure rating. They are for use with ACME-threaded swing joints of the same pressure rating. These service tees eliminate potential problems with cross threading, wedging, or leaking connections of standard pipe threads.

Mechanical Joint Fittings

For large-diameter pipe, 14 in. and greater, ductile iron mechanical joint fittings are used (Figure 4.2). A mechanical joint fitting consists of a Class 350 (350 psi working pressure) ductile iron fitting with a shallow bell socket, a gasket, and a retaining gland with bolts. The gasket is typically available for IPS size plastic pipe, ductile iron pipe, and cast iron pipe. The retaining gland and bolts are used to mechan-

FIGURE 4.2
Mechanical joint fitting.

ically connect the pipe to the fitting by creating a compression connection when the bolts are torqued to the appropriate amount.

The bolts are made of a high-strength, low-alloy steel. Mechanical joint fittings are available in configurations similar to those of ductile iron push-on fittings.

Solvent-Weld and Threaded Fittings

Solvent-weld fittings are used to join PVC materials with the use of a solvent (pipe cleaner) and bonding cement. When these materials are used properly, a weld between the fitting and the PVC pipe is created. PVC fittings are available in a wide variety of configurations, in sizes of ¼ in. to 12 in., in either Schedule 40 or Schedule 80 PVC. In golf course applications PVC solvent-weld fittings are generally used on pipe sizes only up to 2½ in.

Solvent-weld fittings do not conform to a standard pressure rating. The physical process of creating the bond between materials should be in accordance with the manufacturer's recommendations, and only approved chemicals should be used. Threaded connections are also available on Schedule 40 and Schedule 80 fittings. Typically, a combination welded end and thread connection is used to attach valves and sprinklers to the piping system. The threaded outlets usually have female pipe threads.

Threaded Pipe

Threaded pipe, also called threaded nipples, is often used in golf course irrigation systems where valves and other threaded devices are attached to the system. Many products are available, including Schedule 80 PVC, galvanized steel, brass, and ductile iron. Because of its higher rate of deterioration, galvanized steel is seldom used. Most threaded pipe applications are for pipe sizes 3 in. and smaller with lengths ranging from 2 in. to 14 in. or more.

Schedule 80 PVC is available with threads on both ends of the pipe length or threads on one end while the other end is plain. In the latter configuration the pipe nipple is referred to as a threaded one end (TOE). A TOE nipple is very useful in creating the transition between pipe threads and a PVC pipeline, as a threaded connection can be made with an irrigation component and the plain end facilitates the use of a glued connection.

Ductile iron pipe nipples are also available and are used to make vertical and horizontal transitions between a pipeline and a valve. Ductile iron nipples are made of ASTM A-536 ductile iron with a tensile strength of 65,000 psi. They are available only with threads on both ends (TBE).

Saddles

Pipe saddles are used to create smaller service outlets to a piping system; they provide a fast and easy way to tap into an existing pipeline (Figure 4.3). Saddles are commonly available in PVC and ductile iron. PVC saddles are available to 8 in., and ductile iron saddles are sized to 24 in. or more. The tapped outlet of a saddle is available in sizes ranging from 1 in. to 2½ in., depending on the pipe size.

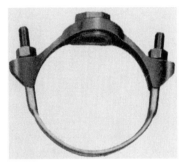

FIGURE 4.3
Saddle.

Saddles are available for a variety of piping materials, including IPS PVC, C-900, C-905, and PE pipe. The specific outside diameter of the pipe must be known so that a presized saddle can be used that will properly conform to the pipe and prevent any undue stress to the piping material.

A ductile iron saddle has three components, an upper piece, the saddle casting, which includes the service gasket material that is centered over the drilled outlet on the pipe; a single or double strap assembly connecting the saddle casting; and connecting bolts. The bolts are torqued to the appropriate foot-pounds (ft lb) to ensure the proper connection to the pipe. Special saddles with resilient gasket materials and spring-grade stainless steel washers are available for HDPE pipe to help counteract the problem of pipe contraction during temperature and pressure changes.

ISOLATION VALVES

Mainline Isolation Valves

The first mainline valves are located at the water source(s) (Figure 4.4). They are responsible for shutting down the entire irrigation system. As the mainline piping network extends from the water source, additional valves are placed on the mainline.

Mainline gate valves are sized to the pipes on which they will operate. These valves must be of high quality, durable, and dependable, as a mainline valve is normally needed only to isolate the system

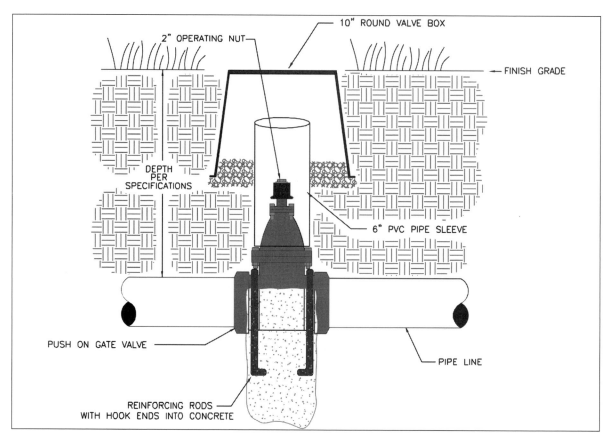

FIGURE 4.4
Mainline gate valve, push-on.

for maintenance or service. As with many irrigation components, new operating criteria and product specifications have spawned the development of new and improved gate valve products. Valve manufacturers have developed new valves that meet higher operational standards. The valve most commonly specified in larger pipe sizes, 3 in. or 4 in. and larger, is a cast iron valve. The current American Water Works Association (AWWA) specification for gate valves is AWWA Standard C-509 for Resilient Seated Cast Iron Gate Valves. Buried cast iron gate valves 4 in. and larger are normally attached to a poured concrete anchor block. Two $\frac{5}{8}$ in. rebar straps extend over the inlet of the valve and down into the concrete. The concrete should not interfere with any of the bolts or nuts on the valve. An appropriately sized mechanical restraining device designed for the piping material in use can also be used in lieu of an anchor block. A valve box and sleeve of rigid PVC should be placed over the manual operating nut for access with a gate valve key. The location of all mainline gate valves should be recorded on the Record Drawing.

Lateral/Sub-Main Isolation Valves

Smaller valves are used to isolate remote control valves, specialty valves such as air/vacuum release valves, and manual drains. Depending on the application, isolation valves can be sized from ½ in. to 3 in. They are typically the same size as the lateral or sub-main pipe they serve. Many different types of valves are used for these applications, including gate, ball, globe, and angle valves, each of which has its own merits. Regional preferences often affect the valve type selected to be used on a golf course.

Lateral/sub-loop isolation valves are typically made of cast bronze. Bronze materials have higher copper content and lower zinc content than the brass used ill-advisedly in some valves, which yields in higher tensile strength and hardness. Bronze materials are very resistant to pitting and are less susceptible to corrosion.

Considerations in selecting a valve include operating pressure, frequency of use, water quality, and serviceability; again, each type of valve havs its own merits.

GATE VALVES

A gate valve is a manual multiturn valve that provides bidirectional flow and is used for on-off operation (Figure 4.5). Its straight flow-through design concept is similar to that of a resilient-seat cast iron gate valve, except that the gate wedge and valve body make metal-to-metal contact when the valve is closed. Bronze gate valves with bronze gate wedges are not considered bubble tight unless the gate is rubber coated. The gate operates along a set of guides within the valve body and seats in a recess at the base of the body. Flow characteristics through gate valves are considered very good. Valve stems are available in rising or nonrising designs. The nonrising stem designs are more compact. A packing material located between the valve stem and the valve body seals the valve stem and is typically replaceable. The top of the valve is normally removable, thus facilitating service.

Hand wheels for gate valves are available in multiple configurations. Aluminum, zinc-plated steel, malleable iron, and bronze wheels are available, as well as bronze cross handles. A cross handle is commonly used, as it is of a durable material, small in size, and easily operated with a valve key. The valve is attached to the pipeline with threaded inlets, available in NPT or BSP thread styles. Bronze gate valves should meet ASTM B-62 specifications for Composition

FIGURE 4.5
Bronze gate valve.

Bronze and conform to MSS-SP-80 (Manufacturer's Standardization Society) standards for bronze valves. Valves should have a minimum pressure rating of 200 for nonshock cold water, oil, or gas (WOG).

ANGLE VALVES

An angle valve, also known as a manual angle valve (MAV), is a valve in which the outlet is configured at 90 degrees from the inlet (Figure 4.6). Its open flow passage provides low friction losses. A rising stem is connected to a seat disk that incorporates a Buna-N, EPDM, or Vitron rubber seating surface to create a positive seal. A packing material is used between the valve stem and valve body and is replaceable. The internal assembly of an MAV is removable from the top for service and maintenance. A bronze cross handle is typically used on top of the valve stem for actuation of the valve with a key; hand wheels are also available. Threaded inlets facilitate the connection of an MAV to the piping system and are available in NPT or BSP threads. The 2½ in. and 3 in. MAV models are available with union connections. MAVs are typically made of bronze meeting the standards of ASTM B-62 and are available in ratings of 150 to 600 psi (WOG).

BALL VALVES

Ball valves, also referred to as 90-degree turn valves, as a quarter turn of the valve handle will either fully open or close the valve, are typically bronze bodied with a straight-through design. An internally mounted ball with a hole in its center is connected to the operating handle for actuation. The ball is available in various materials, including brass; chrome-plated brass, and stainless steel. Chrome-plated brass meeting the specifications of ASTM B-584 Alloy 844 or stainless steel is generally used because of their resistance to corrosion. When closed, the ball seals against a self-lubricating Teflon seal.

Ball valves are available in full or partial port designs, which refers to the size of the flow through the opening (Figure 4.7). Full port designs have less pressure loss across the valve. Ball valves are also available in one-, two-, or three-piece bodies; both two- and three-piece bodies facilitate service once the valve is removed from the line. Because only a quarter turn will fully open a valve, opening speeds of ball valves are much greater than those of gate or MAV values, requiring users to be very cautious when operating these valves. The valve handle is available in several materials, with plated

FIGURE 4.6
Manual angle valve.

FIGURE 4.7
Ball valve.

steel or stainless steel handles being the most durable over time. A ball valve is often installed with the handle on its side to aid in its operation. Pressure ratings of 400 and 600 WOG are typical for golf course applications. Ball valves are available with NPT and BSP threaded inlets.

There are many considerations in choosing the appropriate lateral/sub-main isolation valve. Many commercially available products that work well in residential and commercial applications may fail when used in a golf course irrigation system. Only those isolation valve products that have a proven history of use for golf course irrigation system applications should be used. An understanding of unique site conditions pertaining to soil and water is important, as they may require the specification of valves made of special materials.

SPECIALTY VALVES

Air Release Valves

An air release valve is a valve that is specifically designed to eliminate trapped air from pipelines without permitting the loss of water (Figure 4.8). These continuously acting mechanical valves are typically positioned on the high points of the irrigation system mainline piping and where there is a change from a positive uphill slope to a negative downhill slope. An air release valve automatically releases air from the pipeline through a small vent on the top of the valve.

Air enters an irrigation system during the filling and draining processes. Because air is very compressible, it can accumulate in pockets

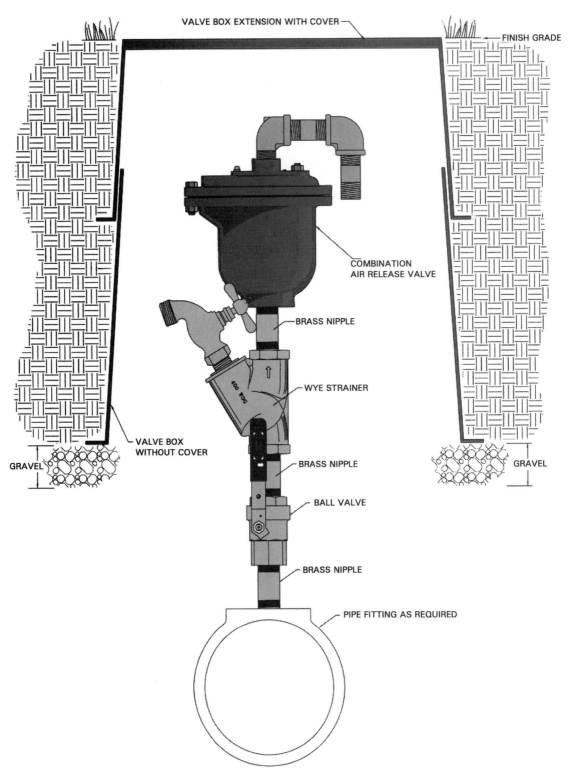

VALVE BOX EXTENSION WITH COVER

FINISH GRADE

COMBINATION
AIR RELEASE VALVE

BRASS NIPPLE

WYE STRAINER

BRASS NIPPLE

BALL VALVE

BRASS NIPPLE

PIPE FITTING AS REQUIRED

VALVE BOX
WITHOUT COVER

GRAVEL

GRAVEL

FIGURE 4.8
Combination air release valve assembly.

throughout the system. A small pocket of air can grow as air entrained in water begins to separate and accumulate. Without an air release device that vents air slowly, the activation of sprinklers or valves causes the compressed air to rapidly evacuate the pipeline, and a surge of water rushes to fill the void in the pipeline. This effect can create water hammer, which can be very destructive to pipe, fittings, and other irrigation components. Accumulated air trapped in a piping system can also restrict the flow of water and create additional pressure losses in the system.

Air release valves are also available as single bodied devices combining air release with a vacuum valve. A vacuum valve is designed to allow air to reenter a pipeline when it is being emptied or drained. These valves are generally referred to as combination air release valves (CAV).

To protect an air release valve or CAV from contaminants, a wye strainer and flush valve are typically installed beneath the inlet of the valve. An isolation valve, to facilitate service and maintenance as well as to isolate the CAV during the winterization process in freezing climates, precedes the strainer and valve. Extruded brass pipe nipples are typically used between the pipeline, wye strainer, and the air release valve or CAV. The entire assembly is enclosed in a large, deep valve box with vent holes in the box cover.

A CAV is typically available with an operating pressure of 150 to 300 psi. The valve body and top construction are typically cast iron, with corrosion-resistant stainless steel internals and float. Buna-N seating material is used on the air and vacuum seating surfaces.

The location and sizing of a combination air/vacuum release valve is best left to an experienced golf course irrigation systems designer.

Pressure-Relief Valves

Pressure-relief valves are used in golf course irrigation systems to discharge excessive pressure or surges and to protect the piping network and its components. These valves are designed to be fast opening and slow closing so that pressure rises are quickly recognized and vented and a rapid close does not create additional surges that result in water hammer.

Pressure-relief valves are commonly used in golf course pumping systems, but are also used in a piping system where a sudden change in pressure can occur because of a change in elevation, the operation of a booster pump, or a sudden change in flow (water hammer) creating a momentary rise in the pressure of the system.

An external pilot valve that is plumbed to the bonnet of the valve is available with pressure-setting ranges of 0 to 75 psi, 20 to 200 psi, or 30 to 300 psi. A pilot valve hydraulically operates a pressure-relief valve. A pressure-relief valve is available in sizes from 1¼ in. to 24 in. with flow ranges of 93 to 6300 gpm. Valve bodies are available with screwed or flanged inlets up to 3 in., and with flanged bodies only for 4 in. and larger. Bodies are available in angle or globe configurations. The valve body is cast iron, and the internal components are bronze and stainless steel. A fabric-reinforced diaphragm reacts to the pressure setting of the externally mounted pilot valve and facilitates the opening or closing of the valve. Valves are available with pressure class ratings of 150 lb or 300 lb. With the addition of further controls, a typical valve body can easily be modified to perform other functions.

Pressure gauges should be placed on both the upstream and downstream sides of the valve to aid in setting the valve and monitoring its operation.

Pressure-Reducing Valves

A pressure-reducing valve is designed to automatically reduce a higher inlet pressure to a steady lower downstream pressure, regardless of the changes in pressure or flow at the valve inlet (Figure 4.9). A pressure-reducing valve is similar in construction and operation to a

FIGURE 4.9
**Pressure-reducing
valve.**

pressure-relief valve; however, instead of venting excess pressure to atmosphere, a pressure-reducing valve reduces the pressure for safe operation of the irrigation system.

Pressure-reducing valves are used at a pumping system or on the piping system on a golf course. At locations where the system operating pressure may damage the piping system or any of its components, pressure-reducing valves are used to regulate pressure. These locations include areas where a negative downhill slope may increase the system pressure or where fluctuations in pressure from the water supply are encountered. When installed in the field, the valve should be enclosed in an access vault. An isolation valve should be installed on each end of the valve to facilitate maintenance and service. A bypass flow line with an isolation valve is commonly installed around the pressure-reducing valve to allow for temporary bypass flow in the event the valve is removed.

Pressure gauges should be placed on both the upstream and downstream sides of the valve to aid in setting the valve and monitoring its operation.

Pressure-Sustaining Valves

A pressure-sustaining valve is used to maintain the upstream pressure of the valve at a predetermined level. Pressure-sustaining valves are commonly used on municipal water supplies, where a minimum pressure in the municipal supply line must be maintained. Fixed-speed or conventional pump systems also utilize pressure-sustaining valves to keep pumps operating efficiently.

Pressure-sustaining valves are of similar construction and size as pressure-relief valves. Often two or more valve features are combined with a pressure-sustaining valve, such as pressure control or check-valve functions.

Pressure gauges should be placed on both the upstream and downstream sides of the valve to aid in setting the valve and monitoring its operation.

Drain Valves

Drain valves are installed in golf course irrigation systems to aid in winterization, flushing, servicing, and maintenance of pipelines and system components. A small 18-hole, double-row irrigation system will hold more than 25,000 gallons of water in its pipelines, equivalent to the volume of a standard in-ground pool. Manual drains provide a means of removing some of the water when required.

Manually operated isolation valves are installed on the underside of pipelines and are accessible through a valve access box and reach tube. To be most effective, drain valves are located in areas that will drain to atmosphere. If necessary, the valve is piped to a drainage line or low area that can accept a given volume of water. Gravel sumps are also used to accept the water.

The number of drain valves on a golf course can vary according to the terrain and the requirements of the system. On new irrigation systems the irrigation system designer specifies the number and/or the location of drain valves. Positioning a drain valve between two mainline isolation gate valves provides a lot of flexibility. On irrigation systems that have large sub-mains, laterals, or sub-loops, drain valves may also be beneficial.

Check Valves

A check valve is a device that is installed on a pipeline for the purpose of allowing flow in one direction. Check valves are typically classified by the type of check mechanism and by the body style of the valve.

The most common check valves are swing check valves and silent check valves. A swing check valve utilizes a freely moving disk or flapper that swings open in the direction of the flow of water. The pressure loss across the valve is relatively low. These valves are available in sizes ranging from 2 in. to 12 in. or more. Swing check valves rely on the force of the water for operation. The reaction time to close a swing check valve is often not quick enough to prevent damage to some irrigation components; in such cases, a faster-closing valve is required.

Fast-acting check valves are available for applications where flow reversal may cause damage to the system. A special spring-loaded "silent check valve" or nonslam check valve is typically used in these situations. A stainless steel spring facilitates the valve closure prior to flow reversal. Silent check valves are typically used in pumping systems to protect pumps and/or suction lines from the potential damaging effects of flow reversal. Silent check valves open at a very low forward flow pressure and will completely close while the forward flow still has a pressure of approximately $1/2$ lb per sq in. on the discharge side of the valve. The pressure loss across a silent check valve is only slightly greater than the loss across a swing check valve.

Check valves are available in multiple body configurations for different applications. Flanged, wafer, and grooved check valves are available from various manufacturers. Valve bodies are typically ductile iron with internal components of bronze and stainless steel.

Remote Control Valves

A remote control valve (RCV) is an automatic valve that, when electrically or hydraulically actuated, allows water to flow through it to activate a sprinkler(s) or other device (Figure 4.10). Remote control valves are often referred to as block or battery valves, as they can trigger the operation of blocks of sprinklers. Remote control valves have been used on golf courses for more than 60 years.

Most remote control valves are configured as globe valves. When the (normally closed) valve is at rest (closed), upstream pressure is present both above and below a flexible diaphragm. Because the surface area of the upper side of the diaphragm is greater than that of the lower side, the diaphragm is forced down, the valve disc attached to it is held on the valve seat, and water cannot flow through

FIGURE 4.10
Brass electric remote control valve.

the valve. When the pressure above the diaphragm is relieved by the opening of a solenoid port or a hydraulic tube, the diaphragm rises, the valve disc lifts off the seat, and water flows through the valve. When the pressure-relief port is closed, the diaphragm is forced back down, reseating the valve disc, and flow is stopped.

Light-duty remote control valves are widely used in residential and commercial irrigation systems with much success; however, the challenges of a golf course environment require the use of heavy-duty valve products. The key components of a golf course remote control valve are as follows:

- *Valve body*—The body of a remote control valve is either cast brass or glass-filled nylon plastic. Each body material should have an operating pressure rating of 200 psi or more. Valves are available in 1 in., 1¼ in., 1½ in., and 2 in. models, providing flow ranges of 5 to 200 gpm. Larger valves are also available, but seldom used for the remote control of sprinklers.

- *Manual actuator*—The valve typically has at least one means of manual operation. Most electric RCVs can be operated manually with a quarter turn of the valve solenoid, which allows the water on the top of the valve to port downstream; this operation is known as internal vent operation. An external vent screw can also be used to actuate either an electric or hydraulic RCV by loosening a screw in the upper body cavity. The loosening of the vent screw allows water to flow from the upper valve chamber, externally venting water and relieving pressure from the upper cavity. Opening a manual vent screw will allow water to flow out through the top of the valve continuously until the vent screw is tightened.

- *Flow stem*—A flow stem or flow control stem is located on the top of the valve. Its purpose is to provide a means of regulating flow by manually adjusting the position of the diaphragm. It is also used to manually turn off the valve; however, it is important to exercise caution when using a flow control stem, as the valve diaphragm or valve seat can be permanently damaged if forced against a small rock or debris.

- *Filters*—Filter systems are normally available as standard or optional equipment for RCVs. At a minimum, the water to the upper valve chamber is filtered through an internal flow-through screen or a filter at the base of the valve diaphragm.

For dirty water applications valves with dynamic scrubbing mechanisms are available.

- *Pressure regulation*—Pressure regulating modules are normally available as options for RCVs. A pressure regulator is typically installed between the valve body and the solenoid assembly. Normally adjustable between 15 and 100 psi, the pressure regulator is designed to maintain a constant downstream pressure as long as the inlet pressure remains 10 to 15 psi above the desired pressure setting. The pressure regulator is equipped with an adjustment screw with a pressure scale that allows for the visual verification of the adjusted pressure. The pressure can also be checked at the Schrader valve, which is similar to the valve on a tire, with the use of a hose and pressure gauge.

- *Solenoid assembly (electric models)*—The valve solenoid assembly is normally rated for 24 volts alternating current (VAC); however, latching direct current (DC) solenoids are available, as well as 115 VAC solenoids for special applications. The electrical characteristics of the solenoid should always be verified before designing or troubleshooting the system.

Remote control valves are top serviceable, and when installed in a valve box, most troubleshooting and repairs can easily be performed. Manual isolation valves are commonly installed upstream of the RCV to help facilitate service.

VALVE BOXES, REACH WELLS

Many golf course irrigation system components are buried with the piping system and require access for operation or maintenance. Gate valves, remote control valves, quick couplers, air/vacuum valves, drain valves, ground rods/plates, and wire splices are examples of buried irrigation devices that call for periodic access. When enclosed in a valve box (Figure 4.11) or reach well, they are protected from traffic and can be accessed for service or use.

FIGURE 4.11
Valve box installed at grade.

Valve boxes are available in many different sizes and shapes, making it convenient to select the appropriate box for a particular application. Among their various features are the following:

- *Materials*—Valve boxes typically have two or three pieces: cover, body, and extension (if required). These separate pieces are available in high-strength high-density polyethylene (HDPE), acrylonitrile-butadiene-styrene (ABS), concrete, steel, or cast iron. For most golf course applications the HDPE material is used as it normally provides enough strength for most applications and is half the weight of concrete. HDPE valve boxes and covers should conform to the ASTM D-638 test method for Tensile Strength of 3,100 to 5,500 psi and the ASTM D-790 test method for Flexural Modulus of 160,000 to 210,000 psi.

- *Sizes*—Valve boxes are available in a variety of sizes and shapes. Round boxes with 6 in., 8 in., and 10 in. round covers are used to enclose smaller components, and larger rectangular boxes with covers measuring 10 × 12 in. to 14 × 19 in. and larger are used to enclose large components such as remote control valves and specialty valves. Valve boxes are also available in standard depths ranging from 6 in. to 18 in. Extensions are available and are used to extend the depth of the valve box, providing access to equipment at greater depths of bury. To reach deep isolation valves, a 4 in. or 6 in. diameter PVC pipe sleeve is often used with a round box over the pipe. A special telescoping curb box is commonly used to enclose cast iron mainline gate valves.

- *Covers*—Covers are available in multiple colors. The use of different colored covers can help communicate their use for different irrigation components. Although green is typically the standard plastic color, plastic covers are also available in back, gray, tan, and violet. Violet valve box covers are often used when reclaimed water is being used. When a valve box is used as an enclosure for a wire or cable splice, different colored covers are often used to indicate the type of cable or voltage at the wire splice, such as 24 VAC, 115 VAC, 230 VAC, or communication cable. A cover is attached to the body with a snap-lock mechanism or a twist top or can be locked with the use of a stainless steel bolt. Although valve boxes are typically installed at grade, they can be lost. Detectable covers are available to help locate a lost valve box. Detectable covers have a steel disk either incorporated into the mold of the valve box cover or attached to the underside of the cover to aid in detection with a metal detector. Concrete covers are often used in place of HDPE in areas that are subject to heavy traffic or are adjacent to paved roadways. Round boxes with grated detectable covers are used to access ground rods and plates.

The location of all valve boxes should be recorded on the Record Drawing.

SPRINKLERS

Among the many products required for the construction of a golf course irrigation system, the sprinkler is the device that actually distributes the water to the turfgrass. The purpose of golf course sprinklers is to distribute water uniformly over its entire wetted diameter of throw. There are many types and styles of sprinklers available that share common modes of operation, but what separates a golf course sprinkler from a residential, commercial, or agricultural sprinkler is durability. The use of aeration equipment, verticutting equipment, top-dressing, spiked golf shoes, mowing equipment, and golf carts, as well as sand from bunkers, make a golf course environment a harsh one for sprinklers. Additionally, the number of cycles golf course sprinklers experience can be much higher than that experienced by other sprinklers.

Golf course sprinklers are considered "pop-up" style sprinklers; that is, the actual sprinkler will elevate, or pop up from a housing when activated and retract back into its protective case, or housing, when not in operation. When activated, a sprinkler rotates as it distributes water across its radius of throw.

Golf course sprinklers are defined by their mode of operation. The golf course industry has seen many different sprinkler drive mechanisms over the years: ball, cam, gear, and impact drive mechanisms, all of which have had some degree of success. Today, however, the two primary types of sprinklers typically used are impact sprinklers and gear drive sprinklers.

Impact Sprinklers

The principles behind the operation of an impact sprinkler have not changed since its introduction to the golf course irrigation industry in the 1930s. The typical impact sprinkler utilizes a one- or two-nozzle assembly to distribute water. A weighted, spring-loaded swing arm is attached to the nozzle assembly, which is deflected sideways upon entering the stream of water exiting the nozzle. The swing arm recoils and returns, creating an impact with the nozzle assembly, which causes the sprinkler to rotate. This action continues, with the sprinkler slowly rotating, until the source of water to the sprinkler stops. The nozzle and swing arm assemblies of impact style sprinklers are typically made of a cast bronze material.

A one- or two-nozzle configuration is typically used by an impact sprinkler, depending on the diameter of throw of the sprinkler. Short-radius sprinklers can achieve adequate water distribution with a single nozzle, whereas larger sprinklers require a two-nozzle system. A two-nozzle sprinkler includes a long-range nozzle and an inner nozzle for close-in coverage. The long-range nozzle is sized to provide the diameter of throw that is required and provides little breakup of the water stream close to the sprinkler, and the inner nozzle provides close-in watering, extending out to the point at which the long-range nozzle begins its distribution. Nozzles are specially sized to complement each other, and care should always be taken to match the long-range and inner nozzles if system adjustments are required, as an improper nozzle combination can result in poor water distribution.

Impact sprinklers are available in full-circle, 360-degree, models and adjustable part-circle models. The part-circle models are typically adjustable from 20 to 340 degrees with small stainless steel adjustable rings that are manually set to lock in an arc setting. The large nozzle assembly design of impact sprinklers necessitates the need for a large open sprinkler case to house the sprinkler when it is not operating.

Impact sprinklers are generally easy to work on, providing replacement parts are available. Because of their straight "flow through" design, they tend to operate at low pressures. The impact motion of the swing arm into the water stream actually improves the water distribution of the nozzles, and a high level of uniformity in application can be achieved. The rotation speeds of impact sprinklers can be quite variable, and, in some cases, if a sprinkler is rotating too quickly, can contribute to poor uniformity of water distribution. Typical rotation speeds vary from 90 to 240 seconds, depending on sprinkler radius.

Gear Drive Sprinklers

The first rotating sprinklers to be mass-produced and commercially available in the United States, in the late 1890s, were gear driven sprinklers. However, gear drive sprinklers held only a small share of the sprinkler market as compared with the impact sprinkler until the late 1950s, when gear driven sprinklers made of plastic were introduced. Throughout the 1960s and 1970s impact sprinklers increasingly gave up market share to gear drive sprinklers (Figure 4.12), which now dominate the golf course irrigation industry.

The gear drive sprinkler derives its name from the series of gears and turbines that converts the water entering the base of a sprinkler's case (body) to a rotational force, driving the sprinkler's nozzle housing. A stator, or flow-regulating device, located in the base of the sprinkler directs a predetermined volume of water past the turbine to ensure that the precise turning torque is applied to the geared assembly. This helps to maintain a consistent, slow rotation speed.

Gear drive sprinklers are available in full-circle, 360-degree, models and adjustable part-circle models providing as much as 30 to 360-degree coverage. Part-circle models utilize a reciprocating mechanism that facilitates the reversal of the nozzle housing. The gear assemblies are contained in separate oil- or water-filled housings within the sprinkler case, which protects them from debris.

FIGURE 4.12
Gear drive sprinkler.

Sprinkler Features

Most impact or gear drive sprinklers are available in various sizes, which typically relate to the sprinklers' radius of throw. Smaller sprinklers are used for tighter spacing from 30 ft to 50 ft, midrange sprinklers provide a radius of 50 ft to 75 ft, and larger sprinklers provide a radius of 70 ft to 90 ft. Some manufacturers also make sprinklers that provide a long radius of throw, from 90 ft to 115 ft.

There are a multitude of common and optional features available for most golf course irrigation sprinklers. Some of these features affect sprinkler performance, and others affect sprinkler serviceability. The individual features and benefits of different sprinklers should be weighed so that the right sprinkler is selected for its intended application.

NOZZLES

Sprinklers are generally available in multiple nozzle configurations, with each nozzle representing a radius of throw and a flow rate at a given sprinkler inlet/base pressure. The radius of throw is used as a guide for irrigation system designers in determining the suitability of a sprinkler/nozzle combination for a particular spacing. The sprinkler's flow is also used to aid the designer in determining sprinkler precipitation rates and safe flow in irrigation pipelines. A sprinkler's inlet pressure aids the designer in the calculation of the overall system's operating pressure or the ability of the sprinkler to operate at a given available pressure. It has become common practice for manufacturers to publish sprinkler performance data in accordance with ASAE Standard S398.1, which outlines the proper testing and reporting criteria for a sprinkler's radius of throw.

The discharge rates of golf course irrigation sprinklers can range dramatically, based on the nozzle size and operating pressure. Small-radius sprinklers can have discharge rates of 5 gpm or lower, and larger sprinklers can have discharge rates of more than 65 gpm.

Manufacturers can also provide independent testing laboratory results indicating each sprinkler/nozzle combination's distribution profile. This profile data is extremely helpful to an irrigation system designer, as it will allow the designer to simulate different sprinkler/nozzle combinations with the use of a simulation software package, such as the SPACE program (available from the Center for Irrigation Technology at California State University in Fresno, an independent testing facility) and thus to select the proper sprinkler/nozzle combination for the application.

Nozzles are often color coded so that they can be visually identified while in operation. The nozzle number or size, as well as its directional orientation, are also communicated on the top of a sprinkler. Some sprinklers are available with a series of low-angle nozzles that can be used to help combat the effects of wind on sprinkler performance. Some part-circle sprinklers are available with a short-radius rear nozzle that is designed to provide a small stream of water, 20 to 30 ft long, to areas behind them, where a full-circle sprinkler would provide too much coverage. For example, consider a part-circle sprinkler positioned close to an access road or tree. A full-circle sprinkler would not be necessary here; however, a part-circle sprinkler can fill the void in coverage. The nozzle or nozzle assembly should be easily accessible so that changes in the field can be made easily.

BODY STYLES

Different sprinkler body styles or cases are available for different operational applications. The most common body styles are check valve, electric valve-in-head, and hydraulic valve-in-head.

- *Check valve*—Sprinklers that operate from a remote control valve or manual control valve typically incorporate a check valve, or stop valve, in the base of the sprinkler's body. This valve is designed to hold back water in a pipeline that is located above any sprinkler on the piping circuit, so that it does not drain out from the lowest sprinkler. These valves are typically rated to hold back water from elevations of 10 ft to 25 ft or higher than the sprinkler.

- *Electric valve-in-head*—Electric valve-in-head (EVIH) sprinklers incorporate an electrically activated valve in the sprinkler itself, eliminating the need for remote control or activation. These sprinklers are actuated by a 24 VAC 50- or 60-cycle solenoid, providing individual sprinkler control. By incorporating the electric pilot valve assembly on the side cases of the sprinkler, along with the valve at the base of the sprinkler, additional functionality is gained:

  - The sprinkler incorporates its own pressure-regulating device to ensure the proper operating pressure. Pressure settings are preset by the manufacturer and can be changed in the field, either by changing the regulator spring within the pilot assembly or by adjusting a set screw at the top of the sprinkler with a small flat-blade screwdriver. Pressure settings are normally available in 60, 65, 70, 80, 100, and 120 psi settings, depending on the sprinkler and nozzle combination.

  - A top-mounted selector switch allows the sprinkler to be activated manually, placed in the automatic mode in which the sprinkler will operate from a 24 VAC power source, or placed in the off position so that the sprinkler does not operate electrically.

  - All sprinkler valve parts and electrical components are located in or on the sprinkler. Most components are top serviceable, eliminating the need to excavate to service the valve or valve seat.

  - The case of a VIH sprinkler has a large lip that is designed to act as protection for the electric pilot valve assembly. This lip also helps keep debris and tall grass away from the nozzle housing so that its discharge stream is not distorted by obstructions.

- *Hydraulic valve-in-head*—For hydraulically operated irrigation systems, normally open hydraulic valve-in-head (HVIH) sprinklers are available. These sprinklers are similar to electric models in that a control valve is incorporated into the base of the sprinkler. However, the control valve is actuated by hydraulic control tubing that originates from a field controller with a hydraulic actuation module instead of from a 24 VAC wired field controller.

Service Features

- *Sprinkler case*—Most gear drive golf course sprinklers are manufactured with a closed case, which means that the internal assembly is designed to seal against the rising sprinkler nozzle assembly once the sprinkler is activated. The closed case design protects the internal assembly of the sprinkler from debris and, on new construction, allows the sprinkler to be set to grade or slightly above grade without fear of contaminating internal components. The inlet size of the sprinkler case can vary from 1 in. to 1½ in., depending on the manufacturer, with threaded inlets available in NPT, BSP, or ACME configurations.
- *Screens*—A screen is incorporated at the base of the sprinkler to prevent debris from entering the sprinkler case and possibly damaging or contaminating internal components such as the valve seating area or a nozzle. A top serviceable rock/debris screen, common to many sprinklers, traps debris before it enters the sprinkler case and is accessible from the top of the sprinkler for cleaning or replacement. Additional fine-mesh screens are typically available that prevent smaller particles from reaching the nozzle assembly.
- *Pop-up height*—The pop-up height of a sprinkler's nozzle assembly is important in managing an irrigation system. A greater pop-up height ensures that nozzles will clear tall grasses and that their discharge streams will not be altered. Pop-up heights can range from ½ in. to 4¼ in. or more.
- *Snap rings*—Most sprinkler components are accessible from the top of the sprinkler. To facilitate accessibility, service snap rings are used to retain internal components. The sprinklers' internal drive and nozzle assembly, as well as the lower valve, can be accessed and removed, serviced or replaced with the removal of the snap rings. Pressure must be relieved from the bottom of the sprinkler prior to removing the snap ring from the lower valve, so as to avoid injury.

The popularity of gear drive sprinklers has led to the introduction of several gear drive retrofit internal assemblies for impact style sprinklers so that golf courses can convert an impact style sprinkler to gear drive operation without replacing the sprinkler case.

Sprinklers for Small Areas

There can be many areas on a golf course where a 30 ft sprinkler provides too much coverage and a smaller sprinkler is required. These areas include the interface between a bunker and the putting surface, bunker slopes, and even small teeing surfaces, where overspraying beyond the tee is not permitted. Commercial irrigation products must be considered for these applications. The use of pop-up style small-radius spray sprinklers operating at low pressure is sometimes the only choice.

There are relatively few parts to a spray head (Figure 4.13). The major components include the following:

- *Spray body or case*—The body of a spray head is commonly made of a plastic material. The body itself is relatively small in diameter (about 2¼ in.), and it houses the internal components. Models are available in multiple sizes for different pop-up height requirements, 4 in., 6 in., and 12 in. The inlet to the spray body is typically ½ in.

- *Riser or flow tube*—The riser assembly supports the spray nozzle and houses the nozzle screen. The nozzle screen is relatively large and is accessible for cleaning by entering the riser through the nozzle. Also made of plastic, the riser pops up under water pressure and retracts once pressure is relieved. At the base of the flow tube is a check-valve that holds back water in the pipelines up to 8 ft or more. A spring is attached to the riser body to retract the sprinkler while not in operation.

- *Nozzle*—Spray nozzles are available in brass or plastic. Brass nozzles are typically used for golf course applications for greater durability. A pressure-regulating cartridge is available on most spray sprinklers. The pressure-regulating device is designed to regulate the pressure to each nozzle from as much as 100 psi to 30 psi to prevent misting and to ensure consistent operation of spray heads on the same piping. However, a pressure-reducing valve should be used to decrease the operating pressure of the zone.

FIGURE 4.13
Spray head.

Spray head nozzles have proportionally high discharge rates, given their short radius of application, which results in high sprinkler precipitation rates of 1½ in. per hour or more. Because these application rates are so high, spray heads are usually scheduled to operate only a few minutes at a time, with one or more repeat cycles, depending on the plant water requirement. Available in a wide variety of nozzle configurations, a spray head can accept nozzles with a radius of throw ranging from 3 ft to 18 ft.

Because of the relatively low flow rates of a spray head, a series of spray heads are normally operated by a remote control valve or manual valve. Although a pressure regulator is installed in a spray head, a pressure-regulating device should be placed at the source of the spray zone to protect the spray heads from a sudden pressure spike.

Verifying the proper operation of spray heads should be part of the routine maintenance and testing procedures, as they are particularly vulnerable to damage in a golf course environment.

QUICK COUPLING VALVES

Long before the pop-up sprinkler was developed, a quick connection system utilizing a buried-at-grade valve (quick coupling valve) and a valve activation key was used to manually connect aboveground rotating sprinklers to belowground pipelines. Although this system required manual operation, wherever a quick coupler was located, water could be delivered. This technology is still widely used today to provide a means of connecting to the irrigation piping system, primarily for hose end watering, and for accessing a temporary water supply, for flushing pipelines, and for draining pipelines, as well as allowing air to vent when empty pipelines are filled.

A quick coupler is activated by inserting the key into the valve and turning the key clockwise; a heavy-duty stainless steel spring-loaded valve seat is forced open, allowing flow through the valve and key. For hose end use, a hose swivel is attached to the end of the valve key; if sprinkler operation is desired, a sprinkler head is attached directly to the top of the valve key.

Most quick coupling valves have similar components, with slight variations to enhance functionality. A typical quick coupling valve assembly has the following components:

- *Valve body*—The valve body is typically made of a cast red brass material for strength and durability. The body inlet size is available in ¾ in., 1 in., and 1½ in., with the size dictating the maximum flow. Flow ranges are available up to 125 gpm. Some valve bodies incorporate antirotation wings that help stabilize the quick coupler and stops the valve from unthreading. The valve body is available in either one-piece or two-piece construction. A two-piece valve body facilitates the replacement of the valve key seal and the valve keyway channel while the system is pressurized. For projects that use quick couplers continuously, the two-piece valve is typically used; however, the flow rate of a 1 in. two-piece valve is significantly less than that of a similar one-piece unit. A keyway channel, which accommodates the valve key, is cast in the throat of the valve body, along with several indentations that allow for regulating water flow.

- *Cover*—Valve covers protect the valve and its internal mechanisms from the accumulation of debris. Different types of valve covers are available for quick couplers. A metal cover is typically used if extra protection for the valve is required. A large self-closing cover made of yellow thermosplastic rubber is commonly used with or without an optional locking mechanism. For systems using nonpotable water, a purple vinyl locking cover with "Do Not Drink" markings is available.

- *Valve key*—The valve key is also made of red brass and is sized to the quick coupler it operates. It is available with one or two lugs that follow the keyway channel in the valve body. An ACME threaded valve and key are also available, which help in allowing slower opening and closing of the valve and permit regulation of the amount of flow. Each valve key has a handle to assist with its manual operation. The valve key can be specified with male or female pipe threads to facilitate the connection of a hose swivel adaptor or sprinkler. Pipe threads, per current ANSI B2.1 specification, are expressed as NPT, in which N stands for National (American) Standard, P stands for pipe, and T stands for taper. Several terms in common usage are widely employed to express male and female pipe threads; however, they are not legitimate terms and have no basis in any standard.

Special lateral fittings that connect a mainline pipe to a manual isolation valve incorporate a special 1 in. outlet to facilitate the installation of a swing joint for a quick coupling valve. Sometimes these outlets are plugged for potential future installation of a quick coupling valve. Some irrigation designers prefer to have a small valve box installed over a quick coupler valve to protect it and to aid in its identification and location.

Quick coupling valves are normally rated for 125 to 150 psi and are available with NPT or BSP threaded inlets.

SWING JOINTS

A swing joint is used to connect a sprinkler or quick coupling valve to the piping system (Figure 4.14). The purpose of a swing joint is to protect the pipeline from the forces of heavy equipment and traffic and to allow a sprinkler to be easily adjusted and set to its intended grade. The most common swing joint material used today for sprinklers is polyvinyl chloride (PVC) and PVC, brass, or bronze for quick coupling valves.

Until the early 1990s a series of Schedule 40 galvanized steel nipples and fittings were commonly used for the assembly of swing joints. A swing joint typically had at least three 90-degree elbows, which allowed for rotation in any of the three axes. Unfortunately, the rapid deterioration of the steel created leaks in the swing joint and rust flakes would clog sprinkler nozzles or disrupt the operation of valves. In addition, once the galvanized steel was in the ground, it

FIGURE 4.14
Sprinkler on swing joint.

would seize up fairly quickly and would no longer provide the desired flex or rotation between the sprinkler and the pipe.

PVC swing joints began to replace galvanized products in the late 1980s and early 1990s because of the high number of failures and associated problems with the galvanized materials, especially on valve-in-head systems, where the swing joints are continuously pressurized.

The early PVC swing joints were made of straight pieces of glued pipe and threaded fittings and were not without their own problems. For years an entire industry, being used to assembling galvanized steel swing joints with pipe wrenches, attempted to work with PVC products that were not designed to handle the same torque as steel products. PVC threads are manufactured and tapered in accordance with threaded pipe standards (ANSI B1.20.1). A threaded male fitting acts as a wedge when coupled with a threaded female fitting. Once these fittings were tightened beyond finger tight, a force, known as hoop stress, of 1780 psi per full turn could be exerted on a typical 1 in. female threaded fitting (which has a maximum hoop stress rating of 7000 psi), resulting in premature failure. However, if the fittings were not tight enough, they would leak. Glued connections between the swing joint riser and the threaded outlet fittings were also subject to failure if a poor joint was made.

Contemporary PVC swing joints have addressed the issues of the past and, when installed properly, are reliable components in a golf course irrigation system. The following features are common to most PVC swing joints:

- *Manufacturer assembled*—½ in., ¾ in., 1 in., 1¼ in., and 1½ in. manufacturer-assembled swing joints are available and should include both inlet and outlet fittings, eliminating the need to assemble units on-site.

- *Pressure rating*—Swing joints are typically rated for 315 psi at 73°F when tested in accordance with ASTM D 3139. Testing should include a 60-minute test at 790 psi and, for short-term exposure, to 1000 psi without leaks.

- *Length*—Different riser lengths are used to maintain an installation angle of 30 to 45 degrees where the depth of pipe varies. Riser lengths (lay lengths) of 8 in., 12 in., and 18 in. are commonly available.

- *ACME threads*—Problems associated with threaded PVC fittings are eliminated with the use of ACME threads. A typical pipe and fitting thread is tapered with a grooved, "V" type notch. In addition to the hoop stress created in joining tapered fittings, the notch in the root of the thread profile reduces the fitting pressure rating by up to 50 percent. An ACME thread design is relatively square, eliminating the notch in the root of the fitting, providing free movement between fittings, and maintaining fitting strength while also maintaining rotational movement. ACME threads are used on threaded connections of swing joint fittings and are available on most outlets to sprinklers and inlets to fittings on a pipeline. A physical stop is molded onto the various threaded fittings of an ACME swing joint, preventing the potential of overtightening a fitting. A rubber O-ring, which is preinstalled in a sealing groove, facilitates the actual seal of an ACME threaded connection. Sealing compounds are not required for ACME fittings.

- *Inlets and outlets*—A wide variety of inlet and outlet configurations are available to facilitate the following connections: ACME, NPT, BSP, spigot, and metric spigot. In addition, if a sprinkler manufacturer recommends a larger-diameter swing joint with a smaller outlet, special enlargement fittings are available to reduce the total number of fittings required to make the transition. Single- or triple-top outlets are available. A triple-top outlet provides a greater degree of flexibility for final height adjustment of a sprinkler and is especially useful on new construction sites where sprinklers are often installed slightly above grade until the turfgrass is established.

- *Integrated service fittings*—Some manufacturers offer an optional service fitting attached to the swing joint to facilitate a connection to lateral or sub-main piping. These 2 in. or $2\frac{1}{2}$ in. gasket or solvent-weld service tees can be ordered with the swing joint assembly including an ACME inlet for the swing joint.

Special PVC swing joints are also used for quick coupling valves. These swing joints are very similar to sprinkler swing joints, with the exception of the final outlet fitting, which is a threaded brass insert and is designed to have a locking mechanism to prevent the rotational force caused by the use of a coupler key from removing the valve from the swing joint. Some outlet fittings to a quick coupler must be anchored and supported by $\frac{5}{8}$ in. rebar.

Quick coupling valves can also be installed on brass and bronze fittings and pipe nipples. The fittings are typically cast bronze class

125 or 250 per ANSI B 16.15 and Federal Specification WW-P-460. The pipe nipples are made from extruded brass pipe per Federal Specification WW-P-351. The fittings are coupled with the use of a nonhardening, non-petroleum-based, antiseize compound for threaded connections to protect against galvanic reaction.

CONTROL SYSTEMS

Control systems, of all the irrigation system components, have probably been most impacted by technology. The first automatic sequencing hydraulic controller was invented in the early 1920s, and the first control systems for golf courses were introduced in the 1950s. The controls were timers or "stand-alone" controllers. The concept of a central controller was still years away. Stand-alone control systems were a significant advance in the industry. Before they were available, an irrigation system manager had relied on manual valves and quick couplers to activate the system. These early controllers utilized a series of clock motors, relays, dials, and switches. The dials were used to program a single start time, the day the controller was scheduled to start, and individual station run times. If the irrigation manager did not want a particular controller to run on a certain night, it was manually turned off with a switch at the controller. As simple as this sounds now, only the wealthiest golf courses could afford this technology.

The first central control systems came to market in the 1960s and offered the ability to start an irrigation system from a single location. Different groups of field controllers were wired to a single central control panel (central controller). The irrigation manager scheduled the central controller to send an impulse at the desired irrigation start time. If an attached controller had a run time entered on any station, it activated that station, and the subsequent stations followed. Each central control panel activated its own group of controllers. Not only did this technology provide a means of starting all the field controllers, it provided the first effective means of managing the system flow. Both repeat cycles and syringe cycles could be programmed and activated from the central controller. The field controllers themselves were still mechanical, and the actual station run times were often very different from the entered run times.

Solid-state controllers introduced several new features to the industry: accurate station timing, multiple operating programs, multiple simultaneous station (multi-manual) operation, and independent start days (schedules) for each program. These features allowed green, tee, and fairway sprinklers to be assigned to the same controller. The multi-manual feature allowed efficient, electronically controlled spot watering and syringing.

The introduction of the personal computer (PC) accelerated the evolution of the automatic irrigation system. The PC provided the means to store and manage irrigation system schedule and program information at a single location. The irrigation manager would create all the operational information at the PC and, depending on the communication protocol, would either download to the field controllers or allow the PC to communicate the operational commands to the field controllers during the entire irrigation cycle. In some cases, the field controllers could communicate critical information to the PC, such as which stations are operating and fuse status.

Field Controllers

Field controllers are available in a variety of configurations. Most have the ability to operate as a stand-alone controller or as a satellite under the management of a central controller, communicating with the central via a cable or radio control (Figure 4.15). A small percentage of field controllers lack field programming capabilities and operate solely as switching units.

Most field controllers have five common components: faceplate, output terminal strip, transformer, enclosure, and the device used to communicate with the central programmer. The faceplate is the programming interface of the controller in which data is directly entered and is viewed on a liquid crystal display (LCD) or light-emitting diode (LED) screen. The output terminal strip is the portion of the controller that accepts the valve field wiring. The controller's transformer accepts the higher incoming voltage from the power supply cable and reduces the voltage to a usable level for the controller's electronics and valve solenoids.

A field controller usually has a wall mount or pedestal type enclosure of plastic, metal, or stainless steel. The communication mode dictates what type of hardware is required at the field controller. If radio control is used, an antenna will be required; if hardwired, a communication module is usually required.

Most manufacturers have developed expandable controller hardware so that a basic controller can be upgraded with the addi-

FIGURE 4.15
Field controller.

tion of plug-in modules. The typical hardware capabilities include the following:

- *Expandable station configurations.* Older style controllers came in only one size. This often made it difficult for an irrigation system designer to properly group stations at a controller site. The designer would have to either add additional controllers or pair stations together in an undesirable manner. Field controllers today are expandable with the use of modules that are normally manufactured in 8- or 10-station increments. For example, a 16-station controller can be expanded to 48 stations by simply adding four 8-station modules. All field changes must be noted in the central programmer so that it can accurately manage any hydraulic and electrical limitations.

- *Communication modules.* Most controllers can operate either as a stand-alone field controller or as a satellite controller within the control of a central programmer. Most field controllers may be upgraded from stand-alone to central control with the addition of a communication module. Many golf courses are unable to install a central programmer because of budgetary constraints. Communication modules provide the means to upgrade a control system from stand-alone to central control at a future date.

- *Selectable power supplies.* Field controllers are typically powered by 115 VAC or 230 VAC. Most controllers today use transformers that can utilize either voltage simply by having a switch turned to the proper setting. This eliminates the need to buy special transformers for different power supplies.

- *Station switches.* Station switches are mounted on the station output modules; they have three positions; auto, off, and on. The auto position allows the station to operate from either a local program or a central-based program. The off position prevents any electrical activation of the station. The on position manually activates the station, which will remain on until turned off. These switches can be a very useful addition to a field controller, as they allow station activation without the need to access the controller's faceplate.

- *Surge protection.* Varying degrees of surge protection are offered, depending on the controller manufacturer and the model. Surge protection devices are available for the power supply, zone wire, and communication cable. Because it is inconvenient and expensive to repair surge-damaged controllers, in most parts of the world it is worth the additional expense to purchase all of the manufacturer's suggested surge protection devices.

Golf course field controllers have many operational and hardware features. Typical operational features include the following:

- *Electronic operation.* A digital LED or LCD screen allows the user to view irrigation programming data and operational status. Electronic operation also allows for accurate programming, eliminating the problems seen in mechanical controllers, such as inaccurate station run times.
- *Multiple program capability.* Different turf areas can be wired to a single controller and then programmed separately within the controller. Controllers can be scheduled to operate several independent programs.
- *Multiple start times.* Rather than providing one heavy application, this feature allows the irrigation system manager to call for several light applications within any program or station. This helps to prevent runoff.
- *Water budget.* A percentage multiplier, ranging from 0 to 300 percent or more, assists in the scaling of station run times. This is useful in trying to modify a series of station run times without completely reprogramming the controller.
- *Multiple station operation.* Solid-state field controllers can activate multiple stations and multiple valves per station. It is also possible to run several programs concurrently. The transformer size limits the total number of stations that can be run simultaneously.
- *Controller self-test and diagnostics.* To aid in troubleshooting, the controller self-test feature provides a thorough test of the controller and its associated hardware. A self-test typically checks the software version, checks for communication between the faceplate and the communication module, and tests fuses. The field controller displays any found issues, thus saving time in troubleshooting.

Decoder Systems

An alternate to a field-controller-based irrigation control system is a decoder system. Because all the components of a decoder system are buried, it is ideal for areas that are prone to vandalism or flooding, as well as for sites where there are objections to field controllers.

Decoders were first introduced in the early 1970s. The early decoder systems utilized DC power. The DC current accelerated the failure of the system's wiring through electrolysis, which is similar to the corrosion seen on car batteries. Later manufacturers of decoder systems switched to AC current and began utilizing cables with a polyethylene (PE) jacket, which has better insulating properties and higher resistance than PVC cables. The higher resistance in the cables also helps prevent damage due to lightning and its associated high voltage.

A decoder system has four major components: decoder, communication wire, decoder controller, and surge protection, each playing a vital role in the operation of the system.

DECODER

A decoder is a small printed circuit board that is encapsulated in a waterproof material and is either directly buried or placed in a valve box at or near the valve it is to activate (Figure 4.16). Each decoder is either preprogrammed or programmable with an identification code, also known as an address, so that it can be distinguished from the other decoders on the golf course. The decoder address is very much like a phone number. Just as multiple phones share the same line, multiple decoder addresses may share the same communication path.

The central or field controller will issue commands that only a decoder with the correct address will utilize. Decoders are available in a variety of sizes, ranging from one to six addresses, and some have the capability of activating multiple solenoids per address. A single address decoder has two sets of wires: the input wires that accept the power and signal current from the communication wire, and output wires that go to the solenoid the decoder is going to activate. If the decoder is capable of operating multiple addresses, it will have a pair of output wires per address, usually color coded, with a reference guide located on the decoder body. Some decoders may also contain wires for grounding.

COMMUNICATION CABLE

The communication cable of the decoder system carries the decoder's activation code and the power supply to activate each decoder within the system This cable typically includes two or three #14 AWG or #12 AWG copper conductors that are color coded and individually jacketed, with some encased in a UF outer jacket.

Because the decoder cable is supplying both the power and the communication signals, it is important that all irrigation requirements be known before sizing the cable. It is very easy for an inexperienced irrigation designer to undersize a decoder cable and thus prevent it from accommodating the peak electrical demands of the system.

FIGURE 4.16
Decoder.

Depending on the manufacturer, a decoder system may consist of a single communication cable (wire path) or may contain multiple communication cables. If multiple wire paths are to be used, it is typical to segment the system in an easily understood manner. A simple approach would be to put six holes on each wire path for a total of three paths in an 18-hole course. It is often a good idea to use a different color jacket for each wire path originating from the central controller to help differentiate wire groups in the field. Creating a system with multiple wire paths often helps in the maintenance of a decoder system, as well as any necessary troubleshooting.

Good waterproof connections to the communication cable are imperative for the reliability of the system. A poor splice toward the beginning of the wire path may affect the operation of decoders that are farther along that path. Any splice to the communication cable, whether at a decoder or at a three-way junction, should have sufficient slack so that the splice can be lifted at least 2 ft above grade for inspection and repair.

If the decoder is located at a distance from the solenoid(s) for which it is responsible, it is necessary to use cable to connect the solenoid(s) with the secondary side of the decoder. For example, consider a fairway lateral with multiple valve-in-head (VIH) sprinklers and a multistation decoder in a valve box in the rough. It would be necessary to run two wires between the multistation decoder and each VIH sprinkler on that lateral line. The distance between the decoder and the farthest head is of primary concern. As with the communication cable, it is important that the electrical limitation regarding maximum distance be observed. This information should be readily available from the decoder manufacturer.

It is important to know the electrical capability of each size of decoder, as the operation of the system will be affected by such capabilities. For example, a green may be piped so that four valve-in-head sprinklers can be operated simultaneously. Because some decoders can operate only one address at time, a decoder or combination of decoders must be selected that will allow the activation of the four sprinklers. The location of each decoder and its address should be noted on the irrigation system Record Drawing.

DECODER CONTROLLER

The decoder controller applies the power and signals to a group of decoders or to the entire decoder system. The controller activation device can be a typical field controller from which the decoder communication cable is routed and, in turn, connected by cable or radio link to a central controller interface, or to a single central control site that accepts the various communication cable wire paths.

Manufacturers have developed central control systems that operate the decoder system in a manner similar, if not identical, to a field controller system. A central controller is typically equipped with the same type of programming and hydraulic system management as a field controller system. Some central control software systems are capable of operating decoders and conventional controllers, in some cases simultaneously. Each decoder address is entered into the central controller's operating system so that it can be identified, operated, and monitored by the software. For system troubleshooting, centrals commonly offer system diagnostic software that can test the electrical operation of every decoder and solenoid in the system and report whether it is operating within the proper electrical tolerances.

SURGE PROTECTION

As in any irrigation control system, the ability to resist the effects of lightning-induced electrical surges is important to the reliability and operation of the decoder system. Poor splices, improper maintenance of the communication cable, and damage resulting from electrical surges are the main causes of problems with decoders. Surge protection is available in several forms; it can be placed at the decoder, on the communication cable, and at the central and/or field controller. Many decoders have built-in surge protection and/or self-resetting thermal fuses. These devices provide some degree of protection, but dedicated surge protectors placed on the communication cable offer a higher degree of protection. These units connect directly to the communication wire, like a decoder, with the secondary wiring attached to an adjacent ground rod. Surge arrestors are typically installed at all communication cable dead ends, as well as along the wire path at intervals of 500 ft to 1000 ft, depending on the manufacturer.

Each surge arrestor is connected to a ground rod. Earth ground readings should be taken at each ground rod to verify that it meets the manufacturer's recommendations. Each surge arrestor should be placed in a valve box, preferably with a color-coded lid, to facilitate service and troubleshooting. The location of all surge protection devices should be recorded on the Record Drawing.

An additional earth ground grid must be installed at the central computer and/or the field controller(s) to protect the electronic components. A surge protection device is also installed in-line on any cable coming to the central or field controller(s) to help prevent surges from entering the equipment from the field.

REMOTE CONTROL

Most irrigation equipment manufacturers offer remote control devices. There are also a number of companies that offer after-market devices. Remote control devices are normally grouped in one of the following classifications:

1. Manual station activation devices—work independently of any central equipment
2. Remote radio controls—work in conjunction with the system central and/or field controller
3. Pocket PC remote controls—provide central-type features in a mobile device
4. Remote computer controls—allow remote access to the central controller

Manual Station Activation Devices

Manual activation devices consist of a radio transmitter and receiver that provide access to individual controller stations across the golf course. These devices work independently of the controller faceplate. The simplest devices provide on/off station commands with no station timing. More sophisticated models may include station timing and station advance features as well as voice communication capabilities. This type of remote control is typically used in stand-alone control systems that do not utilize a PC-based central programmer.

The transmitter is typically a two-way radio, with a keypad, operating on a business/industrial radio frequency (UHF or VHF). It is usually necessary to obtain an FCC license. The keypad is used to transmit activation commands to receivers located at the controllers.

The receiver is typically a portable unit, assigned an identification number, which attaches to a wire pigtail at the controller. The pigtail may be wired directly to the controller's station output wiring, or there may be an access adapter, provided by the manufacturer, to facilitate the addition of these radio activation devices. The receiver uses the controller's power supply to power its radio and any stations it activates. A single receiver may be capable of operating one or more controllers in a cluster, depending on the total station count.

Because these radio control devices are usually low powered, their range is limited to direct line of sight to the controller. However, they can provide a low-cost solution for remote system activation and are handy tools for spot watering, irrigation system maintenance, and winterization or for just testing the system.

Remote Radio Controls

Most equipment manufacturers offer the option of a radio remote control device. Depending on the manufacturer, radio remote controls will provide the ability to access or activate program data that is stored at a field controller or at the central programmer. These devices offer the irrigation system operator more flexibility in system activation than a basic manual activation device. Some central programmers log the system run time of stations that were activated by the remote control system, which permits accurate record keeping.

Radio remote control systems consist of a central base receiver, its antenna, and portable field radios (Figure 4.17). The base receiver receives radio commands via the antenna from the portable field radios, and the commands are transmitted through the central programmer to the field controllers. The field radios utilize a keypad to transmit the operational commands to the central receiver. The field radios can also be used for voice communications.

These systems require an FCC license to operate, which means a thorough site survey should be performed prior to the installation of a system. The site survey involves identifying frequency in use and checking radio communication from numerous locations on the property to the potential base station location. This assessment is crucial for proper selection of the operating frequency and antennas.

Remote radio control systems typically share the following programming capabilities:

- Turn stations on/off with station run time
- Turn groups of stations on/off
- Advance stations and/or groups
- Pause or resume stations
- Turn programs on/off

FIGURE 4.17
Remote radio.

In addition, to protect the system, some control systems ensure that activation commands from the portable radios are hydraulically managed by the central programmer's software. For example, suppose the irrigation system operator calls for all the heads on a par 5 fairway to be activated. The central will activate only those stations that will not exceed the system operational criteria, maximizing the flow potential while preventing an excessive flow condition. Stations that are not activated will be placed in a pause mode until the first set of heads activated turn off, at which point the next set of stations start operation.

Some remote radio controls require the operator to identify the field controller number and then the station number, whereas others activate stations by identifying hole number, area code (i.e., green, tee, fairway, etc.), and station number. Most handheld radios provide a confirmation tone, assuring the irrigation operator that commands issued to out-of-sight stations have been successfully executed. The central software usually verifies that all transmissions have been received through the handheld radio so that the operator knows that commands have been received even if he or she is out of viewing sight of the stations that were activated.

Pocket PC Remote Controls

A recent development is the use of pocket PC devices on irrigation systems (Figure 4.18).

These small computing devices offer the same operational functionality as radio remote control systems, with the added feature of allowing the operator to view programming data and, if available, a map of the irrigation system.

Pocket PC systems also provide the same operational functionality as a desktop computer. The ability to download system database information into the pocket PC and access it on the golf course makes this a valuable tool. Various site adjustments can be made on the pocket PC in the field and uploaded to a desktop computer:

- Station run times
- Area adjustment factors
- Station adjustment factors such as crop coefficient, shade, soil type, compaction, and slope

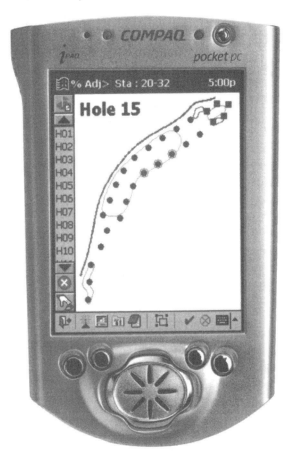

FIGURE 4.18
Pocket PC.

Some irrigation software allows the downloading of entire irrigation programs to the pocket PC, which can be edited and downloaded directly to the field controller.

If the desktop irrigation programming software is map based, some pocket PC systems allow for the entire Record Drawing to be loaded so that the different irrigation map layers can be viewed in the field. Some software packages also have map tools that allow for distance and area measurements on the pocket PC. This can be a great aid in finding lost irrigation components or calculating feature areas.

The pocket PC transmits activation commands to the central programmer through a portable field radio via either a hardwired or wireless link. As a station is activated in the field by the pocket PC and verified by the central, that station is illuminated on the pocket PC, providing visual verification of station activity across the golf course.

Remote Computer Controls

The ability to communicate remotely with computer-based central control systems is easily achieved through the use of telephone modems and remote control software. Remote control software, a telephone modem, and a telephone line must be available at both the host computer (the computer that is being accessed at the golf course) and the remote computer (the computer that is off-site). An off-site irrigation system operator can use the remote computer to access the host computer and actually run the host computer as if he or she were there.

Remote computer control is relatively inexpensive, and many manufacturers bundle this software with their irrigation programming software. With remote system access, a manufacturer or regional irrigation service technician can perform the following services without ever being on-site:

- Update software
- Transfer files
- Provide remote system tutorial
- Troubleshoot the central computer and field controllers
- Provide system maintenance and monitoring

Many golf course superintendents want the ability to dial in to the irrigation system from a remote location to view its operational status. The operational status of the system, including flow, which programs are active and which have completed, system alarms, and weather information from an on-site weather station, can easily be viewed. Remote computer control also allows the superintendent to cancel irrigation programs and scale any scheduled irrigation programs based on current weather information.

LINE CONDITIONERS/VOLTAGE STABILIZERS

Solid-state irrigation control equipment requires a constant and clean power supply for reliable operation. This includes the power supply to field controllers and central control equipment. When sized properly, a line conditioner or voltage stabilizer provides a power supply with a tightly regulated voltage, usually within 1 percent, for power supply input variations of +10 to –20 percent of the required circuit voltage. Although line conditioners/voltage transformers do not provide a power supply in the event of a power failure, they can protect irrigation components when there are variations and surges in the power supply.

A decrease in voltage to the field controllers will result in additional amperage draw; this can generate heat and potentially shorten the life of an electronic component. It is imperative that the power supply be as stable as possible; otherwise, components can fail prematurely as a result of the unstable power supply.

Power supply problems are usually associated with brownouts and sags attributable to the utility company or caused by harmonics and surges associated with switch mode power supplies. A constant voltage transformer can regulate the secondary voltage that feeds the electronic equipment and, with the use of capacitors, make up deficiencies in the available voltage up to 65 percent of the nominal voltage while supplying surge suppression for surges as great as 6000 volts. Line conditioners/voltage transformers should be UL listed for systems in the United States and CSA (Canadian Standards Association) certified for Canadian systems.

UNINTERRUPTIBLE POWER SUPPLIES

In order for the central to react to alarm conditions, it not only needs a clean power supply but an uninterruptible power supply (UPS) so that in the event of a power failure the central can initiate any of its alarm responses. With a UPS, if power is lost during operation of the irrigation system, valuable programming data is not lost. Power-related problems vanish and the system components return to their normal operating condition once the power is restored to the UPS unit.

Most UPS units are available with input voltages of 110 to 120 VAC and an output voltage of 120 VAC. A UPS typically offers line conditioning abilities and surge protection similar to those of a line conditioner/voltage stabilizer, such as protection against power surges and sags, spikes, and brownouts. A UPS is usually wired to a dedicated circuit breaker to help eliminate line problems caused by other electrical devices. Depending on the manufacturer of the UPS and its size, standby power in the event of a power failure may be available for 5 to 20 minutes or more. Some manufacturers of UPS units provide insurance to cover the cost of replacement for any device wired to the UPS that is damaged. UPS units should also be UL listed and CSA certified.

WEATHER STATIONS

An on-site weather station provides the most effective means of obtaining site-specific evapotranspiration (*ET*) data. When a weather station is used with a central control system, the *ET* data it calculates can be downloaded directly into the central computer's programming software to assist with the scheduling and programming of the irrigation system. The utilization of a weather station eliminates guessing in determining daily plant water losses and provides the irrigation system manager with a tool to program the system.

Climatic conditions are recorded at intervals, usually not exceeding five seconds, and stored at the weather station. This climatic data is then imported into a modified Penman equation, a time-tested *ET* model for determining turfgrass water use requirements, before it is imported into an irrigation systems operating program. A weather station monitors the following climatic conditions with the following values:

- Wind speed in miles per hour (0–110 mph) and direction (0–359 degrees)—Instrument type: anemometer and vane
- Air temperature in degrees Fahrenheit (–40° to +122°F) and Celsius (–40° to +50°C)—Instrument type: temperature/relative humidity probe

- Relative humidity in percent (0 to 100 percent)—Instrument type: temperature/relative humidity probe
- Solar radiation in langleys   (0 to 1.2 kW/m²)—Instrument type: solar pyranometer
- Rainfall in inches (0 to 2 in. in .01 in. increments)—Instrument type: tipping bucket rain gauge

Rainfall is not used in the equation to determine an *ET* value but is used to reduce the amount of irrigation required.

Types

Weather stations can typically communicate via hardwire cable, telephone modem, or radio, making it easy to locate the weather station on any site. The communication cable is generally two or three pairs of 20 AWG wire with color-coded jackets twisted together, each pair in its own shield with a drain wire. All three wire pairs are typically encased in an outer PVC or polyethylene jacket. Although most manufacturers require only two pairs of wires to communicate with a weather station, a third pair is typically used as a spare wire or to communicate with any additional sensors that could, potentially, be placed on the weather station. Hardwired weather stations are usually located within 2000 ft of the central control system. Weather stations with modems are typically used if the distance between the weather station and the central exceeds the manufacturer's maximum recommended distance or if a communication cable cannot be installed. The modem system communicates utilizing standard dedicated phone service. Radio communication methods are also available and, as with any radio communication equipment, should be thoroughly tested prior to installation.

Weather stations are generally powered by a power supply of 16 VAC. To eliminate the possibility of any sensor's being affected by the heat of an onboard transformer, the transformer is usually located away from the weather station. Solar-powered weather stations are also available for sites where power supply is a problem.

Maintenance

The proper maintenance of a weather station and its components is essential to obtaining accurate data. It is recommended that a maintenance log be established for every weather station, with maintenance intervals of every month, every six months, and every year. The date of service and a detailed description of the service required is necessary to track the performance of the weather station. Some maintenance is basic, such as checking to see whether there are any obstructions or contamination of any of the sensors. However, some sensors require periodic recalibration and others have parts that require annual replacement. Because most weather stations utilize an on-board battery to store data in the event of a power failure, it should be tested every six months. A weather station should also be checked periodically for structural damage and proper alignment and a visual inspection made of cables and connections. The electronic components of a weather station are particularly vulnerable to humidity. Desiccant packs are placed in a weather station's electronic compartment to keep humidity at an acceptable level

Installation

As with any electronic equipment on a golf course, proper installation and grounding are required for the reliable operation of a weather station. Because they are fairly tall pieces of equipment (7 ft to 9 ft), most weather stations are equipped with a lightning rod to protect against damage from lightning surges. It is extremely important to follow the manufacturer's directions for the installation of the lightning rod, the earth ground grid, and the sensors. Special surge arrestors are generally required for all incoming communication cable wires and power supply wires. These surge arrestors are typically attached to the earth ground grid. All weather station connections should be checked on a regular basis, especially the connection of the lightning rod to the earth ground grid.

Operation

The operation of a weather station is facilitated by the use of an irrigation programming software package. The irrigation software communicates with the weather station to provide real-time weather data or to retrieve data for inclusion in hourly or daily summaries generated by the software. A typical weather station is capable of storing up to 20 days of weather data.

Most irrigation programming software packages provide weather station reporting features that assist in generating weather reports.

The reporting feature allows weather data to be presented in an hourly, daily, weekly, monthly, or yearly display with totals or averages for each climatic value. Reports can also be generated for multiple days. This data can be printed in a tabular form, or daily data can be plotted in a graphic form.

WIRE

Conductors/Cables

Copper wire with an insulating jacket is typically used for golf course irrigation systems. Although aluminum is available at a lower cost than copper, copper is generally used because it has 35 percent greater conductivity. The outer jacket of the conductor protects the copper conductor from mechanical damage during installation and handling and provides electrical insulation. The National Electrical Code (NEC) requires that all wire used in applications covered by the code, which includes the applications found on golf courses, must be listed by a recognized testing laboratory. In the United States the Underwriters Laboratories, also recognized by its trademark, UL, is the recognized agency.

A UL listing for wire and cable implies that the manufactured product meets the requirements of the NEC for the intended application. This conformance is noted directly on the wire, with a UL trademark and the manufacturer's listing number. A UL listing does not ensure that each run of wire has been tested. However, it implies that the UL, on a systematic basis, inspects the manufacturing facilities to ensure that the wire is made to proper standards and with the proper compounds, processing methods, and testing procedures.

The recognized method for defining the size or thickness of a conductor in the United States is a numbering system called American Wire Gauge (AWG). The numbering system is established so that the larger the number, the thinner the conductor. For multiple conductor cables, a slash and the number of conductors follow the wire size.

Wire is available with solid or stranded conductors. Solid conductors are used in applications where there is no repetitive handling or flexing of the wire and it is not moved very often after initial installation. Stranded conductors, as the name suggests, are actually smaller strands that are twisted together, with the total mass equaling that of a solid conductor. Stranded conductors are used where flexing, coiling, or handling is anticipated. For practical manufacturing purposes, #6 AWG and larger wires are generally stranded.

Wire Types

Two basic types of insulation are used in golf course applications: thermoplastic and thermosetting. Examples of thermoplastic insulations are PVC, PE (polyethylene), polypropylene, polyurethane, nylon, and Teflon. Thermoplastic insulations are cured and ready to use once the material cools. They do not require vulcanization or further curing before use. Thermosetting insulations include rubbers and cross-linked polyethylene. These insulations require a vulcanizing or curing cycle and therefore are more expensive.

Wire that is used for direct burial applications of 600 volts or less is classified by the NEC as Type USE, Type UF, or PE wire.

Type USE (underground service entrance) cable is manufactured with thermosetting compounds. Most Type USE cable today is made of cross-linked polyethylene, and it may be buried between the utility's transformer and the user's main electrical panel. Type USE cable is also used for power supply wiring to submersible pump motors. It is generally available in single conductors, but it can be made in jacketed forms as well.

Type UF (underground feeder) wire is manufactured with a jacket of polyvinyl chloride insulation. UF wire is available in both single conductor form and in jacketed cables, with or without a ground wire. UF wire does not propagate flame and is self-extinguishing, so it is suitable for installations that terminate indoors. Valve wire, communication cable, and 120 or 240 volt power wire generally have the UF designation.

PE (polyethylene) insulated wire is available with a UL listing for golf course valve wiring. PE wire is rated for 600 volts, and, although its insulation thickness is less than that of PVC, it has better mechanical and insulating characteristics. PE wire also has superior abrasion, chemical, and cut-through resistance and is 28 percent lighter than PVC-jacketed wire. PE wire is typically used for valve wiring and communication cables for field controller and decoder systems. PE wire will propagate flame and is not approved for inside wiring.

Buried conductors, whether in conduit or directly buried, must have a "wet" rating, which is indicated by a "W" on the conductor marking. Conductors marked USE, UF, or PE can also be directly buried. All other conductors (usually Type THHN/THWN) must be buried in conduit.

Valve Wire

The valve wire between the controller and solenoid should be sized for the total maximum load at inrush current, the distance between the controller and the solenoid(s), and the maximum allowable voltage loss. The wire is typically single conductor UF or PE wire.

Zone wire (also known as control wire or hot wire) is typically available in a multitude of colors (Figure 4.19). Many irrigation system designers use a color-coded wiring scheme, coding different turf areas with different colors. This can make maintenance and troubleshooting easier. Spare wires are also color coded so that they can easily be identified in the field and at the controller.

Power Wire

Power wire is required between the power source(s) and the field controllers. The wire is sized to the maximum load it must supply at solenoid inrush conditions and in accordance with NEC requirements. Several types of wires and cables are used to supply power to field controllers. Power wire is usually direct buried, but in some cases local code dictates that power wire must be placed within a conduit or metal armor.

FIGURE 4.19
Zone and power cable on wire rack.

Power wire is typically installed as individual single conductors or as a cable in which all three conductors are encased in a single outer jacket. Because installing three separate single conductor wires can be unwieldy, the individual conductors can be ordered in a twisted configuration so that the three wires are available on the same spool. Although there is an increased cost, it is partially offset by a simplified installation and reduced amount of scrap. This cable is usually Type UF-B, also commonly referred to as "flat cable," and is available in sizes ranging from #14/2 AWG (two conductors, size #14 AWG) with ground to #6/2 AWG with ground.

For cables larger than 6 gauge, Type TC, or "Tray" cable, is generally used. Tray cable is available in a wide range of sizes and with multiple conductors, each individual wire having black insulation. Because the encased wires are usually not color coded, they are typically labeled with either numbers or letters to aid in determining which conductor is the hot, neutral, and equipment ground. With three-conductor Tray cable, all the conductors are the same size, which means that the ground conductor is larger than the minimum required by the NEC. This provides additional safety, with faster circuit breaker response to lightning and power surges. The outer jacket on Tray cable is 33 to 100 percent thicker than UF-B cable, depending on the wire gauge of the conductors. Some irrigation system designers and consultants use Tray cable for power wire of all sizes. Conductors in Tray cable are stranded.

Communication Cable

The central control system must communicate with a variety of devices. A different type of communication cable may be required for each use. For example, field controllers may communicate via a 14/2 cable, whereas the weather station may use a #20 AWG-3 pair cable with drain wire. Communication cable must be sized in accordance with the manufacturer's recommendations. The cable is typically sized to a total circuit length and/or the maximum number of field controllers or decoders on an individual cable.

Communication cable can vary dramatically between control system manufacturers. In some cases it consists of only a single twisted, color-coded pair of #16 AWG wires, each in its own jacket, wrapped in a shielding foil with a drain wire. Both wires are then encased in an outer jacket of polyethylene. Sometimes specifications call for armored cable, which includes a stainless steel helically wrapped jacket wrapping all conductors or conductor bundles, and is commonly used if there is potential for rodent damage to a conductor.

Another manufacturer may require two twisted pairs of #18 AWG wires, with each wire being color coded, as well as an aluminum shield and a #20 AWG tinned copper drain wire that is in contact with the shield. The aluminum shield is designed to drain off electromotive force (EMF) interference. Still a third manufacturer may require two color-coded #14 AWG (also available in sizes up to #8 AWG, depending on the distance of cable run and the electrical load) tin-coated copper conductors, to prevent corrosion and facilitate soldering, in individual PVC jackets encased in a high-density polyethylene outer jacket. The outer jacket is available in multiple colors to help distinguish individual communication cables in the field.

Some manufacturers recommend installing an extra pair of wires to devices such as weather stations and pump stations for additional insurance in the event of damage to the cable or to accommodate future technology. These wires are often contained in the cable initially installed for the device. For example, a weather station typically uses four wires, but a #20 AWG-3 pair cable is often installed, helping to prevent unnecessary work at a later date.

Telephone cable often consists of three to six color-coded, twisted pairs of #19 AWG wires. The wire bundle is typically encased in an electrically continuous corrugated aluminum shield. A flooding compound (gel) is applied over and under the shield to fill voids and produce a cylindrical core and to provide moisture resistance. The manufacturer's identification, pair count, conductor size, and year of manufacture appear on the outer black polyethylene jacket.

Splice Kits

All below-grade splices to direct-bury irrigation wire and cable must be placed in a UL-listed or CSA-certified waterproof wire splice kit designed for direct bury or submerged applications whenever possible. Splice kits typically have maximum voltage ratings of 30, 600, or 1000 volts. This maximum voltage rating is usually the determining factor in choosing the proper splice kit for a particular application. Manufacturers of wire and irrigation equipment often list the recommended splice kits and methods of connection and wiring for their products.

All wire connections can be classified as one of the following: soldered, insulated wire connection, or crimp connector.

- *Soldered*—A soldered connection, if done properly, provides the best bond between conductors. All conductors that are to be soldered together must be thoroughly cleaned, and all oxidation must be removed prior to making the connection. A soldered connection should be visually inspected before it is placed in a waterproof splice kit. Only solder intended for electrical applications should be used, not plumbing solder. Solder joints are often made on communication cable and power wire splices because of the permanence of these splices. A different connection method is typically used on zone wiring because of the additional time required to make a proper solder joint.

- *Insulated wire connection*—For most golf course irrigation applications, an insulated wire connector (wire nut) is the most common type of connector. A wire nut provides a quick and simple connection. A good connection between conductors can be made as long as the manufacturer's recommendations are followed and the appropriate wire nut is selected for the number and size of the conductors that are being connected. Wire nuts should be UL listed. Wire nuts can be used for most splices in golf course irrigation applications and are particularly popular for use in connecting zone wires to a valve solenoid. An insulated wire connector should always be placed in an approved waterproof splice kit prior to burial.

- *Crimp connector*—Crimp connectors are either insulated or uninsulated and require a special tool to make the physical connection between conductors. Crimp style connectors are typically used on multiconductor cable, and the crimp connections are staggered apart, making a low-profile cable splice that will fit a multiconductor waterproof splice kit.

- *Insulation displacement connectors*—Used in splicing some communication cable, insulation displacement connectors are utilized to make waterproof connections between two or three #16 AWG copper conductors.

Among the most popular types of golf course irrigation splice kits, used for splicing valve wire, are gel filled tubes. These splice kits consist of an electrical spring connector (wire nut) and a specially designed tube filled with a waterproof insulating gel. The gel-filled sealant material does not harden and allows the splice to be reworked without the wires having to be cut. The tube is specially designed to hold the wire nut in place, using locking fingers in the tube. The tube lid also presses against the wire insulation to provide strain relief and to assist in preventing the connection from being pulled out of the waterproofing material.

Two different kits are designed for different sizes of wire. The wire nut and tube should be sized to the number and gauges of the wires they are connecting. The smaller wire nut typically accepts two to five #8 AWG wires through two #12 AWG wires, plus one #16 AWG solid or stranded copper wire, which is typically the wire to the valve solenoid. This splice kit is generally used for a two-wire connection, and the larger kit for the common three-wire connection.

The larger version is designed to accommodate either larger or more wires. The larger splice kit will accept five #16 AWG wires through three #10 solid or stranded copper wires. This splice kit is generally used for valve common wire.

There are currently two different voltage ratings for gel-filled tube splice kits, 30 volts and 600 volts. The 30-volt splice kits are typically used for splices on wire and cable where the operating voltage will not exceed 30 volts. These splice kits are often used on zone wiring, as well as some manufacturers' communication cables and decoder systems. The 600-volt splice kit is commonly used on decoder systems for the connection between the decoder and the communication cable where the line voltage may be in the 30 to 45 volt range, depending on the manufacturer. The 600-volt splice kit can also be used on smaller-gauge field controller power wires.

A resin type or bag type splice kit is often used for multiconductor communication cables and power wire greater than #10 AWG. A resin style splicing kit contains a plastic cast, available in a number of configurations and sizes, as well as two materials, separated within a bag by a seal. When the seal is broken, the two materials are mixed to form the insulating epoxy resin.

The installation of a cast kit is a little more involved than installation of a splice tube. Following the manufacturer's recommendations, individual wires are paired together and properly connected with the appropriate wire nut or connector. Then the two-piece plastic mold is used to encase the entire cable, or the splice is prepared for insertion into the plastic bag. The two-part epoxy is mixed within the bag when a seal is broken, thus releasing the two materials. Once the epoxy has been sufficiently mixed, the bag is cut open and either the epoxy is poured into the two-piece cast, or the wire splice is placed into the epoxy bag and sealed with electrical tape. The epoxy will cure and harden in a period ranging from approximately 20 minutes to 80 minutes.

For low-voltage communication cables some manufacturers recommend all individual splices be placed in the same plastic mold. All splices should be placed in a valve box with at least 2 ft of slack so that the splice can be lifted above grade for inspection, testing, or repair. On power wires and communication cable it is also a good idea to mark each wire with a permanent marker or with a tag listing both the point of origin of the wire and where the wire is going. All splices must be recorded on the irrigation system's Record Drawing.

Fiber Optics

The use of fiber optic cable has become very popular in the telecommunications industry because of the very high speed, low distortion, and clean data transmission it affords. Fiber optic cable is a glass conductor with a plastic coating. Transmission over fiber optic cable is done with light and light sensors. Because the cable does not have any electrical conducting properties, it is virtually immune to damage due to electrical surge.

Although the properties of fiber optics are very attractive, they are offset by high cost and difficulty of repair. Service is available only from highly trained technicians who use special repair equipment. Fiber optic cable is also expensive and must be installed in conduit. It may be some time before it is widely used in golf course irrigation systems.

Sleeves

A sleeve is a pipe that is used to accommodate another pipe or wire for the purpose of protecting it or to facilitate repairs. In irrigation systems separate sleeves are used for pipe and wire. Local code often dictates the type of sleeving material, as well as depth of bury and separation between sleeves.

Care must be taken in choosing the size of a pipe sleeve, as its inside diameter must be large enough to accommodate the outside diameter of the material it is protecting. The ends of sleeves are often plugged to protect them from filling with soil or water. A sleeve is usually installed with a slight pitch so that water does not build up within the pipe. A sleeve is generally installed at the same depth as the pipe.

The sleeving material that is commonly used for irrigation pipelines is often the same material as the pipeline itself, however, using pipe of a different class can help to identify it as a sleeve. It is normally two or three nominal sizes larger than the pipe it is protecting. The sleeving materials for road crossings are normally specified by local code. Schedule 40 galvanized steel pipe or Class 150 ductile iron pipe is often specified.

Conduit

A conduit is an enclosed channel of metal or plastic material designed to hold wires or cables. A conduit is used to protect wire or cable from abrasion and mechanical and environmental damage. National and local codes dictate where conduit is needed on a golf course irrigation system. Typically, conduit is used to protect wire or cable under roads, cart paths, parking lots, bridges, streams, areas with unsuitable fill, and areas in which it is impossible to maintain the proper depth of bury.

Nonmetallic conduit is typically made of PVC and should be marked, showing that it has been approved and tested for use as a wire or cable conduit. According to the NEC, only listed (by the UL or other recognized organization) conduit can be used. Colored, rigid nonmetallic pipe that is used for water transmission is not permitted for use as a conduit. The approved product for golf course irrigation systems is typically Schedule 40 rigid, nonmetallic electrical PVC; however, some local codes require schedule 80 PVC conduit if an area is classified as a high-abuse area.

Schedule 40 PVC conduit is available in sizes from ½ in. to 4 in., is typically gray in color, and can easily be distinguished from irrigation piping. When conduits are required in a golf course irrigation system, separate conduits should be used for wires and cables of different voltages. When conduit(s) are installed in the same trench as a water pipeline, there should be at least a 6 in. separation between the conduit and the pipeline. Often a pull wire is installed in the conduit to aid in the installation of additional wires. For maintenance and other practical reasons conduit should always extend at least 5 ft in both directions beyond the area where the wire or cable needs protection. The NEC specifies, on the basis of conductor type and conduit size and material, the maximum number of conductors that can be used in a conduit.

Open ends on conduit piping materials should be sealed with an approved sealing material, duct seal or foam, to keep debris out and to prevent insects and animals from making a home.

LIGHTNING PROTECTION

The equipment and devices used for lightning protection on golf course irrigation systems can be classified as either "active" or "passive" protection systems. An active lightning protection system is one that reacts to the threat of lightning, and a passive system reacts to the effects of lightning once it has entered the irrigation system's wiring.

Lightning Detection Devices

A lightning detection device is a form of active lightning protection. These devices are designed to protect the central control system, field controllers, pump station, and weather station by physically disconnecting these components from all of their associated wiring, including power supply, communication cables, 24 volt zone wiring, and telephone lines if the threat of lightning is detected. In addition, when the threat has subsided, these devices reestablish all the wire connections to the equipment so that their function can resume. A lightning protection system is not a warning or detection system designed to alert players of a possible lightning strike; it is a protection system for the electrical components of an irrigation system.

The triggering device for a lightning detection system is the lightning detection unit. A typical golf course has a single lightning detection unit that is positioned in a building, typically the building where the central equipment is located. Large sites may have two or more of these detection units. A lightning detection unit is designed to sense radio energy, which is distinct from man-made frequencies, as far away as 30 miles and then trigger a series of disconnection devices to protect the irrigation equipment. The number of disconnects triggered by the detection unit is displayed at a user-resettable counter. The equipment is protected by a series of relays that are wired in series, with the wiring leading to the components of the irrigation control system.

The relay devices used in a lightning detection system rely on a connection to a good earth ground in order to protect the irrigation equipment attached to them. A poor earth ground creates the possibility of lightning jumping from the switching contacts that are performing the various disconnect functions.

Lightning protection systems cannot protect an irrigation system from a direct hit. However, they can provide a vital role in protecting the electrical components of an irrigation system. The cost of this type of equipment must be measured against the frequency of lightning activity, the cost to repair damaged components, and the loss of system service. For central control systems the use of lightning protection/detection devices for the protection of the central equipment alone is usually worthwhile.

Player Warning Systems

A player warning system is designed to activate an alarm or a series of horns if a detection system senses lightning activity. These systems are similar to the lightning protection devices that are used to disconnect the wiring of an irrigation system, but instead activate external alarms that can be heard from a long distance to warn players of potential lightning strikes.

Warning systems anticipate, rather than detect, lightning and provide advanced warning of a possible lightning strike. These systems are fully automatic and provide alert and clear alarms for players on a golf course.

Air horns are powered by either an external low-voltage power supply or a solar panel that trickle charges a battery cell. The solar-powered horn systems are popular, as they can be installed at any time without the installation of cables when radio communication is used.

Irrigation system designers are often asked to include player-warning systems with their system designs so they can be installed at the same time as the irrigation system itself. Liability issues should be thoroughly discussed with the owner prior to installation.

Surge Protection

Surge protection is a form of passive protection, in which a surge protection device(s) is placed in line with the conductor (zone wire, communication cable, power supply cable, and telephone line or radio antenna cable) and the electronic component it is designed to protect. Where a lightning detection system reacts to the threat of electrical surges induced by lightning, surge protection devices react once the lightning induced surge is on the conductor. A surge protection device is most effective in protecting the electronic components of an irrigation system when connected to a good earth ground network so that it can divert lightning energy into the earth.

In golf course irrigation systems, surges are typically produced by lightning strikes. However, surges can also be created by the energizing or deenergizing of transformers, power source shorts, the dropping of an electrical load (such as a pump), or switch arcing.

A given square mile can expect 2 to 30 lightning strikes per year. Lightning strikes are very fast and are measured in milliseconds, or thousandths of a second. A typical lightning stroke produces a peak current within a few milliseconds, which is followed by a reduced current, and successive high currents separated by reduced currents, which last up to a quarter of a second.

Irrigation systems are particularly susceptible to lightning damage because of the large amounts of buried wire. An 18-hole golf course can have 150 to 400 miles of wire or more, with most of the wire terminating at a field controller. Lightning seeks the path of least impedance, and underground cable can offer such a path. Transient surges due to lightning can be induced in electrical wiring from a lightning strike up to 3 miles away.

There are two basic types of electrical surges that are induced on the wiring of a typical irrigation control system:

1. *Metallic surges.* A metallic surge enters a circuit on one of the wires, causing the wire to go to a high potential voltage. The result is current flow from the high wire to the low wire through the electronic circuit, which causes component failure.

2. *Longitudinal surges.* A longitudinal surge comes in on both wires, causing both wires to flow high current simultaneously. The result is a current flow in both wires, which arcs over the electronic circuit to the earth ground. The combination of the high current flow and arc to ground causes component failure.

To protect electronic circuits from metallic surges, a surge arrestor of proper capacity is placed across both wires and ahead of the electronic circuit. This causes the current to flow through the surge arrestor and to the earth ground rather than through the electronic circuit. An electronic circuit is protected from longitudinal surges by placing a surge arrestor of proper capacity ahead of each wire and the electronic circuit and connecting each surge arrestor to the earth ground. This prevents the surge from flowing through the electronic circuit.

Surge arrestors are widely used in golf course irrigation systems. Most manufacturers provide a number of surge suppression devices on their irrigation equipment as standard hardware. However, other manufacturers offer optional surge equipment at a higher cost. It is generally wise to purchase the surge equipment at the time of installation, as retrofitting or upgrading the surge protection equipment in the future can be labor intensive and costly. In addition to the surge protection equipment available from the control system manufacturer, the manufacturer often recommends optional third-party surge protection equipment. The recommended equipment is often described in installation manuals for field controllers and centrals.

The most common surge arrestors used for golf course irrigation applications are spark gaps and varistors (commonly referred to as metal oxide varistors, or MOVs).

A spark gap arrestor consists of a gas tube filled with an inert gas at a reduced pressure. Inside the gas tube are metal electrodes. At the designed spark-over voltage the electrodes break down the gas and allow current to flow from one electrode to another. The spark gap shunts the excess energy away from the vulnerable circuit. Spark gaps are designed to handle larger currents than an MOV but are slower acting.

Spark gaps are simple and reliable devices that have a low voltage drop during the conducting state. They have large power-handling capabilities and are bilateral devices, having the same polarity on both sides. Spark gaps have a longer life expectancy than MOVs and can survive after conducting higher levels of energy than a comparable MOV device.

A varistor is a solid-state unit that clamps a transient voltage surge at a safe level by shunting the excessive energy away from the circuit at a rate much faster than a spark gap. Varistors are also bilateral devices and are relatively small in size. Very small varistors are used on the printed circuit boards of most field controllers. Varistors are self-healing and because of their ability to react quickly and handle moderately high power surges, are widely used in irrigation control systems.

Because spark gaps and varistors have complementing operational characteristics (high current capacity spark gaps and fast-acting varistors) they are sometimes packaged together as multistage lightning protection circuits and used in various applications in golf course irrigation systems. Other surge arrestors utilize several metal oxide varistors, each protecting a line to the grounded neutral.

A surge arrestor should be considered for the dedicated circuit breaker supplying the power to the central equipment, each field controller and weather station power supply, each weather station, field controller or field controller cluster, and each communication cable wire to the central, pump station, and weather station.

Fuses and circuit breakers are not surge arrestors. Their reaction time to a surge is approximately 3 million nanoseconds; an electrical force traveling at the speed of light can cause serious damage by the time a fuse or circuit breaker can react.

Surge arrestors are typically rated with a maximum operating voltage and phase, response time, and discharge capacity. Surge response time is usually expressed in nanoseconds and discharge capacity in amps. The color-coded leads of a surge arrestor aid in its installation. Surge arrestors should be UL listed or CSA certified for their application.

Ground Rods and Plates

Surge arrestor equipment must be attached to a good earth ground network to operate effectively. Many different types of equipment and materials are used in golf course irrigation systems to help achieve a good earth ground.

Generally, two types of electrodes are used to create earth ground grids for golf course irrigation systems: ground rods and ground plates.

GROUND RODS

A minimum-size ground rod as specified by the NEC is ⅝ in. × 8 ft. Other diameter sizes include ¾ in., 1 in., 1¼ in., 1½ in., and 1¾ in. Ground rod resistance is a function of the surface area in contact with the surrounding soil. Because the diameter of a ground rod has only a slight effect on resistance and the resultant effectiveness, the ⅝ in. rod is typically used. For example: A 10 ft long by ⅝ in. diameter ground rod has a resistance of 6.33 ohms; when its diameter is increased to 1¼ in., the resistance is lowered only to 5.6 ohms.

Ground rods are also available in various lengths. The most common ground rods are 8 ft long, having 188.5 sq in. of copper surface, and 10 ft long, with 236 sq in. of copper surface. Because the depth to which a ground rod is driven has a greater effect in lowering resistance than does the diameter of the rod, the longer 10 ft rods are typically used.

A UL-listed ground rod is constructed of high tensile steel and "copper clad" with a 10 mil copper skin (10 thousandths of an inch) in accordance with 2002 NEC Article 250-52 (5). Sometimes ground rods are connected together, end to end, to achieve a deeper rod installation; however, this can drastically increase inductance. (It is not unusual for grounding rods adjacent to utility poles to be 40 ft in length.) In those cases the rods should be connected through a permanent welding process, or rods threaded on both ends should be used with threaded couplings. Ground rods are typically installed in the vertical or near vertical position and an access box installed over the top to facilitate inspection and periodic testing.

GROUND PLATES

Ground plates are also available in various sizes. A typical ground plate is 4 in. × 96 in. × 0.060 in. of solid copper, meeting the requirements of 2002 NEC Article 250-52 (6). Each plate must expose a minimum of 2 sq ft of surface area to the soil. Ground plates are usually available with 25 ft of #6 AWG bare solid copper wire welded to them. Any connection to a plate should be made by a welding process, with the welding rod containing a minimum of 5 percent silver. Plates are typically installed in the horizontal position, at a depth of 30 in. to 48 in., or below the frost line, whichever is deeper.

Ground plates are commonly used in earth ground circuits for electronic controllers. They are often used in conjunction with a ground rod. Ground plates exhibit lower inductance and impedance characteristics than ground rods. Ground plates are often installed with a ground enhancement material that decreases the resistance between the plate and the soil. Maintaining a proper moisture level at any ground electrode is crucial. If an electrode is surrounded by dry material, its effectiveness is greatly diminished. A 4 in. drainage pipe and grate are typically installed vertically, directly over the plate, to allow surface water to reach the plate, which assists in maintaining an adequate moisture level at the plate. Drip emitters, sprinklers, or bubblers may also be used to maintain moisture levels.

Connectors

Ground rods, plates, and conductors may be joined in two ways: with mechanical clamps or with exothermically welded connectors.

- *Mechanical clamps.* A ground rod clamp, also known as an acorn clamp or a two-piece clamp, should be sized to the rod. These clamps should be made from a copper alloy and be UL listed.
- *Welded connectors.* A preferred method for creating permanent connections in metallic grounding equipment is to use an exothermic welding connector. This type of connector is not subject to galvanic corrosion and will not loosen as a mechanical connector will. It is important to select the appropriate disposable ceramic mold pattern, given the number of conductors and/or type of electrode to be connected. A special weld metal is poured into the mold, and the mold is covered. An igniter is used to activate the weld metal, which bonds the metallic parts.

Welded connectors are available in multiple configurations for cable-to-cable or cable-to-ground rod welds. They must be UL listed or made to NEC requirements.

Ground Conductors

A ground conductor is a stranded or solid bare copper wire or copper strap that is used to connect the various ground electrodes within the earth ground circuit. Irrigation equipment manufacturers typically recommend the type and size of the copper wire that is to be used for an earth ground circuit.

Copper wire is available solid or stranded, in any size, of either insulated or bare copper. For direct bury applications bare copper wire is typically used. Copper wire should conform to UL Standard 719.

Ground Enhancement Material

Soil resistance varies with different soil types and structures. Clay soils, partly because of their higher water-holding capacities, have lower resistance than sandy soils, which have lower water-holding capacities. Many different chemical treatments have been used to improve soil resistance. Some chemicals were found to be corrosive to the electrodes in the earth ground circuit or detrimental to the health of the turfgrass or to the environment. Many others were not permanent, as they gradually washed away and required additional applications.

There are some products specially designed to lower the contact resistance to earth through chemical enhancement, and are environmentally safe and stable. These products are long-lasting, eliminating the need for periodic replacement or enhancement. In addition, these specially manufactured products have good moisture-retention characteristics that help maintain a desirable moisture balance regardless of the seasonal moisture variation in the surrounding soil.

Ground enhancement materials are typically placed above and below a ground plate. They are also used as backfill material for ground rods and buried copper conductors. These materials are available in both a nonhardening formulation for clay soils and a hardening formulation for coarse soils, such as sand and rock, to prevent material migration. Some materials require mixing with water to properly set them and to facilitate installation (3½ gallons per 50 lb bag of material). The manufacturer's instructions should be followed throughout the installation and handling of these materials.

SOURCES

American Society of Agricultural Engineers. 2000. *ASAE standards 2000*. 47th ed. St. Joseph, MO: ASAE, pp. 849–863.

National Fire Protection Association. 2002 *National Electrical Code (NFPA 70), 2002 ed*. Quincy, MA: NFPA.

Uni-Bell. *Handbook of PVC pipe*. 5th ed. 2001. Dallas, TX : Uni-Bell PVC Pipe Association, pp. 12–20.

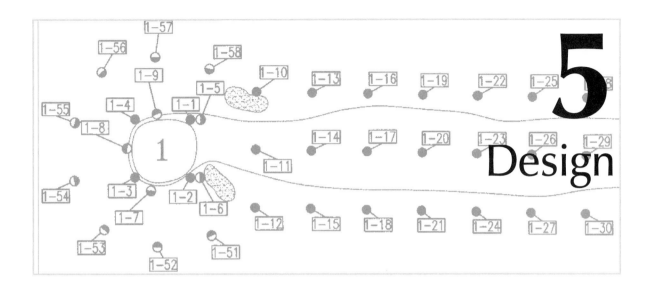

This chapter explains the complete design process, from initial collection of site data through preparation of final plans and other bid documents. Basic principles of hydraulics and electricity are introduced. Flow, pressure, and velocity in pipe are discussed, as are voltage, amperage, and resistance in wire. Head location, coverage, spacing and uniformity, pipe and wire sizing and routing, isolation capacity, grounding procedures, and the calculation of system demand are covered in detail. Drafting procedures and symbols are also addressed. Specification writing is discussed in terms of format, precision, and clarity, and in relation to legal, liability, and regulatory requirements. The importance of knowing and referencing codes and standards is explained. Scheduling and programming for maximum efficiency and for conservation of water and energy are also detailed.

PRELIMINARY PROCEDURES

Site Conditions

Many physical elements and conditions of a site will affect the irrigation system. Information about these conditions must be collected and evaluated early in the design process because some of the most basic elements of the design depend on site conditions. It is also important to understand that, within the 120 to 180 acres of an 18-

hole golf course, many conditions (soils, topography, drainage, exposure to wind, sun, and shade, etc.) will vary substantially. It is rare, for example, to find a course with completely uniform native soils throughout. In addition, modern construction techniques include manufactured seedbeds and perched water tables on greens. Even in an area of heavy clay native soils, the putting surfaces will be primarily sand. At many courses the tee surfaces are also covered with a predominantly sand seedbed mix.

Soil texture and structure have a significant effect on the water-holding capacity and infiltration rate of the soil, and these, in turn, affect the precipitation rate and control system programming that are key elements of system design. A heavier soil, for example, will have a lower infiltration rate but a higher water-holding capacity than a soil that is primarily sand. The irrigation design for the heavier soil must have a lower precipitation rate, or soak times programmed into the station run times, to avoid puddling or surface runoff and the resultant waste of water.

Site topography can affect many elements of the design. For example, a fairly level area (coupled with uniform soils and exposure) may allow the combining of two (or more) long-radius fairway or rough heads on a single controller station. On the other hand, steep slopes, swales, ridges, and mounds, especially when they are in close proximity to each other, may require shorter-radius heads and individual head control to provide the precision necessary to address the different moisture requirements of relatively small areas without over- or underwatering adjacent areas. Further, the steeper areas may require lower precipitation rates or longer soak times for the same reasons heavier soils do.

If heads in an area of steep topography are combined, the combinations must follow the contour lines, not the fall line. Thus, a head on a slope or the top of a mound cannot be paired with one at the bottom of a swale. On holes with a cross slope, the upper-side heads are paired with upper heads, and the lower-side heads with other low heads.

Different turfgrass varieties have different water requirements. Obviously Bermudagrass on a southwestern course requires more water than a cool-season grass in the northeast, for reasons of climate as well as the needs of the actual plant. However, different cool-season grasses on the same course can also have different requirements. Bentgrass fairways and bluegrass roughs have different moisture needs, both because of the plant requirements and because of the different heights of cut. Even when a fairway and the adjacent approach area are of the same grass, they will have different moisture requirements. On many higher-quality courses approaches are treated more like a putting surface than a fairway. They are cut shorter and more frequently, they are fertilized differently, and they usually get more concentrated traffic, so they cannot be irrigated the same way as fairways.

Knowledge of local climate and weather patterns in the growing season is critical in the early stages of a design. Local rainfall and evapotranspiration data is important. Also helpful are water use figures from nearby golf courses, if the irrigated acreages are similar.

Turfgrass exposed to significant winds will require more water than the same type of grass that is sheltered from the wind, so the two areas must be controlled separately. In many designs wind sensors are installed at key exposed areas. When wind speed exceeds a preset limit for a set time, a signal is sent to the control system. With the use of if/then logic in the control software, irrigation in the area of the sensor is paused. When the wind speed falls below the limit for a set time, irrigation in that area is resumed. This may be a mandated requirement for systems using effluent. Temperature sensors and rain gauges are used for similar applications.

Exposure to sun and shade is another issue. Certainly, shaded turf requires less water than the same type of turf that receives full sun all day. Early design decisions will be needed, at least in the area of control. On a tree-lined golf hole aligned east-west, one side of the fairway is in the sun all day and the other in the shade much of the day. If all other conditions (soil, topography, etc.) allow, the design could pair adjacent fairway heads. However, the pairing would have to be sunny side versus shaded side. Combining heads across the hole (i.e., heads that cover both shady and sunny turf areas) would lead to unacceptable conditions. Either the shady-side turf would be too wet, or the sunny side too dry. The same guidelines apply to greens and tees.

Maintenance and management procedures in use on an existing course or proposed for a new construction project must be known early in the design process. If fertigation will be used, the system must be designed to accommodate it, in terms of components as well as in the areas of control and head location. Different turf areas (green, perimeter, approach, fairway, rough, etc.) are fertilized differently, so the system must allow them to be irrigated separately. Other maintenance considerations include grass type and height, frequency of cut, desired "water window" (the time available for irrigation), and applications relating to special procedures such as hand watering, syringing, dew removal, and the timely watering in of hot or expensive chemicals, fertilizers, and other granular materials. Watering in occurs after a product is applied by spraying or spreading, and irrigation (or rainfall) water takes it off the plant leaves and carries it into the soil. Hot chemicals or fertilizers are those that cause foliar burn if they are not washed off the plant leaves. Management practices relating to irrigation priorities, duration, and frequency must also be considered.

Restrictions imposed on a site by legal or environmental issues or by the architect's design concepts must be factored into the design early in the process. Property lines, setbacks, rights-of-way, wetlands, and easements must be identified and their restrictions determined. These can have a significant effect on head locations and the routing of pipe and wires. The crossing easements for buried utilities, such as gas and electric lines or fiber optic communication cables, are governed by the utility companies, which usually have very strict requirements concerning location and installation of irrigation components.

Local, state, and national codes and ordinances can affect design. Local electric codes dictate type and size of materials, minimum burial depths, grounding requirements, and so forth. Noise ordinances can affect the location of pump stations. Many codes require specific procedures when irrigation pipes cross potable water lines, and all jurisdictions have very strict backflow prevention codes.

The use of fertigation brings many regulations into effect, which vary according to the location of the site. Secondary containment around storage and mix tanks and injection points is mandated in many states, with specific guidelines as to capacity and structure. Safety features such as electrical control interlocks, low-pressure drains, and vacuum breakers are also required by a number of states. (Note that a responsible designer includes all these elements even if they are not required by law.) There are also restrictions on where irrigation water injected with chemicals or fertilizer can be applied. For example, a design accommodating fertigation may need part-circle heads along a wetland or pond, whereas a system without fertigation could have full-circle heads.

The use of effluent or wastewater in a golf course system is closely regulated. Some authorities prohibit wastewater irrigation when wind speed exceeds a set maximum. Local and state regulations often dictate areas where wastewater cannot be applied.

Restricted areas can include buffers along property lines or around buildings, streams, ponds, wetlands and adjacent buffers, well fields, septic fields, and so-called natural areas where existing native vegetation is to remain.

Environmental issues are a serious concern in all aspects of a golf course project. The irrigation designer must be aware of all environmental restrictions very early in the process. Some jurisdictions do not allow spray into waterways, regardless of the irrigation water quality. Some do not allow heads, pipe, or wire to be installed in wetland buffers. Others allow pipe and wire to cross wetlands, but only if they are attached to bridge or causeway structures.

Of course, the most critical environmental restrictions are those limiting the amount of water a course is allowed to use. Some authorities limit water consumption by gal per day, some by gal (or acre-ft) per month, and some by gal (or acre-ft) per year, and others have limits on all three. Many states do not even require diversion permits or usage reports if daily consumption is below 100,000 gal, although this would be unusual for a golf course. Over that amount, each course must apply for its own diversion or withdrawal permit, and the state has final authority on how much water a course is allocated. Arizona has a straightforward rule: No golf course can irrigate more than 90 acres to a fixed depth. Withdrawal permitting may require specific equipment, such as central control including flow management, weather stations, and flow meters, to be incorporated into the system design.

Early knowledge of local electric power company costs, policies, and rate structures is important. The desire or need to irrigate only during off-peak hours may shorten the water window to the point that larger pumps, mains, and controller power wiring are required. Pump station starters and controls can also be affected.

On a new construction project, early knowledge of the golf course architect's design concepts is essential to the irrigation design process. Questions must be answered, such as whether the plant secondary rough and out-of-play areas will be planted in fescue or buffalograss. Are there areas that will remain natural and therefore should not be irrigated? Are there waste bunkers or tall grass areas?

Perhaps the most significant site condition is the budget. Clearly, the irrigation designer must be aware of the budget on day one. Better yet, he or she should be involved in establishing the budget. Although this is not always possible, it may avoid serious problems as the project evolves. An unrealistically low budget is a recipe for disaster.

The irrigation system requirements of a golf course (and those of specific areas within the course) result from a combination of all these factors. All must be investigated and evaluated as the first step in the design process.

Water Requirements

Early in the design process, the system water requirement must be estimated. In addition to its use in the basic irrigation design, this estimate will be needed for selecting water resources, for permit applications, and for the design and location of storage ponds. In fact, the estimated system water requirement can be the factor that ultimately determines whether a project is feasible, depending on the availability of local water sources and the financial realities of the project.

Plant water use must be known before the system water requirement can be estimated. As previously discussed, the calculation of plant water use is based on turf type, growth stage, appropriate crop coefficient, and the local reference evapotranspiration (ET_O). The results will vary for different areas of the course (greens, fairways, rough, etc.) when turf types and height of cut in those areas differ. Plant water use is typically described in inches per day, per week, per month, or per year. "Inches" describes average application depth over the coverage area.

The calculation of the system water requirement starts with an estimation of the highest weekly turfgrass water needs; that is, how much water the system will require during the peak demand week of the season. This estimate will be modified by factors such as projected system efficiency and area to be irrigated. The system water requirement is usually expressed in terms of gallons per day (gpd), per week (gpw), per month, or per year (gpy). Also used are acre-ft (325,848 gal) and acre-in. (27,154 gal) per day, week, month, or year.

Estimation of the average system water requirement includes effective historical rainfall and can be the basis for consumptive use permit applications. Average monthly effective rainfall can be estimated from Table 2-43 in Part 623 of the *National Engineering Handbook,* produced by the Natural Resources Conservation Service of the Department of Agriculture. This table is based on historical mean monthly precipitation and historical average evapotranspiration, so it should not be used for day-to-day scheduling or programming. The table is reproduced in the appendix to this book. Estimation of the maximum (net) system water requirement assumes no rainfall and is the basis for calculating initial irrigation system capacities (source, storage, and pump station capacities, main line pipe sizes, etc.).

Preliminary Estimate of Gross System Water Requirement

INPUTS

- Area (acres) to be irrigated (from golf course architect's preliminary estimate or field measurement of existing course)
- Plant water requirement = *ET* or projected turf water use (average local *ET*—usually inches per week, multiplied by average crop coefficient for turf types to be planted)
- Projected system efficiency (typically 80 percent for new design)
- Length of irrigation season (local sources)
- Effective rainfall during irrigation season (local historical records)

THEN

Plant water requirement × number of weeks of irrigation
       – effective rainfall during irrigation season
    = preliminary net water requirement (in inches).

And

Preliminary net water requirement divided by projected system efficiency = preliminary gross water requirement (inches).

And

Preliminary gross water requirement × area to be irrigated (acres)
    = preliminary gross system water requirement (acre-inches).

EXAMPLE 5.1

For

- 72 acres to be irrigated
- ET_C of 1.5 in. per week (average through season)
- 6 month (24-week) season
- 15 in. effective rainfall in irrigation season (note that effective rainfall is not total rainfall)
- 80% system efficiency

1.5 in. per week × 24 (weeks) = 36 in.

36 in. − 15 in. (effective rainfall) = 21 in.

so the preliminary net water requirement = 21 in.

21 in. divided by 0.8 (80% system efficiency) = 26.25 in.

so the preliminary gross water requirement = 26.25 in.

26.25 in. × 72 acres (to be irrigated) = 1,890 acre-in.

Converting to gal,

1,890 × 27,154 = 51,321,060 gpy,

so the preliminary gross system water requirement is 51,321,060 gpy.

This is the value to be used for initial planning purposes such as hydrogeologic investigation of existing resources, diversion or withdrawal permits, storage capacity, and the like. Additional quantities must be added for grow-in and leaching requirements, and water loss in storage (seepage and evaporation).

As more information becomes available, these estimates can be refined. When the golf course architect determines the types of turf to be used in different areas (greens, approaches, fairways, tees, primary rough, etc.) and the acreage to be planted in each, the calculations are run again, using a different crop coefficient for each turf type and the corresponding surface areas.

SAMPLE 5.1

Refined Estimate of Gross System Water Requirement

Type	Acres	Turf	ET/wk (inches)	Acre-Inches per Week	gpw	gpy
Fairway	35	Bluegrass	1.5	52.5	1,425,585	34,214,040
Greens	3	Bentgrass	2.0	6.0	162,924	3,910,176
Tees	4	Bentgrass	1.75	7.0	190,078	4,561,872
Rough	30	Bluegrass	1.25	37.5	1,018,275	24,438,600
				Totals	2,796,862	67,124,688

(Note that the different turf types have different weekly water requirements because they have different crop coefficients.)

When the 15 in. of effective rainfall (15 in. × 72 acres × 27,154 gal per acre-inch = 29,326,320 gal) is subtracted, the estimated annual net requirement is 37,798,368 gpy. Dividing this total by the projected system efficiency of 80 percent results in a refined gross system water requirement of 47,247,960 gpy.

For initial planning of the actual irrigation system capacities, the usage during the peak demand week of the season must be calculated. The ET_O and crop coefficient for that week are used, and no rainfall is included. The result will be the "worst case" amount the system (source, pump station, piping, etc.) must be capable of delivering in a week.

Water requirement is one factor in the calculation of irrigation system capacities. The other key factor is the available (or allowed) time for an irrigation event, usually referred to as the "water window." In its simplest form, the water window is the number of hours available for irrigation between the close of play in the evening and the start of maintenance operations (usually mowing of greens) the next morning. If play ends at 7:30 P.M. and greens mowing starts at 5:30 A.M., there are 10 hours (or 600 minutes) available for irrigation. If the daily water requirement is 450,000 gal, the system could operate, theoretically, at 750 gpm (450,000 gal ÷ 600 min = 750 gpm). This example assumes that the programming and control software and hardware can provide a constant flow of 750 gpm for 10 hours, which may not be valid.

Actually, an even lower capacity may satisfy the requirement. Irrigation might be started on the first nine holes before 7:30, because all play by then will be on the closing holes. This, in effect, would extend the water window to 12 or more hours (in the example) and further reduce the (theoretical) required system capacity to (450,000 ÷ 720 =) 625 gpm.

In the real world, the equation is more complex. Some superintendents want to water the greens as early as possible. Others want to irrigate them just before they are mowed. In some cases, the flow management capability of the control system does not allow the system to operate at the optimum flow rate for the entire cycle. Power company rate schedules, especially as they apply to lower off-peak rates, may dictate when the larger hp main pumps can and cannot be operated.

Among the key factors affecting the water window on today's courses are the requirements of special applications. These determine system capacities more than the requirements of a complete irrigation cycle. An example is the rapid syringing of greens and approaches, or even fairways that are stressed in the afternoon of a day with high *ET*. Another is the rapid watering in of a "hot" chemical or fertilizer. This is necessary to prevent leaf burn and to avoid exposing golfers to the product. It is also necessary to ensure positive control over the application. If a granular product is applied and an unexpected thunderstorm follows, the product may be washed off into ponds or streams. This results in the loss of the effect and the cost of the product, and in the pollution of the adjacent waterways.

Special applications must be completed within short periods of time, both to minimize disruption of play and to ensure the desired effect of the chemicals and fertilizers. Thus, the water window is shortened, and the system capacities must be proportionally increased. If a system needed to run 1200 30 gpm heads for three minutes each to syringe greens, approaches, and fairways, 108,000 gal (1200 × 30 × 3) would be required. If the allowable time is one hour, the system must be capable of producing (108,000 ÷ 60 =) 1800 gpm.

After the irrigation system design is completed, the initially estimated water requirement is further refined according to the actual number of heads, their flow rates, and the precipitation rates of the various patterns in the design. (At courses where regular leaching is necessary because of saline soils or water, or other factors, the leaching requirement must be calculated and added to the basic system water requirement.) The following example is based on the actual precipitation rates, sprinkler quantities, and so forth, used in the design and shown on the plans.

SAMPLE 5.2

Final Estimate of Gross System Water Requirement

Head Type	Quantity	Requirement (in./week)	gpm	pr	min/wk	min/yr	gpy
1	230	1.25	28.6	0.65	115	2,769	18,216,000
2	606	0.9	28.6	0.65	83	1,994	34,556,544
3	207	1.25	24.6	1.12	67	1,607	8,183,893
4	67	1.5	22.6	0.60	150	3,600	5,451,120
5	23	1.5	20.2	1.08	83	2,000	929,200
6	87	1.5	12.0	1.02	88	2,118	2,210,824
						Total	69,547,581

When the 15 in. (29,326,320 gal) of effective rainfall is subtracted, the net requirement becomes 40,221,260 gal per year. Dividing that total by the projected system efficiency of 80 percent results in a final gross system water requirement estimate of 50,276,575 gpy.

Available Water Sources

Common sources of irrigation water are identified and discussed in Chapter 2.

The water source(s) available to a given project can have a significant effect on the design of the irrigation system. Obviously, the quantity of water in a source is critical, and it must be accurately identified very early in the preliminary design process. A limited quantity can affect decisions concerning the total area to be irrigated, the type(s) of turf to be planted, and even the feasibility of the entire project.

Pumping directly from a source into the irrigation system requires a high flow rate in order to irrigate a golf course in an acceptable period of time. This can range from a minimum of 800 gpm for limited coverage on a course with cool-season grasses to 4000 or more gpm for an elaborate, multiple-course system in a desert climate.

Pumping from a reservoir or tank still requires a high flow rate into the system, but the recharge rate from the source into the reservoir can be much lower. For example, if a system requiring 750,000 gpd pumps from a pond at 2,500 gpm, the full irrigation cycle can be completed in 5 hours. The recharge rate from the actual source may be as low as 550 gpm if the storage capacity and surface area of the pond are adequate. A 550 gpm well can produce 750,000 gal in less than 23 hours.

The storage capacity must be at least large enough to provide the difference between the irrigation system flow rate and the recharge rate from the source. In actuality, calculation of storage capacity is based on many factors. The key determining factor is almost always the amount of water needed to prevent loss of turf in the event of a temporary failure of the recharge source. This requirement will always be much larger than the amount needed to accommodate the difference between the system flow rate and the recharge rate.

In discussing storage capacity, it is important to remember that, usually, not all the water in a reservoir is available for pumping.

Intakes (suction pipes or flumes feeding wet wells) are set some distance off the bottom of tanks or ponds to minimize the pumping of accumulated silt or organic matter that settles to the bottom. Floating intakes usually have some type of structure mounted beneath them so they cannot reach the pond bottom. Vertical turbine pumps require a minimum submergence (specified by the pump manufacturer) to avoid cavitation and vortexing. Sometimes the topography of the pond bottom prevents all the water from reaching the pump intake. In order to be meaningful, storage capacity must be calculated as usable capacity, that is, the amount of water that can actually be pumped, given the configuration of the pond and the intake structure, and the submergence and net positive suction head (NPSH) requirements of the pump(s).

In addition to adequate storage capacity, a pond (especially one visible to golfers) must have adequate surface area to avoid excessive drawdown. If the surface area is too small and/or the recharge rate too low, large portions of the pond banks will be exposed before the pond is refilled. Exposed mud banks are unattractive. They can promote erosion and the growth of undesirable aquatic plants. They can also slow up play on the course and even become a problem in terms of the Rules of Golf. Vertical pond banks, made of stone or wood bulkheads, can resolve some of these issues, but they are expensive.

If a system that uses 750,000 gpd is pumping from a pond whose surface area is 1 acre, the drawdown (with no recharge) will be more than 2 ft. If the pond surface is 5 acres, the drawdown will be only 5½ in. With a fixed recharge rate, both ponds will be refilled in the same amount of time, but the smaller pond has much more bank exposed and it is exposed for a longer time.

Table 5.1 illustrates the relationship between pond surface area, drawdown, and recharge rate. This example is based on a daily usage of 750,000 gal, average pond depth of 8 ft, five hours of recharge, and usable storage of 70 percent (to allow for sloped pond banks and intake structure 1 ft above pond bottom).

The ideal source is one that recharges the pond before the start of play, so golfers never see the unsightly exposed pond banks. With an adequately sized source, the draw-down can be completely made up during non-play hours. With a marginally adequate source, it may be necessary to start recharge (i.e., going above the normal water level) before the end of play and then complete it during the early hours of play the next morning.

TABLE 5.1
Pond Storage and Drawdown Effects

Surface Area (acres)	Theoretical Storage Capacity (gal)	Usable Storage Capacity (gal)	Drawdown (in.) No Recharge	Drawdown (in.) 300 gpm Recharge	Drawdown (in.) 550 gpm Recharge
1.0	2,606,784	1,824,749	27.62	24.31	21.54
1.5	3,910,176	2,737,123	18.41	16.21	14.36
2.0	5,213,568	3,649,498	13.81	12.15	10.77
2.5	6,516,960	4,561,872	11.05	9.72	8.62
3.0	7,820,352	5,474,246	9.21	8.10	7.18

Storage and recharge calculations must also consider the requirements of special applications. If the 108,000 gallon syringe requirement on a day with high *ET* is added to the 750,000 gal regular irrigation requirement, can the source completely recharge the pond before the start of play? The "worst case" situation should be the basis for sizing the storage capacity in relation to the recharge rate.

The quality of water in the available source(s) is critical. Water quality can be affected by a wide variety of factors. In areas with even and adequate rainfall, water of marginal quality is usually not a significant issue except in times of drought. In areas with minimal rainfall, however, water quality must be higher.

Water quality must be accurately determined by testing as early as possible in the initial planning stages of a project. Water of poor or marginal quality may necessitate ongoing treatment, entailing significant costs. The possibilities range from a simple injector for correcting pH to a complex and very expensive reverse osmosis plant. The latter is also costly to operate.

Poor-quality water in the primary source on a site may force the use of parallel systems. In some cases marginal-quality water is satisfactory for irrigation of the rough and fairways, but unacceptable for greens and tees. A completely separate system, using good-quality water from a separate source, can be installed to irrigate only the critical green and tee areas. Sometimes local authorities require parallel systems on courses using effluent. Regulations often prohibit the application of effluent near well fields, wetlands, or property borders. One solution is a parallel system using potable water from a clean source to irrigate these areas.

The location of available water sources on-site must be considered. In terms of the irrigation system layout, pumping from a central location can minimize the amount of large and expensive pipe needed. However, a central location is not usually close to an existing power source, and installing a new electric service over any significant distance can be expensive. Pumping from a pond located on the highest elevation of the site may be desirable, as it may reduce pressure and horsepower requirements, but most ponds are located in the lower parts of a site.

The location, size, and depth of a pond are determined by the golf course architect. Golf strategy, aesthetics, and feature fill requirements are all essential in the design decisions, but the irrigation storage capacity and recharge rate must not be overlooked.

Long-term reliability is an important consideration in evaluating available sources. Historical data is available on aquifer levels, stream flow, and lake water levels, and it must be considered in choosing an irrigation source. If the potential source is a dammed lake, it is important to know who controls the level, when it is lowered, and for how long. If the potential source is a municipal water system, under what conditions can the municipality stop delivery of water, and what is its track record with golf courses in the past?

Finally, the long-term costs associated with potential water sources are important. Although the cost of drilling a well can be high, it will probably be cheaper in the long run than buying potable water year after year from a local purveyor.

Extent of Coverage

The extent of coverage in a golf course irrigation system depends on many factors. As in most design decisions, budgets (both for construction and for ongoing operation) are key issues. The extent of desired coverage must be defined before budgets can be established for both construction and long-term maintenance. Additional capacity to accommodate future expansion should also be considered in this process.

The amount and quality of water in the source(s) available to the project can affect the extent of coverage for a variety of reasons. Restrictions dictated by regulatory authorities may come into play, as in the case of the 90 acre limit in Arizona or the specific methods of calculating projected usage mandated by many local water authorities. The cost of water, in extreme cases, can also be a determining factor in decisions concerning the extent of coverage. Even the cost of electric power can be an issue.

Geographic location and local climate have a large effect on such decisions. If green secondary rough is desired on a course in the desert southwest, it must be irrigated. On the other hand, many courses in areas of adequate precipitation rely on rainfall and do not irrigate the secondary rough. They are willing to accept the occasional brown color and weak turf that accompany prolonged dry periods.

In new construction projects, the type of course will affect the extent of coverage. Daily fee and resort courses may opt for larger greens and tees, and wider fairways with less rough, to improve the speed of play. Courses associated with real estate developments frequently elect to provide complete irrigation all the way to the edges of the lots, or well beyond the typical golf course coverage area, in order to maximize the value of the lots.

The course architect's design concept, however, may be the biggest factor in determining the extent of coverage. Some designs call for irrigation of the entire property except for thickly wooded areas. Augusta National Golf Club is probably the best-known example of this type of coverage. At the other extreme are the so-called target courses that grass (and therefore irrigate) only tees, landing areas, approaches, greens, and green surrounds. The areas that would be classified as rough on other courses, and on all other parts of the property, are left without irrigation. Although this scheme clearly irrigates less area than many courses do, the cost may not be lower in simple proportion to the area covered. If precise edges of the irrigated areas are required by the design concept, by regulatory issues (wetlands, buffers, easements, etc.), or by any other criteria, part-circle heads must be installed to achieve the clean edges and the cost will rise accordingly. If, on the other hand, soft edges (a gradual transition from irrigated to nonirrigated area) are acceptable, the cost difference will more closely reflect the proportional difference in area covered.

Most courses fall between the two extremes, but the extent of irrigation coverage still varies widely. In many cases coverage is designed to avoid areas of "tall grass," or native grasses. Areas left to native vegetation and so-called waste areas must not be irrigated because moisture beyond natural rainfall encourages the growth of weeds and other plants not native to the area. Some courses want to irrigate only the green or fairway side of a sand bunker and let the turf on the far side of the feature gradually transition into unirrigated rough as the distance from the sprinkler heads increases.

The width of rough irrigation will depend on the turfgrass planted there, the type of course, and input from the owner, architect, and superintendent.

Some designs irrigate only the tee tops and leave everything else as nonirrigated rough. Others use larger full-circle heads to add coverage in adjacent traffic areas and the rough. The area surrounding tees, and the distance from the front tee to the start of the fairway, can be treated in several different ways. If coverage is desired from the forward tee to the fairway, is it just a green stripe for players to walk on, does the width increase to match the fairway width, or does it start from the back tees at fairway width?

There are similar alternatives for coverage at greens. Some designs include a horseshoe of heads around the sides and rear of a green. They are spaced so they do not throw onto the putting surface, but they do provide good uniformity of coverage in conjunction with the heads (part-circle, throwing away from the green) on the edges of the putting surface, and they obviously increase the width of effective coverage. Some architects are now adding pitching or "collection" areas, cut at collar or approach height, alongside or even behind greens. Some courses want the ability to irrigate these areas separately from the putting surface and the surrounding rough. At the other extreme, there are systems with only part-circle heads throwing toward the putting surface, and nothing outside the collar is irrigated.

Maintenance of the approaches in front of greens is becoming increasingly intense, and some high-end courses now treat these areas nearly the same as putting surfaces. In any course the approach is the second most important area (after the putting surface) on the course in terms of consistency and uniformity of playing conditions. Uniform irrigation within the approach itself is a critical necessity and seldom open to discussion, but decisions must be made about the amount of control and the width of coverage desired to the sides of the approach.

Special or additional irrigation treatment may be required for high-traffic areas, including some in out-of-play parts of the property. On some golf holes, many shots land in an area of the rough, or even beyond the rough in places that are not normally irrigated because of topography or the location of trees and hazards. Many courses want these areas irrigated in order to maintain acceptable turf.

There is also the issue of irrigation for aesthetic reasons, as opposed to irrigation for reasons strictly related to the game of golf. Many courses want wall-to-wall coverage near the clubhouse and around the first and tenth tees, the ninth and eighteenth greens, and the practice green and driving range tee. Some want full coverage for all areas that are visible from the clubhouse. Others want to highlight visual features in out-of-play areas throughout the course and require irrigation to maintain turf or other landscape plantings in those areas. Some courses want green turf between a green and the next tee, even if it is several hundred ft away.

Irrigation is frequently requested in parking lots and along entrance roads. In development and resort courses, coverage near greens and tees is often extended to the edges of adjacent roads for strictly aesthetic reasons. Many of these projects water virtually all common areas throughout the entire property. Many country clubs and resorts include swimming pools, tennis courts, lawn bowling greens, croquet courts, and even polo fields and want them and the adjacent turf areas watered. All have their own specialized irrigation requirements.

Finally, discussions about the extent of coverage must include consideration of future expansion needs. It is very short-sighted to install a system with minimal coverage and minimal capacity in the mains and the pump station. Golf courses are notorious for adding coverage long after an irrigation system has been installed. This may be done to correct deficiencies in the initial coverage, for aesthetic reasons, or because of a change in philosophy on the part of the course's ownership, membership, or management. Remodeling, however, is probably the most common reason for the addition of coverage. Holes are lengthened, new tees and sand bunkers are added, and greens are relocated and reconstructed. Both modification of an irrigation system in response to changes in features, and additions to coverage in response to construction of new features, require additional coverage, which includes the installation of new piping, wiring, sprinkler heads, and possibly controllers. If the mains, power wire, and pump station capacities were not originally sized for these eventualities, problems will occur. In the worst case, the total cycle time will increase to the point that irrigation is required during hours of play.

Decisions on the extent of coverage to be included in an irrigation system must be made early in the planning process. Those involved in the decisions should be the owner, the architect, the irrigation consultant or designer, and the golf course superintendent. Owners are often, and understandably, reluctant to start paying the salary of a superintendent that early in the project. Nonetheless, the experience and insight of the person who will grow in and eventually maintain the course will be extremely valuable in decisions concerning irrigation as well as virtually every other aspect of the project.

The preceding paragraph applies primarily to new construction projects, but the point is just as important in a replacement system on an existing course. The superintendent, the greens chairman, the golf professional, and one or two key members should provide input to the consultant on coverage. If a replacement system is being installed in conjunction with a remodeling project, the architect should also be involved.

Precision of Control

Early golf course irrigation systems relied on large-radius impact-driven sprinkler heads that had been adapted from agricultural applications. Typical fairway spacing on the predominantly single-row systems was 90 to 100 ft, and sometimes even more. A 100 ft radius head covers an area of 31,416 sq ft, or nearly three-quarters of an acre. Certainly, the use of long-radius heads reduced the number of sprinklers needed to cover a given area and therefore reduced the cost (in equipment and installation) of irrigating that area, but it also ignored important considerations such as uniformity of coverage and efficiency. Water and power were relatively inexpensive then, so operating costs were not the issue they are today. Nonetheless, water and power were being wasted and coverage was not uniform, so playing conditions were inconsistent.

Within the large area covered by a single long-radius sprinkler there can be wide variations in many site conditions, including the soils, drainage, topography, turfgrass type and height of cut, exposure to sun and wind, traffic and compaction. Each of these conditions has an effect on a turf's water requirements, and as they change, so will the water requirements. The changes can occur within a small area or a short distance. A south-facing steep slope has irrigation requirements different from those of the swale at the base of the slope. The moisture needs of the intensely maintained and closely mown turf on a USGA putting surface are different from those of the adjacent rough, which is located in native soil and is cut higher (even if both areas have the same type of turf). The pro tee located in a shady slot in the woods requires less water than the front tees that are outside the tree line and exposed to full sunlight all day, even though the soil, turf type, and height of cut are identical. Even if they have the same turf, a fairway and the adjacent rough will have differing water requirements because of differing heights of cut. In the landscape irrigation industry, areas of similar plant material, site conditions, and water requirements are called hydrozones. The irrigation system must allow for separate control of each hydrozone.

Just as there is variation in water requirements across a course, there is variation in application rates in systems with poor uniformity of coverage. Typically, systems with heads spaced at 90 ft to 100 ft will be much less uniform than those with heads spaced closer together. Persistent high winds will further exacerbate the low levels of uniformity. Poor uniformity means that the system must over-irrigate some areas in the pattern to apply enough water in the dry areas to keep the turf there healthy.

The optimum irrigation system allows the operator to respond accurately to the varying needs of small areas of turf. Thus, in recent years consultants and designers have been utilizing heads of shorter radius and tighter spacings to provide more precise control. Many of today's systems have three-row fairway coverage, using 60 ft to 65 ft radius sprinkler heads. A 65 ft radius head covers an area of 13,273 sq ft, or slightly less than one-third of an acre. This area includes many fewer site condition variations than an (more than twice as large) area covered by a 100 ft radius head. It should be noted that although a three-row layout at 65 ft spacing adds some width of coverage (versus a two-row system with 80 ft heads at 80 ft spacing), the main benefits are improved precision of control and a greater width with uniform coverage.

Individual head control is a related and important concept. The benefits of using shorter-radius heads with closer spacing are diminished or eliminated if two or more heads are run together on the same controller station, because of the larger area covered. The optimum system has short-radius heads that are properly spaced and individually controlled.

Some golf courses have relatively uniform conditions throughout, and they may be candidates for systems with two or more heads per station. Some Florida courses have uniform soils, very little elevation change, few trees, and Bermudagrass everywhere. In this case it may be acceptable to install a system with two (or more) heads per station. A system that mixes paired and individually controlled heads can also be effective, depending on conditions across the course. Cost savings can be achieved by pairing heads, but the corresponding loss in precision and efficiency of irrigation must be clearly understood and evaluated.

The use of part-circle sprinkler heads can add to the precision of control. Obviously, they are necessary along "hard" edges or borders, beyond which irrigation is either undesirable or prohibited. Examples include the limits of wetlands, buffer zones, property lines, and rights-of-way. Part-circle heads are also used to provide precise control when there is a clear dividing line between adjoining areas with different irrigation requirements. The approaches and green collars in many of today's systems have part-circle heads that throw away from the green, and thus the surrounds can be irrigated without unnecessary water being applied to the putting surface. The same is true of many tee complexes. In some high-end systems, fairways are covered by a so-called five-row layout. There is a row of full-circle heads in the center of the fairway. Near the fairway edges (sometimes in the step cut or the rough) is a row of back-to-back part-circle heads. One sprinkler throws only into the rough, and the other throws only into the fairway. All are individually controlled.

Over a given area, a layout of individually controlled short-radius heads is much more efficient in terms of water and power usage than a system of long-radius heads, because it can more precisely respond to the moisture needs of small areas. In this case, the use of more heads equates to less water and power.

Budgets and Cost Estimates

As is the case in preliminary planning for every other aspect of a golf course project, cost estimates and budgets for irrigation (both for construction and for ongoing operation) are key issues. They must be established very early in the design process, and they must be realistic. Ideally, an experienced irrigation consultant or designer should be involved in preliminary cost estimates and in the initial establishment of budgets. In new construction projects (and even some remodeling jobs) the golf course architect is frequently asked to help establish budgets, often before initial routings are completed. Most architects are qualified to accomplish this task. Experienced golf irrigation installers are another good source of costs for the geographical regions in which they normally operate.

Mistakes are often made when developers, course owners, private clubs, or superintendents attempt to generate construction cost estimates or budgets based on rules of thumb, surveys of average costs, or the experiences of other courses. Just as golf courses are different by virtue of topography, soils and other site conditions, design, and a host of other variables, so irrigation systems and their costs will vary from course to course.

The construction budget must account for the extent of irrigation coverage the owner desires and is willing to finance, and the extent of coverage the course designer's concept requires. Any discrepancy between the two must be resolved and communicated at the earliest possible date so that all involved have a common understanding of the scope of intended coverage.

Cost estimates and budgets for construction must be based on realistic schedules. Because of increasingly extensive delays caused by permitting and code issues, many projects do not actually break ground until several years after the initial planning and cost estimates have been completed.

A cost estimate done today for a system to be installed three to five years from now must project as accurately as possible what the real costs will be when they are actually incurred. Planners must consider inflation and increases in material and labor costs. Annual cost increases for basic irrigation components (sprinkler heads, remote control valves, quick coupling valves, control systems, pump stations, etc.) are fairly easy to project on the basis of changes made by the manufacturers in the past.

Estimates of increases in the cost of wire and PVC pipe and fittings pose a different problem. Copper is traded as a commodity, and the market can be volatile. The same is true of oil and petroleum derivatives, the basic materials from which PVC pipe and wire insulation are manufactured. Any number of global or national political, economic, or supply/demand issues can affect these markets. As a result, projection of future costs of pipe and wire is a very difficult proposition. Depending on the complexity of the design, wire plus PVC pipe, fittings, and swing joints can represent 20 to 30 percent of the total (non-pump-station) material cost of the system.

Estimating future labor costs is also difficult. The projected state of the national economy will have some effect, but regional and local issues are probably more important. The local supply of labor and the local unemployment rate are very difficult to project into the future, but they will have a significant effect on the labor costs an installer includes in a bid.

The projected condition of the irrigation industry must also be considered. Again, there is a national effect, but the regional aspect will probably have more impact. The number of local projects occurring in a given year will influence the competition between distributors and other material providers. If there are very few projects in a given area, distributors and contractors may lower their profit margins to get their share. On the other hand, there is no incentive to lower costs in a year when many projects are scheduled.

Estimates of irrigation installation costs must consider all the elements of the system, as well as related issues. Unless experienced people are involved and good coordination among them is ensured, some elements can fall through the cracks between the areas of responsibility of the architect, the irrigation consultant, the owner's engineer, and other planners.

Installation of electric power to pump stations is an example, especially when it is not included in the irrigation installer's contract. Depending on the type of power available and its proximity to the proposed pump system, substantial costs can be incurred in this area. A related subject is the availability of temporary power when planting starts. If permanent power will not be available, estimates must include the cost of electric-power-generating units. Generators and diesel fuel are expensive, and with a total pump system of 150 to 300 hp and more, large generators and lots of fuel are required.

Construction costs for pump system buildings are sometimes overlooked, as are those associated with rock or other deleterious materials encountered in trenching. Although the extreme solution, blasting, is usually avoided for reasons beyond cost, rock removal is very expensive in terms of specialized equipment and labor costs. It is also difficult to estimate accurately the quantity of rock that will be encountered.

The effects of permit issues on the irrigation system must be considered in estimates of construction costs. Restrictions on the installation of pipe through wetlands or buffer zones can cause expensive rerouting. Some jurisdictions have unusual and costly special requirements. An example is the requirement in some western counties to install all wiring in conduit. Another is the requirement to install a separate freshwater irrigation system along the property lines (and wetland buffer zones, well fields, etc.) in a course to be irrigated with treated effluent.

Construction cost estimates must include a realistic contingency factor to accommodate unexpected conditions. Unstable soil conditions can add costs in terms of thrust blocking or joint restraint systems. Modifications to course design are common during construction, both on new courses and on remodeling projects. Features are moved or enlarged, tees and bunkers are added, and holes are lengthened. The irrigation system must cover the course as it is constructed on the ground, which may differ significantly from what was shown on the original plans.

The estimated costs for long-term operation and maintenance must accommodate the needs of the proposed irrigation system and the anticipated level of maintenance. The superintendent should definitely be involved in preparation of these figures.

In the case of a minimal (single- or double-row) system, the budget may anticipate that the superintendent or an assistant will maintain and repair the irrigation system in addition to his or her primary duties. On the other hand, the maintenance budget for an elaborate system with several thousand heads must include the salaries of one or more full-time irrigation technicians whose sole function is the maintenance and repair of the system. The budget for the more extensive system will have to accommodate a larger inventory of spare and repair parts and, possibly, excavation equipment such as backhoes or trenchers.

The projected level of maintenance also impacts the estimated operating costs. If a superintendent insists on hand-watering for precision irrigation of putting surfaces, a corresponding number of man-hours must be included in the estimated cost. The same applies in the event of hand-syringing of greens or hand-watering of steep bunker faces.

Base Mapping

All irrigation designs and plans must start with a base map. For new construction projects the map is usually created from the architect's route plan, sometimes combined with a grassing plan. Such maps show the proposed location of features (greens, tees, bunkers, water features, etc.), proposed fairway outlines and grassing schemes, proposed landscape areas, and trees or tree lines. They should include the proposed location of the clubhouse, pro shop, pump station, and maintenance buildings; property lines, easements and rights-of-way; cart paths and bridges, and paved roads. They must also include any areas that could restrict or limit construction or irrigation, such as wetlands and mandated buffer zones along wetlands, well or septic system leach fields, or property lines.

For replacement or modification projects on existing courses the base map must depict the actual location of all these elements. There are many possible sources for base mapping of an existing course. The most accurate horizontal mapping is that done specifically for the project using GPS data collection. Global Positioning System (GPS) equipment, data collection, and mapping procedures are discussed in Chapter 6. The use of this method can have added benefits for the irrigation consultant or designer, especially if he or she intends to do the design or the drafting using computer-aided design (CAD) software.

The next most accurate source of base mapping information for existing courses is aerial photography. The photo must have a recent date, verifying that it shows the latest modifications to the course (added or removed tees, bunkers, trees, etc.). The preferred print scale is 1 in. = 100 ft.

The photo must be taken by an experienced and recognized professional aerial photography firm that uses precision cartographic cameras mounted in specially equipped airplanes. Aircraft attitude, altitude, and flight path must be carefully controlled for maximum accuracy. The cameras and magazines must be calibrated by the U.S. Geological Survey (USGS) on a regular basis, and the firm must have a certificate from the USGS, proving that it is currently in compliance with this requirement.

The desired map scale (on the finished print) dictates the negative scale at which a photo must be taken. The negative scale, in turn, dictates the elevation at which the plane must fly. For a map scale of 1 in. = 100 ft, the required negative scale is 1 in. = 800 ft.

The accuracy provided by a photo taken as described here is acceptable for purposes of golf course irrigation design and construction without ground control (a system of points established by a ground survey crew that is used as a fixed reference to position map features and to confirm accuracy). This control is not necessary, and it can significantly increase the cost of the mapping. Even if aerial photos are used to generate topographic mapping, ground control is not necessary for irrigation design and installation purposes. However, if the photo or any derived mapping is to be used for other purposes, such as planning a building or a road or obtaining site plan approvals, ground control may be necessary to meet the requirements of local codes.

In some locations (often those where development and construction are active) aerial photographers will "fly" entire counties regularly on a spec basis. Prints of these negatives are readily available, and they are much cheaper because the costs associated with aircraft, cameras, and processing are spread over many customers. These photos can be obtained from the photographer directly or sometimes from local or county engineering or tax offices. However, some investigation is necessary because accuracy can vary widely. Negative scale and aircraft elevation must match the requirements of the desired final map scale. If either is incorrect, the final print will be fuzzy and difficult to read accurately. The mapped area must be centered in the negative, because distortion increases as distance from the center of the negative increases. Anyone who chooses to use this type of aerial photo should verify accuracy by carefully checking the distances between several points on the print against the same distances measured on the ground.

Aerial photos can be taken only at certain times of the year. Foliage can obscure important features on golf courses, so a photo must be taken when leaves are completely off the trees. Sun angle is another consideration, and a generally accepted rule is that it must be more than 30 degrees for best results. The combination of these two requirements often limits the photography window to a short period in the fall and several months in the late winter and early spring. The windows vary with the geographic locations of the projects.

From a 1 in. = 100 ft scale print, a photogrammetrist can generate a finished map on a variety of drafting media. Alternately, a competent draftsman can trace the information onto a reproducible sheet, or a skilled computer operator can digitize the information into a digital map format. Regardless of which process is used, this map becomes the base sheet for the irrigation design and, eventually, for the installation plans.

The base map should include a title block with clear notation of the project name, scale and contour interval, a North arrow, and a reference to the source of the information. If the map is generated from GPS data collection, the data file name is listed. If the original was an aerial photo, it should be identified by the photographer's file number and the date the photo was taken.

Accurate topographic mapping is just as important as horizontal mapping. The preferred contour interval (at 1 in. = 100 ft) is 2 ft, although 5 ft is sometimes acceptable. The accuracy of hydraulic calculations for the distribution system and for pumping installations depends to a large extent on accurate topographic information. However, contour lines can clutter up base maps, so they are not usually shown on installation plans for reasons of clarity.

On a new construction project the architect needs topographic mapping to do his or her route plans, so it is usually available before preliminary irrigation design begins. The architect indicates proposed contours at features and in cut-and-fill areas, as well as proposed water levels and pond bottom elevations, on the grading plan. These two sources will provide all the elevation data needed for the irrigation design.

For irrigation design on an existing course, topographic mapping can come from several sources. Although GPS data collection is quite accurate in the horizontal plane, it is much less so in the vertical plane. Accuracy is at least three times less in the Z coordinate than in X and Y. In addition, generating accurate 2 ft interval topography over a golf course would first require laying out an extensive grid over the entire site and then collecting data for all the grid points. This would be an extremely labor-intensive and costly operation, and the vertical accuracy would not be acceptable.

Probably the most accurate (and most cost-effective) source for topographic mapping on an existing course is aerial photography. The desired map contour interval determines the negative scale, but the 1 in. = 800 ft negative scale required for a 1 in. = 100 ft horizontal map scale also accurately produces a 2 ft contour interval.

Again, a professional aerial photographer, with the proper aircraft and calibrated cameras, must be engaged. For topographic work a series of negatives is taken, and the amount of overlap must be carefully controlled. Precisely calibrated instruments create the contour lines by simultaneously observing two adjacent photo negatives. The results can be digital files or hard copy reproducibles on a variety of drafting media. One set of negatives can be used to generate both the planimetric (horizontal) details and the topographic information.

In some cases the base maps provided by a project owner or golf course architect do not show all the information needed for the irrigation design and installation. Additional maps, such as plat plans or other plans recorded with deeds, may be necessary to accurately locate property lines, buried utility easements, or rights-of-way.

STANDARDS AND CODES

The American Society of Agricultural Engineers (ASAE) defines the purpose of standardization as follows:

1.1 Standards, Engineering Practices, and Data (hereinafter referred to collectively as standards) are normally generated for one or more of the following reasons:

- to provide interchangeability between similarly functional products and systems manufactured by two or more organizations, thus improving compatibility, safety and performance for users;
- to reduce the variety of components required to serve an industry, thus improving availability and economy;
- to improve personal safety during operation of equipment and application of products and materials;
- to establish performance criteria for products, materials, or systems;
- to provide a common basis for testing, analyzing, describing, or informing regarding the performance and characteristics of products, methods, materials, or systems;
- to provide design data in readily available form;
- to develop a sound basis for codes, education, and legislation; and to promote uniformity of practice;
- to provide a technical basis for international standardization;
- to increase efficiency of engineering effort in design, development, and production.

1.2 Standards are developed and adopted because of a need for action on a common problem. Their effectiveness is dependent upon voluntary compliance with the standards adopted. It is, therefore, essential that affected groups be invited to participate in the development of such standards.

The American National Standards Institute (ANSI) accredits standards-developing organizations in the United States, and approves certain standards they produce as "American National Standards." Standards are reviewed on a regular basis, so it is important to ensure that the most current version is being used or referenced. The names of standards include the date of the latest revision. Codes are lists of standards and guidelines which are the legal requirements under which irrigation (and other) systems must be designed and installed.

Standards

Material standards provide a recognized and generally accepted description of various components and their performance. ASAE's

Engineering Practices, and the design guidelines published by other standards organizations such as the American Society of Testing and Materials (ASTM) and the American Water Works Association (AWWA) provide recognized and generally accepted methods for material assembly and installation and for the design of systems. The standards are developed by volunteer committees of industry people involved in the design, manufacture, installation, operation, and regulation of the components or systems involved. Knowledge of all applicable standards is important to irrigation system consultants and designers, and even to end users. The former must actually read the main standards and be familiar with their content. Not only are the standards efficient and accurate tools for the design and preparation of specifications, but they often form the basis for the state and local codes that govern the design, installation, and operation of irrigation systems.

Referencing recognized standards in designs, plans, and specifications is similar to speaking a universal language: Everyone involved, from the manufacturer to the distributors, installers, and end users, will understand the terms. If they do not understand, they know where to find and read the actual standard.

In addition to providing clear communication, designs and specifications based on standards promote the proper application and installation of materials. They provide for the safety of installers, system operators, and even the golfers and maintenance personnel who will spend hours on the finished course. Finally, they will help in protecting consultants, designers, installers, operators, and course owners from exposure to liability.

Key material standards for golf irrigation systems include those related to the manufacture, design, and installation of all applicable types of pipe and fittings, valves, wire and cables, electric and electronic components, motors, and pumps. An example is ASTM D2241-00, PVC Pressure Rated Pipe (SDR Series), which specifies the classification, chemical compounds, dimensions and tolerances, workmanship, product markings, water pressure ratings, and test methods, conditions, and requirements, and so forth, for the pipe named in the title. It also references many related ASTM standards. Other ASTM standards provide the same information for different types of pipe, such as Schedules 40, 80, and 120 PVC plastic pipe. The American Water Works Association publishes standards AWWA C-900-97 and C-905-97 for certain sizes and applications of PVC pipe.

Although all these standards have many similarities, they also have significant differences. The critical differences are in dimensions (wall thickness and inside and outside diameter), water pressure ratings, whether a safety factor was incorporated into the calculation of pressure capability, and what surge factor was used. These disparities and their ramifications must be thoroughly understood by designers and specifiers of irrigation systems because misapplication of the products can result in inadequate irrigation, waste of water and power, product and system failures, injury to installers and operating personnel, and liability risks.

Applicable examples of design guidelines include AWWA C-605-94, Underground Installation of PVC Pressure Pipe and Fittings for Water, and ASAE S376.2 (JAN98), Design, Installation and Performance of Underground, Thermoplastic Irrigation Pipelines. Both are approved by ANSI as American National Standards. ASAE S376.2 includes guidelines for the design, specification, and installation of PVC and PE (polyethylene) pipe for irrigation. Dimensions, pressure ratings, and material compounds are discussed, along with minimum installation requirements. Key among the latter is the section on thrust blocking, which includes procedures for determining the area of load-bearing surface needed for a specific application and provides detail drawings of typical thrust blocking.

Codes

Designs and specifications for irrigation systems must be based on recognized standards; they must also meet the requirements of all applicable codes. Codes list minimum requirements for the materials, design, and installation or construction of nearly everything made by humans. Most codes are developed by trade groups, associations, or government bodies. They are updated on a regular basis to stay current with new products and methods. They do not have any legal status until they are adopted by a state, county, or municipal government. When that is done, the code becomes law in the jurisdiction of the government that adopted it.

An example is the National Electric Code (NEC), which is published by the National Fire Protection Association and updated every three years. Its purpose is to protect people and property from hazards that may result from electrical installations. It covers the installation of electrical equipment and conductors in domestic, industrial, and agricultural applications. Specific subjects applicable to golf course irrigation systems include types of cable and their permitted uses (direct burial cables, high- and low-voltage wires, conductors and insulation requirements, allowable ampacities, the size and color of equipment grounding conductors, etc.); required burial depths for wires and cables; grounding methods, ground rods and plates; requirements and sizing for conduits; clearance requirements around electrical panels; allowable voltage loss in circuits; and full-load currents for electric motors.

The NEC has been adopted by many government bodies throughout the United States. Some authorities adopt it as written, and others modify or add sections. Some jurisdictions have adopted other electrical codes. It is incumbent upon the consultant or system designer to be completely familiar with the codes that apply to his or her designs and projects.

Another set of codes important to irrigation installation is found in the applicable portions of the regulations promulgated by the Occupational Safety and Health Administration (OSHA). OSHA is part of the U.S. Department of Labor and concerns itself with the safety of workers on the job. Trenching and excavation, for example, are covered in depth by the regulations. Trench depth and soil conditions dictate whether banks must be sloped or benched, and whether trench shoring or the use of trench boxes or shielding is required to prevent collapse or cave-in. Similar regulations pertain to the installation of wet wells and inlet flumes at pump stations. These often reach depths of 20 ft or more, so workers must be well protected.

Local building and electric codes apply to the design and construction of pump station buildings and to the bridges that may carry pipe and wire conduits. Highway codes regulate how pipes must be installed at road crossings. Local plumbing codes regulate backflow protection and connections to potable water systems. Codes based on environmental concerns can affect the location of sprinklers and other components, as well as the routing of pipe and wires. Other codes, often promulgated by state agricultural departments, govern requirements for secondary containment of chemigation and fertigation materials.

Irrigation systems are required by law to be designed and installed in accordance with all applicable codes. To ensure such adherence, consultants, system designers and specifiers, and installers must have a good working knowledge of the codes and the standards on which they are based. In the event that there is no code relevant to a given situation, a design or installation procedure based on a recognized standard will usually fare better in court than will one that is not.

Foreign and International Standards and Codes

The International Organization for Standardization (ISO) lists among its member bodies the one organization in each country that ISO deems most representative in that country. Approximately 90 countries are represented. ANSI is the U.S. member. Other members include the Standards Council of Canada (SCC), IRAM in Argentina, AFNOR in France, DIN in Germany, BSI in Great Britain, SII in Israel, UNI in Italy, JISC in Japan, and Standards Australia (SAI). Web sources for identifying standards organizations throughout the world include the European Committee for Standardization (CEN) at and the World Standards Service Network (WSSN) at www.wssn.net.

ISO has developed and promulgated a series of standards in an attempt to promote international standardization. Approximately 25 address testing methods and construction and performance requirements for irrigation equipment. Although the titles of these standards indicate an agricultural application, the content is equally relevant to golf course irrigation in most cases. The International Electrotechnical Commission (IEC) also produces some standards with relevant international applications.

The legal status and enforceability of ISO (and IEC) standards depend on the country in which they are being applied. Nonetheless, their use in plans, specifications, and bidding documents will help to clarify communications on projects that are international in scope.

Many countries have national codes and standards that can be applied to golf course irrigation. They are by no means consistent from one country to another, and there is little indication that truly international consistency or standardization is coming soon. Therefore, it is important that consultants and system designers who chose to work in foreign countries learn what standards and codes apply in each country, and to what extent those standards and codes are enforced.

COMPUTER SOFTWARE (CAD)

There are a number of computer programs available that can assist with both the drawing and design of a golf course irrigation system.

These high-technology programs have been developed mainly for full-time professional irrigation designers. However, there are simpler and less expensive programs available for those not wishing to make a significant investment for what may be a one-time use.

Drafting

As in any design field, it is now commonplace for the design of a golf course irrigation system to be done with some type of computer aided design (CAD) software (Figure 5.1). CAD software provides an electronic image of the golf course and, subsequently, the irrigation system. This allows for an accurate drawing that is easily reproducible and changeable. The electronic drawing provides a readable design that uses precise symbols and line types to clearly indicate the designer's intent. In an electronic format, the drawing can be easily sent to other people or devices through e-mail or other forms of electronic communication. A CAD drawing can also act as a base of the golf course features for the Record Drawing. Some CAD software will automatically do a materials takeoff from the drawn plan. The software may also interact with other software that assists in the design of the system. Most of all, the CAD software is a drafting tool for the designer that can save time and eliminate repetitive work.

Irrigation Design Software

There are several different types of irrigation design software available on the market, although none are specifically designed for golf course irrigation systems. Nonetheless, design software can be helpful in golf course irrigation design, as it includes many of the same components and concepts as agricultural or landscape irrigation design. This type of software commonly spaces sprinklers automatically, assists in routing pipes, sizes valves automatically, assigns control zones, and uses various assemblies to quickly and accurately show the irrigation design. The software may have a set of checks and balances to make sure errors are not made. Some also have a hydraulic component or flow zoning capabilities. The design software may be a stand-alone program or may work in conjunction with the CAD software as an add-on. Again, it is primarily a tool to save time by replicating repetitive work, such as sprinkler layout.

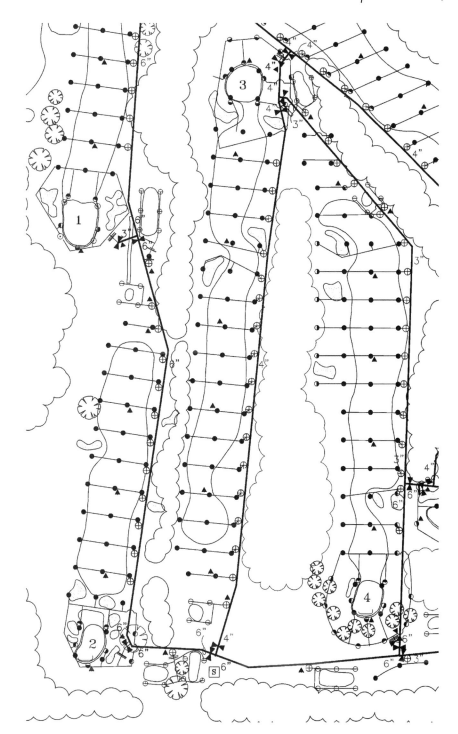

FIGURE 5.1
Example of golf course irrigation design generated with CAD software.

Hydraulic Modeling

Using hydraulic software to size pipes and to determine velocities and friction losses is a necessity in golf course irrigation design. Doing hydraulics calculations by hand results in a more expensive system that may have unknown limitations because of improper piping loops or safety factors built into the manual calculations. Although not written specifically for irrigation, most water distribution software is adequate for golf course irrigation designs. This type of software takes into account elevation, loops, pipe sizes, velocities, and friction losses. The software can simulate specific sprinklers turning on and off throughout the irrigation system, showing the designer the direction of flow, velocity, and pressure at any point (Figure 5.2). Other flow equipment, such as pump systems, booster pumps, check valves, and pressure-regulating and relief valves, can be included in the analysis to model the effects. The designer can size and route

FIGURE 5.2
Example of tabular data typically generated with hydraulic analysis software.

Pipe Table

Id	Up Node	Down Node	Length	Diameter	Roughness	Flow	Velocity	Headloss	Status
			ft	in		US gpm	ft/s	ft	
2	38	98	335.828	3.166	150.	37.97	1.547	1.022	☑
3	39	98	15.081	3.166	150.	125.5	5.115	0.4201	☑
4	98	63	193.876	4.072	150.	163.5	4.028	2.587	☑
5	63	58	118.245	4.072	150.	72.6	1.789	0.3509	☑
6	58	99	591.823	4.072	150.	72.6	1.789	1.756	☑
7	99	14	65.2561	3.166	150.	0.	0.	0.	☑
8	99	33	158.628	4.072	150.	72.6	1.789	0.4708	☑
9	33	57	84.5544	4.072	150.	72.6	1.789	0.2509	☑
10	57	13	291.152	4.072	150.	72.6	1.789	0.864	☑
11	13	32	44.419	3.166	150.	-27.4	-1.117	7.392e-002	☑
12	32	56	473.55	3.166	150.	-27.4	-1.117	0.7881	☑
13	31	56	596.788	3.166	150.	27.4	1.117	0.9932	☑
14	12	31	43.6127	3.166	150.	27.4	1.117	7.258e-002	☑
15	55	12	531.878	4.072	150.	27.4	0.6752	0.2598	☑
16	97	55	630.784	4.072	150.	27.4	0.6752	0.3082	☑
17	40	100	375.11	3.166	150.	47.08	1.919	1.7	☑
18	41	100	25.8181	4.072	150.	150.3	3.703	0.2948	☑
19	100	101	33.5179	5.993	150.	197.4	2.245	9.652e-002	☑
20	101	30	177.541	4.072	150.	82.75	2.039	0.6715	☑
21	30	97	89.2831	4.072	150.	82.75	2.039	0.3377	☑

[OK] [Cancel]

114 items sorted in ascending order of Id

pipes in different ways and model different sprinklers operating, such as a green syringe, to provide for the most economical but efficient piping system for the golf course irrigation system. The designer can make sure that pressures at each point in the system are not too high or too low, that velocities are within the required 5 ft or lower fps parameter, and that all elevation changes have been taken into account. This type of software can work in conjunction with a CAD program or can be incorporated into an irrigation design software program. The software analysis model can be checked in the field with a pressure gauge after installation or can be used as base data to determine how well the system is maintaining its design intent. It can also be used as a troubleshooting tool when problems arise by comparing actual pressures to those that were intended. Moreover, hydraulic modeling software is a great aid in evaluating existing piping systems and locating hydraulic problems and limitations, provided accurate information on pipe size and routing is available. Some hydraulic software is also available in a spreadsheet form with no CAD software required.

COVERAGE

Greens

The putting surface of a green experiences more concentrated player traffic and more intense maintenance operations than any other area on a golf course. It is also the most critical area in terms of play. The uniformity and precision of irrigation are more important on the putting surface than on any other part of the course.

The earliest automatic systems had four (sometimes three or five) full-circle heads on a green. They provided coverage for the putting surface, the collar, the green surrounds, and at least part of the approach. If the spacing was correct for the heads and pressure available, and if most of the putting surface was inside the parallelogram formed by the heads, the coverage on the putting surface was reasonably uniform. The run time for these heads was normally based on the requirements of the putting surface. The drawback was that the moisture requirements of the other areas covered by these heads were not the same as those of the putting surface. Therefore, the other areas were underirrigated in almost all cases, because they had greater heights of cut, different soils, different types of grasses, and so on. If the run time was modified to meet the needs of the surrounds, for example, the putting surface would be overwatered and playing conditions there (and possibly the health of the turf) would suffer.

The addition of part-circle heads, throwing away from the putting surface, solved part of the problem. In most (but not all) cases the surrounds require more water than the putting surface. The theory is that the full-circle heads are timed to satisfy the putting surface, and the surrounds are watered for the same amount of time. Any additional moisture the surrounds need is provided by the part-circle heads without applying unnecessary and excessive water to the putting surface. However, the application rate is low and the uniformity of coverage is very poor in the surrounds because there are no heads forming an overlap pattern with the part-circle heads. In effect, the area in the surrounds covered by the part-circle heads has the same problems as one side of a single-row system: poor uniformity and widely differing application rates throughout the pattern.

An alternative to this approach is a system using only part-circle heads, some throwing into the putting surface and others throwing away from it. Because of the irregular outline of most putting surfaces, it is difficult to precisely limit the throw of the "in" heads to the putting surface. In fact, the attempt to do so often requires the addition of one or more heads and complicates the spacing and head location problems.

To improve coverage in the surrounds, a row of heads is often installed around the sides and rear of the green complex. These are located so that they do not throw onto the putting surface, but they do combine with the part-circle (out) heads to provide good uniformity and total coverage. They can be full- or part-circle heads, depending on grassing patterns and the proximity of tree lines, adjacent tees, restricted areas, and the like.

In some cases spray heads are installed just outside the collar on the sides and to the rear of the putting surface to accommodate the interface between the (high sand content) greens mix and the adjacent native soil. When cool-season grasses are planted on putting surfaces in hot climates, a syringe system, separate from the regular irrigation heads, is often installed. This consists of low-gallonage, fast-rotating heads, which can cool the turfgrass canopy without soaking the putting surface or providing irrigation to the plant. Syringe systems are also installed on some transition zone courses.

Several issues unique to greens complicate the placement of heads. First, heads should not be located in the approach or near the line of flight of an incoming shot. The heads covering the front of the putting surface should be kept as far to the sides as possible, yet frontal bunkers often force a compromise on this issue. Second, heads should not be located in the putting surface or the collar. Third, pipe should never be located under the putting surface (or under sand bunkers) because of the high cost of repairs to the feature if a pipe or fitting fails. However, the proximity of bunker edges or bulkheads to the putting surface sometimes leaves no choice but to pipe under the green.

The slopes in the framing mounds around a green can also present a problem in terms of head location. If a slope is too severe, the profile of a head set flush with grade will be distorted and the uniformity of the pattern will be degraded. Installing the head plumb may eliminate the adverse effects on the profile and uniformity, but is unacceptable because it will conflict with mowing. Locating a head (flush with grade) on a gentle slope is acceptable because the effect on uniformity is minimal. However, in the case of a severe slope, compromising spacing to get the head on level ground is preferable to setting a head so far off horizontal that its profile is distorted.

Another difficulty can be the extreme size of some greens. This problem most often occurs at practice greens, where architects frequently design very large putting surfaces to accommodate many players and to minimize the effects of concentrated traffic and wear. Some courses (and architects or superintendents) allow placement of head(s) in the putting surface of practice greens to maintain proper spacing throughout. (At least one manufacturer produces a head with a sod cup on the lid to camouflage the head.) Others forbid it for fear of damage caused by pipe or fitting failures. A means of minimizing the potential of damage from leaks is the installation of block style heads (with check valves) in the putting surface. These heads are activated with remote control valves located well off the green. The lateral pipe between the valve and the head(s) is pressurized only when the head is operating, as opposed being pressurized constantly in an electric valve-in-head system. Drawbacks to the installation of any head in the putting surface include the difficulty of installing the pipe in (or below) the greens mix, the difficulty of thrust-blocking or anchoring the swing joint and head, and the possible effect on the roll of a putted ball.

In most cases the installation of heads inside the putting surface will not be allowed. Long-radius heads on the edges can provide a solution to a certain degree, but their high flow rate and slow speed of rotation are far from ideal for green irrigation. Often the only solution is installation of regular green heads at normal spacing around the perimeter, and supplemental hand-watering of the weak areas in the center of the pattern. This situation should be clearly explained to the client's representative during staking and before the installation of the heads is begun.

Because of the location of cart paths, steep slopes, and bunkers, player traffic is often concentrated into very narrow "walk-on" areas leading to a green. The heavy traffic can cause severe compaction and wear, and special irrigation may be required in these areas.

Approaches

After the putting surface, the approach is the most important area on a course, in terms of both play and maintenance. Any deficiencies in turf and playing conditions are just as visible and annoying to golfers here as they are on the green.

The approach is adjacent to the putting surface, the fairway, and the rough. Because of differences in soil, turf type, slope, height of cut, and other maintenance procedures, it has irrigation requirements different from those of the adjacent areas. If only full-circle heads are used to irrigate the approach, there will be inefficiencies because the heads will be covering three areas (approach, rough and putting surface or approach, rough and fairway), all of which have different moisture requirements.

Part-circle heads at the borders between the areas allow irrigation of one without getting unwanted water on the adjacent area. A common scheme has part-circle (out) heads near the front corners of the putting surface. A 90 degree arc, from the front of the putting surface to the edge of the fairway, is the most accurate setting for the part-circle heads. Some courses open the arc to 270 degrees, running from the front of the putting surface around to the collar on the side of the green (Figure 5.3). The latter assumes that the irrigation requirements in the approach are the same as those in the rough. The first (typically full-circle) fairway heads are located where they will not throw on the putting surface and where they will provide highly uniform coverage of the approach in combination with the part-circle heads. Back-to-back part-circle heads (180 degrees toward the

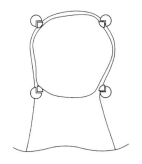

GREEN

LEGEND

SYMBOL	DESCRIPTION
○	360° ARC SPRINKLER
☍	270° ARC SPRINKLER
◠	180° ARC SPRINKLER
◠	90° ARC SPRINKLER

ALL SPRINKLERS INDIVIDUALLY CONTROLLED

FIGURE 5.3
Part-circle heads throw onto putting surface, surrounds, and approach.

approach and 180 degrees toward the fairway) at the border between the approach and fairway can provide more efficient coverage of the approach.

A more precise layout has three heads near the front corners of the putting surface: a full-circle (or 90 degree part-circle head) for the putting surface, a 90 degree part-circle head for the approach, and a 180 degree part-circle head for the rough (Figure 5.4). Figures 5.5 through 5.7 show other coverage options for the green, approach, fairway, and rough borders.

Some high-end courses maintain (and irrigate) the approach in the same way they do the putting surface, except for a slightly longer height of cut. In this case the two clusters of three part-circle heads are located at the borderline between the approach and the fairway. For irrigation purposes in this situation, there is only one demarcation line because green and approach are irrigated in the same way (see Figure 5.8).

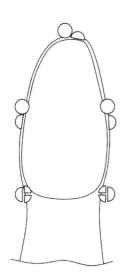

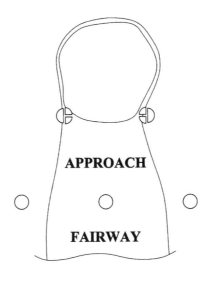

GREEN

FIGURE 5.4
Full-circle heads with part-circle heads throwing away from green. At front corners are three part-circle heads, separately covering putting surface, approach, and rough.

APPROACH

FIGURE 5.5
Part-circle heads at front green corners cover putting surface, approach, or rough separately. First row of fairway heads covers approach, fairway, and rough.

APPROACH

FIGURE 5.6
Part-circle heads at front green corners cover putting surface, approach, and rough separately. Part-circle heads at approach/fairway border cover approach and fairway separately.

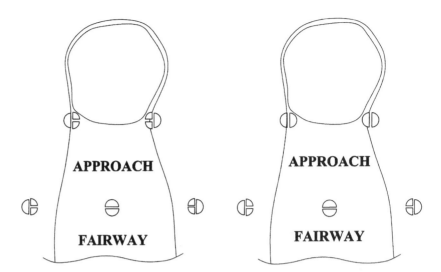

APPROACH

FIGURE 5.7
At front green corners, PCs cover putting surface, approach, and rough separately. At approach/ fairway border, PCs separately cover approach, fairway, and rough.

APPROACH

FIGURE 5.8
Putting surface and approach are maintained identically. At front green corners, one PC covers putting surface and approach, the other covers rough. At approach/ fairway border, PCs cover approach, fairway, and rough separately.

Although the preceding discussion bases the need for dedicated irrigation in a given area on that area's specific irrigation requirements, it should be noted that greens, approaches, fairways, rough areas, and so forth, also have differing fertilizer requirements. In irrigation systems designed to accommodate fertigation, the fertigation can also affect the placement of the part-circle heads.

Tees

Early automatic systems usually had single-row coverage for tees. Because tees are much narrower than fairways, the problems that are so obvious in single-row fairway coverage are not as evident, but they still exist. The area closest to the line between the heads gets the most water, and the edges of the pattern get a lot less. To provide adequate water near the edges, the system must put an excessive amount of water near the center. Conversely, if the run time is set to match the requirements of the center of the coverage area, the edges will be underirrigated. The edges of the coverage pattern at many tee complexes are often slopes, and they may well require more water than the tee surface.

When a head is located within the tee surface, it reduces the area available for placement of the tee markers. For this reason (and because many courses do not have enough tee area to start with), heads should not be placed within the tee surface. The Rules of Golf provide a little help here. They define the teeing ground as a rectangular area two club lengths in depth, the front and sides of which are defined by the outsides of two tee markers. Therefore, the markers will always be set at least two club lengths from the rear edge of the tee surface. Because golfers tend to tee up the ball close to the line between the markers, a head may be placed at the rear edge of the tee surface without interfering with play.

When single-row coverage is used, heads are located along one edge of the tee surface, usually the side on which the players approach the tee. If the tee is exposed to a prevailing wind, the heads should be placed on the upwind side. This placement also keeps pipe away from the center of the tee, where a leak would require costly repairs. In a few cases the head spacing, the length of the individual tee boxes, and the distance between them fortuitously combine to allow head placement on the centerline of the tees, but outside the tee surfaces.

Locating heads along one side of the tee surface does not provide uniform coverage across the tee. With typical tee width (25 ft to 35 ft) the weakest coverage areas will be beyond the far side of the tee box. In the case of elevated tees the weakest area will be a slope, which requires more water than the tee surface. On the wider tees often found on par three holes, the weak coverage areas may well fall inside the tee surface. In this case, two rows of heads will be required.

Two-row coverage is the best way to achieve uniform coverage across a tee box, regardless of its width. It also ensures that the slopes will receive adequate coverage. In the case of a 25 ft to 35 ft tee width, the choice of heads is limited. The major golf irrigation manufacturers produce heads both in the 25 ft to 35 ft radius range in their residential or commercial lines. These heads do not stand up well to use on a golf course. At a radius of 40 ft and greater, golf style heads are available, and they perform well on tees when properly spaced. In the case of narrow tees, some heads may be located off the tee, and beyond the toe of the slope, to maintain optimum spacing.

As is the case with greens and their surrounds, the surrounds adjacent to tees usually have water requirements different from those of the tee surface. The most accurate and efficient irrigation is provided through the use of full-circle and part-circle (out) heads, or part-circle heads throwing only on the tee and others covering only the surrounding rough.

The large practice tees on driving ranges present some unique issues. Their depth (up to 100 yd) forces the placement of heads inside the tee surface, but this is not the problem it is on tees of actual golf holes. In addition, practice tees are subject to very concentrated wear. When an area of turf is worn out, the tee markers are moved and the worn area is prepped and reseeded. During germination and establishment of the new seeds, the area must be irrigated regularly during the hours of play. Short-radius part-circle heads are often installed so that a newly seeded area can be irrigated without disrupting play on the rest of the tee. A common layout is a line of back-to-back part-circle heads across the middle of the tee. Players can use the front half while the rear half is being irrigated, and vice versa.

Fairways

The shortcomings of single-row coverage are well known. Uniformity is poor with this kind of coverage, so coefficient of uniformity (*CU*) and distribution of uniformity (*DU*) values are low, and scheduling coefficient (*SC*) values are high. The application rate can vary by a ratio greater than 3:1 across the pattern. The lack of uniformity forces the operator to set the run time based on an estimated average of the moisture requirements at the poorly covered edges of the pattern and those of the heavily covered center of the pattern. The results are inefficient irrigation, waste of water and power, and nonuniform playing conditions. Most single-row fairway systems use long-radius (90 ft to 100 ft) heads and space them accordingly. As previously discussed, this layout compounds the inefficiency because of the many variables in site conditions found in an area covered by a large head.

If single-row coverage is to be used, there must be additional coverage in landing areas to accommodate the increased fairway width. At least two rows are needed, and possibly more if there are sand bunkers on one or both sides of the fairway.

Double-row coverage provides much better uniformity between the rows than single-row coverage. With typical spacing of 75 ft to 90 ft, it also adds to the width of effective coverage, so more rough is irrigated. The area outside the rows, however, still has all the problems of one side of a single-row pattern. The argument can be made that in this area, usually the rough and the edges of the fairway, precise irrigation is not critical. Nonetheless, water and power are being wasted and playing conditions are not as uniform as they could be.

Three-row fairway coverage is typically configured with 55 ft to 65 ft spacing. One row is on the centerline of the fairway and the others are in the step cut or the primary rough, except in the case of unusually wide fairways (Figure 5.9). The area with good uniformity (i.e., between the outer rows) is now 110 ft to 130 ft wide. Equally important, the radius of the heads is shorter. With individual head control, the operator can respond more accurately to the moisture requirements of a small area.

A modification to three-row coverage is the so-called five-row layout shown in Figure 5.10. There are still three rows of heads, with the middle one on the fairway centerline. The outside rows, however, have back-to-back part-circle heads. This system has the ability to irrigate only the fairway, or only the rough. Although it provides a high level of accuracy and efficiency, the added cost (in heads, wire, and controllers) of a five-row system puts it beyond the reach of many courses.

It should be noted that the coverage in an irrigation system can be as varied as the course design requires. Different types and widths of coverage are frequently mixed, even within a single hole, to properly cover the fairways and features.

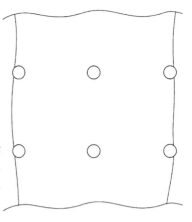

FAIRWAY

FIGURE 5.9
Three-row full-circle fairway coverage.

Rough

In many cases, the coverage of the rough provided by the fairway heads is considered adequate. If, however, improved rough turf is desired, additional coverage may be necessary. USGA and PGA tournaments often feature tall, thick, and uniform turf in the rough. This condition is difficult to establish and maintain without good irrigation coverage. If the heads that water the rough also cover portions of the fairway, it is nearly impossible to improve the rough without adversely affecting (overwatering) the fairways.

The design of a given hole can require precise irrigation of key rough areas. A shot hit off-line should be penalized. Yet a shot hit into a poorly irrigated area of rough may well roll much farther along the hole than a similar shot hit into the fairway. If a shot carries 200 yd in the air and then rolls another 30 yd in the fairway, the same shot

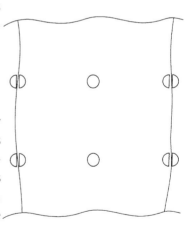

FAIRWAY

FIGURE 5.10
Five-row fairway coverage. Back-to-back PCs at the edge of the fairway allow separate coverage of fairway and rough.

landing in the rough should get much less roll. Weak rough turf will not provide the necessary penalty.

Fairway bunkers are usually framed by mounds on the rough side of the sand. The mounds are maintained as rough, but are highly visible and definitely in play. Proper irrigation of these areas often requires heads placed outside the mounds. Steep slopes and southern exposure can further complicate the issue.

Wall-to-wall systems cover the entire property, including areas where irrigation is not required for reasons directly related to golf. They are often laid out as a geometric grid, and then individual head locations are adjusted where they conflict with greens, tees, or bunkers. Although this allows for rapid staking, it does not necessarily provide the most accurate coverage within the primary areas of play. A better idea is to accurately lay out the irrigation in each hole and then fill in the areas between holes. Uniformity in the latter areas is not as critical, so adjustments to make the coverage fit will not be as problematic as they would be within fairway, approach, or primary rough areas.

Special Areas

The edges of sand bunkers often require special treatment. Spray heads (either part- or full-circle or a combination) are frequently used for this application. A group of sprays is operated by a remote control valve. The spray heads must have integral check valves, and the remote control valve must have a pressure-regulating feature, because system pressure will always be too high for proper operation of spray heads. Ideally, the spray heads are equipped with an adjustment screw to allow for adjustment of the radius and to allow an individual head to be completely shut off.

Spray zones provide effective irrigation of bunker edges, but there are drawbacks. The precipitation rate of spray heads is typically much higher than that of other patterns in a golf course system, so run times must be carefully set and observed. There is also a maintenance issue. Spray heads tend to stick in the up position after the valve has closed, often because sand from the bunker gets caught in the riser seal. Then, because spray heads are small and difficult to see, mowers often damage the risers and nozzles. Although the replacement parts are not expensive, there is a cost for the man-hours needed to make the repairs.

Small rotary pop-up heads are also used for bunker edge irrigation. Again, groups of heads are activated by a pressure-regulated remote control valve, and check valves are needed in the heads. In some cases subsurface drip irrigation is used along bunker edges. The drip lines should be installed no more than 4 in. below grade for maximum efficiency. This means that aerifying cannot be done in the area near the drip lines, but that is seldom a problem.

The consistency of bunker sand is a serious issue in the play of the game. As a result, there are differing opinions about whether and how the sand area of a bunker should be watered. Some courses want no water in the sand areas, which complicates the design of the surrounding irrigation. Others may want full watering of the sand to minimize the effect of strong winds. Islands and narrow peninsulas of turf create special problems. These issues must be addressed in the design process.

Steep slopes and south-facing (or north-facing if a course is in the Southern Hemisphere) slopes often require special irrigation. The heads located on a slope must be controlled separately from those on surrounding areas. If multiple heads are controlled together on the slope, the zones must be laid out along the contour line because the top, the middle, and the bottom of the slope will have different irrigation requirements.

In some cases special-purpose sprinklers are installed with no relationship to the pattern and spacing of the regular heads. Rather, they are located where they are needed to solve a special problem. Examples are heads that cover south-facing slopes, those covering slopes exposed to a (constant direction) prevailing wind, and those that cover known dry spots.

Landscaped areas (trees, planting beds of ornamental shrubs and flowers, ground cover, etc.) require special irrigation. Golf course heads are typically too big for these areas, so smaller (usually residential) sprinklers are used. Landscape irrigation must be zoned according to hydrozones with similar requirements, and sprinklers must be properly located and elevated to accommodate the growth of the plant material. Drip irrigation is also used in many landscape applications. In either case, the smaller heads or emitters operate at pressures much lower than those typically found in a golf course system, so pressure-regulating valves must be installed.

Other areas requiring special irrigation treatment include tennis courts (both grass and artificially surfaced), lawn bowling and croquet areas, and polo fields. Designers of irrigation systems for these areas must have a thorough knowledge of the special requirements of each activity and of the maintenance practices for each surface.

Wind

Wind of any speed distorts sprinkler profiles. When wind speed exceeds 5 mph, the area covered begins to suffer. The upwind throw of a head is shortened and the downwind throw is lengthened. Equally important, the distance of throw across the wind direction is reduced. The results include lower uniformity throughout the pattern (which equates to lower efficiency and increased waste of water and power) and out-and-out dry spots. The latter occur not only on the upwind side of the covered area, but throughout the entire coverage pattern.

Reducing the spacing in general, and especially across the prevailing wind direction, can help combat the effects of wind. Operating heads at lower pressure (staying within the manufacturer's recommendations) causes larger droplets, which fare better in wind than the finer droplets that result from higher pressures. The use of heads with all nozzles aligned in one direction can also help combat wind.

Offsetting heads to the upwind side of a fairway (or any area to be irrigated) is risky. Unless the wind direction and speed are very constant, including during the night hours when most irrigation is done, offsetting heads is not recommended.

Input from Superintendents and Architects

The extent of coverage is important to both the architect and the superintendent who must maintain the course. The latter usually wants more coverage, and the former may want to limit irrigation for design, budget, and aesthetic reasons. A compromise between the two must be achieved. A superintendent may also have specific ideas about irrigation coverage and control based on his or her individual methods of irrigating. Although a design can cater to these preferences, the system cannot be based exclusively on one person's ideas. Other superintendents will operate the system during its lifetime, and it must have the flexibility to accommodate different ideas of how a course should be irrigated.

SUBSURFACE DRIP IRRIGATION

The use of subsurface drip irrigation (SDI) is beginning to find its way into golf course irrigation. Initial installations have been in high-traffic areas such as those found around tees or along cart paths. SDI has also been used for the edges of sand traps. SDI differs from sprinkler irrigation in that it distributes the water underground directly to the roots, rather than overhead as with sprinkler systems. This can cause some cultural changes in how the turfgrass is managed. For instance, fertilizers, which are watered in by sprinklers, would be dependent on rainfall in an SDI system.

The idea of applying water directly to the root zone via drip irrigation has been studied extensively for the last 15 years. During this time root intrusion and back siphonage were identified as major concerns to the long-term viability of the SDI method. Chemical barriers have been successful in preventing root intrusion. The likelihood of back siphonage can be significantly reduced by proper installation of vacuum/air release valves.

Design

SDI systems are designed to operate at relatively low pressures (15 psi), as compared with conventional sprinkler systems (60 to 90 psi). Experience has shown that spacing emitters 15 in. to 18 in. along the length of the tubing and spacing the tubing 18 in. apart will provide sufficient coverage in most soils. This should, however, be verified at site-specific locations. Emitters are typically placed 4 in. to 8 in. deep, with the greater depths selected for areas where mechanical aeration may be desired. (Note: Tubing must be placed deeper than aeration equipment will reach, so some parts of a golf course cannot use SDI.)

With the use of emitters that deliver ½ gallon per hour (gph), this design criterion will produce an application rate approximating 0.5 in. per hour. Emitters are typically preordered at the desired spacing and installed in-line in the tubing during the manufacturing process. Most emitter designs incorporate a pressure-compensating feature, with some now even providing a low-pressure check valve to stop drainage of the system at system shutdown.

The ends of the drip lines are usually tied together with a smaller pipe that is used on the supply side to facilitate periodic line flushing. The flush valve can be a manual valve, an electrically operated hydraulic valve, or a self-flushing valve. Depending on the quality of the source water, flushing frequency will vary.

The control head typically consists of an electrically activated hydraulic valve, followed by a disc filter, or in larger installations a sand media filter, and a pressure-regulation valve. It is recommended that all valve zones allow for measurement of flow rate, total flow, and pressure readings.

Installation

In small installations, drip tubing can be installed with a small trencher or conventional vibratory pulling equipment.

Operation and Maintenance

It is important to monitor a drip system during the first month of irrigation. The water has a tendency to move up rather than laterally. Short, frequent irrigations, rather than long irrigation run times, will help mitigate this effect.

At system start-up, the system should be flushed thoroughly. Soil and other contaminants must be purged from the system before operation. After flushing the system, the system flow rate and operating pressure should be noted. This becomes the baseline to determine whether the system is becoming plugged. Because it is not possible to see the water being delivered, as it is with sprinklers, the irrigator must depend on readings of pressure and flow to verify that the system is operating correctly. Reduced flow rates are an indication that the filter is plugging or, more critically, that the emitters are plugging.

The turfgrass should require approximately the same gross amount of water applied as required with sprinkler irrigation. Because the SDI is dependent on the soil to move water away from the emitters, longer, less frequent irrigation events are recommended. The turfgrass should be observed frequently until the operator is comfortable with the irrigation run times.

SURFACE DRIP—MICRO-IRRIGATION

Surface drip or micro-irrigation is a proven method for irrigating ground cover, shrubs, and isolated trees where sprinkler or spray irrigation methods are not desired. Because drip irrigation is not affected by wind, overspray on sidewalks and other traffic areas is eliminated. This not only improves the aesthetics of the area, but also reduces slip-and-fall hazards. Applications on golf courses include planting beds around clubhouses, tennis courts, swimming pools, and ornamental plantings in out-of-play areas throughout the course.

Drip irrigation emitters come in two basic installation designs, on-line or in-line. The on-line design emitters are manufactured with an insertion barb. Blank tubing is installed along the ground, and holes are punched at desired emitter locations with a specially designed tool. The barbed end of the emitter is pushed into the punched hole.

In-line emitters are installed at the factory during the manufacturing process at preset repeating intervals. The emitter is actually installed inside the tubing, with only the emission hole being visible. Because the tubing emits water along its entire length, it should not be used to transport water across nonirrigated areas. Blank tubing should be used for this purpose.

Small plants and shrubs may require only one or two emitters. Large trees and shrubs will require numerous emitters placed around their bases to encourage wide root growth to support the plants. If plants of various sizes are to be irrigated on one drip line, the irrigator must be sure to calculate the water requirements for each and provide the appropriate number of drip emission devices. Because shrubs and trees grow over time, additional emission devices may be warranted.

There are other low-volume types of emission devices used to deliver water to trees and plants. Small micro-sprayers attached to stakes can be used to irrigate near the bases of trees. These are available in an assorted mix of arcs and wetting patterns. Multioutlet heads can also be used. These are commonly attached to ½ in. risers and can irrigate up to eight individual plants via spaghetti or small-diameter tubing. The multioutlet heads are available with a variety of discharge rates, and most are pressure compensating.

Filtration is the heart of any drip irrigation system. If the filtration system fails, the entire drip system will soon follow. For most drip systems that use municipal or well water supplies, the filtering needs for inorganic material may be sufficiently met with a manually flushed filter system. Small bits of sand or rock will eventually cause small emission paths to plug if not protected. The filtration requirements for these areas can typically be met by the use of a screen or disk filter.

For drip irrigation systems that use surface water supplies, it is important that the water be treated with chlorine or other organic growth inhibitors. Algae and other aquatic plants will continue to grow in the drip lines if they are not treated and will eventually cause plugging to the emission devices. Water supplies with medium/heavy organic loads may require automated back flushing filtration systems. Sand media filtration has proven effective with organic contaminants.

The head works of a properly designed drip irrigation system includes filtration device, a flow meter, a pressure gauge (downstream of the regulator), and a pressure-regulation valve. These are typically installed aboveground for ease of maintenance, or in some cases they are installed belowground in large valve boxes for aesthetic purposes.

Maintenance is key to a long life of a drip irrigation system. Periodic inspection of the head works, drip lines, and emission devices will ensure proper operation. Manual cleaning of the filtration system will be required if the system is not automated. Frequency will depend on the water quality and amount of irrigation applied. The ends of drip lines should also be periodically flushed. Frequency will vary depending on water quality.

SPACING

Accurate analysis of sprinkler spacing patterns is an important tool. The Sprinkler Pattern Analysis & Coverage Evaluation (SPACE Pro) software program provides the user a number of analytical tools. It is not intended as a designed system, but rather an objective measure of important variables that should be considered before purchasing or changing a sprinkler irrigation system. SPACE Pro is designed to provide additional information that may be critical in the selection process.

As discussed in a later section, SPACE Pro software provides calculations of coefficient of uniformity (*CU*), distribution uniformity (*DU*), densograms, and scheduling coefficient (*SC*) for any given sprinkler, nozzle, pressure, or spacing combination. Data files are available free on the Center for Irrigation Technology (CIT) website or provided by the manufacturer, or they can be generated by the end user.

SPACE Pro can graph uniformity over a range of spacings, allowing for estimates of how forgiving or sensitive the selection is to spacing changes. SPACE Pro can also evaluate the mix and matching of various sprinklers, nozzles, pressures, and spacings for their effect on uniformity.

The economics of various sprinkler/spacing combinations can be compared with the use of the SPACE Pro Irrigation Survey (SIS) routine. This allows for comparing existing and/or proposed sprinkler irrigation designs and estimating differences in run time based on providing a minimum amount of water to the dry area for each system. The program uses the SC as a run time multiplier, the estimated cost of water (including energy), and an estimated water requirement to produce desired turf quality.

The difference in run times between various systems becomes the variable to measure water and energy costs. Systems with larger *SC*s require longer run times to apply similar amounts of water to the driest area and therefore incur higher operating costs for water and energy.

There are a number of other benefits provided by more uniform irrigation, including a reduction in excessively wet spots, which are more difficult to mow and can affect playability. Disease and other turf health problems are also associated with overirrigation. Chronic wet spots are often "roped off" or require the costly installation of drainage.

Sprinkler Head Spacing

Selecting the proper sprinkler spacing is critical to optimizing irrigation uniformity. Traditional irrigation system design is based on spacing sprinklers head-to-head. That is, the sprinklers' radius of throw dictates the spacing. The basic premise behind head-to-head coverage is that water is contributed from two or more sprinklers in the coverage area.

This approach can be best described as a "rule of thumb" and does not take into account the actual profile of the sprinkler. The profile is the application rate along the radius of the sprinkler. The profile is affected by four main variables: the size of the nozzle, the shape or design of the nozzle, the operating pressure, and the rotation speed of the sprinkler. If any one or more of these variables is changed, the profile is changed. Changing the profile will change the uniformity and may affect optimum spacing.

The nozzle size and operating pressure are interrelated. Operating at pressures below the recommended range will produce a "fire hose" effect. Water will shoot to the end of the sprinkler radius, leaving a visual donut pattern. Pressures above the maximum desired pressure will begin to atomize the water jet and destroy the desired profile. For all nozzle sizes there is a target pressure range in which the desired radius and profile can be achieved. Nozzle pressure is used to created turbulence in the nozzle. This turbulence is used to distribute water along the sprinkler radius and produce the desired profile.

The relationship between nozzle size and pressure is a sliding scale. The smaller the nozzle, the lower the pressure range required to achieve maximum efficiency. Conversely, in larger nozzle sizes, a higher range of operating pressures is required to produce the desired sprinkler profile.

Nozzle shape or design is critical to producing the right sprinkler profile. Traditional taper bore nozzles required relatively high pressure to induce enough turbulence to develop the desired profile. Newer, or so-called low(er) pressure, nozzles use a variety of geometric shapes to induce turbulence through mechanical means, rather than excess pressure, to achieve the desired profile.

This is why a straight bore sprinkler/nozzle combination rated for 70 psi can achieve similar breakup and coverage, as compared with the same sprinkler and a low-pressure nozzle at 60 psi. The first 55 or 60 psi of pressure provides for the maximum radius of throw, with the additional 10 psi or so used to create turbulence in the taper bore nozzle and breakup along the radius of the sprinkler. The lower-pressure nozzle uses the first 60 psi to achieve distance of throw, but uses mechanical turbulence to provide the breakup along the radius, rather than pressure. Thus, the sprinkler can operate at lower pressure.

Once the user has determined the profile and radius of the sprinkler, he or she will want to know how far apart the sprinklers should be spaced. SPACE Pro allows users to model the coverage from any profile over a range of field spacing and configurations. Field spacing is the distance between the sprinkler heads, and configuration is the arrangement of the heads.

Figures 5.11 and 5.12, as well as Figures 5.13 and 5.14, illustrate the effect of changing only one variable, in this case the nozzle shape, on the sprinkler profile and application uniformity. The same sprinkler, operating pressure, and field spacing are used in both cases.

The boxes in Figures 5.12 and 5.14 show the driest contiguous 5 percent of the coverage area. The average application rate in the box is compared with the average application rate of the repeating coverage area. This produces an *SC* of 1.07 in Figure 5.14, a significant (18 percent) improvement over the *SC* of 1.25 in Figure 5.12. Figure 5.14 demonstrates corresponding improvements in uniformity measures in the *CU* of 95 percent and *DU* of 94 percent, as contrasted in Figure 5.12 with a *CU* of 83 percent and *DU* of 78 percent. This example

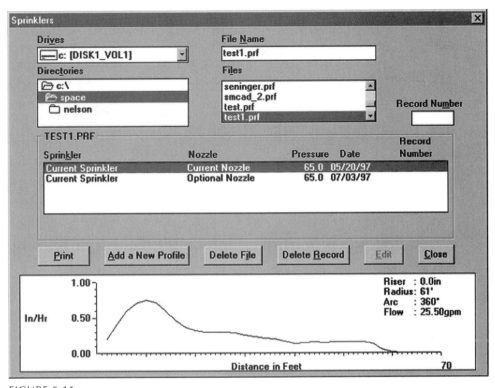

FIGURE 5.11
The profile is generated from a common rotor sprinkler operated at 65 psi.

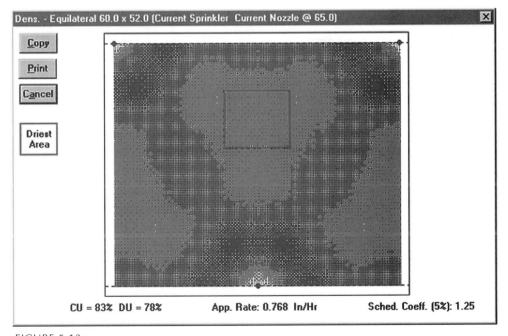

FIGURE 5.12
The denso-gram shows the sprinkler uniformity in shades of darker (wetter) and lighter (drier) areas.

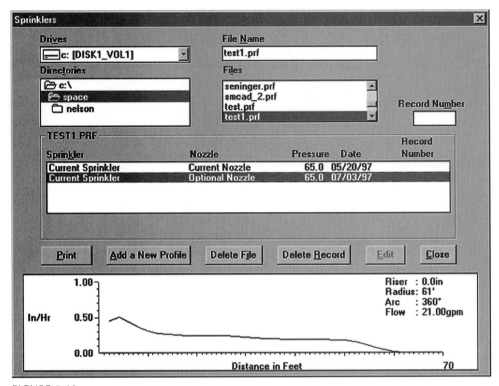

FIGURE 5.13
The profile is changed significantly by use of an after-market nozzle while operated at the same pressure, 65 psi.

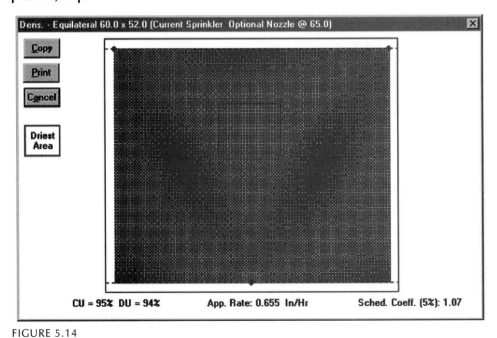

FIGURE 5.14
The denso-gram reflects significant improvement in coverage uniformity by changing nozzles.

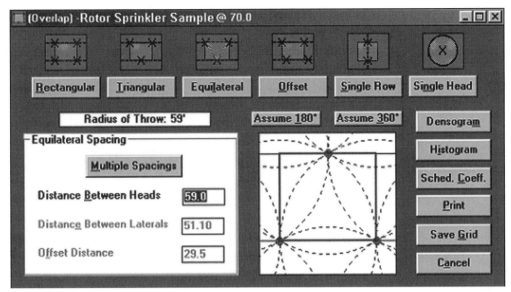

FIGURE 5.15
Users can model sprinkler uniformity over a range of field spacing.

clearly demonstrates the importance of sprinkler profile shape on the ultimate sprinkler application uniformity.

Some sprinkler systems are designed with an equilateral head configuration (see Figure 5.15). As the name suggests, the sprinkler heads are placed in a triangular configuration. The distance between the heads is equal along the three legs of triangle. Other designs commonly found in the field are square or rectangular spacing, offset spacing (parallelogram), and single-row spacing.

An important consideration in selecting a sprinkler/spacing combination is to look at how "forgiving" it is to small changes. It is fairly easy to select a single spacing where any sprinkler will provide adequate coverage. However, in many cases, moving the spacing slightly in one direction or another will have a significant negative impact on uniformity. This is a reality of placing sprinklers in the field, where obstacles such as trees, bunkers, and other hazards require head placement to be something other than as designed.

Ideally, a sprinkler is selected that provides high uniformity over a wide range of probable field spacings. This is what is meant by a forgiving sprinkler. The sprinkler shown in Figure 5.16a illustrates the performance of sprinkler rotor A and how forgiving this product is over a wide range of field spacings.

However, when sprinkler rotor B (Figure 5.16b) is used at the same spacing shown in Figure 5.16a, it is clear that changes in field

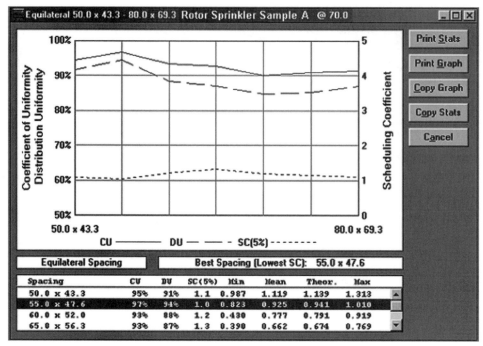

FIGURE 5.16A
The selected sprinkler rotor A maintains relatively high measures of uniformity as expressed in *CU*, *DU*, and *SC* and plotted against various field spacings.

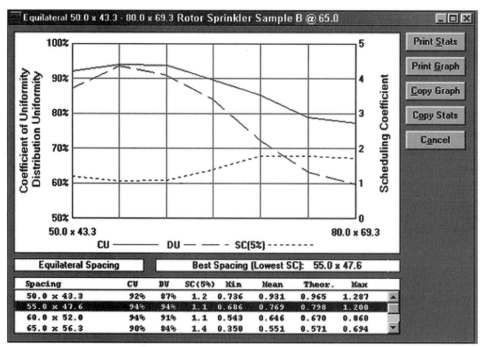

FIGURE 5.16B
The selected sprinkler rotor B shows changes (decline) in *CU*, *DU*, and *SC* as plotted against similar field spacings as shown in Figure 5.16A.

spacing can produce a dramatic decreases in uniformity. This is why knowing how a sprinkler performs at various spacings can be important in the product selection process.

Selecting the proper spacing for greens is dictated in large part by the size and shape of the green. Sprinkler heads are placed off the putting surface to avoid interfering with play. Nonuniform irrigation of the green area is mitigated by the high infiltration rate designed into green construction. Although the design accommodates over-irrigation on large sections of the green, it also allows for the movement of chemicals and fertilizers below the root zone. Improving the uniformity of application in an irrigation system can reduce the impact of drainage and deep percolation. These are key considerations in good environmental stewardship and keeping regulatory agencies from getting involved.

UNIFORMITY

Evaluating the irrigation system for uniformity is critical to managing the system. With increased costs of power and water, irrigation managers can realize direct financial benefits from irrigation systems with greater uniformity. The basic objective behind irrigation uniformity is to apply water as evenly as possible. If every square inch within the pattern area were to receive an equal amount of water, it could be said that the system is applying water with 100 percent uniformity. Unfortunately, neither man-made irrigation systems nor nature-provided rainfall distributes water with 100 percent uniformity. Thus comes the need for irrigation managers to measure and interpret their irrigation systems' performance.

Uneven or nonuniform water distribution creates areas that are too wet or too dry. This situation causes havoc with irrigation scheduling. If a superintendent manages turf by irrigating the dry spots, far too much water will be applied in the wet spots. If the superintendent manages the wet spots, the dry spots will likely become dead spots. To avoid the latter, many irrigation managers have succumbed to the notion of hand-watering.

Data to evaluate the uniformity of an irrigation system is available from two main sources. One is published performance data, which is available from the manufacturer or an independent source such as the Center for Irrigation Technology (CIT). This sprinkler performance data is usually developed in a test building under no-wind conditions. Although sprinklers rarely operate under no-winds conditions, data collected in this manner allows for a wide range of comparisons under various conditions and between different products.

The range of variables is almost limitless, but includes different sprinkler models, nozzle sizes and configurations, operating pressures, rotation speeds, nozzle discharge angles, and sprinkler spacing. If any one of these variables is changed, it will affect the uniformity of the sprinkler system. The trick is to select the variables that are right for a particular system's needs. Computer modeling of these variables allows for a better understanding of the limitations of any given irrigation design.

This type of analysis is not foolproof and must be verified under field conditions. Nor should it be considered a substitute for field experience. The effect of wind is not addressed in this type of evaluation. Significant amounts of water caught under no-wind conditions, particularly small water drops, may fall outside the desired target area under prevailing wind conditions. However, the use of no-wind data does serve a purpose. Rarely, if ever, does sprinkler uniformity improve under wind conditions. Thus, computer analysis of no-wind sprinkler data will help identify those conditions that do not appear favorable to achieving high uniformity.

Moreover, in analyzing an existing sprinkler system, proposed changes can be modeled quickly to determine whether those changes are worth exploring in more detail. For instance, simply changing the nozzle on any existing system has shown uniformity improvements of 15 percent or more. This has been more common in older systems with stretched spacing. Their overall uniformity was relatively low in the beginning, so there was substantial room for improvement. Financial payback on this kind of investment can be less than one year, and there is also the benefit of improved playability and turf quality.

The second way to evaluate the uniformity of an irrigation system is for the superintendent to collect his or her own catch can data. The Irrigation Association, through its Certified Golf Irrigation Auditors (CGIA) program, as well as other organizations, have developed protocols for collecting field data. This type of field measurement is designed to take a "snapshot" of a system's performance and may not include enough data to make technical changes to improve uniformity.

The superintendent may want to collect a more comprehensive data set that requires more catchcans than an audit may require.

Typically, there should be a grid of catchments spaced evenly throughout the repeating area of the sprinkler head layout. The more catch cans used in the grid, the more complete the data set.

Once the data has been collected, how should it be used? The answer starts by deciding which uniformity measurement is best for turfgrass managers. The short answer is, "It depends." Historically, one of the most frequently referenced measures is coefficient of uniformity (*CU*) as defined by J. E. Christiansen. The following formula shows how *CU* is calculated:

$$CU = 100 \, (1 - D/M)$$

$$D = (1/n)\sum |X_i - M|$$

$$M = (1/n)\sum X_i$$

where

CU = Christiansen's coefficient of uniformity (%)
D = Average absolute deviation from the mean
M = Mean application
X_i = Individual application amount
n = Number of individual application amounts
$\sum$ = Symbol of summation
| | = Symbol for absolute value of quantity between the bars

The absolute value of deviation or difference between the mean value and the individual application amount measures only the magnitude, but not the direction (more or less water).

There are several weaknesses in the use of *CU* as the measure of sprinkler uniformity. First, by mathematically treating over- and underirrigation the same way, we do not know whether the problem areas are wet or dry spots. Most turf managers are more interested in the dry spots, though certainly wet spots present their own set of management problems.

A second weakness in using *CU* is defining the size of the problem areas. For example, two sprinkler patterns that both measure a *CU* of 80 percent may present significantly different management challenges. One sprinkler pattern may have the dry and wet spots evenly distributed across the entire coverage area, whereas the second sprinkler pattern may have all the dry spots grouped in one area and all the wet spots grouped in another area. *CU* gives only the measure of the average uniformity across the sprinkler pattern, with no reference to the location, size, or cause of nonuniform spots within the coverage area.

The use of distribution uniformity (*DU*) has been the chosen method among programs or procedures that "audit" irrigation systems. *DU* is a measurement of the underwatered area within a sprinkler coverage area. It is calculated by taking the individual data points from a catch can test and sorting them in rank order (lowest to highest values). The 25 percent of the catch cans that have the lowest values are then averaged. This is sometimes referred to as the "low quarter." The average of the low quarter is then divided by the average or mean application of the entire coverage area and multiplied by 100 to convert to percent. Thus, a *DU* of 80 means that the average water applied in the low quarter was 20 percent less than the mean application over the entire area. (See System Audits in Chapter 6.)

Although *DU* does focus on the underirrigated areas, which is a significant concern to most turfgrass managers, the use of *DU* has its drawbacks. First, the objective is to characterize an entire coverage area with a single number. Second, the average application rate within the low quarter may be known, but there is no reference as to size and shape of the underirrigated area(s).

Third, the selection of 25 percent as the measurement for uniformity is purely arbitrary. It may not bear any relationship to the management needs of the turfgrass. For instance, this would be far too coarse a measurement for determining the irrigation needs of a putting green.

Another method of interpreting irrigation uniformity is to use a denso-gram, which is produced by a dot matrix shading technique. The wetter areas receive more shading, and the drier areas receive less. The result is a graphic representation of the water distribution throughout the pattern area.

A denso-gram is considered a nonquantitative measurement, because the absolute values of wet and dry areas are not expressed. It is more a relative measure that gives the turfgrass manager an understanding of where the problem or wet and dry areas are to be expected. It provides the user with a general understanding of how uniform the water application is. A denso-gram can be used as a quick review of uniformity improvement in considering nozzle and/or pressure changes. The SPACE Pro program depicts sprinkler coverage in the form of a denso-gram.

The use of the scheduling coefficient (*SC*) is a targeted approach to measuring uniformity that closely represents the needs of turfgrass managers. *SC* differs from the other methods described because it allows the user to define critical areas. Conceptually, the *SC* uses a sliding window of designated size (e.g., 1, 2, 5, or 10 percent of the coverage area) to locate the driest contiguous area within the repeating pattern area.

The *SC* was developed to help irrigators manage dry spots. Because situations vary, the user needs to determine the size of the dry spot he or she wants to manage. On a fairway, for instance, larger dry spots may be acceptable, whereas the same-sized dry spots would be unacceptable on a green. This is really an economic decision; that is, what is the minimum amount of water required to provide a desirable playing surface?

One of the strengths of the *SC* is its direct relationship between irrigation run time and turf quality. Because the turfgrass manager can designate the size of the dry spot to manage, he or she can also determine how much water to apply to the dry spot.

There has been significant research done in correlating the percentage of evapotranspiration of a crop (ET_C) with the amount of water applied. Applying 100 percent of ET_C will provide for a fast growing, healthy turf. Lesser amounts will slow the growth and cause a reduction in vigor and color. However, to minimize the total amount of water applied, dry spots should not receive more than the desired amount (typically less than 100 percent ET_C). This limitation is necessary because all other areas will naturally receive more water than the dry spot.

Most grasses will respond with an acceptable green appearance even when receiving less than 100 percent of the estimated *ET*. Thus, targeting dry spots to receive a predetermined amount of water less than 100 percent can ensure that a minimum amount of water is applied, but still yield turfgrass with an overall healthy appearance.

Use of the *SC* can help determine irrigation run times. The *SC* is defined as the ratio of the average amount of water applied in the coverage area divided by the average amount of water applied in the driest part of the coverage area. If both areas were to receive the same amount, the result would be an *SC* of 1.0, indicating perfectly uniform coverage.

However, no irrigation system is perfectly uniform. An *SC* of 1.3, for example, indicates that the irrigation system will have to run 30 percent longer for the driest area to receive the minimum amount of water desired. An *SC* of 1.5 will require a run time of 50 percent longer, and so on. Most managers, obviously, want their irrigation systems designed to achieve an *SC* as near 1.0 as possible.

Several pieces of information are needed to determine the proper run time. The required information includes the system uniformity (*SC*), the *ET* of the crop (*ET*$_C$), and the percentage of *ET*$_C$ to be applied in the dry part of the pattern area (usually less that 100 percent).

The following example uses an *SC* of 1.3 (based on 5 percent window size) and an *ET*$_C$ of 0.30 in. (daily), and it has been determined that 70 percent of *ET*$_C$ is acceptable in the driest part of the pattern area.

EXAMPLE 5.2

The calculations are summarized as follows:

$$\text{Set time} = \frac{(ET_C) \times (\%ET_C) \times (SC)}{\text{Mean application rate}} \times 60 \text{ minutes}$$

where:

ET_C = evapotranspiration crop

$\%ET_C$ = minimum acceptable turfgrass quality expressed as percentage of ET_C

SC = mean application rate divided by the mean application rate in the sliding window (driest area)

And based on the example given:

$$33 \text{ minute set time} = \frac{ET_C\,(0.3) \times \%ET_C\,(0.7) \times SC\,(1.3)}{\text{Mean application rate }(0.5)} \times 60 \text{ minutes}$$

Additional run time will likely be required to offset the effects of wind (spray drift) and heat (evaporation). However, this approach is useful to establish a fundamental baseline for run times. This allows for an economical comparison of potential changes or competing designs.

SC is the only uniformity measurement that allows for economic comparisons. The difference between an *SC* of 1.3 and an *SC* of 1.6 is 30 percent. This means that the system with an *SC* of 1.6 must operate 30 percent longer to provide the same amount of water to a dry spot. The additional operational cost can be calculated in minutes of operation. Using the precediing example, an *SC* of 1.6 would require a run time of 40 minutes, or 7 minutes longer than an *SC* of 1.3. Thus, it requires 21 percent more power and water to irrigate with an *SC* of

1.6 than with an *SC* of 1.3. It is then clear that an investment in the lower *SC* (1.3) at the initial design stage would pay for itself in a very short time period.

Far too often the terms *irrigation uniformity* and *irrigation efficiency* are used interchangeably. They have different and distinct definitions. Irrigation uniformity measures only how uniformly water is applied to the ground. Equipment selection and the design of the irrigation system affect the uniformity of an irrigation system. This includes sprinkler types, nozzle size, operating pressure, pipe size, installation, and system maintenance.

Irrigation efficiency, however, measures the ratio between how much water the plant beneficially used as compared with how much water the system applied. It is really accounting for all the places where water is lost in the distribution and management process, measured against the water beneficially consumed by the plant.

$$\text{Percent efficiency} = \frac{100 \times \text{water used beneficially by the plant}}{\text{applied water}}$$

System design and management are key to the efficiency of an irrigation system. This means that to get optimum performance from an irrigation system, it must be properly designed, maintained, and managed. If all of these variables are not optimized, system efficiency will be reduced, wasting water, energy, and time.

COMMUNICATION ALTERNATIVES

Central-satellite control systems communicate through two basic means: direct burial multiconductor communication cable or wireless technology. Decoder systems communicate only with cable.

Communication Cable

Major controller manufacturers specify the type and construction of the communication cables to be used with their systems. All have copper conductors with either PE or PVC insulation. The outer jacket is usually PE, sunlight resistant and suitable for direct burial, according to National Electric Code (NEC) requirements. Individual conductors (and often the outer jacket) are color coded. Some cables have an aluminum shield and a drain wire to protect signals from electromotive force (EMF). Slightly different cables are often (but not always) used for communication between central controllers and weather stations or pump station control panels.

Communication cables are usually installed in open cut trenches and below mainline pipe for protection. They can be installed by vibratory plowing, but that is seldom done because of the possibility of nicking the insulation, stretching the conductors, or installing the cable against a sharp rock. Control signals are very weak (low voltage and low current), and current leakage resulting from any defect in the insulation or splices can cause ongoing and unacceptable problems. This is also the reason that installation specifications must insist on minimizing the number of splices in communication cables.

Direct burial cable (including installation) is usually less expensive than the cost of the transmitters, receivers, and antennas needed for wireless communication systems. It provides for 25 percent or more faster communication between central and satellite units. However, it is also more susceptible to damage from lightning strikes. The costs resulting from lightning damage to a "hardwired" (communication cable) system can range from the inexpensive but frustrating nuisance of replacing many fuses, to several thousands of dollars in repair and replacement of sensitive and expensive solid-state electronic components. The communication cable itself is often the culprit, because it can carry the surge current from the spot of the initial strike to many other solenoids and controllers.

Controller manufacturers are constantly improving the surge protection in their products, so this problem is being addressed. Systems that detect approaching lightning storms and disconnect communication cables (and other system components) are also available. If properly designed and installed, they can provide added protection against damage.

Another problem with communication cables is their susceptibility to physical damage, suffered either during installation or in subsequent renovation or repair operations. Nicked insulation or improper splices made during installation will cause problems for the life of the system. Later trenching for drainage or irrigation modifications frequently cuts or damages communication cables. Excavation—for tree planting, installing cart paths, or renovating other features—is a further source of problems. Finally, troubleshooting and repair of a buried cable system may be more difficult than the same operations in a radio system, whose components are all readily visible and accessible above ground.

Wireless Communication

UHF narrow-band radio and paging technology are the two most common types of wireless central-satellite communication available at present.

The first step in ensuring successful wireless communication is a site survey. The survey should be done by experienced technicians. It includes both an evaluation of communication conditions within the golf course site (handheld units to central, and central to satellites, considering proposed controller locations throughout the course) and a scan of available frequencies in the local area. Typically, the procedure will scan as many as 40 frequencies and record usage on them 24 hours per day for several days. The scan period should include weekend days. The site survey should be done during summer months when foliage (potential interference) is at its maximum thickness.

The on-site communication evaluation will dictate the type, height, and size of antenna(s) needed on the site and whether repeaters or other special equipment is required. The results of the scan procedure allow the technicians to secure Federal Communications Commission (FCC) licenses for the best frequency (or frequencies) identified. The golf course holds the licenses, and, in theory at least, there will be no interference on the covered frequencies. FCC licenses must be renewed every ten years.

In 1999, the FCC began a program to improve efficiency in the UHF and VHF bands and to accommodate more users in the future. Part of the program cut the frequency width in half ("narrow-band," 12.5 kHz), to make communication more accurate and to make more frequencies available. Manufacturers of radio equipment have reacted with new units that accommodate these changes. This program has not been completed, and the FCC is expected to make similar changes in the future. Adapting to these changes may add to the cost of communication on licensed frequencies.

The antenna requirements identified by the site survey are important. A wide variety of types and classifications (directional, omni-directional, etc.) of antennas are available, and the selection of the correct application for a given site is critical to the success of the communications system.

Wireless communication is generally more expensive than that using direct burial cable. However, the difference can be reduced by clustering satellite controllers and installing only one receiver/transmitter and antenna for the entire cluster. Communication from the initial unit to the other satellites is done through short lengths of communication cable. It should be noted that adding a satellite in the future will be easier with a wireless system than with a communication cable.

Spread spectrum (900 MHz) radio has begun to appear in golf course irrigation systems in recent years. Operators of spread spectrum radios do not require an FCC license, primarily because transmitter power is restricted by the FCC, and distance capability is limited. The latter, however, can be a problem, as can the presence of foliage or other conditions that prevent direct and completely clear line-of-sight relationships between radios.

Fiber optic cables and infrared communication have been used in a few golf course applications, but to date the cost remains prohibitively high.

Combinations of cable and wireless communication are not unusual. In multicourse projects, it is common to communicate from a single central controller to a receiver in each course, and then use buried cable from there to the satellites. The same is true for courses that cross major streets or highways: wireless for the crossing, then cable to the satellites. There are also instances of combining landline or cell telephones into the communication system.

BASIC HYDRAULICS

Hydraulics is the study of liquids in motion. For purposes of golf course irrigation, it is limited to water (an incompressible fluid) moving in closed vessels (pipes). Pressure, velocity, water hammer, and pressure loss because of friction and elevation are the key elements of hydraulics that must be understood.

Pressure

When discussing water, pressure is the relationship of the weight of water to the height of the column of water, or to the distance below the water surface. The weight of water at 60°F is 62.37 lb per cu ft. Because the surface area on the bottom of a cubic foot (12 × 12 × 12 in.) is 144 sq in., the pressure is computed as follows:

$$\frac{62.37 \text{ lb}}{144 \text{ sq in.}} = .433 \text{ lb per sq in. (psi)}$$

That same cubic foot of water is 1 ft high, so the height of the column is 1 ft. Pressure is expressed in feet of head (of a column of water) or pounds per square inch (psi). The meaning of the two terms is the same. The numerical relationship between them is as follows:

$$1 \text{ ft of head} = .433 \text{ psi}$$

and

$$1 \text{ psi} = 2.31 \text{ ft of head}$$

Thus, 100 psi equals 231 ft of head, and 100 ft of head equals 43.3 psi.

Do not confuse pressure with volume, weight, or total force. For example, a vertical 2 in. diameter pipe and a 6 ft diameter wet well, both filled to a depth of 10 ft, will have the same pressure (10 ft × .433 = 4.33 psi) at the base. The total volume and weight of the water in the wet well are obviously much greater than those in the small pipe, but the pressure at the bottom of both is the same, because the depth (or height of the column) of water is the same (Figure 5.17).

If a city main at 30 psi supplied a storage tank (that is open to atmosphere), the water in the tank would rise to (30 psi × 2.31 =) 69.3 ft. Similarly, if the depth of water (height of column) is known, the pressure at the bottom can be calculated (69.3 ft × .433 = 30 psi) (Figure 5.18).

In a closed system of pressurized pipes the theoretical "surface of the water" is the height to which the pump (or other pressure source) can raise a column of water. If a golf course pump station pro-

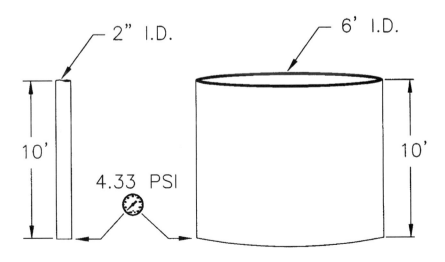

FIGURE 5.17
A vertical 2 in. pipe and a 6 ft diameter wet well, both filled to a 10 ft height. The pressure at the bases of both is the same (4.33 psi).

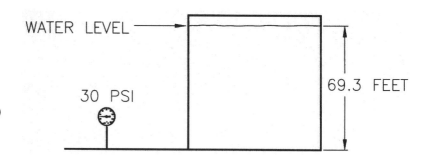

FIGURE 5.18

**If pressure is known: 30 psi ×
2.31 = 69.3 ft. If height (or depth)
of water is known: 69.3 ft × .433
= 30 psi.**

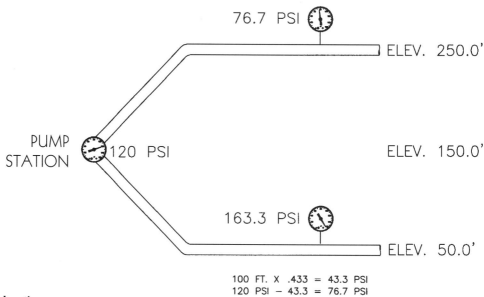

FIGURE 5.19
Static pressure and elevation.

duces 120 psi, the surface of the water is (120 psi × 2.31 =) 277.2 ft
above the pump. The pressure in the system 100 ft above the pump
will be 76.7 psi, calculated as follows:

$$120 \text{ psi} - (100 \text{ ft} \times .433 =) 43.3 \text{ psi} = 76.7 \text{ psi}$$

The pressure at a point 100 ft lower than the pump station will be
163.3 psi [120 + (100 ft × .433 =) 43.3 psi = 163.3 psi] (Figure 5.19).

STATIC PRESSURE

Static pressure is pressure when water is not moving. In a closed
piping system, the components of which are all at the same elevation,
the static pressure will be the same everywhere in the network. A golf
course can have changes in elevation ranging from a few feet to sev-

eral hundred feet. The static pressure at a given elevation (contour line) in a golf course piping system will be the same every place the pipe crosses that elevation, regardless of pipe routing or pipe size. It is important to understand that in a static state, pipe size has nothing to do with pressure. In a dynamic situation, however, that is not true.

DYNAMIC PRESSURE

Dynamic pressure is the pressure at a given point when water somewhere in the system is in motion. The dynamic pressure will always be lower than the static pressure at a given point because of losses upstream of the sensing point. Pressure is lost in a dynamic situation because of friction and turbulence resulting from the movement of the water against the walls of the pipe, fittings, and valves. Friction loss is affected by the flow, the cross-sectional area and geometry of the pipe or fitting, and the roughness of the pipe or fitting walls. Dynamic pressure is static pressure minus the total of all the friction loss between the sensing point and the source. The calculation of friction losses in pipes, fittings, and valves is extremely important in the design of an irrigation system, so systems designers must be completely familiar with the procedures involved. Friction loss calculations are covered in depth later in this chapter. Friction loss tables for sizes of PVC pipe commonly used in golf course irrigation are included in the appendix to this book.

ATMOSPHERIC, GAUGE, AND ABSOLUTE PRESSURE

Atmospheric pressure is the result of the weight of the atmosphere above the earth's surface. It varies with elevation or altitude. Atmospheric pressure decreases as elevation increases, and vice versa. At mean sea level atmospheric pressure is 14.69 psi, which equates to a column of water 33.93 ft high. Atmospheric pressure is also described in inches of mercury, and the value is 29.92 at mean sea level. This is commonly measured as barometric pressure, and it varies slightly at different elevations because of changing weather conditions. To convert from inches of mercury to psi, multiply by .49. To convert from in. of mercury to ft of head, multiply by 1.133.

Pressure gauges are calibrated to report pressure above atmospheric pressure. Thus, a gauge exposed to the atmosphere reads 0 psi. When a pressure gauge reads 120 psi, it means that the pressure is 120 psi above atmospheric pressure. Readings on pressure gauges are sometimes described as psig, meaning pounds per square inch-gauge.

Absolute pressure is gauge pressure added to atmospheric (or barometric) pressure. Thus, a gauge reading of 120 psi at mean sea level equates to an absolute pressure rating of 120 + 14.7 = 134.7 psi. For purposes of irrigation design, absolute pressure is a concern only during calculations of NPSH in the design and selection of pumps, but it is an important element in those calculations.

Velocity

The basic relationship between rate of flow, velocity, and cross-sectional area of a closed pipe is shown in the following equation:

$$Q = AV$$

where

Q = flow rate in cubic ft per second (ft^3/s)
A = cross-sectional area of pipe in square ft (ft^2)
V = velocity in ft per second (fps)

Thus, reducing velocity (V) without reducing flow (Q) requires a larger (A) pipe. If flow (Q) increases and the pipe size (A) stays the same, the velocity (V) will increase.

Restated and modified for commonly used units, the equation is

$$V = \frac{.408 \times Q}{(ID)^2}$$

where

.408 = unit conversion constant
Q = flow rate in gpm
ID = inside diameter of pipe in inches

For 200 gpm in a 4 in. SDR 21 PVC pipe (ID = 4.072 in.) velocity is calculated as:

$$V = \frac{.408 \times 200}{(4.072)^2} = \frac{81.6}{16.58} = 4.92 \text{ fps}$$

Another commonly used form of the equation is the following:

$$V = \frac{Q}{2.45 \times (ID)^2}$$

where

2.45 = unit conversion constant
Q = flow rate in gpm
ID = inside diameter of pipe in inches

Velocity tables are much quicker and easier to use than equations. The tables are computed from the preceding equation and show the velocity for different flow rates in different sizes of pipe. Velocity tables for sizes of PVC and high-density polyethylene (HDPE) pipe commonly used in golf course irrigation are included in the appendix.

The commonly accepted industry recommendation for maximum velocity in PVC pipe is 5 ft per second (fps). Prudent designers will keep velocities well below that level, especially in the larger main line pipes. Larger mains add cost during installation, but they lower pump horsepower requirements by reducing friction loss. The total savings in pumping costs over the life of the system will be much greater than the one-time cost of the larger pipe.

Another benefit of lower velocities is a reduction in the severity of pressure surges in the piping network. Potentially damaging surges, also known as water hammer, are unavoidable in golf course irrigation systems, and the severity of them is a direct function of velocity. Excessive surges can cause failure of pipe and fittings.

Water Hammer

Water hammer is an overpressure surge in a pipe system caused by a sudden change in velocity, which in turn is caused by the rapid opening or closing of a valve. A familiar example of water hammer is the loud thump or rattling noise often heard when a valve in a sink or shower is closed quickly. The noise results from the overpressure waves bouncing back and forth in the pipes. The starting or stopping of pumps can also cause water hammer, as can air trapped in the pipes. An equation for computing water hammer is the following:

$$P_s = \frac{.07 \times V \times L}{T}$$

where

P_s = surge pressure (psi)
.07 = conversion constant
V = velocity (ft per second)
L = length of straight pipe (ft)
T = valve closing time (seconds)

It is important to note that the formula computes surge pressure, which must be added to operating pressure to determine the total pressure on the system during water hammer.

For a 400 ft length of pipe, a velocity of 7 fps, a valve closing time of 0.5 seconds, and an operating pressure of 120 psi, the surge pressure is calculated as follows:

$$P_s = \frac{.07 \times 7 \times 400}{0.5} = \frac{196}{0.5} = 392 \text{ psi}$$

When the surge pressure is added to the operating pressure (392 + 120), the total is 512 psi. If the velocity is 5 fps, the surge pressure would be 280 psi and the total pressure 400. If the velocity is 3 fps, the surge pressure would be 168 and the total 288. Note also that, if the valve closing time is changed to 1 second, the three surge pressures would be 196, 140, and 84 psi, respectively.

The main culprits in a golf course irrigation system are remote control valves and valve-in-head sprinklers. Both types of valves are solenoid activated. They open and close in a short time, causing some degree of water hammer with every cycle. The definition of closing speed is very important. It is not the time from solenoid activation to zero flow through a valve. The correct measurement is from the time the flow starts to slow down to the time it is completely stopped (Figure 5.20). The figure clearly shows flow stopping in less than $\frac{1}{10}$ of a second and going from zero to full flow in $\frac{2}{10}$ of a second.

Research has shown that there are 60 to 100,000 pressure surges per year in a golf course system. Because of the nature of computer-based control systems, the valves open and close separately and in groups in almost infinite combinations and sequences. This fact and the multiple-loop complexity of golf course piping networks make it extremely difficult to calculate water hammer accurately.

Lacking a calculated surge pressure value on which to base the selection of pressure rating for system pipe, the designer must allow for an unknown amount of surge pressure. ASAE S376.2 (JAN98) states that when surge pressures are not known, velocity should be kept below 5 fps, and the operating pressure of the system should not exceed 78 percent of the maximum allowable working pressure of the selected pipe. SDR 21 (200 psi) and SDR 26 (160 psi) are the most common PVC pipes in golf course systems. Seventy-eight percent of 200 psi is 156, and 78 percent of 160 is 125.

Entrapped air is another problem with water hammer. It can both cause hammer directly and, because it is compressible, exacerbate the severity of a surge caused by other factors. Air can enter a system each time a vertical turbine pump starts, when repairs are made after pipe failures or leaks, and during winterization. The air

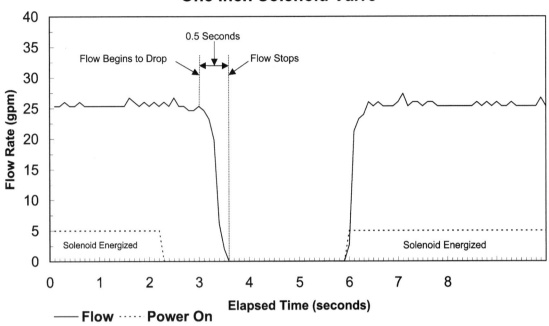

FIGURE 5.20
Closing speed is measured from the time the flow starts to slow down to the time it is completely stopped.

must be removed from the system in a controlled manner or it can damage pipe or fittings. It can also restrict flow. Sprinkler heads allow air to escape much faster than is prudent and cannot be relied upon for this purpose. Continuous-acting air release valves, properly located at high points in the system and fitted with the proper size orifice, are the only safe means of getting air out of the system.

PIPE ROUTING

When selecting the route of mainline pipe, a designer must consider elements of hydraulics, site conditions, the construction and maintenance of the golf course, local regulations and restrictions, the game of golf itself, and cost.

In terms of hydraulics, it is important to loop mains wherever possible and minimize the amount and length of dead-end stubs. Golf course systems frequently have several large loops and many subloops. Loops balance losses and pressures throughout a system and will usually result in smaller pipe sizes, which equates to lower material and installation costs. They also provide multiple paths for water flow to all points in the system. This, coupled with properly located isolation valves, allows most of the piping network to remain in operation when a section of main has to be closed for repairs.

Ideally, the large pipe coming out of the pump station should be split into smaller branches as soon as possible. Especially if the pump station is located near the center of the course, this will divide the flow and reduce the amount of expensive large-diameter pipe. If the pump installation is located at or near one extremity of the course, the large pipes will have to be longer, but they should still be broken down into smaller branches as soon as possible.

Starting from the pump station, the mains should be routed toward the largest concentrations of demand in the system, and they should follow the most direct route possible to minimize the length of the large pipe. However, many elements can conflict with this principle.

Topography and other site conditions can be significant. Steep slopes and narrow ravines cannot be negotiated by trenchers, backhoes, or excavators. It is often cheaper to go around a sharp mound than through it. Routing should go around ledge rock to avoid the costs of blasting or specialized equipment. Areas of unstable soil, such as peat bogs, should be avoided. If that is not possible, special measures, such as the use of butt-fused HDPE pipe, or gasketted PVC pipe with joint restraints, will be required.

Local environmental (and other) regulations frequently limit pipe routing. Most jurisdictions do not allow disturbance (including trench excavation) in wetlands or, in many cases, in 50 or 100 ft buffers adjacent to a wetland's boundaries. Some codes allow pipe to cross ditches or streams only on bridges. Road crossings are expensive, and local regulations sometimes dictate where they can and cannot be located. Restrictions related to utility easements for buried gas lines, fiberoptic cables, and telephone trunk lines can limit routing options. In most cases the installation of pipe through sanitary sewer leach fields is prohibited.

The layout of the golf course can also create problems in pipe routing. Many residential and resort courses have long distances between holes, usually the result of a desire to maximize the number of golf-frontage residential units. Easements to allow cart path access can often be used to route pipe through residential areas. If pipe must be located in nongolf areas that do not have cart path easements, it may be necessary to create an easement solely for the irrigation pipes.

Whenever possible, mainline (and lateral) pipe should not be routed in or across key elements of a golf course. No pipe should be installed under putting surfaces, approaches, tee surfaces, or sand bunkers because of the high cost of restoring these areas if a pipe or fitting fails beneath them. Mains should not be located in fairways for several reasons: Valve boxes and reachwells over (isolation and air release) valves and cable splices can affect play and are aesthetically unpleasant, and excavations to repair leaks or breaks will be located where they are very disruptive to play. Mains and their associated reachwells and valve boxes should be located only in the rough, where their effect on play and aesthetics is minimized. If a main must cross a hole, the preferred location is in the area between the tee and the start of the fairway. If the crossing of a fairway cannot be avoided, every effort should be made to locate any valve boxes or reachwells outside the fairway cut.

ENERGY–WATER RELATIONSHIP (FRICTION LOSS)

With very few exceptions, all water used in a golf course for the purpose of irrigation is pumped. Thus, each unit of water has some unit of energy associated with it as it is delivered to the field. The total annual energy requirements for a golf course are the sum of horsepower required (the amount of energy in each gallon of water) multiplied by the length of operation or hours in the year (the total number of gal of water delivered). Reducing one or both of these variables will reduce the total energy requirements (costs) for the golf course.

The total horsepower requirements are a function of the flow of water (gpm) and pressure (psi) required to operate the irrigation system efficiently. There are many variables that affect the required horsepower of an irrigation pumping plant:

- Is the pump operating at its point of optimum efficiency throughout most of its cycle?
- What is the required pressure to operate the sprinkler efficiently?
- Have the correct pipe sizes been specified and installed?
- Is too much energy being lost through the system, either as a function of improper irrigation design or pumping plant selection?

Reducing operating time is the second area in which energy can be saved. This starts with knowing that the sprinkler system is operating as designed. After correct installation, the irrigation system manager must continue to maintain the system to achieve high application uniformity. The keys to minimum operational run times for the irrigation system are applying the water as uniformly as possible and applying only the water that each type or area of turf requires. This necessitates proper irrigation system design, continued maintenance, and proper irrigation scheduling.

A sprinkler operated below the desired pressure will distribute water nonuniformly, actually requiring more energy because of the extra time the sprinkler must operate in order to meet the minimum water needs of the turfgrass. Operating at too high a pressure also wastes energy and disrupts the sprinklers' uniformity.

A consideration of the relationship between energy and water begins with reviewing changes in operating costs associated with gross application and pressure requirements. Table 5.2 illustrates the sensitivity of operating costs to changes in gross water application, pumping plant efficiency, and the cost of energy if calculated at $0.10 per kWh. The estimate is based on a system designed for operation at 1000 gpm, and pressure is reduced from 100 psi to 90 psi.

Table 5.3 represents the same calculation, but using a cost of $0.14 per kWh. Note that low pump efficiencies contribute to overall higher operational costs, thus producing higher savings when operating pressure is reduced. However, the long-term cost associated with lower pumping plant efficiency is not desirable and should be avoided.

Although each golf course irrigation system will be designed for site-specific requirements, the overarching objective is to reduce the required operational pressure of the sprinkler to optimum performance requirements. It is then important to make sure that the pres-

TABLE 5.2

Annual Energy Cost Savings with a 10 psi Reduction in Operating Pressure Based on 100 Irrigated Acres at $0.10 per kWh

Annual Gross Water Applied (in./yr)	Pump Efficiency 60%	Pump Efficiency 70%
12	$ 394	$ 338
24	$ 788	$ 675
36	$1182	$1013
48	$1576	$1350

TABLE 5.3
*Annual Energy Cost Savings with a 10 psi Reduction in Operating Pressure
Based on 100 Irrigated Acres at $0.14 per kWh*

Annual Gross Water Applied (in./yr)	Pump Efficiency 60%	Pump Efficiency 70%
12	$ 551	$ 473
24	$1103	$ 945
36	$1654	$1418
48	$2206	$1891

sure losses from the pump to the sprinkler head are minimized. There will be some economic tradeoffs between selected pipe sizes and allowable pressure losses. Equipment selection and pipe routing are also important considerations. These calculations are best worked out with the assistance of an irrigation consultant, a professional engineer (PE) or certified irrigation designer (CID). This will produce the best performance from the sprinkler head at the lowest acceptable pumping energy costs.

Operating the system at less than designed flow rate will also cause the delivered water to be more expensive. VFD (Variable Frequency Drive) pumping systems will adjust to changes in flow within a predetermined flow range. A stepped pumping system using a range of available pumps will come on and off line to meet demand. However, operating any pump for long periods of time below its designed operational delivery point will likely result in higher delivery costs per unit of water and should be avoided.

Pressure/Friction Loss

Whether it is called friction loss, head loss, or pressure loss, the act of moving water through a pipe, fitting, or valve will result in a reduction in available pressure. This loss can be masked by elevation changes, either by gains in pressure because of water moving downhill or by additional pressure loss because of water moving uphill. For the purposes of this discussion, it is assumed that there are no changes in elevation.

Moving water through an enclosed structure (pipe) causes the water to rub the pipe wall. The resulting friction causes a reduction in pressure. The rougher the inside pipe wall, the more friction is created, and there is a corresponding increase in pressure loss. Thus, water traveling through a given diameter pipe made of concrete, would result in a higher friction loss (rougher inside wall surface) than when traveling through pipe made of PVC of the same inside diameter (smoother inside wall surface) under similar flow rates.

One of the more popular empirical formulas for estimating friction loss in pipe is attributed to Hazen and Williams. The equation was developed by holding constant the pipe inside diameter, the fluid type (water) being moved through the pipe, and the fluid temperature. Pressure and flow are measured at the beginning and at the end of the pipe section.

Water is considered a noncompressible fluid for the purpose of irrigation design, so if 50 gpm were put through one end of a 2 in. diameter pipe, 50 gpm will flow out the other end (assuming no leaks). However, there will be a reduction in pressure from the beginning measurement to the end measurement. This loss is reported in the standard format of psi loss per hundred ft of pipe. The Hazen-Williams formula estimates what is called a C factor, which is a constant that accounts for the inside pipe wall roughness. The larger the C factor, the smoother the inside wall surface (less rough).

This action can be illustrated by estimating friction loss in 100 ft of 2 in. Schedule 40 pipe. The comparison is between pipe made of steel and pipe made of PVC. Both pipes have the same inside diameter of 2.07 in. The difference in friction loss in the two materials is accounted for in the estimated C factor, or roughness constant. For the steel pipe this value is estimated to be 100. For PVC pipe, the value is set at 150. These C factors hold constant for any diameter pipe made of the same material. Also remember that the higher the C factor, the smoother the pipe surface. Thus, the PVC pipe would be expected to produce less pressure loss than steel pipe when measured at equivalent flow rates.

When the expected pressure loss for water is calculated using the Hazen-Williams equation, that is exactly what is found:

$$f = 0.2083\left(\frac{100}{C}\right)^{1.85} \times \frac{q^{1.85}}{d^{4.8655}}$$

where

f = friction loss per 100 ft of pipe, expressed in feet (multiply by 0.433 to convert friction loss to psi)

C = the estimated constant used to denote the roughness of the inside pipe wall

d = inside wall diameter measured in in.

q = flow rate measured in gpm

The estimated friction loss for 50 gpm in a 2 in. (2.067 inside diameter) steel pipe is calculated at 3.7 psi per 100 ft, using a C value of 100. The friction loss for a similar pipe made of PVC is estimated at 1.7 psi per 100 ft, using a C factor of 150. The friction loss is less than half with the use of PVC at this flow rate. The difference is attributed to the change in C factor, or roughness, of the different materials. Tables in the appendix show friction loss in standard pipe sizes over an expected range of flow rates used in golf course irrigation systems.

Friction loss also changes with pipe diameter. Using the preceding example with 2 in. PVC pipe, the estimated friction loss is 1.7 psi per 100 ft of pipe. If 1½ in. PVC pipe were used, the calculated friction loss would be 5.9 psi per 100 ft of pipe. In this case, the C factor did not change, only the inside pipe diameter. This produces more than a threefold increase in pressure loss. In addition, the recommended design velocity of 5 ft per second has been exceeded and is approaching 8 ft per second. Velocity is discussed further starting on page 198.

Friction loss must also be accounted for in valves and fittings. These losses are most commonly expressed in equivalent terms of psi loss per 100 ft of pipe. This allows for friction loss in pipe, fittings, and valves to be summed together in the calculation of total friction loss.

Depending on the size and type of the fitting or valve, there will be a corresponding estimate of friction loss defined in equivalent length of pipe. As shown in the table on page 438 in the appendix, a 2 in. standard 90 degree elbow will have the equivalent loss of 7.5 ft of SDR 26 PVC pipe at any given flow rate. Therefore, to calculate the friction for one elbow at 50 gpm in the designated pipe (size and type), the estimated friction loss in SDR 26 PVC pipe is 1.31 psi per 100 feet (page 424), and is multiplied by 0.075 (7.5/100). The product is 0.10 psi of loss for the standard 2 in. elbow at 50 gpm. To calculate the estimated friction loss from a 2 in. angle globe valve, the table on page 438 shows an equivalent length of 36.3 ft under SDR 26 pipe. The calculation would then be to multiply the 1.31 psi per 100 feet by 0.363 (36.3/100). This produces an estimated 0.48 psi loss through a 2 in. globe valve at 50 gpm.

To properly estimate the friction loss in the system, every length of pipe, fitting, and valve must be accounted for in the calculation.

Keeping flow rates below the recommended 5 ft per second of velocity reduces pressure loss. Lower pressure losses mean lower energy costs. Optimizing for minimal capital and operational costs should be the goal of every irrigation system design. This can often be best achieved by consulting with a professional irrigation designer.

ISOLATION

When asked, most golf course superintendents will tell you that you can never have enough isolation in a golf course irrigation system. Isolation allows sections of the irrigation system to be shut down for maintenance or to repair problems while the rest of the system remains operational. The more isolation, the more sections. Older systems may have no isolation or isolation of 9 holes at a time. This means that for a small problem, such as a broken sprinkler, the irrigation system for 18 or 9 holes of irrigation will have to be shut down and drained. If the repair takes a long time, and depending on the time of year, such a shutdown can be devastating to course conditions. There are two types of isolation in golf course systems: mainline and lateral, or sub-main.

Mainline Isolation

Mainline isolation is used to shut down sections of mainline piping. It is commonly designed on the basis of number of holes, or an acceptable amount of the irrigation system that can be shut down. Budget is also a consideration. A mainline may be isolated every three holes, every other hole, or at each hole, depending on the piping configuration and budget. It is also common to have isolation on each side of a road crossing and on bridge crossings. Mainline isolation can be accomplished with large ductile iron push-on (Ring-Tite) or flanged gate valves. These types of valves utilize a 2 in. operating nut (painted black to indicate counter-clockwise opening) to open and close and are epoxy coated inside and out with resilient seats. Mainline isolation should be placed so that it accomplishes the isolation of the area desired without having to close a significant number of valves. For example, if there is a 6 in. mainline break, and someone has to close five valves to isolate the break, a significant amount of damage can be done in the meantime. Having to only close two or three valves to isolate the break is faster and less expensive, but may not isolate an area as small as desired.

Lateral or Sub-Main Isolation

Lateral or sub-main isolation usually involves smaller valves, 2½ in. or less, to isolate a green tee, fairway, a number of sprinklers, or an individual sprinkler. In some cases quick coupling valves may also be isolated from the main, especially when they are piped independently from the mainline to a green or other areas. It is common to isolate every tee and green on the golf course. The tees may be isolated individually or per hole. Fairways are isolated differently, depending on how they are piped. A valve may isolate a row of sprinklers, or several valves together may isolate an entire fairway. Some designers require an isolation valve everyplace the mainline is tapped, no matter for what purpose. The quality of these smaller isolation valves varies. Inexpensive valves are fine until you need to use them. Once they are used, the seal leaks, the handle breaks off, or the valve will not seat properly. There are many cases in which inexpensive isolation valves had to be replaced in as little as three or four years. A high-quality brass or bronze gate valve should be used. Some designers use ball valves, but they can be turned on and off quickly, which promotes water hammer, and are difficult to winterize properly. The valves can have different configurations for a handle, but a cross handle is most commonly used on golf courses. All isolation valves should be installed in an access box for locating and servicing and should be precisely detailed on the Record Drawings.

BASICS OF ELECTRICITY

All modern irrigation systems require the use of electricity to operate a variety of components. These components typically include central control systems, field controllers, decoders, electric valves and/or valve-in-head rotors, and pumping stations. Because electricity itself cannot be seen, quite often its importance within the operating system can be overlooked or taken for granted. As with the hydraulic part of an irrigation system, the electrical portion must be properly designed so that the components that require electrical power function correctly. Only those with the proper experience and training should be involved in the design of the electrical system. An experienced irrigation consultant, irrigation designer, or electrical engineer should be consulted before sizing any electrical components on a golf course irrigation system.

It should never be assumed that electricity is available at a golf course with the voltage and amperage that may be required to operate the irrigation system. For this reason it is very important that all potential electrical requirements be identified early in the conceptual design phase of an irrigation system.

Electrical properties are typically identified with the following terms: *voltage, current, cycles per second* (hertz), and *phase*(s).

Voltage refers to the electromotive force available at a power supply and is measured in volts. A common analogy is that voltage is to electricity as pressure is to water.

The rate of electron flow in a circuit is known as *current*. Current is measured in amperes (amps) and is similar to gallons per minute (gpm) in a hydraulic system. In electrical systems with low current, amperage is more commonly expressed in milliamps (mA), or thousandths of an amp.

The type of electricity used in irrigation systems is usually alternating current (AC), but in some cases it is direct current (DC). Direct current, usually supplied by batteries, flows in only one direction. Direct current applications are limited because DC can operate only over much shorter distances than AC. DC applications are typically found in aboveground control circuits and in electronic equipment such as the microprocessors in computers, pump station control panels, and electronic field controllers. In an AC circuit, the electrons flow in one direction, then reverse direction and flow the other way. In the U.S. power system, this reversal of flow occurs 60 times a second; therefore, our power is said to operate at 60 cycles per second. Another common term for *cycles per second* is *hertz* (Hz); the terms are interchangeable. In other parts of the world 50 cycles per second (Hz) is common.

Alternating current is typically available in either "single phase" or "three phase." The phases of an electrical system are like the cylinders of a combustion engine. A single-phase power source is like a single-cylinder combustion engine, and a three-phase source is like a three-cylinder engine. Additional phases provide more "torque" in heavy applications. A three-phase source is generally used where there is a large amperage draw, as in pump motors, and is usually more efficient. Single-phase sources are used in circuits with lower power consumption, such as in the electronic equipment in an irrigation system. It is important to note if single- or three-phase power is available, as the two are not interchangeable without significant equipment modifications. The local power provider should be consulted for specific information on location and availability.

Another term used in discussing electrical systems is *resistance.* Resistance is the opposition to the flow of electrons in a conductor. In irrigation systems resistance is similar to the friction losses in a pipeline. For example, the smaller the pipe size for a given flow, the greater the friction loss: and the smaller a conductor, the greater the voltage loss. Resistance is affected by material type, length of conductor, size of conductor, and temperature.

The relationship between the voltage, current and resistance is expressed in the equation

$$V = IR$$

known as Ohm's law, where

    V = voltage expressed in volts
    I = current expressed in amps
    R = resistance of the conductor in ohms

Ohm's law can be also be expressed as:

$$I = V/R \quad\quad \text{or} \quad\quad R = V/I$$

Ohm's law states that 1 volt will cause a current of 1 ampere to flow against a resistance of 1 ohm.

For golf course irrigation systems, the following voltages may be required to operate irrigation components:

- *24 volt*—Typically supplied by a field controller, used to activate remote control valves or valve-in-head sprinklers.
- *115/120 volt*—This is the most common voltage at which most appliances operate. A typical electrical outlet supplies 115 volts. This voltage is used to power the central equipment components, including the personal computer, central communicating device (interface), uninterruptible power supply (UPS), any dynamic lightning protection devices and the field controllers.
- *208 volt*—This is a somewhat uncommon voltage, more typical in rural areas; its applications are similar to those of 220/240 volt supplies.
- *220/240 volt*—The demands of many larger irrigation systems that utilize multiple field controllers can make the potential electrical loads fairly large. These electrical demands may

translate into larger supply wires between the power source and the field controllers. An experienced irrigation consultant or irrigation system designer may evaluate the benefit of utilizing a greater supply voltage (220/240V) versus increasing the controller power supply wiring. At a higher voltage, a smaller current is required to supply the same amount of energy (power), which will reduce the voltage losses in the wire.

- *440/460 volt*—This voltage is generally used to power large pump motors.

Other standard voltages that can be found are 575 and 2300 volts, both of which typically have three-phase alternating current and are used to supply power to pump motors. The typical Canadian three-phase voltage is 575 volts. These power supplies are typically routed through a step-down transformer to supply the voltage required for an irrigation system.

Controllers

Many types of controllers are used on golf course irrigation systems, and innovations in irrigation system controls continue to become available at a much faster pace than in any other component of the irrigation system. The earliest control systems available were mechanical timers. These timing units were usually composed of a day wheel, a 24-hour clock, and a station run time dial. A series of timing motors, dials, and microswitches provided a controller start command along with station run times. Typically available in 10-station to 24-station configurations, these mechanical devices would operate as stand-alone controllers (without a central) or from a series of central starting panels that activated all the controllers that were wired to each panel. The timing clocks and mechanically operated dials were not very accurate.

Solid-state electronic controllers were introduced in the 1970s, and because of their timing accuracy, extensive programming features, and increasing dependability, they became the most popular means of irrigation control by the late 1980s. Solid-state controllers are available in a wide range of station configurations. Many controllers are expandable: A 16-station controller can be expanded to 64 stations or more, and a communication module can be added to allow communication with a central computer. In addition, manufacturers offer different types of solid-state controllers that can provide varying degrees of field-activated features while offering the same degree of flexibility when managed by a central control system.

No matter how flexible a field controller is, there are several factors that must be considered in positioning them across a golf course.

LOCATION

The location of a field controller can affect the control system operator's ability to take advantage of the flexibility it offers, especially if the controller is not part of a central control system. Among the considerations in locating controllers are the following:

- *Line of sight*—It is often desirable to be able to see all of the stations that are operated from a controller. Line-of-sight from a field controller may be especially important in using a field controller for syringing during the day when the irrigation system operator would want to avoid activating sprinklers that are near golfers. Moreover, in programming a stand-alone field controller it may be helpful to see the stations that are being programmed at each field controller, making it easier to remember the specific watering requirements of each station. With the introduction of handheld radio control devices that allow remote activation of stations, the need to go to the controller for station activation has almost been eliminated and line-of-sight is becoming a less important design consideration, thereby allowing controllers to be located farther out of play.

- *Accessibility*—Controllers may need to be accessed for service, maintenance, and field operation. Many controllers offer three-position station switches that allow for the manual activation of a station without accessing the electronics of the field controller. For these reasons a field controller must be positioned in an area that allows for complete access to its faceplate and other components (Figure 5-21). When field controllers are located in clusters, sufficient space must be provided between them so that doors and panels can be opened without interfering with the accessibility of the adjacent controllers. Many pedestal-mounted field controllers have both front and rear access panels that must be clear of obstructions.

- *Environment*—Field controllers should be located in an environment that is safe for the operation of the equipment. It is recommended that the location be dry and free of excess

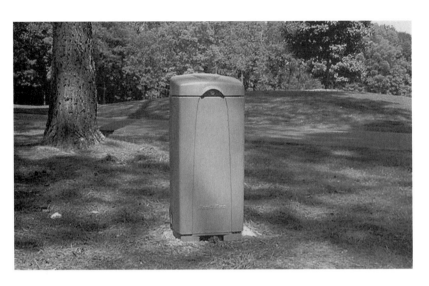

FIGURE 5.21
Typical field controller.

moisture. If flooding is a concern, a field controller should be mounted on a raised concrete base that is higher than any potential floodwater or located at an area away from the flood site (an alternate control method, such as decoders, may be necessary for these areas). The controller environment should provide adequate air circulation to keep components cool. The controller should also be protected from nesting animals and insects. A foam sealant should be used to seal any wire conduits entering the field controller; this will provide a barrier to pests attempting to enter the field controller cabinet. It is also beneficial to position controllers outside the drip line of trees to help in avoiding the root systems during installation, as well as to prevent the roots from intertwining with controller wires. Location outside the trees' drip line can also aid in providing better soil moisture content, which can improve the grounding of the controllers and reduce the possibility of damage to the controllers caused by lightning strikes to the trees. Controllers will stay cleaner, and the chances of the controllers' being damaged by falling tree limbs will also be reduced.

Station Assignment

It is common for many different turf areas (greens, tees, fairways, roughs, etc.), often part of multiple holes, to be wired to a single field controller. A procedure for wiring these various areas to the field controller should be established between the irrigation consultant, designer, superintendent, and irrigation contractor prior to the start of installation. This procedure will dictate the sequence in which valves are assigned to a field controller's station terminal block. By standardizing a wiring procedure, the station assignments between different field controllers across the golf course will exhibit a similar pattern simplifying their management.

A simple station assignment procedure (see Figure 5.22) may be as follows:

1. Start with the lowest hole number.

2. Wire the turf areas in the following order:
   - Greens—front right clockwise
   - Green perimeters—front right clockwise
   - Approaches—front right to left
   - Fairways—right to left, green to tee
   - Tees—right to left, front to back
   - Green surrounds—front left clockwise
   - Roughs—right side, green to tee, then left side, green to tee
   - Bunkers—right side, green to tee, then left side, green to tee
   - Lawn areas

FIGURE 5.22
Typical station wiring sequence.

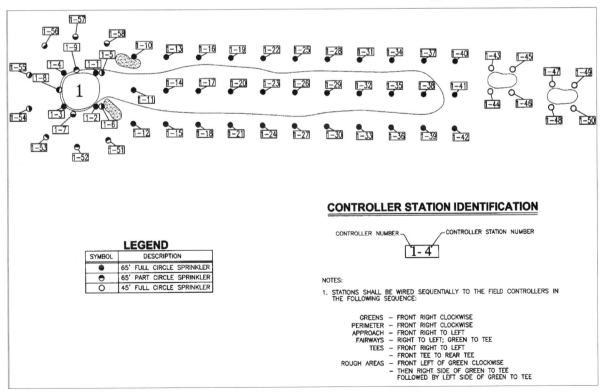

CONTROLLER STATION IDENTIFICATION

CONTROLLER NUMBER — ┐   ┌— CONTROLLER STATION NUMBER

| 1 - 4 |

NOTES:

1. STATIONS SHALL BE WIRED SEQUENTIALLY TO THE FIELD CONTROLLERS IN THE FOLLOWING SEQUENCE:

GREENS — FRONT RIGHT CLOCKWISE
PERIMETER — FRONT RIGHT CLOCKWISE
APPROACH — FRONT RIGHT TO LEFT
FAIRWAYS — RIGHT TO LEFT; GREEN TO TEE
TEES — FRONT RIGHT TO LEFT
     — FRONT TEE TO REAR TEE
ROUGH AREAS — FRONT LEFT OF GREEN CLOCKWISE
     — THEN RIGHT SIDE OF GREEN TO TEE
       FOLLOWED BY LEFT SIDE OF GREEN TO TEE

LEGEND

SYMBOL	DESCRIPTION
●	65' FULL CIRCLE SPRINKLER
◓	65' PART CIRCLE SPRINKLER
○	45' FULL CIRCLE SPRINKLER

Individual Head Control

A typical golf course has numerous microclimates, which can present the irrigation system manager with challenges in matching a specific plant water requirement with the abilities of the irrigation system. An irrigation system that offers individual sprinkler control (individual head control) provides the most programming flexibility. *Individual head control* refers to an individual station wire provided for each sprinkler (one sprinkler, one wire). For example: A putting green has four sprinklers to provide coverage to the putting surface. Individually controlled sprinklers allow each sprinkler to be operated independently, so that the sprinkler that is positioned on the portion of green that has the greatest plant water requirement can be adjusted to supply a greater volume of water to that area. Individual head control is also beneficial when sprinklers are spaced in an odd pattern because of an unusual feature, such as an exceptionally large cape on a green in which an out-of-pattern sprinkler is required to provide coverage. Controlling the sprinklers independently can assist in matching their application rates.

Depending on the size of the irrigation system, individual head control may add only a small percentage to the cost of the irrigation system, especially if it is used in selected areas only, such as in greens and tees and areas with unique microclimates or different soils that would benefit from the additional control.

Grouping Sprinklers

Depending on the irrigation system and the project's budget, individual head control may not be affordable or even necessary. The practice of running two or more valves from a single field controller station output is called pairing sprinklers or grouping sprinklers. It is extremely important to identify sprinklers that cover areas with identical plant water requirements before wiring them together at a field controller. Before pairing sprinklers, the following should be consistent between the sprinklers:

- Precipitation rate
- Soil type
- Slope
- Exposure
- Plant type

The piping network must also be sized to accommodate the additional flow of multiple sprinklers run from a single station output. If operating from a central control system, the flow (or hydraulic) tree must be set up to manage the additional flow that pairing sprinklers will require. At the field controller the activation of additional valves will place a greater electrical demand on a station output. Check with the manufacturer's field controller specifications to ensure that the controller will be able to satisfy the additional electrical demand of any paired stations. The controller may have a station current overload protection feature, which should be set to the actual station demand. This device should be set for each station on the field controller only after it is wired.

The pairing of sprinklers can reduce the number of field controller stations required, thus also reducing the cost of the control system. It is always best to wire each sprinkler or valve individually to a field controller and then pair the sprinkler station wires at the controller, rather than wiring them together in the field. Wiring sprinklers individually will allow for separation of sprinklers in the future if it is determined that there are different water requirements.

POWER WIRING

Power to the central equipment, field controllers, and any additional irrigation components should be supplied from a dedicated circuit breaker. This will help protect the power supply from interruptions caused by other devices. The circuit breaker should be sized to the next highest capacity for the full load of the circuit and in accordance with NEC. When multiple power sources are used on a site, they must never be interconnected, as that would violate NEC requirements. Surge protection devices for circuit breakers are available and should be considered. These UL-listed devices are installed inside the circuit breaker panel of the equipment they are designed to protect. If an electrical surge or spike were to originate from the utility power source, this type of surge protection is designed to divert the surge to the building's earth grounding network.

An uninterruptible power supply (UPS) should be considered for the central equipment's power supply. Such devices provide several minutes of standby power in the event of a power failure. Some of these devices include a software routine that senses the loss of power and automatically diverts to a temporary battery supply. If the battery power supply begins to run down before the utility power supply is restored, some of these devices will activate a Windows shutdown routine that will first save any open file data, safely close any operating irrigation programming software, and then retire the computer itself. Some UPS devices have built-in power supply monitoring software that will track the date and time of any power interruption, aiding in the troubleshooting of power supplies. In sizing a UPS, it is important to know the difference between the *run time* and the *capacity* of each unit. The run time is the amount of time the UPS will be able to provide power from its battery for a given load. Thus, run time tells an operator how long a UPS can provide power during a power outage before the battery runs out. The greater the load, the shorter the standby run time available.

A UPS has a nominal maximum capacity—usually indicated in the name of the unit—for example, APC 650. The 650 denotes that it can provide 650 volt amperes (VA) to the load. The individual loads of all devices being operated from a UPS can be calculated by simply adding the VA requirements stamped on the products' nameplates. These devices are typically the personal computer's central processing unit (CPU) and the computer monitor.

Many manufacturers of golf course control systems recommend the use of a line conditioner, voltage stabilizer, or constant voltage transformer. Such a device is located directly after the circuit breaker at each power source. All are designed to regulate the voltage and provide a constant power supply to the field controllers. They protect against voltage sag and brownout conditions as low as 65 percent of the voltage they are designed to supply. In addition, a constant voltage transformer will act as a surge suppressor. Available in 120, 208, and 240 volt configurations, they are sized by the total demand of the circuit. Taking the full load amp demand and multiplying it by the voltage required for the circuit provides the total volt amp (VA) requirement of the circuit. As a safety measure, the total calculated VA load is increased by 30 percent (multiplied by 1.3) to arrive at minimum size of the constant voltage transformer.

120V, 240V

Because of the increasing complexity of field controllers and irrigation systems, there has been an increase in electrical power requirements. The result can be some very large-gauge power wire. In the

United States, wire is sized by American Wire Gauge (AWG). The lower the gauge number, the larger the wire diameter.

Most manufacturers provide field controllers with dual voltage (120/240) transformers, and power wire design can be based on either voltage. When the voltage is increased from 120V to 240V, the amperage is reduced by one-half. This reduces the wire gauge (size) required for the circuit. It also doubles the allowable voltage loss, according to the NEC.

An economically sensitive power wire design will take into consideration the abilities and requirements of the field controllers and balance them with the hydraulic capabilities of the system.

Sizing

The correct sizing of field controller power wire is essential to the proper operation of an irrigation control system. Power supply, like the system's water supply, is a resource that rarely improves over time. As new demands are placed on electrical services, such as by commercial development and residential expansion, there may be a reduction in the incoming voltage. It is important that the sizing of power wire takes into consideration the possible fluctuations in the incoming supply. For example, a power source may provide 120V during the winter, but during the summer months, when irrigation systems are needed most, additional demands caused by pumps starting or an increase in air-conditioning use may result in the reduction of the available voltage supply to 115V. A conservative wire design should take into consideration the potential variables. Irrigation equipment is typically designed to operate at ±10 percent of its rated voltage. Operating a device at a lower voltage will increase the current demand and increase the heat in the component, thus shortening its life span.

A modern satellite control system provides a high degree of field and central control functionality, and the capabilities of field controllers must be identified. Advanced capabilities can greatly affect the potential load on the circuit. Each field controller has an electrical demand while at rest. This demand is stated as the field controller's draw and is expressed in amps. As solenoids are activated, additional electrical demands are added to the power requirement of the field controller, increasing its total amp load. These demands must be identified by the designer and system operator so that the field controller can perform to the established design criteria. Manufacturers provide charts that show field controller electrical data. Typically, these charts communicate controller model, amp draw when the controller is not operating valve solenoids, and amp draw with solenoids operating. These charts also communicate the maximum number of solenoids that can be operated by the controller.

The following system parameters must be considered in using these charts:

- The maximum number of solenoids operating at one time. This must be identified for each field controller. It is not uncommon for a field controller to have different operating conditions at different times of the day. For example, daytime syringing may require a larger number of stations to be activated simultaneously than would be activated for nighttime irrigation. In addition, radio control of the irrigation system can make it very easy for a system operator to simultaneously activate a multitude of solenoids, thus increasing the demand at a particular field controller.
- The available pipe size to perform the requested function. The flow management element of the central control software will restrict flow to an area based on the pipe sizing in that area. This flow restriction is often the limiting factor in determining the maximum number of stations that can be activated from a satellite.

The total demand for each power supply wire is the sum of each field controller's electrical demand, in amps, on that particular power wire. It is important to follow the NEC in sizing power wire. The 2002 NEC states, in Section 210.19(A), FPN No.4:

> Conductors for branched circuits as defined in Article 100, sized to prevent a voltage drop exceeding 3 percent at the farthest outlet of power, heating and lighting loads, or combination of such loads, and where the maximum total voltage drop on both feeders and branch circuits to the farthest outlet does not exceed 5 percent, will provide a reasonable efficiency of operation.

The designer must choose the wire size that will provide no more than the allowable voltage drop (typically 5 percent) between the source and the power supply to all field controllers on each circuit.

The voltage drop in a circuit can be calculated by the following formula, known as the resistance method of wire sizing:

$$V_d = \frac{2L \times I \times R}{1000}$$

where

V_d = voltage drop in volts

L = distance from source to the load (in thousands of ft) multiplied by 2 for return circuit

I = current in amperes

R = resistance of conductor per thousand ft

EXAMPLE 5.3

Four field controllers are located 1400 ft from a power source that provides 115 volts. Each controller has a maximum operating load of .70 amps. What size should the power wire be?

1. Determine the maximum allowable voltage loss: 115 volts × 5% = 5.75 volts

2. Determine the maximum circuit load: 4 controllers × .70 amps = 2.8 amps

3. Select wire resistance in 1000 ft from the "Conductor Properties" chart in the appendix. For buried wire use the values for 77°F (25°C); for aboveground installations use the values for 149°F (65°C).

4. Apply formula:

$$V_d = \frac{2 \times 1400 \times 2.8 \times 1.015 \text{ (\#10 AWG copper)}}{1000} = 7.96 \text{ volts}$$

Because the voltage loss for the circuit exceeds the maximum allowable voltage loss when using #10 AWG wire, the calculation must be repeated using a larger conductor:

$$V_d = \frac{2 \times 1400 \times 2.8 \times .652 \text{ (\#8 AWG copper)}}{1000} = 5.11 \text{ volts}$$

The total voltage loss for the circuit utilizing #8 AWG is below the maximum allowable loss of 5.75 volts, so it should be selected.

Power wire is available in several forms of wires and cables. Individual power wires are color-coded black (hot), white (common), and green, or bare copper (equipment ground). The black and white wires are sized for the load they are carrying, and are the same size. An equipment ground wire is required by NEC and is used as a safety circuit that causes a circuit breaker to trip in case the circuit is wired incorrectly. The green or bare copper wire must be sized per NEC code for Type UF. Power wire that is placed in electrical conduit is Type THHN/THWN. The 2002 NEC requirements for Equipment Ground Size, Tables 250-122 and 310-16, are as shown:

Black/White	Type UF Green or Bare Copper
#10 AWG	#10 AWG
8	10
6	10
4	8
2	8
1/0	6

Also available is a cable containing all three conductors within a common jacket. When using a multiconductor cable, it is not necessary to size the ground wire because the manufacturer will have already sized it.

Beyond the irrigation control system there may be many other devices that have significant electrical requirements on a golf course. These devices can range from the pumping station, the pond aeration and water treatment equipment, to fans, lights, drinking water fountains, and dewatering pumps. As with the design of the irrigation control system, the proper sizing of the electrical services and supply wiring for these components is essential. An experienced irrigation consultant or electrical engineer should be contacted to size these electrical systems.

Routing

On large irrigation systems it is not uncommon to have multiple power legs originating from a single source. Installing a separate circuit breaker and constant voltage transformer for each leg provides the opportunity to isolate each power leg in the event that trouble-shooting or service is required.

Power wire to field controllers must be installed according to local code. In Table 300-5 of the 2002 NEC, minimum cover requirements for wires carrying 0 to 600 volts are listed. Direct burial cables and conductors of 120/240V are classified as Type 1 wiring circuits and must be buried a minimum of 24 in. deep, or 18 in. if under 4 in. thick concrete that has no vehicular traffic. Because of its depth requirement, power cable is usually placed in the same trench with the pipe, as long as local code permits. Power wire is typically placed on the bottom of the trench and to the side of any pipe in the trench. This helps to protect it from any potential excavations. To allow for service and maintenance, it is desirable to separate controller power wire from other irrigation system wiring, such as zone wire and communication cable (see Figure 5.23). Some irrigation field controller manufacturers specify the safe distance between power wire and communication cables to reduce the possibility of electrical interference.

FIGURE 5.23
Trench with pipe and wire.

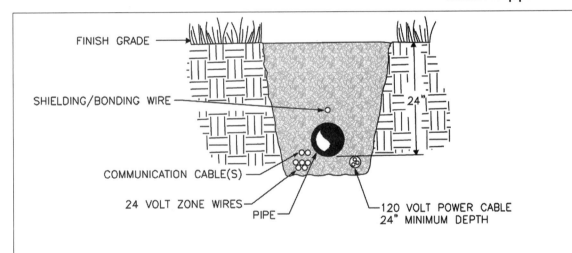

1. WIRE SHALL BE "SNAKED" IN TRENCH WITH MINIMUM 1% SLACK.
2. THERE SHALL BE A MINIMUM 36" EXPANSION LOOP IN ALL WIRES AT EACH CHANGE OF DIRECTION FITTING 45° OR MORE.
3. ALL LIKE WIRES SHALL BE TAPED TOGETHER EVERY 10'.
4. ALL 24 VOLT WIRES AND COMMUNICATION CABLE SHALL BE PLACED A MINIMUM OF 12" BELOW GRADE EXCEPT WHEN CROSSING ROADWAYS OR PARKING LOTS WHERE DEPTH SHALL BE A MINIMUM OF 24" BELOW GRADE.
5. SHIELDING/BONDING WIRE SHALL BE MINIMUM #6 AWG SOLID BARE COPPER PLACED 12" TO 18" BELOW GRADE AND A MINIMUM 4" ABOVE PIPE.

COMMUNICATION WIRING

Central-controlled irrigation systems require a communication link between the central and field controllers. They may also be required to communicate with weather stations and pumping stations. These links provide the flow of program data and/or start commands to and from the field controllers, field switching devices, weather stations, or pumping stations. This is typically accomplished via radio or a hardwire connection. Hardwire communication methods can differ dramatically between control system manufacturers. It is important to follow each manufacturer's recommendations for communication cable sizing and installation before finalizing the communication cable design. Some of the major differences between hardwired communication systems include the following:

- *Types of wire*—Communication wire can vary dramatically from 12-2 PE wire (12-gauge, two conductor polyethylene insulated wire in a UF jacket) to 20-8 multiconductor wire with eight 20-gauge wires, each in an individual PE jacket, with an outer wrapping encasing all the conductors. Some manufacturers recommend a drain wire and shielding within the multiconductor wire to help protect signals from static or transient voltage within the same trench.

- *Signal types*—The communication signals can differ dramatically between equipment manufacturers. Signal voltage can vary from a coded 24VAC source to a low-voltage and low-current digital signal like a telephone signal. Regardless of signal type, most manufacturers recommend separating the communication cable from other conductors carrying a higher voltage.

- *Routing*—Communication wire typically originates from a central location. Telephone and/or radio devices can provide remote communication to the central. Communication wires must be routed in accordance with the manufacturer's recommendations. Some call for multiple wire paths originating from the central. Others require a single wire path that routes through each field controller and then returns to the central controller. Some manufacturers allow their communication wire to be spliced in the field, creating a three-way (or more) connection to various devices, whereas other manufacturers forbid splices except inside controller pedestals. Weather stations and pumping stations typically require their own dedicated communication cable, with no splices.

- *Other considerations*—There are often limitations on the maximum length of a communication path, whether it is a terminal path or a looped configuration. In addition, some manufacturers have limitations on how many field controllers or decoders can be included on a single cable path. As in any design, care must be taken to size the cable correctly so that these limitations are observed.

ZONE WIRING

The power from field controllers to the electric valves and valve-in-head sprinklers is distributed through the zone wire (also referred to as 24 volt wire, or low-voltage wire). Such wires provide the 24 VAC required for the operation of a valve solenoid coil. Zone wires consist of two wires: a single wire from the field controller to each valve or valve-in-head sprinkler, called the control, "hot," or signal wire, and a second wire is routed from the field controller to all valves and valve-in-head sprinklers on the field controller. The second wire is referred to as the common wire. These two wires complete the 24 VAC circuit.

Zone wire is insulated with either a UF PVC jacket or PE (polyethylene) jacket. These wires are typically color coded so they can be easily identified in the field. The signal or "hot" wire is typically colored red. However, a color-coding scheme involving an array of colors is often used to identify different areas of control (greens, tees, fairways, surrounds, roughs, spare wire, etc.). (Note that the NEC states that green wire must be used for equipment ground.) It may also be a good idea to use a different color-coding scheme if a new automatic system is being installed over an older system, to distinguish the new wiring from the old. The common wire is often colored white or yellow and is typically at least one wire gauge larger than the zone wire. The larger size is necessary because the common wire will carry the load from multiple solenoids running simultaneously. If the wire is not larger, with the associated higher resistance, the voltage loss could be unacceptably high.

Zone wire must be sized to provide a continuous 24 VAC (±10 percent) power supply to each valve or sprinkler regardless of its distance from the field controller. This power is supplied by the controller's step-down transformer (secondary transformer). This transformer reduces the 120 or 240 volt power supply to the controller to the 24 volt supply required by most valve solenoids. The total number of solenoids that can be activated by a controller is limited to its transformer capacity. This is typically expressed as its volt-amp (VA) output, which refers to its operating voltage, multiplied by its amp rating.

Some of the considerations that apply to sizing field controller power wire must also be used in sizing the zone wire. The distance between the controller and the valve, as well as the number of valves operating on a single common wire, are sizing variables. An irrigation consultant or irrigation system designer often prepares a project specification that identifies the maximum allowable distance between the field controller and a solenoid. Each field controller should utilize its own valve common wire(s) and should not share a common wire with another controller. This will help in future troubleshooting of the 24 VAC wiring network and meet the requirements of NEC.

The electrical requirement of a typical valve solenoid is expressed in volt-amps (VA) and is known as the "apparent power" of an AC current circuit. The simple calculation is the voltage required multiplied by the amp draw; this is used to determine how many solenoids can be connected to a certain size transformer. For example, a typical solenoid may be rated as follows:

Voltage requirement—24 VAC, 60 Hz
Inrush current—.41 A, 9.84 VA (24 VAC × .41 A = 9.84 VA)
Operating current—.23 A, 5.52 VA (24 VAC × .23 = 5.52 VA)
Resistance—24 ohms

The static pressure of an irrigation system will affect the electrical requirement of a valve solenoid. The higher the water pressure, the greater the inrush current required to actuate the solenoid. Many controllers have the ability to actuate multiple solenoids from a single station output. This potential simultaneous demand must be accounted for, and therefore the inrush current is used for sizing valve wire.

Manufacturers provide charts and electrical data for the electrical requirements of their solenoids. These charts show either the electrical characteristics at various operating pressures, or a single electrical requirement at the maximum operating pressure of the valve or valve-in-head sprinkler.

The total current requirement for the 24VAC (secondary) side of a controller must be added to the controller's operating current to arrive at the total full load for the controller. The secondary current requirement is expressed as the current demand at 24VAC and must be converted to the current requirement at the controller's operating voltage. This conversion is made by dividing the controller's operating voltage by the solenoid operating voltage to arrive at a current multiplier.

EXAMPLE 5.4

A controller has an operating voltage of 115 VAC and a secondary operating voltage of 24 VAC. The controller will operate six solenoids with an inrush current of .41 A each.

1. Calculate the total solenoid current requirement:

   6 solenoids × .41 each = 2.46 A (at 24 VAC)

2. Calculate the interpolation factor between the controller operating voltage and the secondary operating voltage:

$$\frac{115 \text{ VAC}}{24 \text{ VAC}} = 4.8$$

3. Divide the total solenoid current requirement by the interpolation factor to arrive at the solenoid current requirement at the controller's operating voltage:

$$\frac{2.46 \text{ A}}{4.8} = .51 \text{ A at 115 VAC}$$

4. Add the solenoid current requirement to the controller's (at rest) current requirement to find the total full load current requirement for the controller at 115 VAC.

Zone wire to valves and valve-in-head sprinklers must be installed according to code. In Table 300-5 of the 2002 NEC, minimum cover requirements for "Type 5 Circuits for Control of Irrigation and Landscape Lighting Limited to Not More Than 30 Volts and Installed with Type UF or in Other Identified Cable or Raceway" are identified as 6 in. Under streets, roads, highways, alleys, driveways, and parking lots the minimum depth of bury is stated as 24 in. For golf course installations, zone wire is typically buried at least 12 in. in order to avoid damage from maintenance equipment and deep-tine aerators. Because of this depth of bury requirement, zone wire is typically placed in the same trench with the pipe, as long as local code permits.

There are special splice kits especially designed for making waterproof connections in low-voltage zone wires. UL-listed grease-filled tubes are a popular choice and provide a quick and easily serviceable wire connection. These tubes are also easily removed to aid in troubleshooting and system repairs. There should be only one splice per splice kit. All wires should be spliced in accordance with local regulations or by the following procedure: Make all splices by stripping ¾ in. to 1 in. of insulation from the copper conductors, twist the copper conductors together, fasten with the appropriate wire nut, and insert into the appropriate waterproof compound. The waterproofing compound should cover all bared copper surfaces. At the splice location there should be a minimum of 24 in. of slack so the splice can be raised for inspection. All underground splices not located at a control valve site should be housed in a valve box and marked on the Record Drawing. All splices at controller locations should be made inside the controller pedestal or an enclosure, such as a valve box, adjacent to the pedestal pad.

PROTECTION PROCEDURES

Grounding

To protect irrigation equipment from the potentially devastating effects of lightning and other surges, a grounding system for field controllers, weather stations, and central control systems must be installed. Proper grounding is the backbone of any lightning protection system.

Lightning protection and grounding systems are designed to conduct the electrical energy of a power surge or lightning strike to a path away from the equipment. These surges can be caused by the switching or cycling of motors, load switching by a utility company, or lightning strikes on the golf course, or can be lightning-induced surges from several miles away that are conducted over the electrical supply. Such surges can result in costly repairs and irrigation system downtime.

Irrigation systems are particularly vulnerable to lightning-induced surges. The average lightning strike produces a surge of 25,000 volts and 20,000 amps. These surges can be conducted through the irrigation system's zone wire, power wire, and communication cable to the control system. Without a good ground system, the irrigation control system will not survive these surges.

The effectiveness of grounding systems is a function of their resistance and inductance.

Resistance refers to the opposition to the flow of electricity in a circuit and is measured in ohms. A lower ohms reading indicates in less opposition to the flow of electricity and, consequently, a more effective ground. Irrigation system manufacturers provide recommendations for minimum earth ground resistance. These recommendations typically include a goal for earth ground resistance.

Many factors affect resistance:

- *Soil resistance*—A grounding system will discharge the excess energy to the soil around the ground electrodes. The lower the resistance of the soil, the lower the earth ground reading and the greater the potential for equipment protection. Soil resistance is affected by the soil material, moisture content, and temperature. A clay soil has lower average resistance than a sandy soil and will yield a lower resistance to ground, as will a moist soil as compared with a dry soil. A minimum soil moisture level of 15 percent must be maintained. As soil temperature drops, so does the resistance of the soil. The resistance of water increases as it approaches the freezing level and then jumps dramatically lower below freezing.

- *Type and size of the ground electrode*—As a guide, note that the larger the ground electrode, the better the earth ground reading, inasmuch as a larger electrode will have more surface area in contact with the soil. Ground electrodes should be copper coated and UL listed or manufactured to the requirements of NEC for "made" electrodes. The most common ground electrodes are ground rods and ground plates. Ground rods should be made of high-tensile steel with a 10 mil copper skin. Rods should be UL listed with a minimum diameter of $\frac{5}{8}$ in. and a minimum length of 8 ft. Ground rods are usually installed in the vertical position. Ground plates should have a minimum 2 sq ft exposed surface area and be constructed of a copper alloy with a minimum thickness of .06 in. A grounding conductor should be attached to the plate by a welding process. Plates are usually installed in the horizontal position.

- *Connections*—Connections add resistance. Loose connections will not provide a good bond between a grounding conductor and an electrode. Exothermic connections, made by the chemical/molecular bonding of two metals, are the most desirable because they eliminate the mechanical connection between the two materials. Mechanical connections (ground lugs, split bolts, etc.) will loosen over time because of expansion and contraction with temperature changes.

There are several instruments on the market that can test the resistance of a ground system. The two commonly used devices are null-balance earth testers and clamp-on test meters. Each instrument has its own operating principles. The null-balance earth tester (often referred to as a Megger) requires the ground network be disconnected from the equipment prior to testing, whereas the clamp-on type requires the connection to the equipment. The null-balance earth tester is the only effective tester for decoder systems. Regardless of what type of testing equipment is used, the resistance readings should be taken and recorded prior to the permanent connection of the earth ground to the equipment. It is advisable to have the ground network installed several weeks prior to its testing so as to get good soil-to-electrode contact. Because of seasonal variations in soil moisture content, it is a good idea to periodically check earth grounds to ensure that they meet the manufacturer's minimum requirements. Soil amendments can be used to reduce soil resistivity. These materials, often referred to as "ground enhancement" materials or "earth contact" materials, are specially designed to improve earth ground readings while being noncorrosive to earth ground equipment. These materials, if required, should be installed before the permanent connection to the irrigation equipment is made.

The *inductance* of a ground system refers to the geometry (spacing), and shape of the conductors and electrodes of the various ground grid components. This is a phenomenon that is related to the opposition of the flow of electricity, the inductance of the ground grid, and the signal frequency of lightning. The higher the frequencies of the electrical surge, the higher the opposition. Simple grounding geometry (fewer bends and connections) promotes lower inductance.

The *impedance* of a grounding system refers to the total opposition to electrical flow in an alternating current circuit created by its resistance, inductance, and frequency. In grounding systems inductance is the greatest source of impedance.

It is imperative that a good grounding system for a golf course irrigation system be properly designed. The design of a ground system requires knowledge of the laws of physics and electrical engineering principles and is best left to the experts.

The American Society of Irrigation Consultants (ASIC) has developed ASIC Guideline 100-2002 for Earth Grounding Electronic Equipment in Irrigation Systems. This guideline is the most comprehensive document available and is an excellent resource.

Shielding and Bonding

Another means of protecting an irrigation system from the effects of lightning and lightning-induced surges is the installation of a shielding/bonding wire. A shielding wire is essentially a single #6 AWG solid bare copper wire that is placed in the same trench with pipe and wire. It is positioned approximately 4 in. above the pipe, and its purpose is to intercept any transient voltages traveling across the surface of the golf course and to shield the irrigation system wiring. Shielding wire is typically installed 12 in. to 18 in. deep so as to prevent possible damage from maintenance equipment and aerators.

The shield/bond wire is laid in the trench as straight as possible. All bends should be made as a gentle sweep, thereby reducing the impedance. The shield/bond wire is connected to all controller ground lugs. Each power source should have its own shield wire. When shield/bond wires must be spliced, an exothermic connector should be used.

RELATED SYSTEMS

Drinking Fountains

Golf course irrigation designers are often asked to include a system of drinking fountains in their projects. Pipe and wire for fountains are usually installed in the trench with irrigation pipe. Piping to drinking fountains is covered by codes that are different from those covering irrigation piping. Health codes come into play because the pipe carries potable water.

Typically, PE or PVC pipe is installed to supply drinking fountains. Both must be stamped with the National Sanitation Foundation

(NSF) designation "NSF-pw," signifying that they are approved for use with potable water in accordance with NSF Standard No. 14 (NSF/ANSI 14-2002). According to the National Standard Plumbing Code, all pipe used for potable water service piping must be pressure rated for at least 160 psi. The PE pipe typically used is SIDR 9 PE 3408. It is pressure rated at 160 psi, and joints are usually made with brass insert fittings with stainless steel clamps. The PVC pipe used most often is Schedule 40, but SDR 21 and SDR 26 pipe can also meet the code. If the PVC pipe has solvent weld joints, the primer and solvent cement must be NSF approved for use with potable water. If gasket joints are used, the gasket rings and lubricant must also be NSF approved for use with potable water.

Some codes mandate a minimum separation between pipes carrying potable water and those carrying irrigation water. If the irrigation water is treated effluent, the codes are very specific about minimum separation, both in the horizontal and vertical planes.

Obviously, drinking water piping cannot be connected to irrigation piping. If the irrigation and drinking water systems are supplied by a single feed from a city main, the tap for the drinking water must be located upstream of the backflow prevention device, so that there is no way the potable water can be contaminated by water coming from the irrigation system. Valving in the vault or pump house where the taps are located must be clearly labeled to indicate what is potable and what is not. If PVC pipe is used for potable water, it is a good idea to specify pipe of a different color or pressure rating (or both) from the irrigation pipe, so as to reduce the possibility of connecting the two. Most codes require that pipe carrying treated effluent be colored purple for this reason. Designers should check local codes for requirements concerning pipe specifications, pipe separation, backflow prevention, and flushing and disinfection of new potable water piping.

The hydraulics of a drinking water system are similar to those of an irrigation system, except that the pipe in drinking fountain systems is seldom looped. Valves in drinking fountains open and close quickly, so velocities and water hammer must be considered. It is desirable to keep pipes as small as possible (consistent with velocity limits and the pressure requirements of the fountains) to reduce the time water spends in the pipes, because both PE and PVC can impart a slightly offensive taste to water.

Calculations of pressure loss because of friction and elevation must be completed just as they are for an irrigation system. Isolation valves should be installed at all piping tees to facilitate repairs. An isolation valve and a filter should be installed at the base of each fountain. All valves should be installed in valve boxes and accurately located on the Record Drawings. Pressure regulators may be needed at fountains. In northern locations, fittings at the bases of fountains should allow easy disconnect for both water and electricity because the units are usually removed and stored indoors during winter months. Finally, fountain systems in northern climates should be drained or winterized with compressed air, so appropriate fittings should be included in the design.

Drinking fountains (or any other auxiliary equipment) should not be connected to the power wiring supplying the satellite controllers. Controllers are very sensitive to spikes and dips in voltage. The compressors in drinking fountains have a relatively high current demand, and their across-the-line starting can pull voltage down significantly. The separate power wiring for fountains (or other equipment) should be of a different color or a different type (UF vs. TC [Tray Cable], for example) from the satellite power wire to avoid confusion or incorrect connections during installation and later maintenance procedures. If the fountains can operate on 240 volt power, the wire sizes will be smaller and less expensive. If many fountains are involved, several different sources may be needed to keep wire sizes reasonable.

Telephones

Telephone cable is often installed in irrigation trenches. Many golf courses have a network of telephones for emergency purposes. Some have phones at the eighth or ninth tees so that orders can be placed for snacks to be ready at the halfway house. Others have dedicated telephone lines for voice or data links to the pump house. Direct burial cable for telephones should meet the requirements of Rural Electric Authority (REA) PE-39 or PE-54. Cables should be specified with spare pairs of conductors. If splices are necessary in these cables, they should be made only in aboveground junction boxes.

Other Auxiliary Equipment

Irrigation designers are asked to specify and size power wire for a variety of other nonirrigation components, including fans at greens, floodlights, pond aerators and circulators, subsurface airflow systems at greens, and so forth. The procedures for sizing the wire are the same as those used to size controller power wire. Many of these components have high amp loads relative to satellite controllers. They should be on a power cable separate from that supplying the satellite controllers. A cable type or color different from that of the satellite power cable should be specified. All auxiliary equipment and the related wiring should be accurately shown on the Record Drawings.

PROJECT DOCUMENTS

In order for a golf course irrigation system to be bid, priced, or installed, a set of project documents must be prepared to show the installer what equipment is to be used, where it is to be installed, and how it is to be installed. As a minimum, the project documents include drawings and specifications (Figure 5.24). There may also be other documents, depending on the type of project and how it is being contracted for installation.

TABLE OF CONTENTS
FOR
SPECIFICATIONS AND DRAWINGS

SPECIFICATIONS

DIVISION		TITLE
	A.	Table of Contents
	B.	Instructions to Bidders
	C.	Bid Form
	D.	Insurance and Bonding Requirements
	E.	Supplementary Conditions
	F.	Irrigation Technical Specifications

DRAWINGS

SHEET	TITLE
	Cover Sheet
IR-1	Sprinkler and Piping Plan
IR-2	Control and Wiring Plan (Hunter)
IR-3	Control and Wiring Plan (Rain Bird)
IR-4	Control and Wiring Plan (Toro)
IR-5	Irrigation Details

FIGURE 5.24
Project documents including drawings and specifications.

Plans

Plans for an irrigation system should minimally consist of a sprinkler and piping plan, a control plan, and installation details. The sprinkler and piping plan will show the sprinklers, indicate their type, and show the piping that feeds them. The pipe sizing will be shown, as well as the locations of the quick coupling, isolation, drain, and air release valves. The piping plan may also show other accessory items that are part of the system. A separate electrical or control plan must be provided, as it is confusing to have the wiring and piping on the same drawing. The control plan indicates controllers and the sprinklers they control, wire sizes and routes, and power sources, if required. Although one control plan may be used for a number of different manufacturers, there may be several control plans representing the equipment of different golf course irrigation manufacturers. The detail sheet indicates how the various pieces of equipment are supposed to be installed (Figure 5.25). Other drawings can be part of the project drawing too. These may include pond, utility, coverage, pump system, and/or pump house drawings.

Specifications

A set of plans alone is not a good way of presenting the irrigation system design. The plans should be accompanied by a comprehensive set of technical specifications. Specifications complement the plans and provide much more detail about the irrigation system than can be shown in the drawings, notes, or details. The technical specifications detail the equipment to be used, its performance requirements, acceptable manufacturers, and the reference standards and codes that are applicable to the project. Through the specifications the designer dictates the equipment that can be installed to maintain the design intent. Specifications are commonly divided into three sections within a Construction Specifications Institute (CSI) format: General, Equipment or Components, and Installation or Execution. The General section outlines things such as qualifications, storage issues, submittals, permits, and the like, items that are general in nature. The Equipment section outlines all of the equipment that is to be installed. It describes the features required such as the pressure, radius and gpm of the sprinklers. The type of pipe and fittings to be used are also included in this section. The specifications may identify one manufacturer, several manufacturers, or leave it up to the sup-

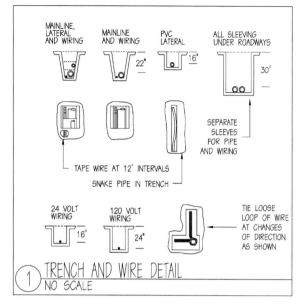

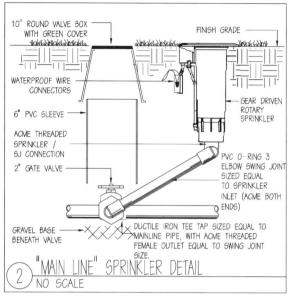

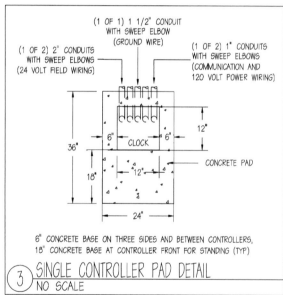

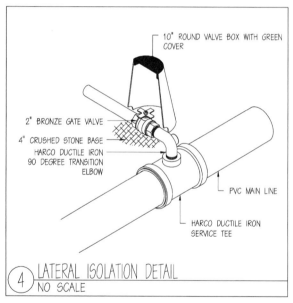

FIGURE 5.25

Detail sheets like these indicate how the various pieces of equipment should be installed.

plier for each piece of equipment. The Execution section outlines how each piece of equipment is to be installed and complements the detail drawings. Rock removal, trenching requirements, and turf restoration are examples of items included in the Execution section of the specifications. Other formats can be used for specifications as well.

Specifications are also the basis for resolving conflicts in the installation of the system. The specifications either state that things must be done a specific way or that specific items must be used, or they do not. They clarify what is expected on what can be a legal or a regulatory basis. Specifications can also be used to determine liability, especially if standards or codes were referenced but not followed. Specifications that reference codes and standards protect the designer to a certain extent, as long as the standard or code referenced was part of normal golf course irrigation design practices.

Other Documents

Depending on the process used to contract the installation, a number of other documents may be included in the project documents. These may include Instructions to Bidders, outlining how to bid the project; insurance requirements for the installing company; and the bid form on which to submit the bid. They may also include general conditions for the overall project, as well as supplementary general conditions specific to the irrigation system or to the project. A sample of the contract may be included so that bidders will be able to see what type of agreement they are going to have to enter into. Reference forms, equipment forms, and bonding requirements are also commonly part of the project documents.

SCHEDULING

The goal of a golf course irrigation system is to apply a precise amount of water when it is needed at the highest possible efficiency, minimizing water losses. This is achieved by the proper design and scheduling of the irrigation system. Irrigation scheduling refers to the calculation of each field controller's station precipitation rate, the amount of water to apply, and when to apply it in order to maintain consistent playing conditions across the golf course.

During the design phase, the designer formulates a water use projection for the golf course, which is typically based on historical seasonal demands. Estimates of station precipitation rates are derived from these projections, and they become guidelines for calculating run times once the system is installed. A revised schedule must be developed once the central or field control system is operational. The most current copy of the irrigation contractor's "as installed" record drawing or an up-to-date GPS Record Drawing is essential in taking this next step. Information from the record drawing will be used to develop a schedule, which can be fine-tuned and adjusted to accommodate seasonal variation.

The efficient delivery of water to a golf course is not simply the application of water 10 minutes a night to each station; it is the application of a precise amount of precipitation from each sprinkler when it is needed. The irrigation system manager should view scheduling in the context of inches of water required for each area, which is expressed as a run time in minutes per station.

The irrigation schedule is developed with the use of the following information:

- Station precipitation rate
- Local or site evapotranspiration rate
- Crop coefficients for the various turfgrass species
- Area adjustment factors (microclimate)
- Station adjustment factors
- Sprinkler application uniformity

This information is required to complete the irrigation schedule and is used to calculate the individual station run time requirement for each sprinkler on the golf course:

$$R = \frac{ET_o \times K_c \times \text{Area}_{(type)} \times \text{Station}_{(adj)} \times 60}{PR \times AE}$$

where

$\quad R$ = the controller station run time in minutes

$\quad ET_o$ = the estimated site evapotranspiration rate in inches

$\quad K_C$ = the crop coefficient

$\text{Area}_{(type)}$ = the golf course area type adjustment factor expressed as a percentage

$\text{Station}_{(adj)}$ = the specific controller station adjustment factor expressed as a percentage

$\quad 60$ = constant that will convert a sprinkler's precipitation rate to run time in minutes

$\quad PR$ = the average precipitation rate of the sprinkler in inches per hour

$\quad AE$ = sprinkler application efficiency expressed as a percentage

Most central control systems provide some means of aiding an irrigation system manager in developing an irrigation schedule. However, even without the help of a central controller, the preceding formula can be used to develop a station run time and total application requirement.

Precipitation Rate

The key to achieving a good irrigation schedule is to obtain, and maintain, an accurate record of all components of the irrigation system. The sprinklers are the prime components of any irrigation system, as they will ultimately deliver the water to the turfgrass plant. The precipitation rate is the average rate at which sprinklers apply water to a given area. Precipitation rate is expressed in inches per hour (in./hr). The factors that affect the precipitation rate are sprinkler flow, measured in gallons per minute (gpm), and the area within the sprinklers' spacing.

A full-circle (360-degree) sprinkler's precipitation rate is calculated with the following formula:

$$PR = \frac{96.3 \times \text{gpm}}{S \times L}$$

where

PR = precipitation rate in inches per hour

96.3 = a constant to convert cubic inches of water per gallon to inches per square foot per hour

gpm = the gallons per minute discharged by a full-circle sprinkler

S = spacing in feet between sprinklers

L = spacing in feet between rows

The constant 96.3 is derived as follows:

1 gallon = 231 cubic inches

1 square foot = 144 square inches

If 1 gallon of water is applied to 1 square foot of area, the depth of water is calculated as follows:

$$\frac{231}{144} = 1.604 \text{ inches per square foot}$$

One of the multipliers in the upper part of the precipitation rate formula is the gallons per minute of a the sprinkler. To convert this to gallons per hour the constant needs to be multiplied by 60 (minutes):

$$1.604 \times 60 = 96.3 \text{ inches per square ft per hour}$$

EXAMPLE 5.5

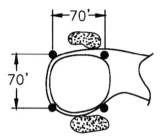

FIGURE 5.26
Square spacing on a green.

Four full-circle sprinklers water a green. Each sprinkler uses 31.3 gpm. The sprinklers are spaced in a square pattern 70 ft apart (see Figure 5.26). The precipitation rate is calculated as follows:

$$\frac{96.3 \times 31.3}{70 \times 70} = .62 \text{ in. per hour}$$

For sprinklers spaced in an equilateral triangle pattern, at equal distances from each other, the following formula is used:

$$PR = \frac{96.3 \times \text{gpm}}{S \times L \times .866}$$

EXAMPLE 5.6

FIGURE 5.27
Equilateral triangle spacing on a fairway.

Full-circle sprinklers water a fairway. The sprinklers are positioned in an equilateral triangular pattern 70 ft apart (see Figure 5.27). Each sprinkler uses 31.3 gpm. The precipitation rate is calculated as follows:

$$\frac{96.3 \times 31.3}{70 \times 70 \times .866} = .71 \text{ in. per hour}$$

For part-circle sprinklers, the following formula is used:

$$PR = \frac{96.3 \times \text{gpm}}{S \times L} \times \frac{360}{\text{Sprinkler arc}}$$

EXAMPLE 5.7

Six part-circle sprinklers water a tee. Each sprinkler uses 10.1 gpm. The sprinklers are spaced in a square pattern 45 ft apart (see Figure 5.28). The sprinkler arcs are set at 180 degrees. The precipitation rate is calculated as follows:

$$\frac{96.3 \times 10.1}{45 \times 45} \times \frac{360}{180} = .96 \text{ in. per hour}$$

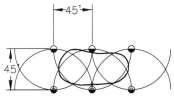

FIGURE 5.28
Square spacing on a tee.

Another variation of the formula is used to calculate the precipitation rate for single-row spacing:

$$PR = \frac{96.3 \times \text{gpm}}{S \times D \times .8}$$

where *D* is the diameter of throw of the sprinkler in feet and .8 (80%) is the coverage multiplier of a single-row sprinkler's diameter of throw.

EXAMPLE 5.8

Full-circle sprinklers water a fairway. Each sprinkler uses 51.0 gpm. Each sprinkler covers a 92 ft radius, and the sprinklers are spaced in a single-row pattern 90 ft apart (see Figure 5.29). The precipitation rate is calculated as follows:

$$\frac{96.3 \times 51.0}{90 \times 184 \times .8} = .37 \text{ in. per hour}$$

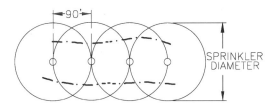

FIGURE 5.29
Single-row spacing on a fairway.

To complete the system scheduling, the precipitation rate for each sprinkler must be determined so that its run time can be calculated.

Before calculating precipitation rates, it is important to check each sprinkler to ensure that it has the correct nozzle and operating pressure, and that part-circle sprinklers have the correct arc setting.

Evapotranspiration Rate

To know how much water to apply, the system manager must know the net water loss in the time since the last irrigation event. The sum total of plant and soil water loss is referred to as evapotranspiration (ET). Evapotranspiration data for turfgrass is referred to as ET_o. Chapter 1 explains ET and indicates sources for obtaining local ET data.

An on-site weather station (or multiple weather stations) is the best source of ET_o data on a golf course because it communicates site-specific environmental data. In using an on-site weather station, care should be taken in choosing its location. The ideal location is open, level terrain at least 30 ft in diameter and at a distance from any nearby obstruction of at least ten times the height of that obstruction, whether it is a tree, a building, or another structure. For example, the weather station should be located at least 300 ft from a 30 ft tree. Proper location will ensure that its multiple sensors will not be affected by nonenvironmental factors.

Crop Coefficient

A crop coefficient (K_c) is an ET_o multiplier. Turfgrass water requirements vary by plant species. The crop coefficient provides a means of adjusting ET_o data for the different turfgrass species on a golf course. Typically, cool-season grasses have crop coefficients of less than 1.00 for most of the year; warm-season grasses have crop coefficients that are substantially less than those of cool-season grasses.

Most turfgrass species exhibit seasonal variations in their crop coefficients, which are typically dependent on their adaptability during different seasonal weather patterns. Studies show some substantial differences in plant water requirements of various cultivars, which can have unique crop coefficient profiles among other turfgrasses of the same species. The developmental stage of a turfgrass plant also affects its water needs. It is wise to obtain local crop coefficient data, expressed in monthly values, for the various turf-grasses on a golf course to aid in scheduling the irrigation system. (Additional information on crop coefficients can be found in Chapter 1).

Area Adjustment Factors

An area adjustment factor is used to fine-tune the identified crop coefficients. Although areas across the golf course such as greens, tees, and fairways, may share the same turfgrass species, these areas usually have different plant water requirements because of different management practices. The area adjustment factor aids in further refining an area's plant water needs. Figure 5.30 shows various area adjustment factors that may be applied to a run time calculation.

No.	Name	ET Adjust. %
1	Greens	55
2	Fairways	70
3	Roughs	60
4	Perimeters	60
5	Practice greens	55
6	Driving range tee	60
7	Green nursery	55
8	Tee nursery	65
9	Practice hole	60
10	Clubhouse	60
11	Tees	65

FIGURE 5.30
Typical area adjustment table.

Station Adjustment Factor

The irrigation schedule can be further adjusted to take into consideration the site-specific requirements of individual sprinklers. These factors define the microclimates in which the sprinklers operate. Microclimates are the individual surface environments in which the sprinklers are located, and they can vary dramatically across a golf course. The factors that can have the most dramatic effect on microclimates include air circulation, amount of shade, exposure to wind, traffic, and sunlight intensity. Many of these conditions can vary on a seasonal basis and may require adjustments throughout the irrigation season.

Sprinkler Application Efficiency and Uniformity

A sprinkler's application uniformity can arguably have the greatest influence on the sprinkler run time calculation. *Sprinkler application efficiency* refers to the uniformity with which water is applied to the turfgrass. Every sprinkler has its own distribution curve, also referred to as sprinkler profile, which is the projection of its application rate over its radius of throw. These profile data are used by the irrigation system designer in selecting the best sprinkler and nozzle combination for a particular sprinkler spacing that will yield a uniform distribution of water across the area being covered. Nonuniform irrigation will either require more water to be applied, in order to provide adequate water to the dry area within the sprinklers' spacing, or result in the subsequent hand-watering of the dry areas. The value of uniformity is calculated by dividing the average precipitation rate within the driest 25 percent of a the sprinkler's pattern by the average precipitation rate of the entire pattern. The procedure is known as determining the low quarter distribution uniformity (DU_{LQ}) of a zone.

System efficiency is expressed as a percentage. A properly designed and well-maintained irrigation system can have an efficiency rating of 80 percent or higher, whereas inefficient and poorly maintained irrigation systems can have efficiencies of 65 percent and lower.

Another component of good uniformity and efficiency is the proper installation and maintenance of the irrigation system, as a poorly installed and maintained system cannot operate at its peak efficiency.

Soil

The final component of irrigation scheduling is the soil. The soil does not affect the total run time required for the sprinkler. However, it does dictate the time between irrigation events, the maximum application rate, and the number of irrigation cycles required to prevent runoff. The soil type, depth, and slope, as well as the turfgrass root depth, all factor into this calculation. It is quite common for golf courses to have many different soil types, compactions, and slopes, and identifying them will aid in the scheduling of the irrigation system.

Once a sprinkler's total operating run time is calculated, its precipitation rate must be compared with the soil's infiltration rate and slope. An application that exceeds the infiltration rate will result in runoff or puddles on the playing surface, both of which waste water and degrade playing conditions. A maximum application time should be calculated for each soil type and slope condition. This maximum application time is referred to as the cycle time. If the required run time exceeds the maximum cycle time for a particular soil type and slope, then a soaking interval must be scheduled to allow for infiltration. Once the soaking interval has been observed, the remaining station run time can be scheduled to operate.

Final Schedule

The use of a central computer can dramatically decrease the time it takes to calculate an irrigation schedule and provide a means to make seasonal adjustments to each controller station throughout the year. Ideally, a central control system automatically downloads daily weather data and applies all the adjustments that have been entered (crop coefficient, area, station, application efficiency) to each controller. It then posts the calculated station run times for the system manager to review and/or edit, before generating an irrigation program. The irrigation system manager can factor in the weather forecast against the calculated station application rate and make any necessary final adjustments to the system.

Efficient golf course irrigation scheduling requires that the system operator pay constant, close attention to the plant water requirements across the site and make frequent system adjustments in order to minimize water use and provide a healthy playing surface. The old saying "Twenty minutes a night is just right" does not describe an efficient irrigation schedule nor one that will promote healthy turfgrass while minimizing water use.

PROGRAMMING

Programming the irrigation system is the final step in preparing for an irrigation event. A water window, which indicates a predetermined start and stop time for the irrigation event, must be established, as well as the operating sequence for all the sprinklers that have been scheduled to operate. Programming entails managing both the electrical and hydraulic properties of the irrigation system. Proper irrigation programming ensures that both electrical and hydraulic systems operate within the parameters of the original system design criteria and is essential to the long-term health of the irrigation system.

The irrigation system designer and the final irrigation system Record Drawings are the best sources for most of the information needed in programming the system. If the irrigation system designer is not the person doing the irrigation programming, then the system programmer should discuss the design philosophy with the designer and obtain all design criteria prior to starting the programming. The designer should approve the programming prior to implementation.

All of the following electrical and hydraulic data must be known in order to complete the system programming. Most of the required hydraulic and electrical data represent "one-time" entries, which will be used to manage the irrigation system for years. Although it is a tedious process, it is important that these data be accurately entered, as all decisions and calculations made by the irrigation software from this point on will rely on these data.

Electrical Data

- Number of stations per controller
- Number of valves per station
- Maximum number of active valves per controller
- Controller assignments to communication cable wire paths or groups

Hydraulic Data

- Controller station flow
- Lateral pipe routes and sizes
- Mainline pipe routes and sizes
- Water supplies and capacities
- Pump operating curves
- Pump station sequencing

Map-based irrigation software provides the opportunity to import Record Drawings that are developed by CAD drafting software packages. If these irrigation software packages are being used, most of the programming data should be available electronically and may be imported directly into the irrigation programming software at the central controller. These data should include the layering and attribute information specified by the manufacturer of the irrigation programming software.

Additional site-specific information that must be known includes time available to irrigate, area operating priorities, and unique area water windows.

Electrical Data

A Controller Data Worksheet should be developed for each controller on the golf course. This worksheet should provide detailed information for each controller that can be referenced to the irrigation Record Drawing. The Controller Data Worksheet should include all the necessary controller information that will be imported directly into the central control system's irrigation management software package:

- Controller/decoder numerical identifier
- Controller/decoder location description
- Station area description
- Total number of stations
- Number of valves per station
- Grouping assignments

These data worksheets should always be kept current. Any changes to the field wiring should be reflected on the worksheets, as well as on the Record Drawings.

Each controller station should be identified as to the area it controls. It is not uncommon to have 75 or more controllers on-site, with as many as 72 or more stations per controller. Memorizing the wiring sequence is not an option. The controller data worksheets will help in identifying the controller stations that control the various areas of the golf course. Many controllers are available in multiple station configurations. Usually these controllers are expandable by adding more station output cards or modules. A golf course may have a variety of different controller station configurations, each of which must be recorded at the central.

An irrigation controller has a maximum electrical output, which is determined by the volt amp (VA) output of its transformer. This output determines the maximum number of valves or valve-in-head sprinklers that can be activated simultaneously. Often, the control system's ability to activate multiple stations exceeds the electrical and hydraulic limits of the irrigation system, with the potential to cause damage to various irrigation components. The designed electrical limitations of a controller should be recorded at the central controller to prevent the activation of more stations than the irrigation designer intended. If valves or valve-in-head sprinklers are grouped together at a controller station, it must be indicated at the central that a station is operating multiple solenoids so that the central controller can recognize the increased electrical load on the system.

Field controllers must be identified numerically and with a location description. The controller keypad or dipswitch terminal block can be used to assign a numerical identity to each controller in the system. This number will also be entered in the irrigation software, enabling communication between the two devices and facilitating system programming.

Some irrigation control systems have limits to the number of controllers or decoders that can operate on an individual communication cable or leg. If this is the case, a field controller/decoder will be identified in the central software with a communication leg identification (ID) number as well as a controller ID number.

Hydraulic Data

The electrical data is only half of the equation. The irrigation system programmer must also consider hydraulic limitations in order to program the system safely and efficiently.

The hydraulic management of an irrigation system is a process whereby individual controller stations are assigned to the piping network. Controller stations are assigned to flow zones or flow groups, which in turn are assigned to larger supply lines, or branches, which are then assigned to their water source. A useful analogy is a comparison of the flow management network to the branching pattern of a tree, in which main trunk lines separate into smaller branches and further separate to smaller twigs, which attach to clusters of leaves, which can be viewed as flow zones.

Flow management begins with identification of the total flow of every controller station. The completed Controller Data Worksheet is the best reference for this information. The individual controller stations are assigned to flow zones, each with a section of pipe supplying sprinklers along its length. Each flow zone is assigned a maximum flow, limiting the number of sprinklers within that zone that can be operated simultaneously. Each flow zone is referenced to its supply source, which is a main section of piping called a branch or pipe.

Each flow zone is hydraulically limited by the size of the pipe that feeds it. The irrigation designer would have considered three factors when originally sizing this pipe: velocity, pressure loss, and the number of sprinklers needed to run simultaneously.

The irrigation system designer's maximum flow criteria, usually indicated in fps, dictates the maximum flow assigned to a flow zone. Assigning a capacity that exceeds the safe flow within a pipeline will result in excessively high velocities and pressure losses, both of which can cause damage to the piping network and reduce sprinkler performance. An example of the piping around a green is shown in Figure 5.31. The green is fed by a pipe that supplies the nine sprinklers around the green. The sprinklers are all assigned to the green feed pipe and are classified as a flow zone.

In this illustration the (feed) pipe to the green loop is 3 in. and the pipe around the green is 2½ in. All piping is class 200 PVC. Each valve-in-head sprinkler has a flow rate of 29.3 gpm, and the design criterion for the maximum allowable velocity on the pipeline is 5 fps.

As shown in the Class 200 pipe sizing chart in the appendix to this book, the following maximum capacities at less than 5 fps are listed for each pipe size on the green:

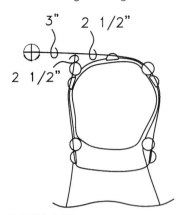

FIGURE 5.31
Typical piping—green.

Pipe Size	Capacity (gpm)	Velocity (fps)
2½ in.	80	4.82
3 in.	120	4.88

The maximum flow potential for the green is 263.7 gpm, (9 sprinklers × 29.3 gpm = 263.7), which would exceed the design criteria of 5 fps. The maximum flow within the flow zone is determined by the maximum safe flow within the zone, and in this case the determining factor is the 3 in. pipe that supplies 120 gpm. With these criteria, a maximum of four sprinklers can be activated simultaneously within the flow zone (4 × 29.3 = 117.2 gpm). In the central programming software this green would be assigned a flow zone number and a flow value of 120 gpm, and it would be assigned to a branch. Each 2½ in. feed off the 3 in. line would carry approximately 60 gpm, well below the maximum threshold for that pipe size. The process of creating branches and flow zones is repeated until every sprinkler is assigned to a specific flow zone and branch.

Each flow zone and branch is identified by the following:

- Name
- Reference number
- Total safe flow
- Supply branch name and number

All supply branches eventually lead to a main supply branch exiting a water source, which is typically one or more pump systems.

The creation of flow management tables is extremely important, and only those with the proper training and experience should attempt to program the system. A mistake in entering flow values of a branch or flow zone may result in the activation of too many sprinklers, potentially causing damage to the irrigation system, or too few sprinklers, unnecessarily causing a longer water cycle.

The final step in creating a flow management database is to assign a sequencing routine to the irrigation system. Irrigation systems are supplied by a water source that can be capable of supplying as much as 3500 gpm or more. A large amount of water put in motion quickly can be very damaging to an irrigation system. For this reason, the irrigation programming software utilizes a flow step procedure, which simply means that the total desired system capacity is introduced incrementally. For example, if the system is designed to operate at 2000 gpm, the irrigation system software may initially call for 500 gpm and step up in increments of 500 gpm until 2000 gpm is realized. Typically, a one- or two-minute time delay is programmed between the flow steps. The objective in stepping up the flow is to maximize the operating efficiency of the pump system or other source while protecting the piping system.

Once all the irrigation system data has been entered into the irrigation programming software, base (initial) irrigation programs are created. Typically, individual programs are developed for specific areas of the golf course such as greens, tees, fairways, roughs, approaches, surrounds, and lawn areas. The irrigation system programmer can create a specific program for each of these different areas. Controller stations are assigned to each program from the software data base or, if map-based software is being used, directly from the map. A default station run time can be added for each station in the program, or the program can be assigned to operate on the basis of evapotranspiration (*ET*).

An irrigation program requires a start time, a stop time, or both, and an operation priority. A start time or stop time is required for each program that is to be added to the next irrigation event. Several programs may be active at any one time throughout the irrigation event. Some programs may have an operational priority over others. For example, a greens program may have a start time of 3:00 A.M., but other programs may be active when it is scheduled to start. By assigning the greens program a high priority, the programmer ensures it will run at the desired time, because, as flow becomes available, stations assigned to program with the highest priority are activated first. The program's priority sequence must be identified in the program database.

Most irrigation software programs provide a dry run, or projected flow routine, in which the irrigation system operator can run an accelerated simulation, without water, of the scheduled irrigation event. The dry run provides an opportunity to view the interaction of the various programs that are scheduled to operate, when they start, when they finish, the total flow for each program, the flow steps of the pump station, the flow graph for the irrigation event, and the total flow of the irrigation event. After reviewing and approving the dry run, the irrigation system operator can, depending on the type of control system, transmit the irrigation programs to the field controllers or leave the central in the automatic mode and allow the central to operate the system.

WEATHER STATIONS AND SENSORS

If weather stations or ET data services are used to provide daily ET_o data, additional information must be entered into the programming software. The weather station must be configured for the elevation and latitude at which it is located. A crop coefficient adjustment factor must also be established and entered into the software. The weather station can be programmed to automatically download the day's ET_o data into the central software. An ET_o source download time must be specified so that the software can wait until the full day's ET data are available before acquiring the ET_o value from the weather station or ET service. The central software can use this data to automatically calculate the net ET_o loss for the day and reschedule run times to satisfy this net loss. If multiple weather stations are used, each controller station must be assigned to the weather station that best represents that station's environmental conditions.

Sensors are generally used in a system to respond to field conditions or to record data such as wind speed, rainfall, soil moisture, temperature, pressure, and flow, or to sense whether a switch is open or closed. Sensors are typically assigned to individual controllers or controller stations. The software uses sensors to acquire real-time information and provide real-time responses. This process usually relies on an if/then premise. For example, suppose that wind speed sensors are installed on a site. Within the irrigation programming software a maximum wind speed condition is entered such that if the maximum allowable speed is reached, then stations assigned to that sensor will be placed in a pause condition until the sensor reports that the wind speed has dropped below the maximum threshold for a set time period. Similar responses can be generated for sensors responding to ambient temperature, rainfall amount, and rainfall intensity.

SOURCES

Adams, R. F., et al., eds, 1999. *Annual book of ASTM standards*, Section 8, vol. 08.04, *Plastic pipe and building productions*. West Conshohocken, PA: American Society for Testing and Materials.

American Society of Irrigation Consultants. 2002. *ASIC Guideline 100–2002*. Chicago, IL: American Society of Irrigation Consultants.

American Society of Agricultural Engineers. *ASAE Standards 1998*. 45th ed. St. Joseph, MO: ASAE, pp. 3, 837–853.

Croft, T., and W. I. Summers. 2002. *American electricians handbook*. 14th ed. New York: McGraw-Hill.

National Fire Protection Association. 2002. *National electrical code (NFPA 70*. 2002 ed. Quincy, MA: NFPA.

National Association of Plumbing-Heating-Cooling Contractors. 1996. *National standard plumbing code illustrated*. Falls Church, VA.

Oliphant, J. C., and D. F. Zoldoske. 1989. *Sprinkler profile and coverage evaluation (SPACE): software and documentation*. CATI Publication No. 890403. Fresno, CA: Center for Irrigation Technology, California State University, p. 39.

United States Golf Association. 2002. *The rules of golf as approved by the USGA and the Royal and Ancient Golf Club of St. Andrews, Scotland*. Far Hills, NJ: USGA.

U. S. Department of Agriculture. September 1993. *National Engineering Handbook: Soil Conservation Service*. USDA: Part 623, chapter 2.

Zoldoske, D. F., G. S. Jorgensen, and S. Genito. 1995. Subsurface drip irrigation in turfgrass: A university experience. *Microirrigation for a Changing World,* ed. by F.R. Lamm. Fifth International Microirrigation Congress, April 2–6, 1995, Orlando, FL. St. Joseph, MI: ASAE, pp. 300–302.

6

Construction Management

This chapter continues with the irrigation project after the design is completed. It discusses methods used to estimate material and construction costs. It then reviews bidding procedures, and prebid and preconstruction meetings. Methods for field staking of head, valve, and controller locations are included. The chapter also covers the procedures for creating accurate Record Drawings and interactive controller maps based on Global Positioning System (GPS) data collection. Finally, it describes the evaluation and auditing of existing systems.

COST ESTIMATING

In setting a budget for a golf course irrigation system, it is important to include accurate and realistic costs, as many system renovations require approval and/or assessment of the membership to pay for them. Accurate estimates prevent the necessity of approaching the membership for more money, which can be difficult and embarrassing. Cost estimates are used in the design process to make sure that adequate funds are allocated. Some clubs' bylaws, however, require actual bid numbers from material suppliers and contractors before approval can be given or funding secured. The installation of a new irrigation system or the renovation of an existing system always involves more than just the cost of irrigation itself. All cost factors must be considered in establishing the budget.

The costs of irrigation materials can be obtained from local representatives of the major irrigation equipment manufacturers. A materials list will be provided, based on the system design. Installation costs can be bid or estimated as a percentage of materials cost, or on a per-sprinkler basis. Many designers have developed per-sprinkler costs for cost estimating, based on their experience with previous projects. These costs can vary, depending on the geographic location of the project. For example, the cost per sprinkler in Miami will be different from the cost per sprinkler in Chicago.

Additional items that may have to be included in the budget are discussed in the following paragraphs.

Pump system—The cost of a pump system can vary dramatically, depending on the number of pumps, their size, and the control technology being used. More pumps will cost more money, and conventional control systems will be less expensive than variable frequency drive (VFD) systems. High-discharge pressures with substantial flows will require greater horsepower and result in more expensive pumps. The costs of safeties, monitoring, alarms, and other special components must also be included.

Wet well—If a turbine pump system is being installed, a wet well, inlet pipe, and screen will be needed. The costs of these items will vary with the depth of the wet well and the difficulty of installing it. In conjunction with a pond dredging project or new construction, these costs will be low, but installation in a pond or lake full of water will raise costs considerably, and a reliable estimate will be needed for this work.

Pump house (new or renovation)—Although a pump house itself is not always necessary, some sort of fencing, roofing, or other protection for a pump is usually constructed. Costs can vary considerably, depending on the type of construction, but should include fans, air inlets, doors, roof, siding, and the like.

Power supply—A new pump system or one of increased size will require work on the high-voltage power supply to the system. Costs will vary, depending on local power utility requirements and how much of the cost has to be borne by the golf course as opposed to the utility. Burying high-voltage lines across the golf course can be prohibitively expensive, and if it is proposed, must be included in all budget discussions.

Electrical equipment—Substantial cost is involved with wiring a new pump system, as well as heaters, fans, lights, and so forth, to the building power supply.

Water supply—If a water supply has to be developed, either through construction of a pond or groundwater development, these costs must also be in the budget. The costs can be relatively small or very large, depending on the location, size, and availability of a water source. If water is transferred from one water source to another (e.g., from well to pond), piping, drilling, pumping, controls, and electrical costs for these items are part of the overall budget. The quality of water will also impact the water supply costs. If pH adjustment, filtering, sulfur injection, or other treatment is needed, the costs of equipment involved, as well as the increased size of the pump house, must be considered. Other types of injection such as fertigation, wetting agents, or biologicals will also have to be included in cost estimates.

Removal of rock—The presence of rock is always an unknown on any construction project, and an irrigation system installation is no different. Rarely is rock removal included in the base installation costs of the installing contractor. The cost of removing rock or other deleterious material (material that cannot be used as backfill) are paid as an addition to the installation costs and must be budgeted, especially for projects that are on rocky sites. These costs can be as low as $1,000 and may be as high as $250,000 or more on certain sites.

Turf renovation—Topdressing, loam, mulch, and fertilizer for renovation of trenches and/or disturbed areas of the golf course must also be budgeted unless included in the installation costs. Even if the contractor does a good job of turf renovation, there will probably still be some areas that will need attention after the contractor has left the project. Seeding versus sodding of the trench lines can have a substantial impact on costs. Cutting and removing the sod from the trenches or buying new sod will cost more than seeding, although these practices are common in many irrigation system installations. Seeding, although less expensive, will require more patience, and it will be necessary to rope off the seeded areas to get a good turf stand, which will also have a cost associated with it. Additional golf course maintenance staff may be required to provide the renovation work or to assist the contractor, depending on how the contract and specifications are structured.

Landscape irrigation around the clubhouse and other buildings, and in planting beds throughout the golf course, may be part of the project. These costs must also be budgeted, including such items as tennis court irrigation.

Additional nonirrigation costs may include water fountain supply (both water and electricity), green fan power, aerator power, restroom power and piping, and telephone wire.

It is helpful to keep all these accessory costs as a separate line item to distinguish them from the irrigation system costs. The amounts can be considerable, but they represent improvements to the facility, not the irrigation system (Figure 6.1).

Installation of an irrigation system can require several permits, depending on the location of the golf course. Permits may be required for water withdrawal, wetland disturbance, stream crossings, road crossings, and so forth. There are fees associated with obtaining permits and additional costs for design professionals to obtain them. Finally, there may be costs for Record Drawings or programming associated with the project if these items are being provided by a third party.

BID PROCEDURES AND DOCUMENTS

There are many different ways to obtain costs for a project and many ways to structure the bidding. The bid can be a competitive bid or a negotiated bid. It may include installation and materials for a pump system and pump house combined, or each may be a separate bid. A

FIGURE 6.1
Budgets should include all costs, not just the hard irrigation costs.

Base Costs:		
Irrigation System (957 sprinklers @ $900.00 per)		$861,300.00
Green Collar/Bunker System		$ 50,000.00
Weather Station		$ 10,000.00
Parking Lot Crossing (1000 feet @ $10.00 per foot)		$ 10,000.00
Demolition of Old System		$ 10,000.00
Lightning Protection System (Add Horns)		$ 5,000.00
Consulting Fees		$ 17,000.00
	Subtotal:	$963,300.00
Other:		
Pump System Renovations		$ 25,000.00
Green Hose Reels (4 @ $1800.00)		$ 7,200.00
Utilities—Fans, Drinking Fountains, Monitoring		$ 25,000.00
Club House Irrigation		$ 8,000.00
Permitting (estimate)		$ 5,000.00
Rock/Deleterious Material		$150,000.00
	Total:	$1,183,500.00

complete set of bid documents must be prepared. The irrigation documents may be part of a golf course construction or renovation package, or may have to stand on their own. The bidding procedure that best fits the specific situation should be chosen. In public bidding specific rules and regulations must be followed. In a private bid there are no rules, but it is important to be fair to all parties bidding the project. No matter what process is used, the following documents should be included as a minimum: instructions to bidders, a bid form, insurance requirements, and the technical specifications for each facet of the project. In addition, general and supplementary conditions may be included in the project documents or as part of the final contract. The technical specifications in most cases will follow a Construction Specifications Institute (CSI) format, although there are other forms. Within this format the technical specifications are further broken down into three sections: General, Materials, and Execution (installation). The General section includes submittal requirements, qualifications, and other job-specific general specifications, such as record drawings. The Materials section provides the specifications for the various equipment to be used, including all the accessory items. The Execution section outlines how the equipment is to be installed, and includes such items as rock clauses, turf restoration, and training and programming. Once the project documents have been sent to potential bidders, a prebid meeting should be scheduled. This will allow

FIGURE 6.2
A prebid meeting allows the contractors to familiarize themselves with the golf course conditions.

the irrigation contractors to see the site and to ask questions of the club and the designer about the project documents. The prebid meeting should be mandatory to ensure that all contractors are familiar with the site when they bid, so as to prevent problems during construction (Figure 6.2). During the bidding phase any changes to the documents will be handled through an addendum.

Contracts must be prepared and must be signed by all parties to protect everyone involved in case of a dispute. Standard forms, such as American Institute of Architects (AIA) documents, are best because they are court proven and do not favor one party over another. They are also inexpensive and do not usually require extensive attorney review.

Following contract signing, a preconstruction meeting may be held to answer any questions of the successful contractor and determine a schedule and a starting point. During the construction phase, changes to the plans are handled with change orders. A change order must be signed by all parties to the contract. It includes an explanation of the change, any additional costs or credits, and any change to the completion date. Although rock removal costs should be paid through a change order, other change orders can become problems because their costs were not budgeted. Many change orders can be avoided by good field work during preliminary design.

STAKING

Although a design may look good on paper, the system will work properly only if it is correctly implemented in the field. The first step is proper staking of the sprinkler locations in the field to indicate the extent and uniformity of coverage outlined in the design. It is common practice to stake a hole from green to tee so that any needed spacing adjustments will occur in the rough between the fairway and the tee. If systems are staked from tee to green and the adjustments are made in the approach, water application in that area will be difficult to manage. Tees are usually staked back to front so that adjustments are made in the rough. Although wind must always be taken into consideration, it is especially important on single-row tee complexes to stake the sprinkler locations with respect to the prevailing wind. The sprinklers should be staked so that they do not have to fight the wind, but use it to their advantage. In wall-to-wall systems, the center of the fairway is staked first to exact spacings so any that necessary adjustments will occur in out-of-play areas. It is a mistake to start at the edge of the property and lay down a grid pattern, because heads will inevitably fall in locations (putting surfaces, sand bunkers, tee surfaces, etc.) where they cannot be installed. The adjustments needed to resolve such issues will distort the specified pattern (and thus reduce uniformity and efficiency) in the areas where the most precise irrigation is required. As good as the base map for the design may have been, there will be changes to the sprinkler layout in the field. As previously discussed, square or triangular spacing, or a combination of both, is acceptable, depending on the layout of the hole. Spacing sprinklers in the field can be accomplished in a number of ways. Most common is the use of several measuring tapes and enough people to carry the basic spacing patterns (Figure 6.3), but the use of GPS technology is becoming more popular for staking. Staking is easier if the participants can take hand direction and are capable of understanding the language of the person directing the effort. Various colored flags, stakes, or "whiskers" should be used to denote different types of sprinklers and different nozzles.

After a hole is staked, the contractor must produce an as-staked drawing, showing the schematic head layout, the total number of the various types of heads installed, and how the totals compare to plan quantities.

The locations of other irrigation components can also be staked. The proper location of the irrigation mainline is important. On existing golf courses it is fairly simple to keep the mainline in the proper location, as there are fairway cuts and existing turf stands. In new

FIGURE 6.3
To be done correctly, staking requires several people and measuring tapes.

construction, however, the mainline must be staked to make sure it is on the property; not under proposed tees, greens, sand bunkers, or structures; and outside the fairway cut. Isolation valves and air release valves should also be staked so that they are installed in the proper locations. Controller locations must be determined with the superintendent to ensure that they are out of play and convenient for operator use. Line-of-sight visibility to all heads may also be a consideration, but the use of remote control (handheld radios and PDA) devices usually makes it a non-issue.

MONITORING OF INSTALLATION

The installation of a new irrigation system must be monitored and observed, no matter how good the contractor may be (Figure 6.4). There are two reasons for this: Someone must be able to assure the client that the system is being installed as specified, and someone must make decisions when unforeseen conditions arise.

Monitoring and overseeing the installation (Figure 6.5) is very straightforward—does or does not the installation meet the requirements of the project documents? Key items to check include pipe depth, trench compaction, sprinkler height and position, swing joint angle, wire splices and tightness, valve box grade, and many others. Materials should also be checked on a continuing basis to ensure that they meet specifications, as they will continue to arrive in after the

FIGURE 6.4
It is important to observe an installation during the construction period.

FIGURE 6.5
Installation of an irrigation system involves specialized equipment and contractors.

initial deliveries and substitutions (intentional or otherwise) occur. With some contractors, there will be very little to comment on during the monitoring phase; with others, there can be a lot, especially at the beginning of the project. This, again, emphasizes the need to check references and select an experienced and reputable golf course irrigation contractor. All comments on the installation should be backed up in writing, with a copy to the contractor and to the owner. This practice protects all parties throughout construction and at the end of the project in case there is a problem.

Another aspect of monitoring is the approval of payment requisitions. Submission of payment requests should be limited to once a month, and specific terms of payment should be set forth in the contract. It is important to ensure that the balance to completion (amount of money as yet unpaid under the contract) is always less than the value of the remaining work. It is common practice to retain 10 percent of the labor portion of all invoices, although this may vary, especially on publicly owned projects. It is also a good idea to request an up-to-date schematic Record Drawing with each request for payment so that the project manager has something to work with and knows that the contractor is keeping Record Drawing field notes as the project proceeds. It must be kept in mind that a paid contractor is a happy contractor and that payments should not be delayed or withheld unless there is a valid reason.

Once installation is completed, a punch list should be prepared. This covers all aspects of the project, including the irrigation and pump systems, the pump house, and any other construction that took place. The punch list should include all items that are installed incorrectly, need adjustment, or do not meet the specifications. All of these items must be corrected by the contractor before final payment is authorized and the accumulated retainage released. Sometimes the retainage may be reduced to the value of the punch list when the list is issued. Punch list items must be backed up by the specifications and a time limit set for their completion. Completion and delivery of the final Record Drawings and operating and maintenance manuals for all installed components are important parts of the punch list.

Record Drawings

The lack of accurate and complete Record Drawings as-built detracts from the completeness and efficient operation of the system. A Record Drawing is used to locate equipment for repairs, for programming, and for the proper scheduling of the system. If there is no Record Drawing, or one that is inaccurate, the system will be harder to manage and will cost more to both operate and maintain.

A good Record Drawing (Figure 6.6) includes all of the equipment installed with the irrigation system. This should also include accessory items such as water fountains, fans, and telephones, and all of their related piping and wiring. The Record Drawing should include sprinklers, specifically detailing the model, nozzle, and arc so that they can be graphically differentiated from each other. The location of a sprinkler should be drawn on the map as precisely as possible, or located with the use of mapping equipment as outlined later in this chapter. The Record Drawings are often divided into a mechanical drawing and an electrical drawing. In addition to sprinklers, the mechanical drawing should include pipe routing and sizes, isolation valves, quick coupling valves, drains, air release valves, and directional change fittings. All wires, including type, size, and routing, should be included on the electrical drawing, as well as high-voltage (120V/220V) wire splices, communication cable splices, 24 volt wire splices, controller locations, power sources, and grounding grids.

All equipment on a drawing should be locatable with the use of a triangular measurement method (Figure 6.7). This allows the components to be located by measuring from two permanent reference points: where the points cross is the location of the item. It is important to use permanent reference points, as other items move with time and the reference point will be lost.

A Record Drawing is worthless unless it is drawn on an accurate base map of the golf course. The base map should minimally include

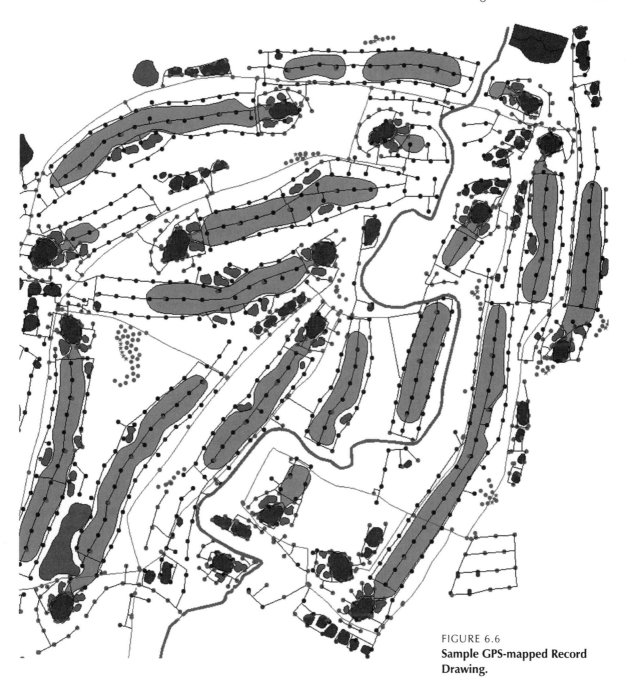

FIGURE 6.6
Sample GPS-mapped Record Drawing.

greens, tees, bunkers and fairways, and stream routings and pond outlines. The inclusion of cart paths, roadways, and buildings greatly improves its usefulness and accuracy. Tree lines and property lines give the map more definition and make it easier to locate the different parts of the golf course.

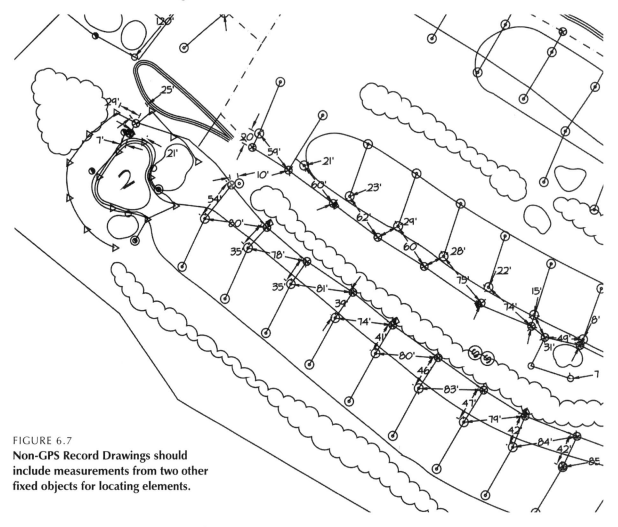

FIGURE 6.7
**Non-GPS Record Drawings should
include measurements from two other
fixed objects for locating elements.**

GPS

The use of the Global Positioning System (GPS) to develop Record
Drawings is fast becoming the standard in golf course irrigation
because of its speed, accuracy, and ability to be imported directly
into a map-based irrigation control system.

Unlike traditional survey equipment that requires a site device
and a rod device, as well as two people to operate the equipment,
GPS requires a single operator utilizing a self-contained unit. In addition, GPS does not require a horizontal line-of-sight, as is needed to
operate traditional survey equipment, making data collection significantly quicker.

As with any technology, there is a learning process involved in
using the equipment, but with proper professional training most

people can readily learn data collection procedures. However, collecting data is only one element of GPS. A good Record Drawing is the result of good data. GPS data must be accurate, organized, and corrected for errors—and a legible map must be generated. Only those with experience should perform these tasks.

HOW GPS WORKS

Various U.S. military units began development of a Global Positioning System in the late 1950s. The goal was an all-weather system that could be used for accurate positioning of fixed or moving objects for military applications. A system was developed consisting of 24 solar-powered radio-transmitting satellites. Four satellites are in each of six fixed orbits. The position of the orbits and the speed of the satellites ensures that several are always visible to rover receivers on the earth's surface. GPS works on the principle of trilateration, through which the position of an unknown point is calculated by measuring the lengths of the sides of a triangle between two known points (satellites) and an unknown point (rover).

President Reagan formally guaranteed civilian access to the GPS signal, without charge to the user, in 1984. In July 1995 the system was declared fully operational, with a full constellation of 24 solar-powered radio-transmitting satellites.

GPS ACCURACY

GPS offers varying degrees of accuracy, ranging from less than 1 cm to more than 100 m. Based on the quality of the equipment being used, data collection techniques, site conditions, and correction procedures, accuracy will vary. The Department of Defense (DOD) deliberately corrupts signals transmitted from the satellites so that hostile forces cannot use this technology against U.S. forces. Other factors can slightly corrupt the radio signals that travel 12,000 miles to earth and can cause enough inaccuracy to make GPS unsuitable for golf course mapping. To a large extent, obtaining accurate data depends on knowledge and skill in using GPS technology.

Terms generally used to specify the level of accuracy are *sub-meter accuracy* and *survey-grade accuracy*. Sub-meter accuracy, fixing a position to within less than 1 m on the horizontal plane (although it is two to six times less accurate on the vertical plane), is the most common level used in golf course Record Drawing development. Survey-grade accuracy is obtainable via a process known as Real Time Kinematic (RTK) GPS, whereby accuracies of less than 1 cm can be achieved. However, with increased accuracy comes significantly increased cost in equipment, training, and time. Although sub-meter data collection may appear to have varied levels of accuracy an experienced GPS data technician collecting the data can minimize the variance in accuracy levels, and maintain consistent sub-meter horizontal accuracies. The vertical accuracy can also be slightly improved, although it is usually accurate enough for irrigation design purposes, but there are better methods for collecting vertical/elevation values on a golf course.

A key to collecting quality data is to understand the factors that affect the accuracy of the data. Several receiver and data collector features and settings affect the data collected:

- Number of satellites
- Satellite geometry
- Satellite elevation
- Logging interval
- Distance between the base and rover receivers
- Differential correction

A minimum of four satellites is required to compute accurate three-dimensional (3D) GPS positions. It is desirable to have five or more satellites visible so that a GPS receiver can use all of them to calculate a stronger solution, which will also aid in canceling out errors. A position can, however, be computed with three satellites if the altitude is provided, and this is known as calculating a two-dimensional (2D) GPS position.

Satellite geometry (position) is very important. It is desirable to have maximum separation between the satellites that are reporting. This separation, known as dilution of precision (DOP), takes into consideration each satellite's location relative to the other satellites. The lower the DOP, the higher degree of accuracy. Position Dilution of Precision (PDOP), the most commonly used DOP, indicates the three-dimensional geometry of the satellites.

The lower the PDOP values, the greater the accuracy of the satellite geometry. Typically, a PDOP value of 6 or less should be maintained to provide the degree of accuracy required for golf course irrigation mapping.

A satellite's elevation will factor into the overall accuracy. If a satellite is low on the horizon, its signal has a greater distance to travel, which, in effect, causes it to have lower signal strength, which then leads to delayed reception by the rover receiver. This slight delay can cause a satellite's distance calculation to be inaccurate, resulting in the potential of a large positional error. Precise timing is crucial because the radio signals the satellites transmit travel at the speed of light (186,000 miles per second). If a satellite's timing is off by 0.01 second, the positional data it is calculating can be off by 1,860 miles. In addition, a low satellite signal may reflect off nearby surfaces, which known as the multipath effect. To reduce these effects, an elevation mask is set in the rover unit. This value usually defaults to 15°, below which signals will not be accepted.

The logging intervals selected can have an impact on differential correction accuracy. The data collector should be programmed to accept several (five or more) confirmed positions for each point. These positions can then be reviewed and averaged to provide a better-fixed point. To obtain sub-meter positions on a second-by-second basis, the measurement-recording interval at the base station and the position-recording interval at the rover must be identical, or the rover's interval must be a direct multiple of the base interval. Experienced GPS field technicians take care to map line and area features slowly, so that no more that 8 ft is collected on line and area features before subsequent corrected data are acquired.

The distance between the base and rover receivers also has an effect on overall accuracy. This is important to understand, especially when performing postprocessed differential correction. The greater the distance between the base and rover receivers, the more the level of accuracy degrades. This level of degradation can vary, depending on the receiver. A process called differential correction helps to eliminate some inaccuracies. *Differential correction* refers to the use of a precisely located GPS receiver (base station) at a known, fixed position. Because such base stations know exactly where they are, they can analyze errors on GPS signals and determine an error-correction value for the data of a user at another, unknown position. (Exact knowledge of the nearest base station position is critical, as the differential correction position accuracy depends on the accuracy of the coordinates of the base station.) This method can be applied to postprocessed and real-time data correction to provide corrected information. Postprocessing is the procedure in which GPS data are brought into a computer and its data compared with those of the base station and then corrected. This process, although cumbersome, is effective in eliminating inaccuracies and increasing the accuracy of a receiver. Postprocessed differential correction is a technique that uses base station error record files, and positional data from the rover. These files are processed together, after the data collector returns from the field, and the output is a differentially corrected rover file.

Real-time differential correction, as the term indicates, is a process in which data are corrected in real time as they are being collected. With real-time differential GPS, the base station(s) calculates and broadcasts (via radio signals) the error of each satellite as it receives the data. This calculation is received by the rover, which applies the correction to the position it is determining. This allows an experienced GPS technician to view the differentially corrected mapping event on a screen-top computer. Any obvious inaccuracy can be seen on the computer screen as the map develops, and corrections can be made in the field. This can also be very helpful with multiple site visits or mapping events, as the last mapping event's data can be viewed as new data is collected, thus eliminating double mapping or the problem of missing components. There are several sources of differential correction data, for both postprocessed and real-time correction. The operator may use his or her own base receiver and locate it over a known survey point, download data from a source near the rover location via a dial-up bulletin board site, access a private vendor using the vendor's satellites and receivers, or contact one of several U.S. government sources, such as the CORS network or Coast Guard differential GPS (DGPS) beacons.

GPS data are nongraphic, descriptive, positional information stored in a database. This data structure is referred to as topology. Topology provides the information that connects points, lines, and polygons to each other. GPS data is just that, data, and it needs a considerable amount of cleanup to make it presentable. An actual drawing itself is generated by the use of a computer-aided design (CAD) or Geographic Information System (GIS) program by someone with a good working knowledge of golf course irrigation systems. This draftsperson will convert the raw corrected positional data into the final Record Drawing. The final drawing can be presented on a series of plans (Hydraulic Plan, Electrical Plan, and Utility Plan, etc.) and/or presented in the form of an electronic file. It is worth the extra time and effort to have an electronic file created that can be imported into the irrigation system's operating software.

A major consideration in the development of a GPS map is whether the map is going to be used in the irrigation system's operating software. Most manufacturers of irrigation programming software have a certain procedure that they recommend so that the import process goes smoothly. For example, all manufacturers recommend that different area features of a golf course be created on their own layers. Layers give the draftsperson the ability to structure data. Layers usually contain information about only one type of feature or a small group of related features. The creation of layers is easily accomplished if the GPS mapping system allows for the collection of feature and attribute data within a Data Dictionary on the GPS system. A Data Dictionary is a listing of all the different types of lines, points, and areas that exist on the site that is being mapped, as well as a list of attributes that describe each feature. For example, there may be several different types of sprinklers on a site. Instead of labeling all the different sprinklers as one type, it is desirable to differentiate them within the Data Dictionary with their own names (labels). In this way, the different labels can be identified and sorted individually. It is not uncommon for a typical GPS map to have more than 100 layers differentiating the various sprinkler types, course features, pipe sizes, and valve sizes and types, as well as the different electrical components of an irrigation system, including wire types, splices, spare wires, and grounding components.

GPS data, which is positional information, can also be used to record descriptive information about lines, points, and areas. This descriptive information is called an attribute. An attribute can be common to all features at a geographic location; however other attributes can depend on the type of feature and the characteristics that are important to that feature. Examples of point attributes used in documenting irrigation systems are sprinklers, valves, satellites, wire splices, ground rods, mainline fittings, and valve boxes. Lines on a golf course can also have attributes, which are represented as pipe size, wire gauge, cart paths, and drainage line size. Areas are a series of points joined together to make a boundary and contain attributes such as a green, tee, bunker, fairway, pond, lake, or building.

The more detailed the Data Dictionary is, the more attribute information can be recorded about a point, line, or area. For example, a sprinkler may be recorded simply as *SPRINKLER,* or, if a detailed Data Dictionary is used, it may be recorded as

Sprinkler, attributes of:
    Model: 750
    Nozzle: 32
    Operating Pressure: 70 psi
    Arc: 270 degrees

This entry provides the end user with a significant amount of data about the irrigation system. The data can also be used within a GIS, which is discussed below.

RECORD DRAWING DEVELOPMENT

A completed GPS Record Drawing is a result of multiple site visits by the GPS technician and a careful review of the Record Drawing. Ideally, the irrigation contractor, system designer, golf course superintendent, and GPS technician should communicate throughout the map development process to ensure that the final product is complete and accurate.

It is best to have mapping events coordinated among all parties involved in the construction of the irrigation system. A member of the installation crew or of the golf maintenance staff should be available to review the as-installed drawings with the GPS operator prior to any field mapping event. Moreover, staking all aboveground components the day of the mapping event will speed up data collection and reduce the potential for omission of any component. The installer should stake all buried elements (fittings, splices, valves, etc.) when they are installed and maintain those stakes until the GPS operator has recorded the position and type of each item.

As the plan develops, the irrigation contractor must be able to provide detailed system information such as satellite station numbers, wire and pipe size, and arc settings of sprinklers. All of this information is crucial to the programming of the irrigation system and should be included on the final drawing.

GIS

An emerging technology in the golf course irrigation industry is the Geographic Information System (GIS). A GIS is a computer-based tool consisting of five components: hardware, software, data, people, and methods for mapping and analyzing things that exist and events that happen. GIS technology integrates common database operations, such as query and statistical analysis, with the unique benefits of visualization and geographic analysis benefits by a map. GIS software can be customized to meet specific needs, and customized menus can be created to choose and explore data. A GIS provides the ability to create site-specific maps, integrate information, visualize various scenarios, solve complicated problems, present powerful ideas, and develop effective solutions.

What is making GIS a beneficial tool in irrigation is the use of maps created from GPS positional information, and the associated attributes (information). GPS collects positional information and tags attributes to the points, lines, and areas that are collected, and GIS provides a means for analyzing the data and projecting the results on a map or in a spreadsheet.

HOW A GIS WORKS

A Geographic Information System links graphic and textual information in a computerized database. It relates information about attributes to a geographic location. CAD drawings, orthorectified aerial photos, or GPS maps are often used as the system's graphic foundation or base map. A GIS converts positional data, such as areas, lines, and points collected via GPS, and the associated attributes into tabular and graphical data. GIS attributes are unlimited in number and variety and provide up-to-date information about a site. GPS data, once converted to GIS tabular data, can be imported and overlaid on the base map.

Geographic data are developed from an exact geographic reference, such as latitude and longitude coordinates, or a secondary reference such as an address, postal code, or road name, which is calculated through geocoding. Many types of data sets are available in real-world coordinates known as a datum or projection; for example, utility plans, soil surveys, topographical surveys, and buildings. If the datum/projection being used is known, as well as the datum/projection these data sets are in, they can be added to the overall GIS map for future use and retrieval.

Geocoded information allows location of features such as hot spots, insect activity, microclimates, topography, and soil information. A GIS allows the development of ever greater knowledge, history, and current configuration of a selected site and all of its elements. It stores GPS features and tabular information as a collection of layers that can be linked together. The utility of a GIS is in the presentation of relationships, or how an action affecting one feature can have an effect on another.

HOW GIS IS BEING USED

Golf course architects, builders, and superintendents are using GIS to assist them in their daily management decisions. Having the ability to evaluate real-world situations present on a golf course gives them a greater understanding of the measures needed to solve a problem and prevent future ones. GIS can help in locating routing plans, tracking disease/insect activity, developing a drainage system by looking at site-specific topography, and assigning irrigation run times based on slope, exposure, and soil characteristics. Having an intelligent map provides the ability to perform a query and create "What if" scenarios. These queries can greatly reduce the potential for improper/unneeded design, renovation, or cultural practices and thus help in developing "precision turf management" practices.

Custom menus can be created to evaluate scenarios typical of individual golf courses, which makies this system even more user friendly. These menus can range from locating soil types and wetland areas to forecasting irrigation system maintenance, calculating the square footage of course elements (greens, tees, bunkers, etc.), scheduling equipment maintenance, tracking weather conditions, and tracking employee performance.

MOBILE MAPPING AND GIS

Small, palm-sized portable touch-screen computing devices, known as PDAs, or Pocket PCs, are becoming a popular option on new irrigation systems. These devices are an easy-to-use, lightweight, low-cost solution for mobile mapping and geographic information systems, yet powerful enough to accept GIS software packages that allow golf course and irrigation specific system maps to be viewed and modified in the field. They are also used to transmit commands via radio signals.

Pocket PC devices can utilize an intuitive map (i.e., GIS and GPS functionality) that makes field data maintenance and collection fast and easy and provides immediate data availability and validation. The ability to compare data directly to geographic features in the real world adds a deeper sense of reality to the GIS database. Currently, a Pocket PC with GIS software can provide the following services for a golf course and irrigation system:

- Access sprinkler information: type, nozzle, pressure, and arc setting
- Access program information: default run times, cycle time, soak time
- Adjust factors for slope, exposure, soil type, etc.
- Access and activates programs or individual stations
- Allow for measurements that can aid in the location of objects such as quick couplers, splices, mainline fittings, gate valves, and catch basins

- Provide field calculation of areas such as greens, tees, bunkers, and fairways

Data that are collected, edited, or created in the field are easily transferred into a desktop computer through a synchronization process A synchronization routine either downloads or uploads data between the desktop and the Pocket PC, depending on which is the more up-to-date data set.

Combining the accuracy of GPS and the power of a GIS will take cultural practices to the next level. The explosion of interest in precision turf management or site-specific management has been made possible by the combined use of these two technologies. Working in a geographic environment assists the user in recognizing patterns quickly and helps in gaining new insights that make better management decisions.

In addition to using a GPS receiver with a Pocket PC, digital photographs can be added to a GIS. A photograph is automatically linked to a GPS position, and a file is created that can be displayed along with other layers in the GIS. Software automatically compares the GPS position information with the images from the digital camera. Each time a stamped photograph is matched with the time-stamped data in the GPS file, it determines an accurate GPS position for the photograph, thereby georeferencing the photograph.

Because viewing graphical data on a map is generally easier than analyzing tabular spreadsheet data, the applications for GIS are growing significantly. Imagine training new employees as to where certain hot spots may be found across a golf course. If a GIS were in place, the map could be queried for the following scenario:

Project sprinklers that were:
Syringed: >10 times
Date: June 15 to August 1, 2003
Time: 11:00 A.M. to 2:00 P.M.

At that point the GIS could create a data set for just those sprinklers that meet the query requirements and provide a graphical tool to new staff members as to where these hot spots are located.

THE NEXT STEP

Having all this GPS and GIS information available is valuable, but today's GIS software commonly defaults to two dimensions, which may result in the loss of detail and clarity. Because GPS collects information in three dimensions, and the number of georeferenced data sets that contain three-dimensional information is constantly growing, these data sets will all soon be viewable in three dimensions. Three-dimensional modeling is the next evolution in GIS technology. This technology will allow for the interaction of data in its true form. Three-dimensional modeling will provide the golf course architect, builder superintendent, and staff to view, monitor, and manage a golf course facility as never before.

CREATION OF CENTRAL CONTROLLER MAP

At present the creation of a central controller interactive map is a fairly complicated procedure that is constantly evolving. Obviously, it would be nice to take an electronic form of a Record Drawing, hit an "Import Map" icon on the irrigation central control computer's software package, and have the entire map import directly into the software and populate all the databases. Although it is on the way, this feature is not yet available.

Ensuring Accuracy

A goal of the irrigation consultant or irrigation system designer is to have the completed record drawing available in an electronic format (AutoCAD drawing/GIS project) prior to the start up of the irrigation central control software package. To achieve this goal, the GPS operator meets with the irrigation contractor, irrigation consultant, or irrigation system designer and the golf course management staff to review the plan. Upon verification of the plan's graphical and positional content, the irrigation consultant or irrigation system designer verifies the accuracy of the attributes, thereby eliminating potential errors in database entries and ensuring that the system will operate as designed. These attributes are typically divided into three main categories, hydraulic, electric, and environmental, which include, but are not limited to, those listed in the table on the facing page.

Much of the information required to populate an irrigation system's database can be assigned to each individual sprinkler. This is accomplished either by assigning GPS attribute values during data collection or by assigning these attributes during the Record Drawing development stage via a CAD or GIS software package. These attrib-

Hydraulic	Electric	Environmental
• Sprinkler location code (hole number, turf area descriptor, zone descriptor). Example 4G1 = hole 4, green, zone 1 • Sprinkler type • Sprinkler nozzle • Sprinkler arc setting • Sprinkler gpm • Sprinkler spacing (head spacing, row spacing); used to calculate rotors' precipitation rates • Sprinkler spacing pattern (square, triangle, single row); used to calculate sprinkler precipitation rates	• Field controller number / decoder identification • Wire path number • Sprinkler station identification • Station valve load • Station sprinkler count • Sprinkler "attached pipe network" (maximum flow capacity); used to calculate hydraulic network flow management • Sprinkler pump station assignment	• Sprinkler site codes (slope, soil types, percolation rates, turf type, crop coefficient, microclimate factors, etc.) • Sprinkler weather station adjustment factors

utes make up the specific properties of each sprinkler, which the central control software uses to make educated decisions for irrigation programming. Once the electronic format of the Record Drawing contains the appropriate attribute information, the Record Drawing can be imported into the central control system software.

Map Import Routine

To import the Record Drawing/golf course map, the host computer must run through several routines to associate this information with the central control system software. Several irrigation software programs have "Installation Wizards" or "Step-by-Step" start-up routines, which include two processes: creating the map and populating the database. The order in which these routines are performed varies by manufacturer. The first, and most critical, step is to transfer the electronic copy of the Record Drawing (typically located on a CD provided by the GPS operator) to a folder/location in the host computer "Root" directory *(C:\).*

Next, course-specific information must be entered, including the course name and software keycodes that may be required to unlock certain software features. (These steps can vary by manufacturer.) Once these steps are performed, a blank database is created within the software for the import routine. To actually begin the map import routine, the map typically must be named; this is usually the golf course name used to unlock the software. At this point the computer will look for the source of the data, which is in the folder in the Root directory. Once the map file(s) is located, the software analyzes the map and creates a list of all the layers embedded within the drawing. These layers can be categorized as either irrigation system information or golf course feature information. The map importer must select the layers he or she wishes to import and identify each feature type as a point, line, or area. Examples include:

- *Points*—sprinklers, field controllers, valves
- *Lines*—pipe routes, wire routes
- *Area*—greens, tees, fairways, bunkers, ponds

Once each layer has been identified and imported, the GPS Record Drawing is located within the central control software. The last step is to specify graphical and user settings. These settings will be used to organize the layers in the map and to assign colors and symbol settings to layers. Map-based central control system software packages closely mimic the organizational structure of many CAD and GIS software packages, so map layers must be organized in a manner that allows the user to view the information/layer stacked beneath it. Once the layers are organized, and color and symbol information is applied, the map import process is complete.

Database Population

In most cases, once the map is imported, the databases can be populated. This is usually performed though an "Import Wizard." To populate a database, attribute information associated with each sprinkler type must be imported. The software will typically display two columns: an Irrigation Programming column with its required fields, and the Map Layers Attribute Data. The map importer matches the listings in the columns so that the attribute data from the drawing is paired with the correct database field within the software. Once all the fields in the irrigation programming software are matched with the appropriate GPS Record Drawing fields' attributes, a *populate* function will automatically merge the two data sets. This series of steps is usually repeated for each of the sprinkler types imported into the map. Upon completion, it is a worthwhile exercise to go through the map and double-check several sprinklers to verify their values. The irrigation consultant or irrigation designer should also verify the hydraulic network, or flow tree, which is the portion of the software where maximum flow values are assigned to each branch and flow zone. Once the irrigation map and databases have been successfully imported, the software can be used to create irrigation programs.

Non-Map-Based Data

Even though the map and database import routines have been completed, it is still necessary to enter/verify critical system information such as site- and user-specific environmental factors and user-defined scenarios/alarm conditions that sensors will report. For example:

- If the site has multiple pumping stations, the system designer will program in their maximum safe pumping rates.
- Weather stations are calibrated within the software. The latitude and elevation are entered so that the software has a reference location and can factor in the sun's angle as it creates evapotranspiration (ET) models.
- Most interactive irrigation programming software has the ability to react to multiple programmable, user-defined if/then scenarios, utilizing "smart sensors." Sensor identification and decision parameters must be inputted.

The creation of the interactive map is a multistep process and the result of the cooperative efforts of the irrigation consultant or designer, the installer, the golf course superintendent, and the map importer. The extra effort required to provide this final step helps ensure that the irrigation software will be fully utilized and the system will operate as designed.

IRRIGATION SYSTEM EVALUATION

In performing an evaluation, the evaluator must identify components that affect the overall operation, performance, and efficiency of the system, both good and bad. The evaluation should be broken into component parts in a logical order that is easy to follow. The evaluator should provide conclusions, recommendations, and the estimated cost of improvements. It is important that an evaluation be factual and not exaggerated. All aspects of the irrigation system should be included. Basically, the evaluator asks a lot of questions about the irrigation system being evaluated. The answers to the questions, along with the data collected, will become the evaluation results. This section outlines the questions that must be asked and the data that must be collected for each component.

It cannot be assumed that the people reading the report know anything about the irrigation system. Many decision makers (owners, board members, green committee chairpersons, etc.) do not know what water source is used for irrigation, whether there is a pump system, or where it is located. A good evaluation takes time, and the finished product should include pictures, tables, and graphs detailing the results.

Background

An evaluation should start with the history of the system:

- When was the system installed?
- What is irrigated, and what improvements have been made?
- Are there any significant elevation changes?
- What equipment is currently installed?

Water Supply

The source, location, quality, and availability of the water supply should be detailed. If there is a problem with any of these, explain the issue and what will be improved if it is solved.

- If there is a withdrawal or diversion permit, what is the amount covered, and is it enough?
- If there is no permit, is one needed?
- What is the process and time involved to secure a permit?
- If the system runs out of water, how often does it occur, what time of year, and what causes it? How does it affect the maintenance of the golf course?

Sprinklers

A discussion of sprinklers should include how many different types are installed on the greens, tees, fairways, approaches, and rough.

- Are they the right sprinklers for those areas?
- Do the greens have a surround system (Figure 6.8)?
- What are the benefits of installing a surround system?

FIGURE 6.8
Collar sprinklers are common on most new irrigation systems.

- Are the sprinklers correctly spaced? The spacings should be measured and the findings explained. A table such as shown in Figure 6.9 is a good way of depicting such information.
- Check rotation speeds. Are they consistent?
- Are the sprinklers pressure regulating, or do they operate at many different pressures?
- Are the sprinklers level, broken, installed on slopes (Figure 6.10) or set too high or too low?
- Do they have consistent nozzles?
- Do they have other problems, and, if so, how much hand-watering is needed?
- Is the coverage adequate?

Location	Spacing (feet)	Comment
#2 Green	59'×66'×82'×73'	Inconsistent Spacing
#6 Green	41'×52'×59'×56'	Inconsistent Spacing
Practice Green	61'×62'×57'×83'	Somewhat Consistent Spacing
#1 Tee	49'	Too Close a Spacing
#10 Tee	56'	Acceptable Spacing
#16 Tee	53'	Acceptable Spacing
#8 Fairway	91'×88'×99'×90'×88'×90'×95'×92'×90'×92'×89'×92'	Inconsistent Spacing
#16 Fairway	91'×88'×93'×89'×92'×93'×90'×87'×87'×91'×92'	Inconsistent Spacing

FIGURE 6.9
Sample sprinkler spacings should be measured to check whether coverage is adequate.

FIGURE 6.10
Sprinklers should not be installed on slopes, as such placement affects their distribution.

- How many sprinklers are replaced or repaired in a year?
- Are tee heads throwing on nearby greens, or green heads on tees?
- Is water being thrown on roads or adjacent property?

Pipe and Fittings

Determine the size of mainlines from an as-built drawing or from repair experiences. Apply the 5 ft-per-second rule to the piping, based on the pump and pipe system capacity.

- Are pipe sizes too small and velocities excessive?
- What type of pipe is it?
- What is the pressure rating?
- Is the system operating pressure within 78 percent of the pipe's pressure rating?
- How often do mainline repairs have to be made?
- Are they pipe repairs or fitting repairs?

Ask the same questions about lateral piping: type, pressure rating, and size:

- Are they fittings, glued joints, pipe or repairs of previous repairs.
- Is the pipe made of steel, asbestos-cement, or ABS (acrylonitrile-butadiene-styrene)? Each of these has its own problems, which should be outlined.
- What types of fittings are installed on the mains and laterals: glued, gasket, epoxy, ductile iron, or mechanical joint?
- Are they causing any problems? If so, explain.
- Are the fittings properly thrust blocked?

Using a pressure gauge, take pressure readings at greens, turning sprinklers on, one zone at a time. The readings will indicate whether the sprinklers are receiving the proper amount of pressure.

- Are there pressure surges? Watch the movement of the gauge.
- Are the surges occurring only on parts of the course?
- Are elevation changes affecting pressures?

Put a gauge in the highest and lowest quick couplers on the golf course, and slowly turn on sprinklers (two at a time), recording the pressures at the high point, low point, and pump system until the pump system capacity is reached (Figure 6.11). Record the flow from the pump system flow meter, or estimate it based on the number and type of sprinklers operating. Track what pumps are operating, as this can also be a test of the pump system logic.

Isolation Valves

Determine the isolation capacity in the system.

- Are the greens and tees individually isolated? What about the fairway sprinklers?
- Are the fairways isolated as a loop, or is each lateral isolated?
- What about mainline isolation? Is isolation provided at every hole, every few holes, six holes, nine holes, or does the entire system have to be depressurized to make a repair?
- How is isolation achieved? With large gate valves, threaded valves, or ball valves, PVC, or metal?
- Are these cheap valves that have broken handles or leaking seals? Do they work? Are they frozen open or shut? What is the access?

FIGURE 6.11
Pressure gauges help in troubleshooting the pump system and analyzing performance.

FIGURE 6.12
Valve boxes are used to service equipment, but should be installed at an appropriate depth.

- Are the valves in valve boxes or reach sleeves? Are they too shallow or too deep, making maintenance difficult (Figure 6.12)?
- If valves are in pits or cast iron curb boxes, does this pose a maintenance problem?

Drains

Drains are similar to isolation valves. It must be determined if there are any, what they are made of, what are they housed in, how accessible they are, and what kind of maintenance they require. Where do they drain to—a sump, daylight, or a wet spot on the fairway?

Quick Coupling Valves

If pressure testing is performed on the greens, it will be clear as to whether there are quick couplers located at the greens.

- Are there quick couplers on the tees, fairways, and other areas?
- How many are broken, have no covers, are at an angle or loose?
- Are they installed directly in the soil or in a valve box or sleeve? Does the sleeve or valve box have a cover?
- Is the key easy to get in and out?
- Are the quick couplers too high or two low?
- If the green quick couplers are being used for syringing, how far are they from the green? Do they interfere with play?
- On what type of swing joint are they installed? Do they turn on the swing joint each time they are used?

Electric Valves

Depending on the type of system, there may be many electric valves or none. There may be some for clubhouse watering, pond fillers, bunker areas, or landscaped areas. There may be one for every sprinkler.

- Where are the electric valves located? What is their purpose?
- Are the valves brass or plastic?
- How old are they?
- Are repair parts available?
- What is the voltage of the electric valves?

- What is their pressure rating?
- What condition are they in, and how much maintenance do they require?
- How often do the valves stick open or closed?
- What size are they, and do they regulate pressure? If they do, is the regulator properly set?
- Can they handle dirty water?

Air Release/Vacuum Release Valves

Are there any air release/vacuum release valves? Most older courses do not have them.

- Are these valves properly located at high points and at dead ends?
- Are they of the proper size and type?
- Do they have isolation valves? Are the isolation valves open?
- Do they have filters or wye strainers?
- Are they in valve boxes or sticking out of the ground (Figure 6.13)?
- How do they direct the air coming out of them?
- Are the plugs still in their tops?
- What condition are they in?
- Is it clear as to why they are there and what their purpose is?

FIGURE 6.13
Air release valves should be installed in valve boxes below grade.

Swing Joints

Determining the type and condition of swing joints is important.

- What kind of swing joints are installed under the sprinklers— galvanized, brass, PVC? Or are they just straight nipples?
- If they are made of PVC, are they glued or prefabricated, with or without rubber ring gaskets?
- Are they leaking or corroding?
- Can they move, or are they locked up?
- Are the quick coupler swing joints stabilized with rods or some other device?
- What about the swing joint position? Is it configured at an up angle, or is it flat or on a down angle?

Valve Boxes

Are valve boxes utilized to access buried components?

- Where are the valve boxes located? Are any in play?
- Are the valve boxes at grade?
- What condition are they in?
- Are the covers or sides broken?
- Are they a potential liability risk?
- Do they have metal parts so that they can be located?

Control Systems

How is the irrigation system controlled?

- Is there a control system or is the irrigation manual?
- Is there a central controller? If so, what type, mechanical or computer?
- If mechanical, what does it control?
- If a computer, is it powerful enough? Does it have enough memory? What is its operating system?
- Are there field controllers, or is it a decoder type system?
- How many field controllers are there and where are they located? Are they in groups or individual (Figure 6.14)?
- What is the condition of the central and the field controllers?
- How old are they?
- What is their technology?
- Are the field controllers keeping accurate time?

FIGURE 6.14
Controllers are often installed in groups at several locations on a golf course.

- Are they susceptible to lightning damage?
- Are there extra fuses stored at the controller?
- Is what the field controller is operating apparent from its location?
- Are there any empty stations?
- What is the control logic for greens, tees, and fairways?
- Are the heads individually controlled, twinned, or worse? Is each tee individually controlled, or are all the tees on a hole operated at once, along with some on another hole?
- Are the enclosures plastic, metal, or stainless steel? Do they provide adequate protection from vandalism and weather?
- What are the age and condition of the field controllers? Are they rusted? Are they secure, at grade, and level?
- Are there nesting creatures such as snakes, mice, ants, or scorpions (Figure 6.15)?
- Are the controllers installed on concrete pads or something else?
- What is their voltage?
- Are the incoming wires separated, or are all the wires coming in through one hole in the pad? Is the pad large enough?
- What options do the controllers have in terms of lightning protection or other features?
- Can they be run by remote control, from the central or directly?
- Is there a weather station?
- How does the central communicate: hard wire, radio, or paging? If by hard wire, how many paths? If by radio, are there any interference problems?

FIGURE 6.15
Many different animals consider controllers to be safe, warm, and dry environments.

FIGURE 6.16
Controller wiring can be difficult to follow when not installed neatly.

- Does the central control system include a GPS-based map or electronic Record Drawing?
- Does it interface with a personal data assistant?
- How are the field controllers, central, weather station and pump system grounded?
- Is there a rod, several rods, or a combination of rods and plates?
- Is ground enhancement material being used?
- Are clamps being used, or an exothermic connector?
- Is there access to the connectors, and if so, how?
- Can the grounding grid collect moisture, or is it irrigated?
- Has the grounding for all the various electronic equipment been tested for resistance to ground?
- Does it meet the grounding and resistance requirements of the controller manufacturer?

Wiring

An automatic system contains many different types and sizes of wire.

- What are the various types of wire installed: communication, power, control, and common? What colors are they (Figure 6.16)?
- What are the voltages, size, and condition?

-
- What kind of wire connectors are being used? Are they water-proof?
- Are there many splices? If so, are they in valve boxes and shown on the Record Drawings?
- Are the wires routed with the mainline, or are they in separate trenches or pulls, making them difficult to locate?

Pump System

- Where is the pump house located?
- What is its capacity in terms of pressure and flow?
- How many pumps are there, and of what size, horsepower, and capacity are they?
- What types of pumps does the system use: centrifugal, turbine, submersible, or some combination of two or three (Figure 6.17)?
- Is there a pressure maintenance pump, jockey pump, or both?
- Are the main pumps all the same size, or do they vary?
- What is the speed of the various pumps?
- Does the irrigation system water in an acceptable period of time, or does it take too long?

FIGURE 6.17
Pump systems are not always installed in buildings.

- Are there performance curves for the pumps? If not, what are the model number and impeller sizes?
- How does the pump system get water? Does it use suction lift, flooded suction, a submersible or a vertical turbine pump?
- Is there a wet well intake or a floating foot valve?
- Is the intake screened?
- Are the wet well and inlet piping big enough?
- Do the pumps lose prime?
- What are the velocities in the intakes? Are they acceptable?
- As discussed, all pump systems need to regulate pressure. How is the pump system regulating pressure: variable frequency drive (VFD), pressure-regulating valve, or pressure relief valve?
- Is there a relief valve, and is it properly sized?
- Are the pumps isolated?
- Where are the isolation valves in the pump system?
- Does each pump have a check valve? If so, where is it located?
- How many pressure gauges are on the pump system? Are they working and readable? Are they in the appropriate locations?
- Does the system have a pressure tank? If so, is it vertical or horizontal?
- Is the tank pressure rated and/or certified? What size is it?
- Is the tank a bladder tank, or does it have an air release valve to maintain the air/water balance?
- How old is the tank, and what condition is it in?
- Are there any transfer pumps in the system? What do they do, and where are they located?
- What is the capacity of the transfer pumps, and how are they controlled?
- Are there injection, fertigation, or other systems attached to the pump system?
- Is the system capable of remote monitoring? How is that accomplished—through telephone, radio, or hard wire?

Pump System Controls

Pump system control technology is constantly evolving.

- How is the pump system controlled, and what is the logic?
- Is it technically up to date, with a flow meter and pressure transducer displayed on the front of the panel, manually turned on and off, or is it using Mercoid and limit switches (Figure 6.18)?

FIGURE 6.18
Gauges and flow meters help in troubleshooting pump systems.

- Does it have a logic controller?
- What kind of starters are being used? Are they across-the-line or some type of reduced voltage?
- Does each pump have a hand-off-automatic switch and an hour meter?
- If it is a VFD system, what is the backup, if any, if the VFD fails?
- How smoothly do the pumps switch, and how well are they operating?
- How much maintenance is the pump system requiring?
- Does the control panel/system include all of the appropriate safeties for the type of system installed (low discharge with bypass, high discharge, low wet well, high temperature, phase failure, etc.)?
- Is the panel UL listed? Is the station UL listed, and what kind of third party certifications does it carry?
- Can the control panel be monitored from a remote computer?

Pump House

Most pump systems are enclosed in a building.

- What is the condition of the pump house—walls, floor and roof?
- Is the pump house big enough? What is it made of—wood, concrete, or something else (Figure 6.19)?

FIGURE 6.19
The pump house should be evaluated for its condition, as well as the pump system.

- Does it meet NEC requirements?
- Are the doors big enough to get equipment in and out? Is there a hatch for turbine removal?
- Is the ventilation forced or static? Is there an exhaust fan? Where is it, and how big is it?
- Is the fan controlled with a switch or a temperature sensor?
- Are there air inlets? How big and where?
- Is there a heater? How is it controlled?
- Is there enough light? What type of light is it, and where is the light switch located?
- Are there any power outlets for servicing the system? Where are they located?
- Is there a containment area for chemicals or fertilizers?
- Is there other irrigation on the system, such as clubhouse or tennis court watering? If so, what is the source, and how is the irrigation controlled?

Management

- What is the level of management required for the irrigation system? How is it measured?
- Is the management intense, fair, or adequate?
- Are the schedules changed on a regular basis?

- Are repairs quickly made?
- Are the irrigation system control features being used?
- Are databases filled out, and are they correct?
- Is the system properly programmed?

Conclusion and Recommendations

An evaluation should end with a short synopsis of the overall condition of the system. It should include the level of maintenance required, the limitations of the current system, if any, and an estimated cost of annual repairs and parts. The recommendations of the report should be outlined in terms of prioritized short-term and long-term needs. A brief description should accompany each recommendation, restating what is said in the report. The conclusions and recommendations should summarize the entire evaluation for its readers. They turn to the body of the report for more detail if they feel it necessary, but most decision makers (owners, green committee members, etc,) will not read the entire report. Estimated costs for each recommendation should be given, as well as a time line for recommended repairs or modifications. The following questions should be addressed:

- Is total replacement the only economical alternative?
- Is a phasing plan needed?
- What is the proposed time line?

An evaluation of the entire system is not always necessary. Frequently, evaluations of specific components are made, such as water supply, coverage, pump system, or hydraulics.

Documentation

The saying "A picture is worth a thousand words" has great merit. The report should include pictures to clarify key issues. How many members have ever been in the pump house? Without pictures, it is hard for them to understand what the report is talking about. It should include examples and name specific areas of the golf course wherever possible so the reader can relate to the problem. Records of past maintenance and repairs as well as hand-watering costs should also be included (Figure 6.20). Data should be presented in graphs, tables, and charts for clarity. Drawings or sketches can be used if needed to illustrate a point. Verbal statements are more credible

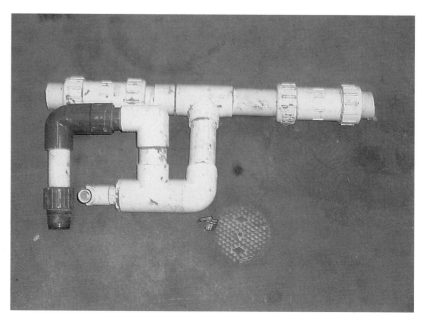

FIGURE 6.20
Often, irrigation system repairs are performed to fix previous repairs made incorrectly.

when backed up with graphic data. The report and its presentation should be professional.

SYSTEM AUDITS

Uniformity in irrigation is defined as the evenness with which a sprinkler applies water to the area being irrigated, for a given spacing, profile, and wind condition. Computer software can be used to determine the theoretical uniformity of a specific sprinkler at a specific spacing, but an audit will reveal the uniformity under actual field conditions. Audits, along with the physical data, provide a visual picture of the uniformity in the field. Audits are applied, not theoretical; they are "hands on." An audit helps the irrigation system manager understand how a sprinkler distributes water either singularly (Figure 6.21) or in a group.

Required Equipment

The items required to perform an audit include flags for marking existing sprinkler locations; a tape measure (100 ft minimum) for measuring area sizes and sprinkler spacings and laying out the catch device grid; a pressure gauge (0 to 160 psi) for operating pressure measurements; and some type of catch device for the collection of

FIGURE 6.21
The distribution profile of the sprinkler determines how uniformly it will apply water at a specific spacing and pressure.

water. Catch devices can be very simple, such as plastic drinking cups, or anything with a fairly large opening (throat area) and relatively straight sides. Several devices are commercially available (Figure 6.22). All of the needed equipment can be purchased as an auditing kit, if desired. A timing device will be needed to measure sprinkler operating time. Finally, several assistants are needed at various times throughout the auditing process to help with measurements, layout, and data collection.

System Tune-Up

Auditing an irrigation system that has not been maintained is not a good idea. Because an audit is intended to measure uniformity, the system should be in its normal operating condition. Therefore, before an audit is done, a system tune-up should be performed. It should address the following problems:

- Plugged or broken nozzles
- Broken sprinklers
- Tilted and sunken sprinklers
- Arc misalignment
- Nonrotating sprinklers
- Closed valves

FIGURE 6.22
There are several manufactured catch devices, such as the one shown here.

FIGURE 6.23
Low operating pressure severely distorts the distribution profile.

All of these problems should be eliminated before an audit takes place. Major problems, such as low pressure (Figure 6.23) or poor spacing, that cannot be easily fixed should be let alone to be documented in the auditing procedure.

Auditing Procedure

Audits are best performed in a set routine under wind conditions similar to those under which normal irrigation takes place. This ensures consistency in the audits, ease of comparability, and efficiency in the time it takes to perform an audit. Because an audit can interfere with play, the faster it can be accomplished, the better. The following steps should be followed in performing an audit:

1. *Flag the locations of sprinklers.* Mark all sprinklers that apply water to the area being audited. This is easily done by operating the sprinklers for a short period of time and marking the locations with flags. Make sure the flags are in a location where they will not interfere with the operation of the sprinklers. Place a flag behind each sprinkler, or lay it down if a catch device is behind the sprinkler.

2. *Find the center of the area being audited, using a measuring tape.* For example, on a green it would be the center point of the width at the widest point and of the length at the longest point (Figure 6.24). On a fairway, it may only be necessary to

FIGURE 6.24
Cups should be laid out in a grid pattern with the use of a measuring tape.

find the center of the fairway, widthwise. Mark the center with a flag or *small* dot of paint if there is play.

3. *Set out the catch devices in a grid pattern.* The grid will depend on the size of the area being audited and the number of catch devices available. The closer the grid spacing, the more precise will be the measurement of uniformity. Triangular or square grids can be used, depending on the shape of the area being audited. For the most part, try to keep the catch devices inside the sprinklers, although that will not always be possible. Place the catch devices so that the sprinkler stream does not knock them over. If the weather is unsettled, put a catch device out of the audit area to measure any rain, which can be subtracted from the collected data. Depending on the distance between sprinklers, catch devices can be spaced from 5 ft on center (for 40 ft to 45 ft sprinkler spacing) to 10 ft (for 80 ft to 90 ft sprinkler spacing) or more to achieve a high level of accuracy. A rule of thumb is to have about 70 catch devices in a grid, which will help determine the spacing (Figure 6.25). Smaller audit areas, such as greens and tees, will use fewer devices. For greens, the grid should cover the entire cut surface and into the approach. Try to audit multiple tees simultaneously, and operate all the sprinklers covering them (Figure 6.26). It may

FIGURE 6.25
A green cup test takes about an hour from start to finish.

FIGURE 6.26
Multiple tees can be tested at the same time.

be possible to audit tees on several holes at once. For a fairway (unless it is a par 3), take a representative section that is on the basic sprinkler spacing of the fairway. For single-row fairways, a single row down the middle and then out to the sides works well (Figure 6.27). For multiple rows, use double rows of catch devices between the sprinklers, and to the sides if checking rough coverage/uniformity. Engineered catch devices are available from several vendors. They offer the convenience of direct readings in inches or milliliters of

FIGURE 6.27
A representative section should be selected when testing fairways.

caught water. The disadvantage is the relatively high cost of purchasing 70 or more. Another option is to buy plastic drinking cups. Look for containers with relatively wide mouths (thin edges) and straight sides. Consider a minimum depth of 3 in., to keep drops from splashing out during data collection. The width of the catch device opening should be at least 4 in., and the opening can be round or square. The sides should be as near vertical as possible. Small, clear, hard plastic cocktail glasses have been used with some success; they are inexpensive and disposable. All catch devices must be of the same size and shape. If nonengineered catch devices are used, a graduated cylinder or similar device to measure caught water will be needed. These can be read in metric or English units. On windy days, the catch devices may have to be weighted with small rocks so that they do not blow away. The rocks will not affect the amount of water caught; it can be poured into the graduated cylinder and measured.

4. Next, measure the static pressure of the area being audited, most easily through the closest quick coupler. Remember that static pressure is the pressure with no water moving, and the system off. Simply insert the key with pressure gauge attached into the quick coupler and read the pressure. If no quick coupler is available, an adapter can be used with the gauge installed in a nearby sprinkler after the internal assembly is removed (Figure 6.28).

FIGURE 6.28
With the appropriate adapter, a pressure gauge can be installed in the sprinkler in place of the internal assembly.

FIGURE 6.29
During testing, puddling can occur while the auditor is trying to get enough water into the catch devices.

5. Operate all sprinklers in the audit area as they would normally be run. This includes operating the same sprinklers and the same number of sprinklers that would normally operate together, even if they are outside the audit area. The test should be run long enough that the driest catch device has a measurable amount (assuming no absolute dry spots) and the fullest cup is not overflowing. Four to five rotations of the sprinklers are usually needed. In some cases, this may be more water than the area can take without puddling, especially on greens (Figure 6.29). For most golf course areas, 9 to 15 minutes is common. Uniformity is not dependent on how long the test is run, but on how uniformly the water is applied. Ideally, the tests should be run under the conditions present when irrigation is normally performed. For example, if winds normally run at 3 to 5 miles per hour during irrigation, conduct the test during similar conditions. Otherwise, test results will not reflect actual uniformity during a typical irrigation event. Conducting a test during higher- or lower-than-normal wind conditions will skew the test results. For example, individual head control on a green requires that each sprinkler be operated separately during the audit, if that is the way it is normally scheduled. The catch device readings that are collected can be dimensionless in terms of time. When uniformity is considered or measured, the concern is the ratio of dry, average, and wet areas. How fast or slowly the water is applied is a function of run time.

FIGURE 6.30
GPS mapping can be used to locate and collect catch device data.

6. While the system is operating, walk around and note any problems with the sprinklers, such as worn nozzles, inconsistent nozzle sizes, or rotation speed, high or low heads, unlevel heads, and sprinkler types and models, especially if they are different. Also note whether full- and part-circle sprinklers are operating together. Document all of the problems with notes and pictures.

7. Next, measure the dynamic pressure of the area being audited for each different sprinkler or set of sprinklers operating, using the same mechanism used to measure the static pressure. To avoid getting wet, remember to watch out for the sprinkler streams while reading the pressure.

8. To document the audit, draw or map the audit area and the locations of sprinklers, catch devices, and quick couplers. This can be done with a measuring tape or using GPS (Figure 6.30). Note all of the sprinkler types, models, and nozzles. Make sure that the grid for the audited area is tied to the sprinkler layout through the map. Measure the spacing of all the sprinklers affecting the audit area. Note the center of the audit area and the direction from which the play comes.

FIGURE 6.31
Errors can occur while auditing, and all such problems should be noted on the field logs.

9. Document problems encountered during the testing, such as cups knocked over by sprinkler streams (Figure 6.31), nonrotating sprinklers, and so forth. Track the desired operating time set on the controller versus the actual operating time, as on older controllers they can vary significantly.

FIGURE 6.32
Temporary tees and greens should be used during catch device tests, as it is difficult to play through an audit.

10. When all of the sprinklers have operated for the prescribed length of time, the catch devices are read. For consistency, the same person should read all of the cups. One person reads while another writes down the values. Read the catch devices in order, following the map sequence.

The entire audit process for a given area will take about an hour and should be scheduled around play. Otherwise, it is very difficult to play through the catch devices, and there may be a risk of a golf ball hitting one of the catch devices (Figure 6.32).

Once the data has been collected, it must be interpreted. Visually observing the catches while there is still water in them is a nonquantitative way to interpret the data. This procedure quickly indicates the parts of the audit area that are overwatered (wet spots) or underwatered (dry spots) and shows the general uniformity of the coverage. It provides immediate feedback and relates the amount distributed to a specific location. This can also be seen on the audit map (Figure 6.33). Any areas that have puddles should be noted and shown on the map as well. If desired, the map can be further refined to provide contours and even section profiles of water application.

Calculations

AVERAGE

The average is the total amount of water collected in all the catch devices divided by the number of devices. For example, a test showed the following 15 numbers in milliliters: 12, 18, 13, 14, 10, 9,

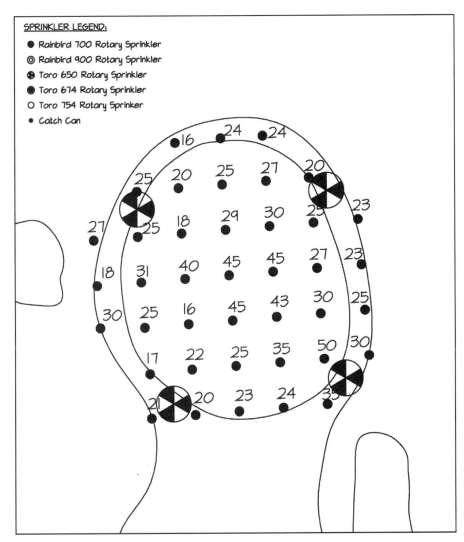

SPRINKLER LEGEND:

● Rainbird 700 Rotary Sprinkler
◎ Rainbird 900 Rotary Sprinkler
✪ Toro 650 Rotary Sprinkler
● Toro 674 Rotary Sprinkler
○ Toro 754 Rotary Sprinker
• Catch Can

FIGURE 6.33
Audit results should be shown on a sketch of the golf course feature, along with the associated reading for each catch device.

18, 20, 23, 22, 20, 15, 19, 15, 16. To determine the average, add up all the numbers and divide by the number of data points:

$$12 + 18 + 3 + 14 + 10 + 9 + 18 + 20 + 23$$
$$+ 22 + 20 + 15 + 19 + 15 + 16 = 244 \text{ ml}$$

$$244 \div 15 = 16.27 \text{ ml}$$

MEDIAN

The median is the number in the middle of the data collected. To get the median, first list the numbers in order: 9, 10, 12, 13, 14, 15, 15, 16, 18, 18, 19, 20, 20, 22, 23. The median is the eighth number, or 16.

DISTRIBUTION UNIFORMITY (LOWER QUARTER)

Distribution uniformity (lower quarter) (DU_{LQ}) is the standard measurement used in field audits, although other techniques may be used. Distribution uniformity (lower quarter) is the average of the lowest 25 percent of measurements divided by the average of all the measurements. Of the 15 measurements, the lower quarter represent fours collection devices:

$$15 \times 0.25 = 3.75 \text{ or } 4$$

$$9 + 10 + 12 + 13 = 44$$

$$44 \div 4 = 11$$

11 ÷ 16.27 (overall average from preceding calculation) = 0.68 or 68% uniformity

SCHEDULING COEFFICIENT

The scheduling coefficient has to be calculated with the use of specialized distribution uniformity software and cannot be calculated manually, but using the actual catch device data provides real-world, as opposed to theoretical, values.

Uniformity and coverage problems that show up in the audit results occur for a reason. Part of the reason for doing an audit is to determine why the results are what they are. The audit shows where; the question is, Why? The problem may be the design—that is, the spacing is not good for the sprinkler, nozzle, and pressure combination being used, or the wrong sprinkler is being used. It may be the hydraulics of the system, with the sprinklers receiving too much or too little pressure because of small pipe sizes, partially closed valves, high elevations, or an improperly sized pump system. It may be a lack of control too, such as when too many sprinklers are operating together instead of individually.

During the audit, watch the pressure gauge to see whether the jockey or pressure maintenance pump is cycling. Often, a system does not operate well with one or two sprinklers at a time. To keep the pressure consistent, an additional sprinkler or two may have to be turned on for the duration of the audit.

The results of the audit can be used to provide a base schedule for irrigation of the golf course, based on the minimum uniformities measured, or for each individual green, tee, and fairway if they are all audited. It can also point out whether adjustments to the nozzles, pressure, spacing, sprinklers, control system, pump system, or hydraulics are needed. Audits can be used to establish a base line uniformity for the irrigation system and, subsequently, as a trouble-shooting method for problem areas by comparing past uniformities to present values.

For example, if, as shown by the audit, the distribution uniformity from the audit for a green is calculated at 68 percent, as indicated in the preceding example, and the desired amount of water to be applied is 0.20 in., then the actual amount to be applied is 0.20/0.68, or 0.294 in. If the system has a precipitation rate of 0.56 in. per hour, the run time would have to be 32 minutes to ensure that all of the area being irrigated gets a minimum of 0.20 in.

Auditing is a great way to obtain both a visual and a statistical indication of how uniformly the irrigation system applies water to a given area. The audit provides an actual measurement of uniformity and precipitation rate, as opposed to the theoretical. It indicates both wet and dry spots and helps in developing schedules that apply minimum amounts of water to all areas.

Installation

7

This chapter describes the common procedures, practices, and assemblies employed to install a golf course irrigation system, looks at the specialized equipment required to implement these procedures, and highlights the various benefits and drawbacks of all. Potential installation pitfalls and problem areas are examined and various solutions suggested.

Installation is the final element of the golf course irrigation system triad (system design, equipment selection, installation). Installation is the keystone to a successful golf course irrigation system. By the time an installation has begun, the design has been completed and the equipment manufacturer selected. State-of-the-art irrigation equipment specified in the finest design can be rendered useless by improper installation.

PRELIMINARY CONSIDERATIONS

An installation begins with the ordering, receiving, and storage of materials and culminates with the final punch list, system documentation, and warranty period. The installation sequence of the various elements and areas of a golf course irrigation system differ widely from one project to another. Financing, permitting issues, utility connections, material deliveries, subcontractor availability, and soil and weather conditions are only a few of the myriad elements that often dictate where the installation will commence and the sequence it will follow. Where an installation is being done on an existing golf course, interruption of play and inconvenience to the members are critical considerations.

There are numerous and undeniable advantages to having the permanent water source completed and operational at the start of the irrigation system installation. A rational look at most golf course irrigation system installations suggests that it is highly unlikely that the permanent water source, whether it is a well, pond, or municipal water supply, can be completed prior to the start of the piping installation. For this reason, connections to a temporary or secondary water source should be considered. This connection can be used to flush, adjust, and test the system. It is also frequently used for initial system operation when the permanent water source is not completed.

MATERIAL TAKE-OFF AND MATERIAL ORDERING

Material orders should be generated from a detailed material take-off based on the irrigation system plans and specifications. The material take-off should begin with the largest pipe size, usually located at the water source, and progress methodically through the system, culminating with the smallest pipe size. Gate valves, electric control valves, sprinkler heads, and field controllers can be counted as assemblies. An assembly includes all the ancillary items required to install a valve, head, controller, and so forth, according to the plans and specifications. Sample 7.1 shows the items typically included in an assembly for a 1½ in. electric control valve (see Figure 7.42, page 357).

SAMPLE 7.1

1½ IN. PRESSURE REGULATING ELECTRIC CONTROL VALVE ASSEMBLY

6 in. × 1½ in.	ductile iron service tee
1½ in.	lateral 90° ell
1½ in.	bronze gate valve
1½ in. × 3 in	ductile iron nipple
1½ in.	electric control valve
1½ in. × 6 in	TOE nipple
2 in.	coupling with 2 in × 1½ in. reducing bushing
1	standard valve box

1   DBY splice kit
1   DBR splice kit
Gravel
Teflon tape

Pipe quantities can be estimated or measured by several methods. The actual pipe route can be physically measured on the course with a measuring wheel. However, actual physical measurement of all the proposed pipe of a golf course irrigation system is time-consuming and impractical. There are more practical methods for doing a take-off and estimating pipe quantities. A map measuring wheel can be used to wheel off the various pipe quantities on the irrigation plan.

As a pipe size is scaled or measured, the pipe leg is highlighted with a colored marker to indicate that it has been measured. A legend is placed on the plan to indicate the different pipe sizes and their corresponding highlighted colors. As the mainline pipe is measured, the mainline pipe fittings are counted and each fitting is indicated at its location on the plan. Sample 7.2 shows a typical 6 in. pipe take-off with fitting designation.

SAMPLE 7.2

TAKE-OFF—6 IN. SDR-21 GASKET JOINT PIPE WITH FITTINGS

2,860 lf 6 in. SDR-21 gasket joint PVC pipe
4 each   6 × 6 × 6 ductile iron tee
3 each   6 × 6 × 4 ductile iron tee
4 each   6 × 6 × 3 ductile iron tee
2 each   6 × 4 × 6 ductile iron tee
3 each   6 × 4 × 4 ductile iron tee
1 each   6 × 3 × 4 ductile iron tee
3 each   6 in. ductile iron 45 degree elbow
2 each   6 in. ductile iron 22.5 degree elbow
2 qt.   pipe lubricant
66   80-lb. bags concrete

The take-off of power wire and communication cable is similar to the mainline pipe take-off. A low-voltage wire or hydraulic tubing take-off is more tedious and time-consuming. Frequently, a rule of thumb is used for estimating low-voltage control wire: 800 ft per head. This can be a dangerous and very inaccurate method for establishing quantities of low-voltage wire or hydraulic tubing. Factors such as field controller location and station capacity, spare wires, and wire routing drastically influence this feet-per-sprinkler-head ratio. The preferred method for establishing low-voltage wire or hydraulic tubing quantities is to do a detailed measured take-off, as is done with the piping. An alternate method is to do a detailed measured take-off of several typical field controllers, tally the total of the various low-voltage wire sizes (or hydraulic tubing), and divide by the number of stations covered by the field controller. This should provide a representative quantity per station of the various low-voltage wire sizes or hydraulic tubing. Multiply that quantity-per-station number by the total number of stations to derive the estimated total quantities required. Experienced estimators add 5 to 10 percent to these quantities to account for waste, slack, and topography. Sample 7.3 shows a typical low-voltage wire estimate derived from field controller sampling.

Today the majority of golf course irrigation systems are designed utilizing any one of a variety of computer-aided design (CAD) and/or irrigation design programs. A completed golf course irrigation system design is composed of data inputted in layers: golf course features, sprinkler head layout, piping diagram, wiring diagram, and so on. Although specialized software programs do not eliminate the need for manual material take-off, the programs can automatically count and measure many of the components of the system when the data has been inputted properly. Field controllers, sprinkler heads, gate, air release and quick coupling valves, electric valves, pipe, power wire, and communication wire are just some of the items that can be counted and measured by many CAD programs. The take-off of other items such as fittings, low-voltage wire, hydraulic tubing, to name a few, is best counted or measured manually.

Once the take-off is completed, the material format should be restructured into purchase orders to be sent to the various material vendors. A copy of each purchase order should be kept on site where the materials are stored. The purchase orders are invaluable for checking in materials, tracking back orders, and general reference during the construction period.

SAMPLE 7.3

LOW-VOLTAGE WIRE ESTIMATE BASE ON TYPICAL FIELD CONTROLLER SAMPLING

	Common 12/1 White	Greens 14/1 Orange	Fairway 14/1 Red	Tees 14/1 Black	Spare 14/1 Blue
Wire measured on:					
Field Controller B	2,890	6,500	28,800	3,360	2,170
Field Controller H	1,880	5,240	9,260	4,380	1,760
Field Controller L	4,370	4,560	30,600	5,170	2,780
Field Controller N	3,775	6,420	29,380	1,590	2,250
Total of wire measured	*12,915*	*22,720*	*98,040*	*14,500*	*8,960*
Stations used:*					
Field Controller B		10	32	4	4
Field Controller H		11	12	6	4
Field Controller L		9	45	5	4
Field Controller N		10	40	5	4
Total	*205*	*40*	*129*	*20*	*16*
Average wire per station:	12,915/205 = 63	22,720/40 = 568	98,040/129 = 760	14,500/20 = 725	8,960/16 = 560
Total number of stations for entire system:	1,350	231	812	116	191
Estimated quantity of wire required based on average per station times total number of stations:	85,050	131,208	617,120	84,100	106,960

* Total stations is the sum of the valve-in-head sprinklers and the electric control valves.

5 to10 percent should be added for slack and waste.

PERMITS

Many aspects of a golf course irrigation system are subject to codes and regulations. These can usually be categorized in two groups: regulatory codes and construction codes.

Some examples of components that may be subject to regulatory codes include the following:

- Water allocation or diversion
- Pond construction
- Land clearing
- Soil conservation/erosion
- Variances and planning board approval
- Wetland or road crossings

Components that may be subject to construction codes include the following:

- Connection to a potable water supply
- Installation of a private well or water source
- Installation of a backflow preventer
- Electric power supply to field controllers
- Electric supply to pump station
- Pump house construction

Although there is a reluctance on the part of many golf clubs to approach municipal planning and building departments, the time to find out whether a variance, planning board approval, or construction permit is required is before the start of a project, not halfway through. Many a project has been stopped or delayed because approvals or permits were not filed for and obtained in advance. Furthermore, in today's litigious society, all parties involved in planning and installing a golf irrigation system are vulnerable to legal action for not filing for and obtaining the required permits.

Construction permits, once issued, require inspections at various stages. Requests for inspections should be promptly called in to the appropriate agency by the contractor and copies of the inspection approvals kept on file. Should an accident related to the construction occur anytime in the future, copies of inspections and approvals by building department officials may prove invaluable in limiting liability.

THE STAGING AREA—RECEIVING AND STORING MATERIALS

A substantial area is required for the storage of installation materials and construction equipment. This area is generally referred to as the staging area. Although the storage of materials and equipment can be split—for example, pipe and trenching equipment in one location and sprinkler heads, valves, and other loose goods in another—it is preferable to have all the materials and equipment stored in one place. The size of the area required for staging will vary with each installation, but all have certain elements in common. The staging area should be accessible by tractor-trailer. The area should be relatively level, drain well, and be accessible in varying weather conditions. The staging area should be centrally located on the course. This will save many man-hours in transporting materials and equipment around the course.

Piping material should be stacked and stored by type and size. Installations frequently call for different classes of pipe of the same diameter: For example, 8 in. SDR-26, Class 160 PVC, for a pond feed pipe and 8 in. SDR-21, Class 200 PVC, as part of the irrigation system mainline. These two different classes of pipes should be labeled and stored apart from one another to prevent the inadvertent use of the wrong pipe. All pipes should be organized so that each pipe type and size is readily accessible without having to move other materials and so that the pipe can be loaded or moved with a forklift. The ability to load and move pipe mechanically during construction will save countless man-hours.

On new construction sites where dust is anticipated, it is advisable to plug or tape both ends of each piece of pipe or tarp both ends of each pipe pallet. Fine dust created by construction equipment can enter open-ended pipe and settle to the bottom of each piece. This fine dust is very difficult to flush effectively from the completed piping system. Leaves are also a problem, not only on new construction sites but on existing courses as well. Taking preventive measures is well worth the time and effort, with the reward being a clean piping system with fewer problems on start-up.

Secure, sheltered storage facilities are needed for most of the remaining materials. In rare situations, an existing building may be available for this purpose, but in most instances storage trailers or containers are rented for the duration of the installation. The amount of sheltered storage space or number of storage trailers needed will vary, depending on the size of the installation and how much of the material requires secure sheltered storage. Items such as ductile iron fittings, large gate valves, and valve boxes can be stored outside when theft or vandalism is not a concern. Materials such as sprinkler heads, electric solenoid valves, quick coupling valves, PVC fittings, and splice materials are shipped in standard quantity packaging in cardboard boxes and require sheltered storage. Power, communication, and low-voltage wire should also be secured and sheltered from the elements.

The materials should be grouped together in the storage area according to function. For example, all the materials required for valve-in-head sprinkler installation, such as the sprinkler heads, swing joints, PVC fittings, and low-voltage wire splice materials, should be stored in the same area. Having the materials grouped by function will save many man-hours when pulling materials during installation.

Additional storage area is required for bulk items such as sand, stone, selected backfill, and topsoil. Multiple bulk storage sites should be provided for installations where large quantities of selected backfill and/or topsoil are anticipated. Where possible, these sites should be dispersed throughout the course and located close to the area that will require the bulk material. Installations that generate quantities of unsuitable backfill material (deleterious material) will also require a disposal site. Having on-site disposal areas in the vicinity of the holes that generate the deleterious materials can minimize cost. Trucking the deleterious material off-site for disposal can add substantial cost.

Irrigation contractors often utilize portable diesel and gas storage tanks for fueling equipment and trucks. The fueling station is frequently located within the staging area. State and local regulations may stipulate whether and how a fueling station may be constructed. However, under no circumstances should a fueling station be located near a public roadway, catch basin, drain grate, body of water, or wetland. Containment equal to or greater than the full tank capacity should be provided around every tank. Even a minor spill of fuel can cost tens of thousands of dollars to clean up, given today's environmental regulations. For installations on an existing golf course, a viable alterative to using portable fuel tanks is for the irrigation contractor to use the club's fueling facility, track the fuel used, and reimburse the club for the expense. This arrangement reduces the risk of contamination from a fuel spill.

The staging area may require access to a variety of utilities. Golf irrigation contractors often include an office or office/storage trailer in the staging area. This office space is used for administrative purposes and for maintaining a current Record Drawing of the installation. The office trailer usually includes lights, electric outlets, electric heat, and air-conditioning, thus requiring a temporary electric service. Sometimes a temporary telephone service is required for a phone and fax machine. Sanitary facilities for the installation crew, whether provided by portable toilets or use of the facilities at the maintenance building, must be considered.

The staging area also frequently includes an area for mixing concrete for thrust blocks. The concrete is usually either ready-mix bagged concrete or a mix of sand, gravel, and Portland cement. In either case, storage for the concrete materials and access to a water supply are required.

The installation process generates a considerable amount of scrap material and refuse. Some of this material, such as scrap wire and cardboard, can be recycled. Other material will require proper disposal. Local recycling and landfill regulations usually dictate what requires recycling and what is acceptable for disposal. Contacting several local carting or container companies can yield information about what must be recycled, what the landfills will accept, and the most cost-efficient method of handling refuse.

INSTALLATION EQUIPMENT

The variety and sizes of construction equipment adaptable for golf course irrigation installation seem unlimited. The equipment best suited for each installation varies according to digging conditions, soil types, and width and depth of excavation. Generally, no one piece of equipment can fulfill all installation and excavation requirements. Rather, a variety of types and sizes of installation equipment is utilized during installation. Excavators, backhoes, chain and wheel type trenchers, vibratory plows, compactors, landscape tractors, and power brooms are examples of typical installation equipment. Forklifts, pipe trailers, and wire trailers are examples of material handling equipment (see Figure 7.1).

FIGURE 7.1
Pipe trailer used for transporting pipe around the course.

FIGURE 7.2
**Vermeer 8050 trencher—
85 horsepower trencher.**

Mainline pipe is usually installed by the open-trench method. Lateral lines and sub-mains are also frequently installed by the open-trench method, particularly on new courses or in rocky soils. Appropriate selection of trenching equipment for a specific digging condition is the key to open-trench production (Figure 7.2). An undersized trencher can slow production and is susceptible to breakdown. Of equal importance to trencher size is the style of the trencher attachment and the configuration of the digging chain. A trencher boom capable of digging 72 in. deep is undesirable if it is required to dig only 36 in. deep. Likewise, the style and configuration of the digging chain should be suitable to the soil type. A carbide bit chain configured to dig in shale is ineffective digging in sand.

Where piping is to be installed by the vibratory plow method, the vibratory plow should be sized to the soil condition and application. Pipe should not be installed by a vibratory plow in hard soils and/or soils that contain rock or shale. This should be avoided even if there is equipment that can handle these soils. When rock or shale is encountered, the ability to restore the turf on existing courses, and the future integrity of the pipe on all courses, renders the vibratory plow method undesirable.

Larger vibratory plows are generally used for fairway installation, with smaller, more maneuverable plows used for green, tee, and bunker installation (see Figure 7.3). The style and configuration of the vibratory plow blade is as important as the size of the vibratory plow. The blade should be configured to provide the specified depth of

FIGURE 7.3
Plywood tracks laid to allow Vermeer LM-42 vibratory plow to operate in sandy soil conditions.

cover over the pipe. Where wire is being installed in conjunction with the pipe, the wire should be laid via a wire chute, not pulled through the ground (see Figure 7.4). The chute should be of sufficient size and radius to handle the bundle of wire without chaffing and bending. Wire chutes can be configured to install the wire either above or below the pipe. Installing the wire above the pipe allows for easier access and splicing. In either case, minimum depth of cover must be maintained. The blade should be configured to provide at least 1 in. separation between the pipe and the wire.

There is a variety of specialty equipment that can be used to backfill, compact, and restore trench lines. Sweeper brooms and auger backfillers are two examples of specialty equipment used for backfilling (Figure 7.7). Jumping-jack compactors (stompers) (Figure 7.6) and sheep's foot wheel compactors (Figure 7.5) are the two most common compactors used for trench compaction. There are numerous landscape attachments that can mount on a three-point tractor hitch and be used for final trench grading and restoration.

For installations on existing courses, all wheeled vehicles must be equipped with turf tires or lug-type tires with nonagressive treads.

CREW

Installation crews vary in number according to the size of the installation and the production schedule. A simple double-row installation with a six-month installation time frame may require only a six-man

FIGURE 7.4
Combination pipe pulling/wire laying blade in use.

FIGURE 7.5
Trench being compacted with a Vermeer TC-4 compactor.

FIGURE 7.6
Trench being compacted with a stomper (jumping jack compactor).

FIGURE 7.7
Trench being backfilled with a Ditch Witch trencher equipped with a sweeper broom.

installation crew. Larger, more complex installations will require bigger crews. It is not uncommon to have a 10- to 20-man installation crew, or even larger. Larger crews are generally divided by function, i.e., mainline, fairway lateral, green and tee, and wiring crews.

Regardless of the size of the crew, a foreman or project leader should be designated, who will be responsible for coordinating the installation with the superintendent or owner's representative. Ideally, the foreman or project leader should not change for the duration of the installation. Moreover, to maintain consistency, one crew member should be designated to oversee the installation of all of the following: power wire, communication cable, field controllers, and central.

SAFETY

Safety should be the paramount consideration on any construction site, and golf course irrigation system installations are no exception. Local construction codes and health department statutes, as well as federal OSHA regulations, mandate that certain safety precautions be followed (Figure 7.8). Prior to starting any installation, all relevant safety regulations should be researched and a plan for compliance adopted.

FIGURE 7.8
Mechanic wearing safety goggles and protective gloves while cutting ductile iron pipe.

The following are potential safety concerns particular to golf course irrigation systems:

Personal Protection
- Ear protection
- Eye protection
- Head protection (hardhat)
- Foot protection (steel-toed shoes)
- Respirator, particularly when cutting asbestos cement (Transite) pipe
- Traffic control (barricades and police officers to control traffic patterns when road crossings are required)

Equipment Safety
- Functional seatbelts on all ride-on construction equipment
- Operating back-up alarms on all trucks and other equipment
- ROPS (roll over protection system) on all required equipment
- Ground fault protection on all electrical outlets and generators
- Grounded plugs on all electrical power tools and generators
- Shoring for deep excavations and wet well installation

Site Safety
- Holes closed during construction
- Construction areas cordoned off
- Open excavations covered nightly
- Stable cover constructed for wet well until pump house construction is complete (see Figure 7.22, page 328)

LAYOUT AND STAKING

Before any installation can commence, the irrigation system should be staked and laid out in the field. It is important to have the proper personnel on the staking team. Key staking team members should include the irrigation system consultant/designer, the golf course superintendent and/or assistant responsible for irrigation, and the irrigation contractor. In new course construction or where an irrigation system is being installed in conjunction with course renovation, representatives of the golf course architect and golf course builder should be present. Staking usually requires the use of a 300 ft tape or multiple 100 ft tapes. The square or triangular spacing indicated on the irrigation plans is replicated in the field with the use of the tapes. Additional team members may be required to hold various measure-

FIGURE 7.9
Staking team flagging a green.

ments on the tapes. All staking team members should be capable of communicating in a common language. A typical irrigation system staking team is composed of four to seven members (see Figure 7.9).

The sequence for staking and layout will vary according to the design and installation priority. Preferably, system layout begins with the staking of sprinkler heads, followed by the routing of mainlines and the location of isolation valves. This sequence allows the mainline and isolation valves to be located relative to the sprinkler heads. However, there are many scenarios that require the mainline and isolation valves to be laid out prior to staking the sprinkler heads. This is particularly common in new construction and systems installed in conjunction with course renovation.

Staking a golf hole requires considerable time and energy, and every effort should be made to preserve the integrity of that staking. Typically, wire marking flags are placed at sprinkler head and valve locations at the time of staking. These flags can be moved or lost or can deteriorate over time. Alternate or supplementary methods of marking may be used in instances when a period of time may elapse between staking and installation. On existing golf courses, marking paint or whiskers may be used to supplement the marking flag or a cup cutter may be used to invert a sod plug at the sprinkler head or valve location (see Figure 7.10). On new golf courses, wood stakes, lath, or PVC pipe can be used to mark the locations.

An "as-staked" plan should be drawn of each hole as the layout process progresses. This plan should indicate the type of spacing, the

FIGURE 7.10
Sprinkler head location being marked with a cup cutter, marking paint, and a flag.

numeric distance between sprinkler heads, and the model number of each sprinkler head and its corresponding nozzle size (Figure 7.11). When the wiring to the field controller has been completed, the designated station number can be added to this plan. Some irrigation consultants and contractors use Global Positioning System (GPS) technology to generate their as-staked plans.

After each day's staking, copies of the as-staked plans should be given to the irrigation consultant/designer, the golf course superintendent, and the irrigation crew foreman.

CONNECTION TO A SECONDARY WATER SOURCE

As previously mentioned, rarely is the permanent water source completed when the system installation starts. Having water available early on to flush, test, adjust, and wire the system has numerous advantages. For this reason, a connection to a secondary water source, whether it is a permanent or temporary connection, is desirable. The secondary water supply can come from a variety of sources: potable (city) water supply, well, pond, or sometimes in the case of an existing course, the old irrigation system water source.

Regardless of the source for the secondary water supply, one issue remains constant: A cross connection between potable and nonpotable water supplies must be avoided. If a potable water source is involved, then *a backflow protection device or air gap is required*. If the secondary water source is only temporary and will be disconnected when the permanent water source comes on-line, the installation of a removable spool piece can allow for reconnection to the secondary supply in case of emergency.

To benefit from and use the secondary or temporary water source, the irrigation mainline must be connected to that source and completed in each direction to the first mainline isolation valve.

CONNECTION TO THE PERMANENT WATER SUPPLY

Permanent water supplies for golf course irrigation systems come from a large variety of sources. The equipment and mechanics of how this water is transferred from the source into the irrigation

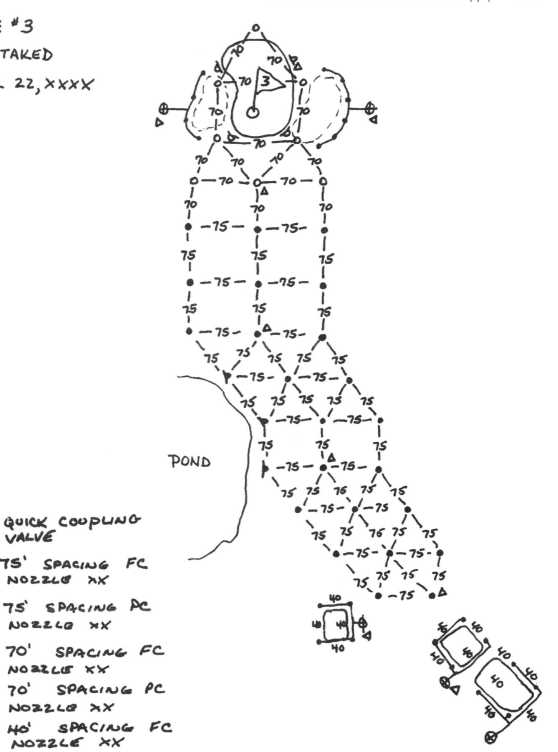

HOLE #3
AS STAKED
APRIL 22, XXXX

POND

△   QUICK COUPLING
    VALVE

●   75' SPACING FC
    NOZZLE XX

⬣   75' SPACING PC
    NOZZLE XX

○   70' SPACING FC
    NOZZLE XX

⬡   70' SPACING PC
    NOZZLE XX

·   40' SPACING FC
    NOZZLE XX

FIGURE 7.11
Typical "as-staked" drawing.

system at pressure vary even more. The configuration of intake structures, pipes, valves, pumps, and accessories is limited only by the imagination.

Wet Well and Intake Installation

Wet wells with intake flumes (with vertical turbine pumps) are probably the most common type of intake structures utilized for golf course irrigation systems. Wet wells can be constructed of a variety of materials—precast concrete, corrugated steel, PVC, high-density polyethylene—to name a few. A typical intake for vertical turbine pumps consists of a vertical column of pipe (wet well) connected to a horizontal length of intake pipe (flume). The majority of wet wells are constructed of round, square, or rectangular precast concrete sections. These sections are stacked one on top of another to complete the wet well. Wet well depths can vary substantially from one installation to another. They are seldom shallower than 12 ft, and most do not exceed 25 ft in depth.

In installing a wet well and intake flume, safety should be the number one priority. The Occupational Safety and Health Administration (OSHA) stipulates that any excavation more than 5 ft in depth requires a mechanical shoring or the presence of an experienced soils engineer. One of the most common causes of construction fatalities is excavation cave-in.

FIGURE 7.12
Wet well excavation in stable red shale soil.

Planning and preparation is important before installing a wet well (see Figure 7.12). Frequently, the soil type that will be encountered when digging to a depth of 12 ft or more is unknown. Money invested in test bores can be well spent, especially if there is the possibility of encountering rock, unstable soils, or groundwater. If a test bore indicates the presence of rock, equipment that can handle the rock can be scheduled or blasting can be anticipated. If unstable soil is discovered, the proper shoring materials can be ready on-site prior to starting the excavation. If groundwater is discovered, dewatering can be done before excavation is begun (see Figure 7.13).

The most difficult section of the wet well to set is the base (bottom) section. The base section must be set at the correct elevation, it must be set level, and it must be set at the greatest depth. In addition, when the intake flume connects to the base section, the base section must be correctly oriented to the water source and pump house footprint. The lifting capacity of excavators and cranes must be considered. Lifting capacity greatly diminishes as the extension or reach increases.

For all of these reasons, the size and weight of the base section should be kept to a minimum, even if this increases the cost of the wet well. For example, precast concrete companies frequently cast a 60 in. high base for a 72 in. diameter wet well. This base section weighs approximately 13,400 lb. The same 60 in. high base can be manufactured in two sections, a 24 in. base section with a 36 in. riser. The 24 in. base would weigh approximately 7,900 lb and the 36 in.

FIGURE 7.13.
Dewatering prior to excavation for wet well installation.

FIGURE 7.14
A 24 in. base section of a wet well is being transported to the wet well excavation. A 60 in. riser section with pipe boot waits to be set.

riser 5,400 lb. The 24 in. high base section is substantially easier and safer to set than a 72 in. high section (see Figure 7.14).

Precast concrete wet wells generally have a boot or gasket precast in the base or in one of the riser sections at the elevation where the intake flume from the water source is to enter. In addition, the wet well usually has ladder steps precast into each section. When properly constructed, the boot or gasket will point in the direction the intake flume follows to the water source and the ladder rungs will fall under the access hatch in the pump station skid (Figure 7.15).

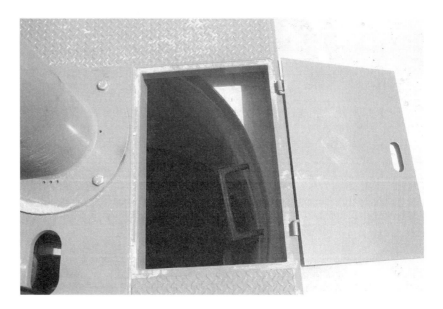

FIGURE 7.15
Pump station access hatch to wet well with ladder rungs properly located under a skid.

FIGURE 7.16
Antifloatation collar poured in place. Stainless steel bolts and rebar secure the collar to the wet well.

Once the base section is set, the remaining sections of the wet well are relatively easy to install. Each section should be checked for elevation, plumb, and level. An antifloatation collar should be considered, particularly in installations where groundwater may be encountered (Figure 7.16). The anti-floatation collar prevents the wet well from floating should it be surrounded with saturated soil.

The intake flume is usually installed level. It is critical not to have any bellies or high spots in the flume, as either will create pockets that will trap air and reduce capacity and efficiency. Another important consideration is the stability of the ground through which the flume is being installed. In unstable ground, measures should be taken to stabilize the intake flume. This can often be accomplished by simply bedding the flume in gravel.

Provisions should be made to prevent water from leaking from the pond along the intake flume excavation. In its simplest form, this can be done by backfilling and compacting the excavation near the water source with a nonpermeable clay soil (Figure 7.17). More complicated solutions involve the construction of an antiseepage collar.

Intake pipes constructed of gasket-joint PVC have been known to pull apart. To prevent this from occurring, the integral bell coupling on the pipe can be drilled and stainless steel lag bolts installed, securing one pipe to another. Several lags bolts should be equally spaced around the circumference of each bell (Figure 7.18). The number of lag bolts required depends on the diameter of the intake pipe.

FIGURE 7.17
Nonpermeable clay is placed around an intake flume penetration into a pond profile to prevent seepage.

FIGURE 7.18
Intake flume sections secured together with stainless steel lag bolts.

It is important to support and secure the intake flume once it exits the soil profile and runs along the bottom of the water source. A common practice is to install support pillars constructed by stacking bags of ready-mix concrete on a gravel base (Figure 7.19). The ready-mix concrete bags harden underwater, forming a stable support for the intake flume. This method should be used only for support pillars of limited height installed in a nonmoving water source. More complex supports can be constructed of concrete block, Sono-tubes filled with concrete, or formed and poured concrete pillars.

The initial point of entry for water into the intake flume is most commonly through an intake screen. Considerations in installing the intake screen include the following:

FIGURE 7.19
Intake flume and strainer supported with concrete bags.

- The best place to filter out contaminants is at the water source.
- The screen should be constructed of noncorrosive materials.
- The screen should be installed so that it is elevated and supported above the floor of the water source.

Where intake screens are installed in a stream or river, the water intake should enter through the downstream or end section of the intake screen. The upstream and top sections of the screen should be solid, allowing no water entry. Where rotating drum intake screens are installed in a stream or river, a diverter shield can be installed to prevent floating debris from becoming entangled in the screen. Likewise, in installations where the water source may be subject to heavy leaf fall, a diverter can be installed over the intake screen to reduce contamination from the falling leaves. Some installations include a gauge to indicate water depth over the flume (Figure 7.20).

Another consideration when installing an intake flume is the inclusion of an intake flume isolation valve (Figure 7.21). This is a large gate or sluice-type valve that is installed in the intake flume.

FIGURE 7.20
Water depth gauge attached to intake strainer.

FIGURE 7.21
Intake flume with gate valve isolation.

FIGURE 7.22
Wet well site secured while waiting for pump house construction.

Closing this valve prevents water from entering the wet well from the water source. Including such a valve allows for the scheduled dewatering of the wet well for examination of the bowl assemblies and pump intake screens. It also allows for the examination of the bottom of the wet well and the removal of any foreign matter. Wet well and intake structures that do not have isolation valves usually require either the intake screen to be suffocated or an inflatable balloon to be placed inside the intake pipe through the wet well and then inflated. Either process curtails the flow of water into the wet well and should be performed by a certified scuba diver. After wet well installation is complete, the opening should be covered and fenced off for safety purposes (Figure 7.22).

Other Common Intake Structures

Two additional types of intake structures are common in golf course irrigation pump systems: flooded suction and floating suction intakes (typically with centrifugal pumps). In a flooded suction installation, the water source is at a higher elevation than the pump. Typically, in a flooded suction installation, the suction line is installed through a bank or a dam into the water source.

PUMP STATION INSTALLATION

The overwhelming majority of golf course irrigation pump stations, whether they are vertical turbine or centrifugal stations, are prefabricated. Not only is a prefabricated pump station usually less costly to purchase than a built-in-place pump system, but it is also easier and less costly to install. Prior to ordering a pump station, there are several items that must be confirmed:

- Obtain written verification of the available power from the utility company.
- Verify the wet well diameter and depth.
- Verify the desired pump column length (pump set).
- Request advance notification of date of delivery.

Items to consider when taking delivery of a pump station include the following:

- Have suitable equipment available to unload the pump station, pump columns, and ancillary equipment.
- Have a representative of the pump station vendor on-site to examine the station. If a representative is not available, examine the pump station and other materials for possible damage sustained during shipping. If damage is found, note the extent of damage on the delivery slip and notify the pump station vendor. Documentation with a digital camera can be valuable.
- If the pump station cannot be permanently set at the time of delivery, provisions must be made for suitable storage. Be sure the pump station is covered by insurance while it is in storage.

There are several key considerations in installing a prefabricated pump station:

- The pump house footing and slab must be completed and properly cured prior to setting the pump station.
- Delivery trucks and/or equipment for off-loading and setting the pump station must be able to access the pump house site.
- The crane or setting equipment must be able to handle the load at the required lift and reach (Figure 7.23).
- The pump station should be set and secured according to the manufacturer's recommendations.
- The pump station should be temporarily covered and protected when a pump house is to be constructed around the newly set station.

FIGURE 7.23
Crane setting prefabricated pump station.

POTABLE WATER SUPPLIES, WELLS, AND EFFLUENT WATER SOURCES

The configuration of materials and the installation requirements for connecting to other water sources, such as potable water supplies, wells, or effluent water sources, vary widely. However, there are two questions that should be uniformly considered and answered prior to connecting to any of these sources:

1. Have all the water allocation and construction permits been approved and issued?
2. Is a backflow protection device required?

CRITICAL CONNECTIONS

The most critical section of piping in a golf course irrigation system is the segment that extends from the point of connection to the pump station or water source to the first group of gate valves where the mainline splits to go in different directions. Should a fitting fail or a leak occur in this section of pipe, irrigation can be lost to the entire golf course. If a leak or failure occurs after this first group of valves, it can usually be isolated so that irrigation is lost only to a limited area of the course. Connections to most pump stations or water sources have several features in common:

- The connection involves the largest, or one of the largest, pipe sizes in the installation.
- The connection usually involves the transition from one pipe type to another.
- The connection may be subject to vibration due to the proximity to the pump station or water source.
- The connection may experience some settling or ground movement due to deep excavations around the pump house or water source.

Any or all of the following measures can be taken to maintain the integrity of the connection:

- Stabilize the ground that surrounds and supports the pipe and connection. This may require importing a more stable soil and/or bedding the pipe and connection in stone.
- The bottom elbow of the Z-pipe should be thrust blocked (Figure 7.24).
- The connection and/or transition should be made with a gasket type transition fitting.
- Movement of the fitting should be restricted or secured by retaining clamps, threaded rod, and/or thrust blocks.
- A photograph or digital picture of this and other key fittings should be taken and kept with the owner's manuals and Record Drawings. The photographs will prove to be a valuable reference should any of the fittings or connections have to be dug up in the future for repair.

IRRIGATION MAINLINE

Trench Dimension

Excavation for the irrigation mainline requires the trench to be of sufficient depth to provide the specified depth of cover. It is important to note that *depth of cover* refers to how many inches of soil are over the pipe, not how deep the bottom of trench is. For example, to provide 24 in. of cover over 4 in. PVC, a trench approximately 29 in. deep is required. To provide the same 24 in. of cover over 10 in. PVC, a trench approximately 36 in. deep is needed. If a uniform

FIGURE 7.24
Connection of irrigation mainline to pump station discharge using transition coupling and thrust block.

depth of cover is required for all pipe sizes, then the depth to which the trench is excavated will have to increase as the pipe size gets larger. The depth of the trench should be checked at intervals to ensure uniformity. The trench width must be sufficient for proper installation of the pipe and fittings; it must also be wide enough to allow the proper placement of backfill material alongside and over the pipe. Trench production is directly related to how deep and how wide the excavation will be. For this reason, it is advantageous to have more than one trencher, set up at different trench widths.

Frequently, more than one pipe may be installed in a trench. Common examples of combination are mainline and lateral pipes, mainline and pond fill pipes, dual water source mainlines, and mainline and potable drinking fountain supply pipes (Figure 7.25). It is important to allow for separation between pipes when multiple pipes are installed in a common trench. This separation allows for independent expansion and contraction of each pipe, and such separation is invaluable if pipe repair becomes necessary in the future. Installation of large (and heavy) size pipe may require special equipment (Figure 7.26).

Mainline generally follows the contour and outline of the fairway edge. It is preferable to gently sweep the pipe rather than install numerous elbows. Each elbow creates additional friction loss and must be thrust blocked or restrained. Pipe manufacturers list the maximum deflection allowed for each size of pipe they produce. The sweeping or deflection of the pipe should not exceed the manufac-

FIGURE 7.25
Cat 307 excavator with 24 in. bucket opening a trench for the installation of multiple pipes.

FIGURE 7.26
Tractor with fork attachment used to transport and lower 10 in. mainline in place.

turer's recommendations. Open pipe ends should be sealed with tape at the end of each day's work to prevent the intrusion of debris (Figure 7.27).

Thrust Blocks

For the installation of standard gasket joint pipe, thrust blocks must be poured for all pipe dead ends, tees, elbows, reducers, and gate

FIGURE 7.27
Fittings sealed temporarily with duct tape.

valves. Whenever possible, mainline dead ends should be avoided. Pipe dead ends are by far the fitting most susceptible to failure. A variety of factors influence thrust block size and construction. Among these are type and size of pipe, fitting configuration, system operating pressure, and, most important, soil structure and stability. The less stable the soil, the larger the thrust block required. ASAE S376.2 has long been considered the standard for thrust block construction. Figure 7.28 shows typical thrust block configurations for a variety of fittings.

Unstable Soils

Certain conditions and/or soils are so unstable that they mandate the installation of special fittings or pipe types to ensure the integrity of the system.

There are several options for dealing with unstable soils. A number of manufacturers make restraining glands that can be used with standard gasket type pipe and fittings. These restraining glands allow for some pipe movement while preventing pipe joint or fitting failure.

Several PVC pipe manufacturers extrude pipe and gasket-type fittings that are locked together by the insertion of a hard plastic spline into grooves in the pipe and the fitting. The spline prevents the pipe from pulling out of the fitting while allowing for some movement of the pipe. The PVC pipe is manufactured in standard pressure ratings. The variety of fittings available with splines and adaptable to

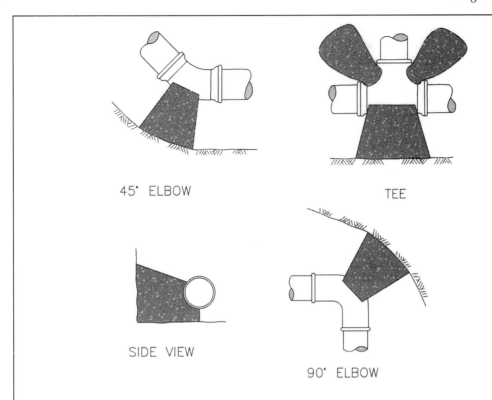

45° ELBOW

TEE

SIDE VIEW

90° ELBOW

THRUST FACTOR

SIZE	DEAD END OF TEE	90° ELBOW	45° ELBOW	22 1/2° ELBOW
2"	4.6	6.5	3.5	1.8
2 1/2"	6.7	9.4	5.1	2.6
3"	9.8	13.9	7.5	3.8
4"	16.2	23.0	12.4	6.3
6"	34.8	49.2	26.7	13.6
8"	59.0	83.5	45.2	23.0
10"	91.5	130.0	70.0	35.8
12"	129.0	182.0	99.0	50.0

BEARING STRENGTH OF SOILS

SOIL TYPE	BEARING STRENGTH (lb/ft^2)
SOFT CLAY	1000
MEDIUM CLAY	2000
COARSE AND FINE SAND	3000
GRAVEL AND SAND	4000
SOUND SHALE	10000

1. TO OBTAIN TOTAL AREA OF THRUST, MULTIPLY FITTING THRUST FACTOR BY THE PIPE DESIGN WORKING PRESSURE.

2. DIVIDE THE TOTAL AREA OF THRUST BY THE BEARING STRENGTH OF THE SOIL TO ARRIVE AT THE TOTAL UNDISTURBED AREA NEEDED IN SQUARE FEET REQUIRED TO RESIST THE THRUST.

3. THRUST BLOCKS SHALL BE POURED AGAINST UNDISTURBED EARTH WITH A MINIMUM CONCRETE COMPRESSION STRENGTH OF 3000 PSI.

4. THRUST BLOCK INSTALLATION AND DESIGN SHALL BE IN ACCORDANCE WITH ANSI/ASAE S376.2 JAN 98.

FIGURE 7.28
Typical thrust block details.

golf course irrigation is limited. Therefore, this pipe is generally used with standard gasket type fittings with restraints.

High-density polyethylene pipe (HDPE) is becoming more widely used for golf course irrigation. This pipe is ideal for golf courses with unstable soil conditions as well as other soil conditions. HDPE is joined by a method of butt-fusing, whereby a thermal heating device is used to fuse two lengths of pipe or a pipe and fitting together (Figure 7.29).

The disadvantages of installing high-density polyethylene are as follows:

- HDPE pipe is more expensive than standard PVC pipe.
- Nominal size HDPE has a smaller inside diameter than the same nominal size PVC pipe. The pressure loss and velocity through HDPE will be greater than the pressure loss through the same nominal size PVC pipe. Consequently, HDPE pipe may have to be one or more pipe size larger than its PVC counterpart.
- Special equipment must be purchased or rented to butt-weld the pipe and fittings together. The variety and configurations of available fittings are limited.
- Labor costs for assembling HDPE are higher because of the time and equipment required to butt-weld the pipe and fittings.

FIGURE 7.29
Butt-fusing 8-inch HDPE pipe.

Removal of Rock

Piping installation in rock and rocky soils presents other challenges, the first of which is suitable trench production. It is important to avoid undersizing the equipment and to see what types and sizes of machines have been used successfully under similar conditions.

Rock and ledge of a certain hardness just cannot be trenched or excavated. When rock is this hard, it is frequently removed by demolition hammer or blasting (Figure 7.30). A local excavating equipment dealer can provide recommendations for suitable equipment outfitted with a demolition hammer. If blasting is required, it is essential that the blasting firm or individual has the required local and/or state credentials and has obtained the necessary permits. The irrigation system installer must ask to see and copy any required state and/or local certifications or licenses and request an insurance certificate.

Once the rock or ledge has been removed, suitable bedding and backfill material must be brought in. For most pipe sizes, a minimum 6 in. of bedding and 6 in. of cover should be provided. Lateral bed-

FIGURE 7.30
Backhoe equipped with a demolition hammer breaking ledge rock for removal.

ding should also be provided between the sides of the trench and the pipe to prevent the rock or ledge from making contact with the pipe. The bedding and cover can be placed either by hand or by machine. However, once bedding has been placed on the bottom of the trench, it should be hand-graded to provide support under the pipe. Even after the select backfill process has been completed, backfilling the remainder of the trench with large rock or ledge should be avoided.

Wet Conditions

Frequently, during the installation of a golf course irrigation piping system, wet areas with localized shallow groundwater are encountered. Installation in these areas should be scheduled when conditions are the driest. Even then, special equipment and provisions may be necessary to install the piping successfully. Planking or plywood may be needed to support and provide traction for rubber-tired equipment. In many cases, the rubber-tired equipment will not be suitable for handling the wet conditions and a track machine will be required for the excavation.

The open trench should be kept free of groundwater during pipe installation. This often requires the use of trash or dewatering pumps. Spending time to properly set up the pumps will ensure safe and proper installation of the piping. A common method often employed to maintain a dry trench is to dig a sump trench at each low area or belly in the piping trench. The sump trench is dug perpendicular to and at a greater depth than the piping trench. This allows the groundwater from the piping trench to run off into the sump trench. To set up the dewatering pump, a crushed stone base is placed in the bottom of the sump trench, the suction hose of the trash or dewatering pump is installed, and more stone is added (Figure 7.31). The sump trench should be monitored periodically during operation, and silt prevented from suffocating the crushed stone intake.

Soil conditions in wet areas are frequently unstable and unsuitable for typical gasket type fitting installation and thrust blocks (Figure 7.32). Prior to installing any change-of-direction fitting (tee or elbow), a stable base must be created to support the fitting. This can usually be accomplished by excavating to a greater depth in the area where the fitting will be installed and then filling that area with crushed stone. Gravel bases may also be constructed to support concrete thrust blocks, provided the soil has sufficient lateral bearing load. The

FIGURE 7.31
Sump trench being utilized to dewater mainline pipe trench.

FIGURE 7.32
Typical thrust blocks formed with lumber.

size or bearing surface of the thrust block is directly related to the bearing load of the soil.

Many wet or unstable soils do not have sufficient bearing load to support the use of concrete thrust blocks. In these situations, retaining clamps or glands are used on all directional fittings. In severe situations, retaining glands or clamps are used on all fittings and the gasket joints of the pipe.

Backfill and Compaction

The first step in backfilling is to hand place clean backfill material under, around, and over the pipe. A minimum of 6 in. of cover should be placed over the pipe and hand tamped. When this is completed, the remainder of the trench can be filled. The backfill material should be free of organic material, debris, rock, and stones with a diameter of 2 in. or larger. Soil type and moisture content, turf condition, and weather determine whether the remaining material can be backfilled by machine or by hand. Trenchers equipped with backfill blades with angle, tilt, and float (refer to Figure 7.2), soil augurs, and hydraulically driven brooms (Figure 7.7) are examples of equipment utilized for backfilling.

If backfill material is to be compacted by hand, it should be placed in maximum 6-in. layers. If mechanical compaction is used (see Figures 7.5 and 7.6), soil layers should not exceed 12 in. The soil should be compacted to a density comparable to that of surrounding undisturbed soil. Under-compacting can result in trench settling and over-compacting can create hardpan and conditions detrimental to the establishment of turfgrass. Over-compacting often exhausts the supply of backfill material and requires the supply of additional materials to completely fill the trench.

Trench Restoration

On existing golf courses, the restoration of trench lines varies according to the specifications and/or expectations of the club. Some installations require the lifting and replacement of sod on all trenches, whereas others limit the sod lifting to fairway pipe crossings. Some installations stipulate that all trenches will be seeded, and still others stipulate that the course will perform all of its own restoration.

The degree and manner of trench restoration on an existing golf course are often directly related to budget. The lifting and replacement of sod can add substantial cost to the installation. Other concerns in considering the lifting and replacement of sod are as follows:

- The sod must be replaced in a timely manner to ensure its survival. The length of time between lifting and replacement will vary according to the time of year and the weather conditions.
- Newly replaced sod will require frequent watering until reestablished. This often necessitates the use of spray tanks because the new irrigation system is under construction and may not be ready to supply water to the newly laid sod when needed.

- Installation activity may be limited, reduced, slowed, or curtailed by adverse weather and for soil conditions.
- The poor quality of existing turf may not allow for the sod to be lifted.
- Sod cannot be cut and lifted where there are heavy tree roots.
- Sod cannot be lifted and/or replaced when the ground is frozen.
- New sod must be purchased to replace poor-quality sod or sod that does not live. The new sod usually does not match the existing turf and may be distinguishable for years.

Seeding the trench lines has some advantages over lifting and replacing sod:

- Grading and reseeding trenches is far less costly than lifting and replacing sod.
- Installation can continue under a variety of weather and soil conditions that would be unacceptable if sod were being lifted and replaced.
- While the trench lines are being graded and raked, adjacent bare and low areas can be filled, graded, and seeded.
- Seed mixtures are available in a greater variety than sod type.
- Seed can be broadcast not only on the bare trench line, but also extended into the adjacent existing turf. This allows the seeded trench line to blend in with the existing turf.
- Pregermination, hydroseeding, and mulching are a few of the methods that can be utilized to shorten the time needed for reestablishment.

The disadvantages to seeding are as follows:

- Seed takes longer to reestablish the turf.
- Seed requires lighter but more frequent irrigation.
- Seed does not provide the "instant green" gratification of sod.
- Areas that are seeded are more prone to washout and erosion.

Road, Stream, and Bridge Crossings

There are areas on most golf courses that present challenges for mainline installation. Road, stream, and bridge crossings are three of the most common.

ROAD CROSSINGS

Road crossings can be completed either by the open trench method or by boring. If the road is a public road, a road opening permit is usually required regardless of the installation method. Because utilities are commonly installed in road rights-of-way, the mark-out of all utilities is critical prior to the start of any road crossing.

With both methods, it is preferable to install the mainline pipe inside a larger sleeve pipe. Wire should not be installed in the same sleeve pipe with the mainline, but rather in separate electrical conduit. In addition, irrigation equipment manufacturers often recommend that field controller communication cable be installed in its own dedicated conduit to prevent unwanted "noise" or contamination from high-voltage electrical circuits. For these reasons, it is not uncommon to have multiple electrical conduits installed with each road crossing. PVC irrigation pipe *should not be used* for conduit for wiring. All electrical conduits should be Schedule 40 or Schedule 80 PVC electrical conduit or rigid steel electrical conduit. All sleeves and conduits should extend a minimum of 5 ft beyond the edge of the road surface or pavement.

The open trench method is usually the less expensive method of installing a road crossing, but it has some disadvantages:

- If the road is in use and cannot be closed to traffic, half of the road crossing will have to be completed, backfilled, and restored before the second half can be started.
- Traffic control officers may have to be hired to direct vehicular traffic around the construction.
- The government agency that maintains the road may require a bond to be posted prior to issuing the road opening permit. The contractor doing the road crossing is usually responsible for the integrity of the backfill, compaction, and pavement resurfacing for the duration of the bond period.
- The pavement patch is always visible and may deteriorate over time.

The advantages to installing road crossings by boring include the following:

- The road crossing can be completed in one step.
- There is minimal interruption to vehicular traffic.
- There is little if any road restoration required with boring.
- Unsightly pavement patches are reduced or avoided altogether.

The boring of a road may be done by any of several methods. Again, the mark-out of existing utilities is critical prior to starting the bore. An observation hole is generally opened over any and all utilities that will be crossed. The path of the bore runs through the observation holes, allowing the contractor to observe the boring equipment and ensuring that no damage is done to the utility. After the bore is complete, the observation holes are backfilled, compacted, and resurfaced.

Smaller pipe sizes can be installed with the use of a compressor and a pneumatic missile. A substantial advantage to installing a road crossing with this method is that the size of the excavation is kept to a minimum. Moreover, multiple bores can be made from a single excavation pit. This method is commonly used for pipe sizes 4 in. in diameter and smaller. However, there are pneumatic missiles that will install much larger size pipe.

Pipe pushing, or ramming, is another common method of boring. This method employs a hydraulically operated ram that pushes a drive rod with a soil compaction bit. Existing soil is displaced and compacted, building a tunnel through which the mainline sleeve can be installed. This method usually accommodates larger pipe sizes than the pneumatic missile but requires a larger excavation for setup.

For many years, the method of choice for installing larger diameter road crossings employed a mechanically driven auger that rode on steel tracks. The auger drills a large-diameter hole under the road while simultaneously installing a steel sleeve. This method requires a large excavation for both the drilling unit and the target hole. However, once the unit is set in place, the actual boring proceeds quickly, barring any unforeseen complications.

Directional drilling is perhaps the most widely used and versatile method of boring. Many utility companies use directional drilling exclusively for the trenchless installation of their electric, telephone, gas, and water lines. Directional drilling employs a specialized boring bit that can be steered and traced from aboveground. Among the unique features and advantages of directional drilling are the following:

- A wide variety of directional drilling equipment is available, making this method cost-effective for a broad spectrum of different pipe sizes.
- Directional drilling allows both changes in elevation of the bore and changes in direction. Bores done by other methods generally have to be in a straight line and either level or at a uniform pitch.

- Directional drilling can accomplish bores of a much greater length than other methods.

Because of its ability to change elevations and direction and perform longer bores, directional drilling can be used for installing pipes and conduits under obstructions that cannot be bored by other methods. Parking lots, culverts, streams, rivers, and ponds, are examples of problems for which bores can be completed by directional drilling.

BRIDGE CROSSINGS

Mainline installation often requires pipe to be suspended or supported from various structures such as bridges and culverts. The first consideration is whether the bridge or culvert will support the weight. The total weight load is the sum of the pipe, fittings, straps or hangers, and the water they will carry. The load-carrying capacity of a bridge can often dictate the pipe material used for the bridge crossing. Welded steel or ductile iron pipe weighs considerably more than comparably sized PVC or HDPE. For courses that have prefabricated bridges, the load-carrying capacity of the bridges can usually be obtained from the manufacturer. On new construction, the added load-carrying capacity for the pipe can be engineered into the construction of a bridge. Often a chase way or hangers can be prefabricated into the bridge. If there is a question as to whether a bridge or culvert can support a certain weight, a civil engineering firm should be consulted.

Other considerations in crossing a bridge or culvert are as follows:

- The pipe will be exposed to the weather and the elements.
- The pipe may be subject to vandalism.
- Provisions are needed for pipe expansion and contraction.
- Electrical conduits may be required for wire crossings.
- Should a drain or blow-off fitting be installed on the pipe?
- Will the pipe interfere with bridge deck replacement?
- Can the pipe and conduits be hidden from the view of players?
- Does the stream or river flood?
- Is the bridge or culvert likely to wash out?
- Are any permits required to install the pipe on the bridge or culvert?

Standard resin PVC pipe is not acceptable for installation where it is exposed to sunlight. Ultraviolet rays will cause its gradual deterioration and eventual failure. Several PVC pipe manufacturers have developed pipe that is UV resistant. This pipe is widely used in the

FIGURE 7.33
UV-resistant PVC pipe being installed under a bridge.

mining industry and is very adaptable for use in bridge and culvert crossings (Figure 7.33). The PVC fittings manufactured for UV-resistant pipe come in different grades. Fittings for bridge and culvert crossings should be permanent connection fittings with spline retainers. Elbows used for change of direction should be sweep elbows constructed of the same UV-resistant pipe material, not adapters solvent-welded to regular Schedule 80 PVC elbows. Other pipe types widely used for bridge crossings are high-density polyethylene (HDPE), Schedule 40 steel pipe, and ductile iron pipe.

Regardless of pipe type, because the pipe is strapped or hung from the bridge or culvert, provisions must be made to prevent longitudinal movement. All UV-resistant PVC fittings must include spline retainers or utilize retaining clamps. Where push-on bell-end ductile iron pipe is coupled together, retaining clamps are also required. All other ductile iron fittings should utilize glands with retainers. Lengthy bridge and culvert crossings may require the installation of special expansion couplings to allow for expansion and contraction of the pipe. These couplings are generally not necessary on crossings less than 200 ft in length.

The pipe should be supported at regular intervals that allow for longitudinal movement, but not latitudinal movement. The intervals between supports or hangers will vary with pipe type and size. The hangers or supports should be coated metal and have a minimal width of 2 in. A hanger or support should be placed within 2 ft of any elbow.

Where wire crosses a bridge or culvert, the crossing should be made with Schedule 40 or Schedule 80 PVC electrical conduit or rigid steel electrical conduit. Appropriate electrical conduit fittings should be used in conjunction with the pipe. As previously discussed in regard to road crossings, separate conduits may be required for different voltages and field controller communication cable. The electrical conduits must be secured at regular intervals, according to the NEC.

STREAM CROSSINGS

Stream and drainage ditch crossings, although similar in many respects to road and bridge crossings, present several unique concerns:

- What environmental permits are required?
- Does the stream flow have to be diverted while the crossing is completed?
- What are the remedial requirements after the crossing is completed?

Many small streams or drainage ditches may not require any environmental permits to cross. Others may involve lengthy environmental studies and a drawn-out application process. For the latter, directional drilling may be a viable option; it may shorten the application process, eliminate the need for stream diversion, and reduce remediation in the area immediately adjacent to the stream. At some stream crossings, pipe and conduit are encased in concrete to prevent damage from future stream maintenance (Figure 7.34).

Diverting the flow of a stream is generally accomplished by one of two methods:

1. Excavating a new temporary stream path around the area where the crossing will be completed.
2. Damming the flow upstream and downstream of the crossing location and pumping the water around the excavation.

FIGURE 7.34
Pipe and conduit crossings being encased in concrete under future streambed.

Most bridge and stream crossings and many road and culvert crossings require vertical offsets in the mainline piping and transitions from one pipe type to another. Vertical offsets are generally constructed of four 45-degree bends or elbows. The pipe "Z's" up, crosses the bridge, then "Z's" back down. The transition from one pipe material to another usually occurs before the first Z and after the second. The offsets present challenges for thrusting or retaining the 45-degree bends. The lower 45-degree bend where the pipe turns up can be secured with a traditional concrete thrust block, conditions permitting. The riser pipe and top 45-degree bends cannot be successfully restrained with thrust blocks, but should be secured with restraining clamps or fitting restraints. Any couplings, whether they are in the riser pipe or in the pipe crossing the bridge, also require restraints. An optional method of securing the bottom 45-degree bend to the top 45-degree bend is to tie the two elbows together with threaded rod (Figure 7.35). Failure to properly restrain any of these fittings will eventually result in a blow-out.

The transition from one pipe type to another is generally accomplished with a gasketed transition coupling. Each flange and gasket must be sized for the pipe it is accommodating. Ductile iron couplings with transition gaskets can also be used for making this transition.

A transition from HDPE pipe to another pipe type requires special attention. HDPE pipe is joined by butt-fusing, theoretically making it one long piece of pipe and thus making it more prone to expansion and contraction. HDPE pipe is also less rigid than PVC and is subject to more latitudinal movement. Transition couplings or ductile iron couplings should be used on HDPE pipe only in conjunction

FIGURE 7.35
Ductile iron pipe offset secured with threaded rod and retaining glands.

FIGURE 7.36
Transition from HDPE to PVC pipe employing threaded rod and restraining glands.

with restraining clamps or glands (Figure 7.36). Furthermore, stainless steel wall stiffeners may be required for certain HDPE pipe of certain Standard Dimension Ratio (SDR). The restraining clamps or glands must secure the transition coupling to both the HDPE pipe and the pipe it is connecting to. Another widely used method of joining HDPE to another pipe is to butt-fuse a flange to the HDPE and use a gasket by flanged adapter on the joining pipe.

VALVE INSTALLATION

Contemporary golf course irrigation designs employ a series of interconnecting pipe loops, each with the capability of being isolated from the rest of the system.

Mainline Gate Valves

Push-on American Water Works Association (AWWA) type gate valves are most commonly used for mainline isolation. Mainline valves 10 in. or larger are frequently AWWA type mechanical joint gate valves. The exact location of the isolation valve should be selected in the field with several considerations:

- The valve should not be located in a cart path or maintenance road, or in greens, approaches, fairways, or tees.
- The valve should be easily accessible by the maintenance staff.
- The valve should not be installed in an area subject to flooding.

The excavation where the gate valve will be installed should be completed prior to placement of the valve. This should include excavating or notching into the trench sides and under the valve location in preparation for the thrust block. It is far easier to dig for the thrust block before the gate valve is installed. A larger excavation will be required for mechanical joint gate valves to allow proper tightening of the bolts that secure the retaining gland to the valve. Once the excavation has been completed and the pipe ends beveled to receive the valve, the valve can be installed. A backhoe should be used to lower larger valves into place. Certain manufacturers' valves have lifting holes built into the valve body; otherwise, a sling can be secured to the valve body or operating nut. The valve can then be lowered into place and pushed onto the pipe end with pry bars. With a mechanical joint gate valve, it is important to remember to put on the retaining gland and gasket prior to installing the valve.

The valve should be visually checked to see that it is plumb prior to pouring the thrust block. The thrust block should extend under the valve and into both sides of the trench. The concrete from the thrust block should not reach the gasket joint or top bonnet of the valve. Commonly, two U-shaped pieces of rebar are installed over the gate valve, extending down into the concrete thrust block. Once the thrust block has been poured, the excavation can be backfilled and the valve access box set. The style and type of valve access box used with mainline isolation valves varies from installation to installation. Figure 7.37 depicts a typical mainline gate valve installation with a reach sleeve and 10 in. round valve box.

Innovative manufacturers have developed joint restraint systems for use with mainline gate valves that eliminate the need to pour thrust blocks. The joint restraint can secure the valve and pipe directly to a mainline tee or directional change fittings (Figure 7.38). A compacted stone or concrete base should still be constructed to support the gate valve, and a thrust block must still be poured for the tee or directional change fitting.

Threaded Gate Valves

Although some systems utilize AWWA type gate valves throughout, it is more common to find Iron Pipe Size (IPS) threaded bronze gate valves and/or ball valves used for smaller lateral line isolation valves, drains valves, and pond fill valves. IPS valves used for these purposes are generally installed on service tees (gasketed tee with a threaded side outlet). The service tee may be constructed of ductile iron or PVC. The depth of cover over lateral pipes and pond fill pipes is usually less than that required for mainline pipe. For this reason, service

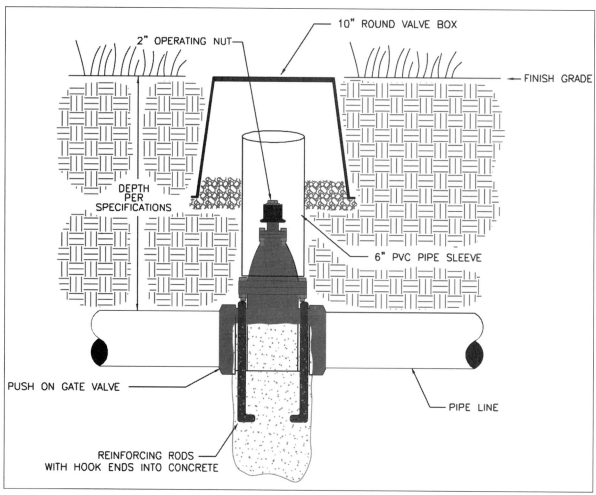

FIGURE 7.37
Typical mainline gate valve assembly with sleeve and 10 in. round valve box.

tees are commonly installed with the threaded outlet facing up. A nipple and elbow are threaded into the service tee, and then the gate valve is installed. Materials used to construct this lateral ell vary from Schedule 80 PVC to brass nipples with bronze elbows. Once again, innovative manufacturing has resulted in the prefabrication of a ductile iron lateral ell that saves time and is stronger than field-fabricated units (Figure 7.39). A PVC threaded connection to the gate or ball valves should be made only with Schedule 80 PVC nipples. The Schedule 80 PVC nipple results in a much stronger connection than can be achieved with the use of male adapters. Schedule 80 TOE

FIGURE 7.38
Mainline gate valve utilizing tie bars and restraint. Trench wall behind gate valve has been excavated for installation of thrust block.

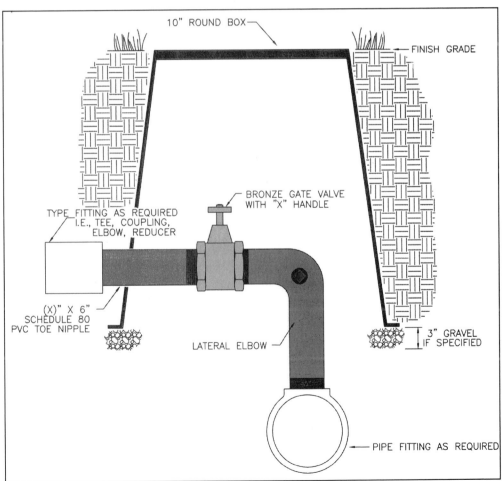

10" ROUND BOX

FINISH GRADE

BRONZE GATE VALVE
WITH "X" HANDLE

TYPE FITTING AS REQUIRED
I.E., TEE, COUPLING,
ELBOW, REDUCER

(X)" X 6"
SCHEDULE 80
PVC TOE NIPPLE

LATERAL ELBOW

3" GRAVEL
IF SPECIFIED

PIPE FITTING AS REQUIRED

FIGURE 7.39
Typical lateral line isolation valve detail employing a ductile iron lateral elbow.

(threaded one end) nipples are used to make the transition from the IPS gate valve to solvent-weld PVC pipe or fittings.

Drain Valves

Drain valves are often installed in a variety of low areas where the discharging water can be piped off without objection. Service tees for drain valves are installed with the outlet facing toward the discharge area, or down. A TBE (threaded both end) nipple is used to connect the gate or ball valve to the service tee, and then the drainpipe is pitched to the discharge area.

Drain valves are seldom larger than 2 in. and are designed to drain down the system to facilitate repairs or prior to winterization in cold climates. Any water system benefits from periodic flushing of the distribution system. When debris enters a large-diameter pipe from a break, it is very difficult to flush out through a 2 in. drain valve. For this reason, the inclusion of flush valves is becoming more common in piping systems. A flush valve is a larger-diameter AWWA type gate valve installed in one or more of the larger distribution pipes. The flush valve is piped to an area where large quantities of water can be discharged without creating problems. When wide open, the flush valve creates higher velocities in the pipe system, allowing built-up sediment and debris to be flushed from the system.

Quick Coupling Valves

Superintendents' philosophies about quick coupling valves run the gamut from "You can never have enough quick coupling valves" to "I never use the things." There may be as many different concepts as to where to install quick coupling valves as there are golf course superintendents, irrigation consultants, and contractors combined. Some irrigation consultants and designers indicate exactly where quick coupling valves are to be located, and others present concepts and numbers in the specifications with the actual locations to be determined in the field at the time of installation. Among the most prevalent ideas about the location of quick coupling valves are the following:

- A quick coupling valve should be located on the live side of each green isolation valve or next to the first fairway sprinkler closest to the green. This quick coupling valve is for emergency watering should the green sprinklers become inoperable.

- One or two quick coupling valves should be located around each green for manual watering of hot spots.
- One quick coupling valve should be located near each sand bunker group.
- One quick coupling valve should be located in the landing area of each fairway.
- One quick coupling valve should be located next to the sprinkler closest to any hot spots on the course.
- One quick coupling valve should be located within a hose length of each tee complex.
- One quick coupling valve should be located near any landscape area that may require supplementary watering.

On an existing golf course, if the plans and specifications call for a set number of quick coupling valves to be located in the field at the time of installation, the superintendent should mark up an irrigation plan showing the desired location of each and every quick coupling valve prior to the start of installation. This exercise allows the superintendent to best allocate the specified number of quick coupling valves and realize at the start whether the installation of additional valves is required. Copies of the marked-up plan should be provided to the irrigation consultant/designer and the irrigation contractor.

Construction details for quick coupling valves vary from installation to installation. A large variety of swing joint and specialty fittings are available for quick coupling valve installation (Figure 7.40). However, several objectives remain consistent with the installation of these valves:

- Every quick coupling valve must be installed on a swing joint to prevent damage to the piping system when hoses are overstretched.
- Every quick coupling valve must be stabilized to prevent unthreading when the quick coupling key is removed.
- A detailed location of every quick coupling valve must be provided on the Record Drawings.

Air Release Valves

Typical air release/vacuum release valve assemblies (see Figure 7.41) consist of the following:

- A ball valve isolation valve

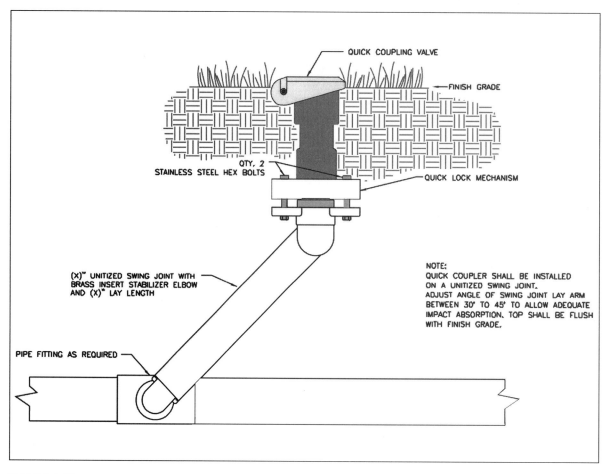

FIGURE 7.40
Typical quick coupling valve on unitized swing joint.

- A bronze wye strainer to keep the air release/vacuum relief valve free of debris
- A purge valve to clean collected debris from the wye strainer and to be used for test purposes
- An air release/vacuum relief valve
- Two threaded street elbows that protect the air release port on the release valve, preventing foreign debris from entering the valve
- A valve access box with vented cover to allow for the free flow of air in and out of the air release/vacuum relief valve

Electric Control Valves

With the current changes in turfgrass management brought on by the greater expectations of golfers and a need for more precise water control, the role of the electric control valve in golf irrigation has wid-

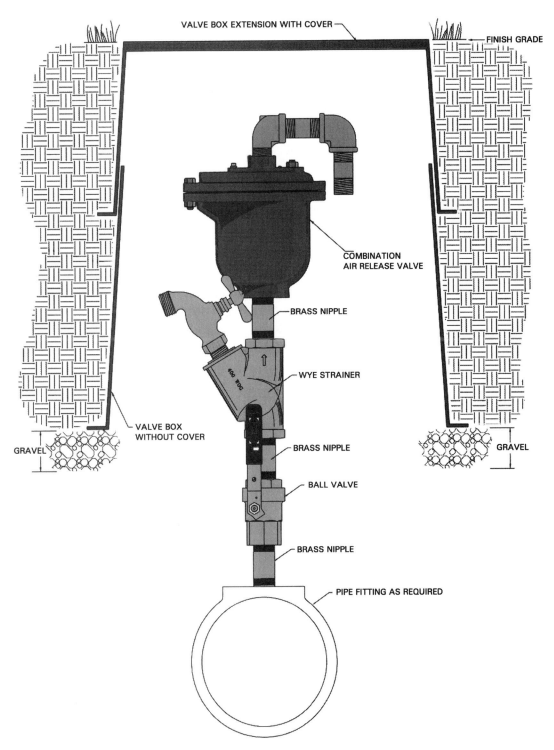

VALVE BOX EXTENSION WITH COVER

FINISH GRADE

COMBINATION
AIR RELEASE VALVE

BRASS NIPPLE

WYE STRAINER

VALVE BOX
WITHOUT COVER

GRAVEL

BRASS NIPPLE

BALL VALVE

GRAVEL

BRASS NIPPLE

PIPE FITTING AS REQUIRED

FIGURE 7.41
Combination air release valve assembly.

ened. Among the common expanded uses for electric control valves are the following:

- Part-circle sprinklers covering green surrounds
- Spray heads on green collars
- Block style sprinkler heads on tees
- Small rotary or spray heads on bunkers
- "Hot spot" irrigation in fairways
- Clubhouse irrigation
- Landscape beds throughout the course
- Automated pond fill valve

Most electric control valves in golf course systems require pressure regulation, and they come preset from the factory. The desired downstream pressure will vary according to the type of sprinkler and nozzle selected. The irrigation consultant/designer generally specifies the desired pressure setting. The pressure regulator setting should be checked and set with a pressure gauge. It is important to note that many manufacturers' pressure regulating electric control valves regulate pressure only when operated automatically through the solenoid. That is, if the valve is manually bled, its pressure regulation function is bypassed. Manually bleeding one these valves can subject the sprinkler heads to full-line pressure.

The following considerations apply to the installation of an electric control valve (see Figure 7.42):

- Preferably, locate the electric control valve where it is out of the spray range of the heads it controls. Do not locate the control valve where there is heavy cart or foot traffic. Avoid locating the valve in low areas, or in in-play areas of the course.
- Install a gate valve or ball valve directly upstream of the electric control valve to isolate the valve from the system for service.
- Install a gate valve or ball valve directly downstream of the electric control valve where the downstream piping from the control valve runs to a higher elevation. Closing this valve will prevent the water in the downstream pipe from flooding the valve box when the electric control valve is disassembled for service.
- Install a valve access box of sufficient size to permit easy service. The pressure-regulating valve assembly should be easily accessible for adjustment. Sufficient room around the Schrader valve should be provided so that a pressure gauge can be

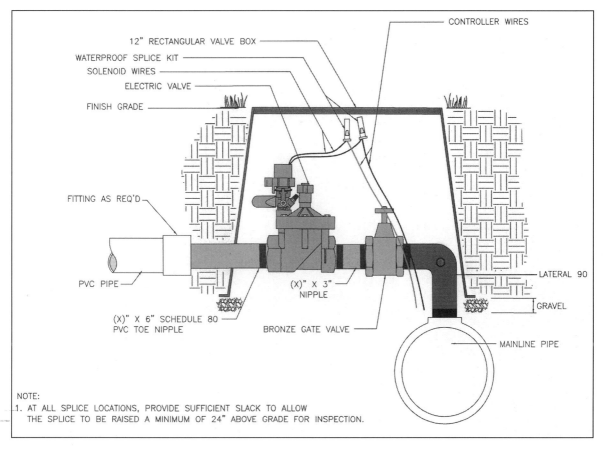

CONTROLLER WIRES

12" RECTANGULAR VALVE BOX

WATERPROOF SPLICE KIT

SOLENOID WIRES

ELECTRIC VALVE

FINISH GRADE

FITTING AS REQ'D

PVC PIPE

(X)" X 6" SCHEDULE 80
PVC TOE NIPPLE

(X)" X 3"
NIPPLE

BRONZE GATE VALVE

LATERAL 90

GRAVEL

MAINLINE PIPE

NOTE:
1. AT ALL SPLICE LOCATIONS, PROVIDE SUFFICIENT SLACK TO ALLOW
   THE SPLICE TO BE RAISED A MINIMUM OF 24" ABOVE GRADE FOR INSPECTION.

FIGURE 7.42
Typical electric control valve.

easily connected. The electric control valve should be installed at a depth that allows for easy service.

- Install the valve box on a bed of compacted crushed stone. The stone will support the valve box and provide some drainage. Some irrigation consultants, designers, and contractors add bricks under the valve box for further support.

- Use waterproof splice connections and leave sufficient slack in the wire to allow an unscrewed solenoid to be removed from the valve box with wires attached.

Pond fill valves often have a manual gate valve bypass installed on the valve manifold (Figure 7.43). Opening the gate valve allows water to fill the pond without operation of the electric control valve.

In some areas of the country, particularly those prone to severe lightning damage, hydraulic valves are commonly used. Much of the preceding discussion is also relevant to the installation of hydraulic

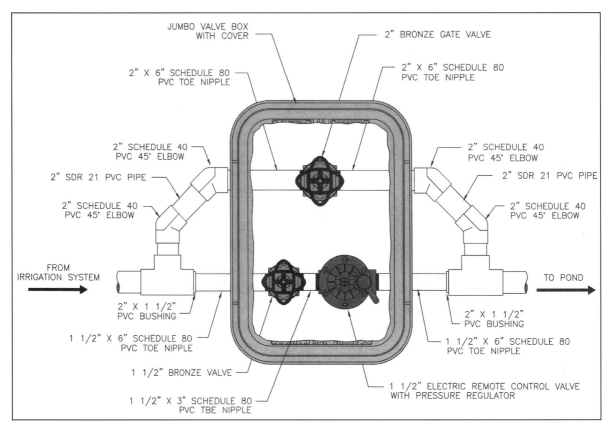

FIGURE 7.43
Typical pond fill valve assembly.

valves. However, hydraulic valves do not come with pressure regulation and the comments in regard to wiring are not relevant. In addition, some in-line hydraulic valves are manufactured as single integral units that cannot be disassembled for service. Systems that employ this type of hydraulic valve should include a union just downstream of the valve to facilitate its removal and replacement.

Backflow Preventers

Perhaps no item installed in a golf course irrigation system comes under more scrutiny and regulation than a backflow preventer (Figure 7.44). State and local codes dictate which devices are acceptable and how they are to be installed.

Regardless of what type of device is installed, the following should be considered:

- A backflow device should be installed according to state and local codes. The required permits should be applied for, and

FIGURE 7.44
RPZ (reduced pressure zone) backflow preventer.

the required inspections made. Copies of all permits and inspection approvals should be kept on file.

• The device should not be installed in a pit or vault or in any area where it may be subject to flooding.

• The device should be protected from freezing temperatures or winterized prior to the onset of subfreezing temperatures.

• The device should not be installed where it is subject to vandalism.

• The device should be installed where it is easily accessible for service. Testing and service should be performed on a regular schedule as called for by state or local code. If there are no state or local codes requiring testing, the device should be tested and serviced no less than once a year, preferably at the start of the irrigation season.

Valve Boxes

Valve boxes are typically installed to allow the following:

• Opening or closing of isolation and drain valves
• Access for the use of quick coupling valves
• Inspection and servicing of electric control valves, pond fill valves, and pressure regulating valves

- Testing and/or servicing of air release/vacuum relief valves
- Inspection and testing of wire splices
- Marking and location of provisions made for future expansion of the system, such as pipes stubbed for future use or the termination points of spare wires

Valve boxes should not be installed where they are likely to come into play. Thus, it is obvious that valve boxes should not be installed on putting surfaces, on tees, or in sand bunkers. Nor should they be installed where they are likely to be struck by a ball, such as on the approach to a green. There are other areas that should also be avoided:

- Heavy foot traffic areas, such as walkways to greens, tees, bridges
- Cart paths and maintenance roads
- Green collars and surrounds
- The faces of steep banks or slopes
- Low areas or areas prone to flooding
- Areas likely to be overgrown with vegetation
- Areas not accessible to maintenance personnel

Lightweight valve boxes, which are designed for use primarily in residential irrigation systems, should not be installed on golf courses. The selection of valve boxes should be based on the ability of the material to withstand daily abuse.

Valve boxes are usually installed over soil that has recently been excavated. To prevent settling, this soil should be properly compacted prior to the installation of a valve box. A minimum 4 in. bed of crushed stone should be provided as a base for the valve box. Many consultants and designers require more than 4 in. of crushed stone as a base. Concrete bricks or blocks are also frequently specified for additional support.

A valve box should be installed true, at or just below existing grade. There should be no high corner, which can be susceptible to mower damage. Valve boxes with locking lids should always be used in areas prone to vandalism or flooding.

The size and style of valve boxes used for a particular purpose should remain consistent throughout the installation. For instance, if a 10 in. round valve box is used for access to a mainline isolation valve, it should be used for access to all mainline isolation valves. It is not uncommon for a basic 18-hole golf course irrigation system to

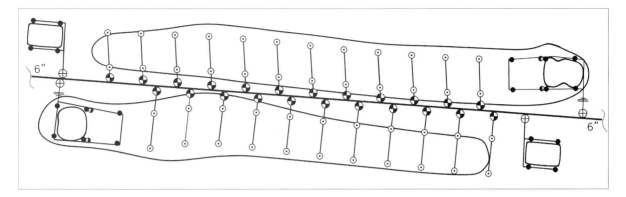

have 300 or more valve boxes. Field identification of what a certain valve box controls is often in question. This uncertainty is compounded when a common mainline supplies water to parallel holes (Figure 7.45). Which valves control the feeds to the fairway left of the mainline, and which control the feeds to the fairway right of the mainline? When an emergency arises, these questions are *real* and very confusing. As-built drawings or Record Drawings are often not available. Labeling of a valve box as to what that particular valve controls goes a long way toward eliminating the confusion. Most valve box manufacturers provide a space on the lid for such labeling. The space may be labeled with an etching tool, a wood-burning tool, or an attached after-market label. The emphasis here is that the valve box be labeled for what the valve controls.

FIGURE 7.45
Parallel fairways with a common irrigation mainline that would benefit from labeling of the lateral isolation valves.

WIRE INSTALLATION

Early automatic golf course irrigation systems were relatively simple to wire. Typically, a 120 volt wire supplied electricity to power a number of "clocks" installed at various locations throughout the course. The clocks reduced the voltage via a transformer and then distributed the reduced voltage to electric control valves through low-voltage control wire for set time periods. With the advent of central controllers, a communication or pulse cable was added to link the central controller to the field clocks.

Wiring a modern golf course irrigation system has become far more complex. A typical modern system employs a myriad of wires, cables, and control circuits that manage the operation of the system, protect the irrigation equipment, and record a history of events. Adding further to the complexity of the wiring is the frequent inclusion of various utilities. Contracts for golf course irrigation installations often incorporate the installation of power wire for drinking fountains, aerators, fans for air movement, and circulating pumps, as well as the installation of telephone cable. Coaxial and fiber optic are other types of specialty cables that are sometimes installed.

Shared Trenches

There are three primary reasons that utility installations are often included in an irrigation contract:

1. Including the utilities in the irrigation contract can reduce costs.
2. A common trench can often be used for both the irrigation system pipe and wires and the utility cables.
3. Combining the utility installation with the irrigation installation can minimize inconvenience to the membership.

The "common trench" concept often means that a single trench will contain a variety of wires and cables as well as multiple pipes. For example, it is not uncommon for a single trench to include the following:

- 8 in. SDR-21 PVC mainline
- 4 in. SDR-26 PVC pond fill line from well
- 1 in. SDR-9, 200 psi polyethylene water service to drinking fountains
- #8/3 AWG tray cable supplying 120V power to irrigation field controllers
- #6/3 AWG tray cable supplying 240V power to drinking fountains
- #16/2 AWG field controller communication cable
- #18/4 AWG pump station communication cable
- #12/2 AWG type UF-B well pump start control cable
- #14/1 and 12/1 AWG wires to control valve-in-head sprinklers
- 6 pair gel-filled telephone cable
- #6/1 AWG bare copper shielding/bonding/bonding wire

Prior to starting installation of any wiring, it is important to have a single wiring plan that indicates what wires and cables run in a common trench. Typically, different line symbols are used to indicate the various wires and cables. It is often difficult to follow and distinguish between these symbols, particularly when the plans have been generated in a black, blueline, or gray scale. Highlighting the various wire and cable types with colored markers and producing a blown-up drawing in a larger scale will help eliminate potential mistakes. Generating as-installed sketches as the pipe and wire installation progresses will aid in the production and accuracy of the final Record Drawings.

It is important to provide space for separation when installing multiple pipes and wires in a common trench. This separation facilitates troubleshooting and allows room for repair. Furthermore, wires and cables used for different purposes and carrying different voltages may require different depths of cover in order to comply with national and local electrical codes. Certain wires or cables may also require separation to prevent interference or distortion of a signal (Figure 7.46). Considering all the functions discussed here, a

FIGURE 7.46
Mainline pipe with power wire on one side and communication cable on the other.

common trench usually has to be excavated wider and deeper than would be required for any one of its components.

Codes

Most electrical components and wiring are subject to codes, regulations, and inspections. Although there are numerous and varied electric codes, the National Electrical Code (NEC) is the most widely used and accepted. Table 300-5 of the NEC specifies minimum cover requirements for wires that carry between 0 and 600 volts. The minimum cover requirement for direct burial power cables or conductors is 24 in. Lesser depths are permitted where cables and conductors rise for termination or splices, or where access is otherwise required. If the cables or conductors are installed in rigid metal conduit or intermediate metal conduit, then the minimum cover requirement is only 6 in. In situations where 24 in. of cover is not easily attainable, installing the power wire in rigid metal or intermediate metal conduit is a viable option. Conduit should be installed at a sufficient depth that it is not damaged by aerification.

The NEC has different minimum cover requirements for circuits that are used for control of irrigation and are limited to not more than 30 volts. The minimum depth of cover for low-voltage (usually 24 volt) irrigation control wire when installed in turf and landscape areas is just 6 in. However, the minimum cover requirement for the same wire when installed under streets, highways, roads, alleys, driveways, and parking lots is 24 in. The 6 in. minimum depth is not practical for golf irrigation because it puts the low-voltage wire in jeopardy of being damaged during aerification. A 12 in. depth of cover is typically the minimum allowed over low-voltage irrigation control wires.

Power Wire

Wire that supplies voltage to operate field controllers is often referred to as "power wire." Power wire requires a 24 in. minimum depth of cover. Three-way splices in power wire are common and often involve wires of different gauges. UL-listed waterproof splice materials should be used in making all power wire splices. The splice should be installed in a valve access box and so indicated on the Record Drawings. With many wire types such as single conductor UF, two-wire type UF with ground, twisted conductors, and power cables, the conductors are color-coded as black, white, and green. With 120 V wiring, the black is the hot leg, the white is the neutral leg, and the green is the equipment ground. With 240 V wiring, the black and white legs are hot and the green is the equipment ground. With products such as Tray Cable (TC), number consistency must be maintained throughout the entire installation. Typically, with 120 V wiring, #1 is hot, #2 is the neutral, and #3 is the equipment ground. With 240 V systems, #1 and #2 are hot and #3 is the equipment ground.

Additional power wires or electric services are frequently installed in conjunction with irrigation systems. Drinking fountains, aerators, water fountains, and circulating fans are common examples of appliances installed on a golf course that requires power wires. Frequently, a different type of wire or cable is used to power these appliances. For example:

Power to field controller—type TC cable (Tray Cable)
Power to drinking fountains—type UF-B, 2 wire with ground

The use of different types of power wires assists in the identification of wires, reduces the number of incorrect connections, and helps in troubleshooting should the power wire be damaged. Appropriate UL-listed splice kits should be used for making all splices (Figure 7.47).

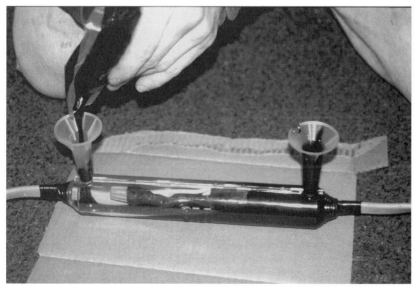

FIGURE 7.47
Power wire splice being made with a UL-listed splice kit.

Low-Voltage Wiring

Wire that runs from the field controller to each individual valve-in-head sprinkler or electric control valve is commonly referred to as low-voltage wiring or control wiring. The common wire runs from the field controller sequentially to each valve-in-head sprinkler and/or electric control valve to be operated from that field controller. The common wire is usually at least one wire gauge larger (typically #12 AWG) than the zone wire. Station or zone wires run from the field controller to one or a group of valve-in-head sprinklers or electric control valves that are to be operated as one station or zone. If two or more valve-in-head sprinklers or electric control valves are to be operated together as one station or zone, it is preferable to run a separate single conductor from each valve-in-head sprinkler or electric control valve back to the field controller. The wires can then be grouped together at the field controller and connected to the desired terminal. Station or zone wires are typically #14 AWG single conductor.

Low-voltage control wires are manufactured in a wide range of solid colors and colors with different colored strips added. Typically, low-voltage control wires are color coded according to function. The following is an example of such color coding:

Red	Fairways
Orange	Greens
Black	Tees
Blue	Spare wires

The use of green low-voltage control wire should be avoided because, in the United States, it is generally accepted that green wire denotes the equipment ground. In many other countries a green wire with a yellow stripe denotes the equipment ground.

Common wire is also often color coded. Specifications frequently call for separate independent commons that are dedicated to a single field controller. In situations where multiple field controllers are installed on a single pad, a trench may contain multiple common wires. Using commons of different colors avoids confusion. Another popular practice is to have a dedicated common wire running to every green and tee. For example, a yellow #12 AWG common wire may run from the field controller to the green and tee, and a white #12 AWG common wire may run to each of the other valve-in-head sprinklers or electric control valves (fairways, bunkers, roughs, etc.).

Single conductor #14 AWG wire is also frequently used as a trace wire in trenches that contain only pipe, but no wires. The following are two examples of where trace wire might be installed:

- Lateral pipes on a spray zone installed to irrigate bunkers
- Lateral pipes feeding small non-valve-in-head rotary sprinklers on a tee

The trace wire is installed along with the lateral pipe. One end of the trace wire is coiled and terminated in a valve access box. Should the piping have to be located, a wire scope can be connected to the trace wire and the wire/pipe path plotted. Trace wires are also frequently installed with drainage pipes. Trace wire should have a dedicated color that is not found on any other wire in the system.

A majority of golf courses use some type of remote sensor to activate a well or pump, which maintains the water level in a pond. Multiconductor UF-B wire or multiple single conductors (#14 or #12 AWG) are typically installed between the sensor and the relay that activates the well or pump. Again, it is advantageous to be able to identify any pond fill or pump start wire. Minimum cover requirements for this wire depend on the voltage it caries.

Communication Cable

Systems that use communication cable exclusively to communicate between the central controller and the field controllers are said to have their field controllers "hardwired." The type of communication cable used to hardwire a system varies according to equipment manufacturer. Regardless of the manufacturer, however, there are several rules that should be followed in installing communication cable:

- Communication cable should be installed according to the manufacturer's recommendation.
- Splices should be avoided. If a splice is absolutely necessary, it should be made by experienced personnel with a splice kit approved by the manufacturer.
- Bends or turns in communication cable should be made gently and gradually—no sharp 90 degree bends or turns. This is particularly critical for shielded communication cable. Making a sharp bend in shielded cable can cause the aluminum shielding/bonding to cut into one of the communication conductors.

- Communication cable should never be installed in a common trench with primary or secondary electric services or other high-voltage services.
- When communication cable is installed in a common trench with field controller power conductors, physical separation should be maintained between the communication cable and the power conductors.
- In areas prone to rodent damage, provision should be made to protect the integrity of the communication cable. This may range from installing a steel-armored cable to installing all the communication cable in electrical conduit. The conduit should be a minimum size of $1\frac{1}{4}$ in., because most rodents have a difficult time getting their teeth around large conduit.
- Labeling each communication cable simplifies the wiring of the field controllers. The labeling can also prove to be invaluable should troubleshooting be necessary. For example, the labeling of the communication cable that enters a field controller on #14 fairway may be as follows:
  - Communication in from Field Controller on #13 Fairway
  - Communication out to Field Controller on #15 Fairway

Such labeling is also appropriate for power wire and, likewise, will help with troubleshooting.

Weather Station Wiring

Weather stations are frequently installed as part of a new irrigation system. Wiring requirements vary according to manufacturer. All weather stations require a source of power—line voltage, low-voltage, battery, or solar power. Most battery chargers require a low-voltage power supply. A transformer is supplied with the weather station that reduces 120 V power to the required low-voltage. There are two options for installing a transformer:

1. The first option is to install the transformer at the weather station location. This often requires the addition of a weatherproof enclosure to house the transformer and electrical conduit to run the power wire in and out of the enclosure. The enclosure and conduit often pose an obstacle for mowing and maintenance equipment.

2. The second option is to install the transformer at a remote location and run low-voltage wiring to the weather station location. Possible remote transformer locations include the nearest irrigation field controller or a nearby electrical supply panel. A transformer draws minimal current. If the transformer is installed at the nearest field controller, the input voltage of the transformer must match the field controller power voltage. If the field controllers operate on 240 V power, the transformer will need to have a primary winding of 240 V. Consulting the manufacturer's literature or checking with its technical department can determine the maximum allowable run for various wire sizes. Typically, a #14 AWG can be run substantial distances and is often of sufficient size. Using a different color of #14 AWG single conductor or a different wire type such as #14 AWG/2 Type UF-B will allow for easy field identification should the wire ever be exposed during a repair.

Communication cable used to hardwire a weather station usually differs from the communication cable used to hardwire the irrigation central controller to the field controllers. The outward appearance of both communication cables is very similar. Caution should be exercised so as to avoid using the wrong cable for an application. Similar-appearing communication cables should be separated in the material storage area, and each reel clearly and indelibly labeled as to use.

Pump monitor cable links the pump station to the irrigation central controller, and often uses the same or similar type communication cable, as does the weather station. Likewise, the pump monitor communication cable should be marked and separated at the staging area.

Telephone Cable

The inclusion of telephone cable installation in an irrigation system contract is very common. For what and how the telephone cable will be used varies widely, ranging from a simple intercom system to sophisticated systems linked to the club switchboard, the local telephone company, and a 911 service. Selection of the telephone hardware and how the system will be used should be determined prior to installation of any telephone cable. These decisions should determine the types of wire that will be used and how they will be installed. Frequently, these decisions are approached after the cable installation is complete. Only then is it discovered that the cable was run to wrong locations or that the incorrect type of cable was used.

Telephone cable is often gel filled and shielded. As with communication cable, all turns should be made gently and gradually. Sharp bends can damage the wire cover, shielding/bonding, and conductors. The bend radius should be no less than ten times the cable diameter.

Cable Length Markings

Power wire, communication cable, and telephone cable often come in large spools containing 5000 ft or more. Many wire manufacturers label the footage on the wire at regular intervals, such as every 2 ft. This is called "sequential footing" and usually appears before or after the wire nomenclature; it may be in ascending or descending order, depending on how the wire was wound on the spool. This information is not usually found on the label or tag that accompanies the wire. Prior to starting use of any of the wire spools, the starting and projected ending footage should be marked indelibly on both sides of the each wire spool.

Say, for example, that the first number found on a 5000 ft spool of wire is 099006 and the following number is 099004. The wire is wound in descending order. On a 5000 ft spool the ending number should then be 094006. Typical labeling would be:

Starting #099006
Ending #094006

As the spool is used, the installer may take the difference between the first number found on the open spool of wire and the ending number on the side of the spool. The difference will tell the installer exactly how much wire is remaining on the spool. This information is invaluable during the installation process, helping to eliminate or reduce splices and ensuring that sufficient wire is on hand to complete the project.

Grounding Grids

Lightning damage has always been a problem with irrigation systems. The more wire installed in a system, the larger the wire grid or target available for a lightning strike. All golf irrigation equipment manufacturers have provisions for lightning protection within their controller equipment. The effectiveness of any lightning protection equipment is directly related to the effectiveness of the earth ground grid to which it is connected. Different grounding grid designs will yield different results. Furthermore, the effectiveness of identical earth grounding grids will vary, depending on soil type and moisture content. The resistance of earth ground grids is measured in ohms. Most manufacturers recommend obtaining readings ranging from 5 to 10 ohms. The lower the ohm reading, the more effective the ground. Ground grids should be tested shortly after installation and every three months thereafter for the first year. Initial readings are frequently higher than readings taken three to six months after installation. Initial ground readings are frequently requested by manufacturers and usually required by consultants. The periodic readings recommended during the first year and twice yearly readings thereafter should be part of the maintenance budget.

Grid Configuration

Materials used to construct earth ground grids are somewhat consistent, but the actual recommended configuration of a ground grid varies from one manufacturer to another. Furthermore, many irrigation consultants/designers expand upon what is required by a manufacturer. Most consultants/designers define a specific ground grid that is to be installed initially. They further define additional grounding measures to be taken if tests indicate that the initial ground grid failed to produce the desired results. In some soils it is nearly impossible and economically not feasible to achieve the desire results. Money would be more wisely spent if it were set aside for future repair of lightning damage to equipment, rather than being spent on expensive upgrades to the ground grids that will not improve results.

Grid Installation

The following are key concerns in installing earth ground grids:

- How and where the earth grounding grids will be installed is a critical factor in selecting a field controller location. Marking paint should be used to indicate the projected paths for all wires and ground grids. Where possible, ground rods and ground plates should be located in irrigated areas or low areas that will collect water.

- Field controllers should be installed outside the sphere of influence of the ground grid. The sphere of influence of an 8 ft ground rod is a circle with an 8 ft radius. The sphere of influence of a 10 ft ground rod is a 10 ft radius circle.

- In ground grid configurations employing multiple ground rods, the sphere of influence from one rod should not overlap the sphere of influence of another rod. Minimum spacing between rods should be at least twice the length of a ground rod.

- When possible, the path of bare copper wire, ground rods, and ground plates should be clear of other wire and cable paths and should not cross over other wires and conductors.

- Solid bare copper ground wire should be installed in a straight line. Sharp turns or bends should be avoided. If bare copper wire must change direction, the turn should be a gradual sweep.

- Dedicated PVC electrical conduit should be installed at each field controller for the earth grounds. This conduit should contain only the earth ground wire(s) and shielding/bonding/ bonding wire (if specified).

- Earth ground wire should be installed by the open trench method and not by vibratory plow. The open trench method results in better soil contact with the bare copper wire.

- UL-listed ⅝ in. copper-clad ground rods should be driven a minimum of 8 ft in a vertical position. Where conditions prevent the ground rod from being driven vertically, the oblique angle at which the rod is driven should not exceed 45 degrees from vertical.

- Ground plates should be installed in a flat horizontal position a minimum of 30 in. below grade. In areas where the frost line exceeds 30 in., the ground plates should be installed below the frost line.

- Some specifications call for the inclusion of ground enhancement materials with the installation of ground rods and plates. The manufacturer's warning labels should be read before any of this material is used. The installer should wear the proper protective equipment when handling and installing ground enhancement materials. Water can be added to the ground enhancement material prior to installation creating slurry that

FIGURE 7.48
Earth ground plate being installed with ground enhancement material.

is not susceptible to wind drift and is easier to handle (see Figure 7.48).

- Temporary connections employing "acorn type" ground clamps may be made to the earth ground grid until such time as satisfactory test results are achieved. At that time, the ground clamps should be replaced with permanent connections made by an exothermic welding process.

Central controllers, weather stations, and pump stations are examples of other irrigation equipment that should have earth ground grids.

Lightning damage to irrigation equipment is frequently the result of lightning following a path created by wire that is connected to the equipment. Installing a bare copper shielding/bonding wire above major bundles of wire often allows the bare copper wire to intercept lightning and dissipate the energy, thus protecting the irrigation equipment. The bare copper shielding/bonding wire should be connected to all the earth ground grids for the area it services to create a shielding/bonding wire grid.

Power for the field controllers in a typical golf irrigation system may come from multiple power sources. The shielding/bonding wire from field controllers serviced by one power source cannot be connected to a shielding/bonding wire from field controllers serviced by another power source. If there are three different power sources supplying power to the field controllers, then there must be three *separate and independent* shielding/bonding wire grids.

Lateral or Sub-Main Installation

Lateral lines, as commonly used in golf irrigation, refers to a system of pipes to which the sprinkler heads are connected. Lateral lines are usually isolated from larger mainlines by closing one or a series of isolation valves. On golf irrigation systems utilizing valve-in-head sprinklers, lateral lines are under continuous pressure and may be more accurately described as sub-mains. On most golf irrigation systems the majority of lateral lines are 2½ in. or 2 in.

Lateral lines can be installed by the open trench method or by vibratory plow if conditions permit. Much of the previous discussion regarding irrigation mainline installation pertains to the open trench installation of lateral lines. However, there are two common differences:

1. Specifications usually allow for a shallower depth of cover over lateral lines, usually 18 to 24 in. In rocky and hard soils this depth of cover is sometimes reduced to as little as 12 in.

2. Most wiring associated with lateral installation is low-voltage control wire to the sprinkler heads and valves. When other wires are installed with a lateral line, the width and/or depth of the excavation is usually modified.

Installation of lateral lines by the vibratory plow method requires many considerations:

- Gasket joint pipe cannot be installed by vibratory plow. Piping material must be solvent-weld PVC, HDPE, or polyethylene pipe.
- Soil conditions must be acceptable. Pipe should not be installed by vibratory plow in extremely rocky soils. Moreover, vibratory plows may not function in extremely hard and compacted soils.
- The vibratory plow must be suitable to the soil conditions and equipped with a combination pipe-pulling/cable-laying blade. The combination blade should have an expanding bullet of sufficient size to allow easy pulling of the pipe. The combination blade must also have a wire-laying chute of sufficient width to accommodate bundles of low-voltage wire. The vibratory plow and combination blade must be capable of pulling the pipe while laying the low-voltage wire just above the pipe. There should be a minimum 1 in. separation

between the pipe and the wire. Both the pipe and the wire should be installed at specified depths.

- PVC solvent-weld pipe should be joined with an approved solvent-weld cement and compatible primer and applied according to the manufacturer's directions. It is important that the PVC cement and primer are appropriate for the ambient temperature range during installation. The PVC cement and primer should be stored in a heated area. Neither should be subjected to extended periods of freezing temperatures. Both must be used before the expiration date stamped on the can.

- The typical procedure for making a solvent weld joint is as follows:

  1. Cut and bevel the PVC pipe at the desired point and remove any pipe burrs.

  2. Coat the outside end of the PVC pipe with primer.

  3. Coat the inside of the fitting with primer.

  4. Apply an even coat of PVC cement to the outside of the pipe. Be sure the coating is equal to the depth of the fitting.

  5. Apply an even coat of PVC cement to the inside of the fitting. Be careful not to apply excess cement; it can accumulate inside the fitting and the pipe.

  6. Apply a second coat of cement to the outside of the pipe.

  7. Insert the pipe to the full depth of the fitting and give a quarter turn. Hold in position until the pipe starts to set, normally 15 to 90 seconds.

  8. Wipe off excess cement.

  9. Allow the pipe sufficient time to set before handling or installing it. The set time will vary, depending on the temperature, relative humidity, cement manufacturer, and type of cement. The colder the temperature, the longer the set time. According to ASTM-D2855, the cure time for PVC pipe of 3 in. and less is as follows:

         60° to 100°F   2 hours
         40° to 60°F   4 hours
         20° to 40°F   12 hours

- Lateral pipe installed by vibratory plow is fitted from the fixed point out. The first connection point is usually at an isolation valve. The pipe is fitted from that point out, sequentially, to the farthest fitting or sprinkler head (Figure 7.49).

FIGURE 7.49
PVC pipe being installed with Ditch Witch 6510 vibratory plow.

- An entrance hole of sufficient size should be dug at the point where the lateral line installation is to start. The entrance hole should allow the pipe to attain the desired depth of cover without putting undo stress on the pipe joints.

- The pipe must be properly aligned with fittings and fixed connection points. Wherever tees and elbows are installed, the pipe must approach the fitting at the proper 90 degree angle. Experienced equipment operators are the key to achieving proper alignment.

- PVC pipe does not have to be vibratory plowed in straight lines. Gentle curves in the pipe are acceptable and necessary, particularly around greens and bunkers. Sharp turns that cause stress on the pipe joints and/or misalignment of fittings should be avoided.

- PVC pipe should not be installed by the vibratory plow method when the ambient air temperatures are so low that they jeopardize the integrity of the pipe joints and pipe. Nor should pipe be plowed when there is 1 in. or more of frost in the ground.

- On existing courses, plow lines should be rolled with a dual-drum vibratory roller.

A major concern with installing solvent-weld PVC pipe by the vibratory plow method is making provisions for pipe expansion and contraction. This is of particular concern when all fittings are solvent-weld PVC. For example, a par 5 fairway may have a 450-yard continuous run of 2 in. PVC, or 1350 ft. The ambient soil temperature may vary during the year from 45° to 75°F. The expansion factor for 2 in.

PVC is .36 in. per 100 ft per 10°F temperature deviation. The expansion/contraction for the 450-yard par 5 would be as follows:

450 yards=1350 ft
.36 in. × 1350/100 × 30/10
.36 in. × 13.5 × 3 = 14.58 in.

The expansion/contraction potential for a 2 in. lateral running the length of the fairway would therefore be 14.58 in.

A remedy for this situation is to install gasketed service tees for the connection of all valve-in-head sprinkler heads. If fairway sprinklers were installed on 70 ft spacing, the gasketed service tees would allow expansion and contraction every 70 ft. Further provisions for expansion/contraction can be made by using gasketed fittings for all changes in direction (tees, elbows). All directional fitting must be thrust blocked.

As with solvent-weld fittings, the PVC pipe must be properly aligned to install any gasketed fitting. The PVC pipe must first be beveled with the use of a mechanical beveller or a file. The gasketed fitting is first put on the fixed or nonmovable side. A light coating of pipe lube is applied to the end of the beveled PVC pipe, and the gasket-joint fitting is pushed on. A pry bar can be used to assist in pushing on gasketed fittings. Lube is applied to the other end of the PVC pipe, and it is pushed into the fitting from the next sprinkler head or fitting hole. As with solvent-weld fittings, assembly progresses from the fixed point out, sequentially, to the farthest sprinkler head or fitting. After all the fittings have been installed, the thrust blocks are poured or installed. If rocky conditions are encountered, lateral pipe must be installed by open trenching (Figure 7.50).

SPRINKLER HEAD INSTALLATION

Modern golf irrigation designs utilize a variety of sprinkler head types for diverse applications. Often, one type of sprinkler head is used for a multitude of different applications. The nozzle configuration and spacing of the sprinkler head frequently change with each different application. The first challenge in installing sprinkler heads is to ensure that the correct head with the proper nozzle is installed where needed. When the system is staked, the "as-staked" drawing should indicate which head is to be installed at each specific location and which nozzle configuration is to be installed. This information can

FIGURE 7.50
Lateral pipe being installed in rocky ground with a Vermeer LM-42 equipped with a rock wheel.

then be written on a marking flag or stake or painted on the ground prior to installation. Separating the different types of sprinkler heads in the material storage area and labeling the boxes for intended use helps eliminate confusion when the heads are selected for installation. The foreman or a responsible crew member should pull the correct sprinkler heads and place them at the specific locations where they are to be installed.

Swing Joints

All sprinkler heads located on a golf course should be installed on swing joint risers. The key considerations for the installation of swing joints are as follows:

- The long riser nipple of the swing joint should be installed at an angle approximating 45 degrees from the horizontal. The swing joint should not be installed with the riser nipple straight up (vertical) or flat (horizontal). Figure 7.51 shows the proper installation of a typical swing joint. If the lay length of the swing joint is too short, it is better to install the swing joint properly and add a coupling and a nipple to the top elbow to raise the sprinkler head to grade.
- Elbows and nipples on swing joints should never be overtightened. The swing joint should move freely when moderate pressure is applied.

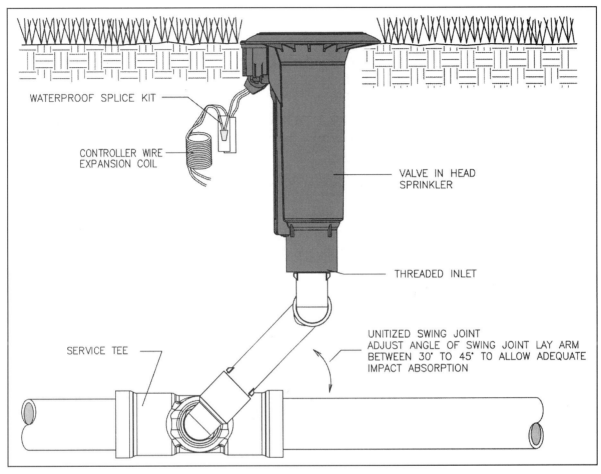

WATERPROOF SPLICE KIT

CONTROLLER WIRE
EXPANSION COIL

VALVE IN HEAD
SPRINKLER

THREADED INLET

SERVICE TEE

UNITIZED SWING JOINT
ADJUST ANGLE OF SWING JOINT LAY ARM
BETWEEN 30° TO 45° TO ALLOW ADEQUATE
IMPACT ABSORPTION

FIGURE 7.51
**Typical valve-in-head sprinkler
and swing joint detail.**

- Teflon tape should be utilized as a thread sealant for IPS threads. Neither Teflon tape nor thread sealant should be applied to ACME or buttress-thread swing joints.

Sprinkler Head Location

Likewise, there are certain considerations common to the installation of all sprinkler heads on golf courses:

- Sprinkler heads should be located to accommodate the game of golf.
- Sprinkler heads should not be located on green collars or putting surfaces. An exception is a green so large that locating all the heads off the green surface would exceed the maximum

allowed head spacing and sacrifice proper coverage. Changes in sprinkler head model, pressure regulation, and/or nozzle that would allow greater spacing should be considered before locating heads in the putting surface.

- If a head must be installed in the putting surface, the following should be considered:
  - Minimize the number of heads in the putting surface.
  - Rather than installing a valve-in-head sprinkler requiring pipe under constant pressure to be under the putting surface, utilize an electric control valve located off the putting surface. The pipe under the putting surface is then under pressure only when the head is operating. Three different combinations of valve and sprinkler head can be utilized:
    1. The sprinkler head model can be changed to a check valve model without valve-in-head. A pressure-regulating electric control valve is installed to control and regulate each head.
    2. Valve-in-head sprinkler(s) are installed without wiring and the pilot valve left in the "ON" position so pressure is regulated. A standard electric control valve is installed to control each head.
    3. Valve-in-head sprinkler(s) are installed, and the pilot valve left in the "AUTO" position. A standard electric control valve is installed for each head. A control wire is run to both the head and the control valve and connected to a common terminal in the field controller. The electric control valve functions as a safety or master valve.
  - Consider installing a sprinkler head with a smaller diameter top. Many athletic field heads can be adapted for this purpose. The top diameter of the head is substantially smaller than that of a valve-in-head sprinkler. With proper nozzle selection, the athletic field head can perform similarly to many valve-in-head sprinklers. The athletic field head is controlled and regulated with a pressure-regulating electric control valve.
- Heads should not be placed directly in front of a green or in any location where an approach shot may strike them.
- Heads should not be installed in cart paths, in walking paths, on sand bunker edges, or at locations prone to flooding.

- A head should be installed at or slightly below grade; it should be installed level and plumb.
- Installation on sloped areas should be avoided whenever possible. Moving a head 4 or 5 ft to get to level ground is preferable to installing it on a slope.
- Where snow plowing is an issue, heads should be installed at least 1 ft from the pavement edge.
- During installation, part-circle sprinkler heads should be dry adjusted so that the arc throws in the general direction intended. Modern designs often have part-circle sprinkler heads installed back-to-back—for instance, part-circle heads that throw in, to water the green putting surface, and part-circle heads throwing out, to water the green surrounds. Dry adjusting the sprinkler head at the time of installation helps to ensure that the correct head is used for each application. Many sprinkler heads have markings on their cases designating the approximate right or left stop of the arc. This feature greatly facilitates the dry adjustment of the sprinkler head and saves time.

Metal Case Sprinkler Heads

Early metal case sprinkler heads were installed on swing joints that were fabricated in the field (as opposed to factory assembled) of galvanized steel fittings and nipples. Almost all modern installations use premanufactured PVC swing joints. There are two concerns in using premanufactured PVC swing joints with metal case sprinkler heads:

1. Many of these sprinkler heads have bodies constructed of bronze or cast iron. The weight of the body creates stress and possible fitting fatigue on the swing joint, especially on the top elbow. A solution is to install premanufactured swing joints that have a brass nipple incorporated in the top elbow.

2. Metal case sprinkler heads are manufactured with holes in the bodies for drainage. Typical installation details include gravel sumps around the head to support it and aid in drainage. When the gravel encompasses the swing joint, it prevents movement in the elbow joints, and renders the swing joint ineffective. The gravel sump should not extend down below the first elbow in the swing joint. This allows move-

ment in the swing joint, which protects both the sprinkler head and the piping system.

Valve-in-Head Sprinklers

The majority of modern golf irrigation systems utilize plastic case valve-in-head sprinklers as the primary type of sprinkler head. The heads may employ gear or impact drives. The valve-in-head sprinkler is typically installed on a premanufactured swing joint. Concerns in installing valve-in-head sprinklers include the following:

- The style and size of the swing joint should be based on the flow of the sprinkler head, not the threaded inlet size of the head.
- Valve-in-head sprinkler heads require the connection of low-voltage control wires for automatic operation. The wiring should be installed in a manner that protects its integrity both during installation and later, should the sprinkler head have to be excavated for service or replacement. Low-voltage wires are frequently damaged during initial compaction and when the sprinkler head is excavated for repair or replacement. To reduce the incidence of damage caused by compaction or excavation, the wires should be installed close to the body of the sprinkler. Several manufacturers make retaining clips that secure the control wire to the swing joint assembly. Another method of securing the low-voltage wiring to both the swing joint and the valve-in-head sprinkler body is the use of zip-ties that are readily available at wholesale electric supply and home improvement centers.
- The design of valve-in-head sprinklers with extended grass flanges makes compaction difficult. During installation, the soil should be hand placed in layers and gently compacted by using something like the handle end of a shovel or a baseball bat. Special care should be taken not to damage the pilot valve or wires.

Smaller Specialty Sprinkler Heads

The installation of small rotary sprinkler heads and pop-up spray heads (mist heads) on golf courses has become very popular because of the demand for more precise water control on special treatment and problem areas (Figure 7.52). These small heads should also be installed on swing joint risers. Premanufactured Schedule 40 PVC

FIGURE 7.52
Spray (mist) heads installed on top of mounds.

swing joints are available from many manufacturers in ¾ in. and ½ in. sizes and with a variety of lay lengths. Installation of these small heads on flexible pipe or "funny pipe" should be discouraged. The flexible pipe connection is not as strong as a standard swing joint.

Some features that are standard on larger sprinkler heads are optional on the small heads. When available, the heads should be installed with optional check valves to reduce low-head drainage and prevent puddled water from reentering the piping system through an open nozzle orifice. Options such as stainless steel risers, heavy-duty wiper seals, stronger retraction springs, and adjustment screws are advantageous.

FIELD CONTROLLERS

Before a field controller (satellite controller) can be installed, an appropriate location must be chosen. The first and most important consideration is that the location must be out of play. Even locations in the rough that are frequented by errant tee shots should be avoided.

Opinions vary on whether a field controller should be visible from the field of play. Some golf course architects and irrigation consultants/designers go to great lengths to ensure that every field controller cannot be seen during a round of golf. This frequently adds cost due to longer wire runs, berming, and/or plantings. Others believe the field controller is part of the golf course landscape. To be consistent, all would agree that it is desirable to hide the field controllers from the golfers' view.

Many superintendents prefer being able to see all sprinkler heads controlled from the field controller location. Seeing the sprinkler heads from the field controller location becomes even more desirable with new course installations. Often, the central computer is not installed or operable until the maintenance facility is completed. The newly installed irrigation system is often operated for a year or more in a stand-alone mode from the field controllers.

Field controllers should not be installed next to sprinkler heads, especially where the upward stream of the head will hit them.

A criterion frequently overlooked during the selection of a location for a field controller is earth grounding. A selected field controller location often hinders or makes impossible the installation of an acceptable earth ground grid. Moving a field controller up or down a fairway, or to the other side, may greatly enhance the possibility of establishing an acceptable grid.

The relocation of a field controller for any reason should be reviewed by the irrigation consultant/designer. Changes in controller location impact voltage loss in power wire and may necessitate a change in wire size.

Field controller station capacity has increased over the years. Some manufacturers now provide the capability of controlling nearly 100 stations from a single field controller. Often, one field controller location will control multiple golf holes. Low-voltage control wire, power wire, and communication cable may enter the field controller location from several different directions. With greater station capacity, specifications often call for multiple earth ground grids. Wiring employed within the ground grid should not cross over other wires and cables. With a variety of wires and cables entering from different directions, common sense dictates that routing of the wiring to each field controller should be a prime consideration in the selection of location.

Field controllers should not be installed near telephone poles, light poles, flag poles, or other structures that are likely to be hit by lightning. Surge and lightning protection equipment often fails to protect field controllers from a direct strike in the vicinity of the controller.

Radio Considerations

Central/field controller systems that utilize radio signals for communication require additional consideration. Field controller locations where the line of sight to the central may be obstructed by buildings, hills, or other structures, should be avoided. Locations next to high-voltage transformers, cell towers, microwave antennas, or other devices that may interfere with the integrity of the radio link, should also be avoided. Prior to ordering the central and field controllers, a radio frequency survey is usually conducted on-site by the manufacturer/distributor to determine which available frequencies are best suited for communication. The integrity of the radio communication path between the central and each proposed field controller location should also be checked at this time. Problems with field controller locations can sometimes be corrected by the installation of different style antennas, a repeater, or a remote antenna. The time to address these potential problems is in the planning stages, not after the system has been installed.

Field Controller Pad Construction

Specifications for poured-in-place pad construction for field controllers vary, depending on the area of the country and the irrigation consultant/designer. The following should be considered:

- Separate conduit sweeps should be provided for low-voltage wiring, power wire, communication cable, and ground/shielding wire. Couplings and extensions generally need to be added to both ends of most sweeps so that they are long enough to protrude through the pad and out from under the pad
- To prevent sharp bends in the wire and conform to the American Society of Irrigation Consultants (ASIC) grounding guidelines, the radius of the conduit sweep ell for the earth ground grid and/or shielding wire should have a minimum radius of 8 in. This can be achieved by installing a standard 1½ in. PVC Schedule 40 conduit sweep elbow or a 1 in. Schedule 40 long-radius conduit sweep elbow. The 1 in. long-radius ell should be used when space within the mounting template is limited. Long-radius ells are often special order items and cost substantially more than standard-radius ells.
- Where multiple field controllers are mounted on a common pad, two or more U-shaped conduits should be installed, linking each controller to its immediate neighbor. These linking conduits can be used to install power wire and communica-

tion wire from one controller to another. Should there ever be a need to move a sprinkler head or a group of sprinkler heads from one controller to another, the conduits can be used, eliminating the necessity of excavating the low-voltage wiring.

- Before excavating and installing the various conduits, it is important to check to be sure that all the conduits will fit within the mounting template provided with the controller and the controller base. The bottom opening in the base of some field controllers is actually smaller than the opening in the mounting template provided with them. Before pouring any pad, the installer must make sure that both the mounting template and the field controller will fit over the conduits.

- Conduit sweeps should be installed to the specified depth of cover for the wires and cables they carry. To comply with the National Electrical Code (NEC), a bushing or terminal fitting with an integral bushed opening must be installed at the end of any conduit that terminates underground where the wires or cables emerge as direct burial.

- On multiple controller pads, conduit groups should be equally spaced so that the completed pad will have uniform gaps between the field controllers.

Once the conduits have been installed, the excavated soil can be backfilled and compacted. A wood form for the pad can then be constructed and installed. The dimensions and construction of field controller pads vary widely and are often determined by the personal preferences of the irrigation consultant/designer or the irrigation equipment manufacturer/distributor. The following should be considered in sizing and constructing field controller pads (Figure 7.53):

- Provide a minimum of 6 in. from the front, sides, and back of the field controller to the edge of the concrete pad. A popular option is to provide at least 24 in. in front of the field controller. This allows the superintendent to operate and service the field controller while standing on a concrete pad.

- Allow a minimum of 4 in. between field controllers. Some manufacturers may require substantially more space for access to the internal components and wiring.

- The depth of the pad will vary according to the preferences of the consultant/designer and the area of the country. However, pads should not be less than 8 in. thick.

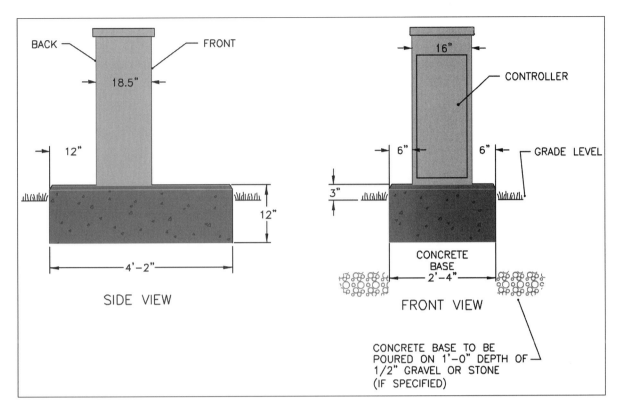

BACK — FRONT

18.5"

12"

12"

—4'–2"—

SIDE VIEW

16"

CONTROLLER

6" 6" — GRADE LEVEL

3"

CONCRETE
BASE
—2'–4"—

FRONT VIEW

CONCRETE BASE TO BE
POURED ON 1'–0" DEPTH OF
1/2" GRAVEL OR STONE
(IF SPECIFIED)

FIGURE 7.53
**Typical field controller pad
construction.**

• The field controller pad should be installed level and approximately 2 in. above grade.

A minimum of 4 in. of compacted stone should be provided as a base for the concrete. There are many situations where additional stone may be required, such as in wet areas or unstable soils. Some specifications require the installation of wire mesh or rebar in the pad construction. Others require that additives such as fiberglass be incorporated into the mix.

Getting concrete to the various field controller locations often presents a challenge, particularly on existing golf courses. The first decision is whether to use ready-mix cement or to mix the concrete on-site at the various controller locations. Mixing concrete on-site can be a time-consuming process, with the consistency and integrity of the concrete dependent on the individual making the mix. However, in some instances it is impossible to get ready-mix cement to a particular location and mixing on-site may be the only option.

In most instances, purchasing ready-mix concrete is the quickest and most economical solution. Delivery should be limited to the amount that can be comfortably poured and finished in a day. Distributing the concrete around a golf course takes time. If ready-mix concrete sits in a delivery truck for extended periods of time and/or if water is added to the mix, the integrity of the mix can be affected. Often, a day's pour is better divided into two deliveries. For instance, a 10-yard pour may be divided into a 5-yard delivery at 8:00 A.M. and a 5-yard delivery at 1:00 P.M. Purchasing the ready-mix in this fashion is more costly, but the sitting time is reduced and the integrity of the concrete is maintained. Typically, controller pads for an 18-hole golf course require more than one day to pour. Preplanning the staging areas and determining which pads will be poured on a given day, the order in which they will be poured, and the route the truck will follow, will facilitate the pour. The ready-mix truck may be able to directly access some controller pad locations, whereas others will require auxiliary equipment to buggy the concrete (Figure 7.54). Front-end loaders, backhoes, and concrete buggies are often used to distribute the concrete.

Once the concrete has been placed, it should be screeded and floated so that it is level or tapered slightly from the templates to the edges of the form. Low areas or pockets should be avoided, to prevent water from pooling on the pad. The mounting template(s) should be positioned and installed while the concrete is relatively wet. On multiple controller pads, the mounting templates should be aligned so that they are in a straight line, equidistant from the back and sides of the pad, and with equal spaces between them. The concrete should be manually worked around each mounting bolt to

FIGURE 7.54
Concrete buggy delivering ready-mix concrete to field controller location.

ensure that there are no air gaps. The mounting templates should then be checked for level with a torpedo level. Once the concrete has started to set, a trowel or broom finish can be applied and the edges finished with an edger (Figure 7.55).

Some irrigation installers suggest prefabricating concrete field controller pads and installing them on gravel bases. Prefabricated controller pads are prone to shifting or settling, resulting in pads that are not level and field controllers that are not plumb. The required depth of cover for conduits is often sacrificed with prefabricated pads. Several manufacturers also produce prefabricated field controller pads constructed of metal or polyethylene. There are similar concerns in installing premanufactured field controller pads.

Special conditions, such as unavoidable location in a flood plain, require special controller pad installations (see Figure 7.56).

The concrete should cure a minimum of 24 hours before the field controllers are installed. Cure time may be longer in cool or damp weather. Excess concrete should be removed from the mounting bolts and template. Before installing the field controllers, any excess conduit protruding through the pad should be cut off. After the field controllers are secured to the pad, the ends of the conduit can be excavated and the field wiring run into the controller. As previously mentioned, to comply with the NEC, the conduit ends in the ground must terminate with a bushing or a terminal fitting with an integral bushed opening. Excess wire in the field controller should be trimmed.

FIGURE 7.55
Edging and finishing field controller pad.

FIGURE 7.56
Field controller installed on elevated mounds above 100-year flood level.

Wiring Connections at Controllers

Before attempting to wire any field controller, the manufacturer's installation manual or instructions should be read in their entirety. Depending on state and local codes, some or all of the wiring may have to be performed by a licensed electrician.

Prior to connecting any power wire, low-voltage control wire, or communication cable, the earth ground wire and shielding wires should be connected. Most field controllers are equipped with a chassis ground lug for connection of the earth ground grid/shielding wires. The earth ground grid resistance should be measured with a ground tester to verify that the earth ground grid is acceptable. Depending on the type of measuring equipment and the procedure used, the power wire connection to the field controller may have to be completed and energized to perform a proper measurement. The measurement should be performed as soon as possible after the earth ground grid is connected to determine whether additional grounding is required. If the measurement indicates additional grounding is required, it should be installed and remeasured.

Before connecting any power wire, the installer should check to see that the power is turned off at the source. An AC voltage meter should be used to verify that the power is off at the field controller location. Before the connection of the power wire is made, the transformer should be checked for proper input voltage rating. It is not uncommon for modern golf irrigation systems to use 240 V power supplies to keep power wire size to a minimum. Many field controllers come with dual voltage transformers that may need to be rewired to accommodate the 240 V power supply. Other field controllers are equipped with an input voltage selection switch.

The NEC requires that where the power wire enters the power supply connection box in the field controller, the wiring must be firmly secured. An appropriate size romex connector or similar approved wire restraint should be installed in the knockout of the power supply connection box. There also is a limit to the size of the power wire that can be installed in most field controller's power supply connection boxes. This wire size is often limited to #10 AWG or smaller. If larger wire or multiple wires enter the field controller, they should be spliced together with a #10 AWG leg run into the power supply connection box.

There are two other critical concerns with power wire connections:

1. Polarity of line and neutral connections must be maintained throughout the installation. Reversing polarity may trip the circuit breaker or cause damage to one or more field controllers.

2. Most golf irrigation systems utilize multiple power sources to power the field controllers. The wiring systems from each power source should remain independent of each other. No interconnection of power wire, equipment ground (green wire), or bonding/shielding wire from one power source with that from another power source should ever be made.

The connection of communication cables varies according to manufacturer. Some field controllers have terminals for "communication cable in" and "communication cable out," whereas others connect the all communication cables to a common terminal board. It is helpful to have the communication cable identified prior to connection. This process can be done as the communication cable is installed along the mainline piping.

If the communication cable was not identified at time of initial installation, it can be identified when it is connected to the field controllers. In this instance, connection of the communication cable should be done in a sequential manner, starting at the central controller location and working out to the most distant field controller. Conductors in the communication cable can be twisted together at the central computer and a continuity test performed at the first field controller location identifying the communication cable in and out. This process can be continued sequentially, identifying the communication cable at each field controller location.

The labeling of both the power wire and communication cable in and out of each field controller location benefits future servicing and troubleshooting. Inexpensive labeling devices are available at most office supply stores.

Connection of Low-Voltage Wiring

Connection of low-voltage control wiring is the most time-consuming part of the wiring process. The preferred station sequence varies among irrigation consultants/designers, superintendents, and contractors. Prior to initiating the low-voltage control wiring, a consensus must be reached on the wiring sequence. This sequence should be recorded and followed throughout the wiring process. The following is an example of a typical wiring sequence for a triple-row irrigation system with additional heads in the rough:

1. Green sprinklers, starting at the front left and proceeding clockwise around the green
2. Center approach sprinkler head
3. Right side approach sprinkler head
4. Left side approach sprinkler head
5. Tee sprinkler heads, starting at the front of the tees and proceeding to the rear of the tees
6. Center row fairway sprinkler heads, proceeding from green to tee
7. Right side row fairway sprinkler heads, proceeding from green to tee
8. Left side row fairway sprinkler heads, proceeding from green to tee
9. Part-circle out sprinkler heads around green, starting at the front left and proceeding clockwise around green
10. Right side of fairway rough sprinklers
11. Left side of fairway rough sprinklers
12. Bunker sprinkler heads

A field controller data sheet should be compiled as each controller is wired. The data sheet should list the following:

- The location of the field controller
- The numeric assignment in the central program for that controller
- The station capacity of the field controller
- Location of each station
- Model of sprinkler head
- Operating pressure
- Nozzle size
- Arc of adjustment for part-circle sprinkler heads

Some manufacturers supply a data collection sheet that can be duplicated and used to collect the data. Simple spreadsheets can be also created. The station assignment number, model of sprinkler head, operating pressure, and nozzle size should be transferred to the Record Drawings.

DECODER SYSTEMS

The installation of a decoder system is very similar to the installation of a central/satellite system, with the exception that a decoder system does not require field controllers or individual station wires to operate the system. The power and control signals required to operate a decoder system are carried over the same cable. There is a great reduction in the amount of wire to be installed with a decoder system, and all, or most, of the field controllers that are used on a conventional centrally controlled irrigation system are not required. There can be some installation time savings in the installation of a decoder system; however, time savings are usually offset by the extra care that must be taken in the documentation and installation of all cable and decoders. In addition, because a poor connection on a cable can prevent communication with decoders farther down the cable, it is imperative that extra care is taken in splicing the cable. Decoders are susceptible to lightning damage, so it is essential that the manufacturer's earth grounding guidelines be followed.

CENTRAL CONTROLLERS

The central controller or central computer is often one of the last items in an irrigation system to be installed. On new course installations, the maintenance building must be completed or a temporary location for the central provided. Most central controllers are PC-based, and manufacturers usually upgrade the software at least once a year. There are advantages to ordering and installing the central shortly before it will be used. Waiting to order the central usually ensures that the system will come on-line with the latest computer and the most current version of software.

Another reason the central controller is usually one of the last items to be installed is that other segments of the system must be fully or partly installed and operable before the central can be used:

- The permanent water source or temporary water source must be in place and operable.
- All or segments of the irrigation mainline must be complete, flushed, and operable.
- Some lateral or sub-main piping must be completed, flushed, and operable.
- Some or all of the field controllers, power wire, and communication cable must be in place and wired.

In contrast, ordering the central early in the installation process allows the superintendent to become familiar with the hardware and the programs before they are actually used to operate the system. In a situation where a superintendent and/or assistant may not be familiar with computers, their operating systems, and irrigation software, ordering the central early is an advantage. In either case, sufficient lead-time must be allowed when ordering the central controller to ensure that it will be available when desired.

Central controller/computer installation details vary by manufacturer and the specifications developed by the irrigation consultant/designer. The following guidelines apply to the installation of a central controller/computer:

- Select a location where the central is not exposed to extreme temperatures or excessive dust.
- Provide a dedicated electric circuit to power the central.
- Install all wiring to the central in electric conduit for protection.
- Include an uninterrupted power supply (UPS).

- Install maximum lightning/surge protection and connect to earth ground.
- Follow the manufacturer's installation recommendations.

Handheld Radios

Most modern central controller/computers integrate a handheld radio into the system that allows the superintendent to operate the irrigation system remotely from the keypad. The radio usually comes equipped with at least two frequencies, one that operates the communication with the central controller/computer and at least one other dedicated to a channel for voice communication. There are a number of considerations in installing a handheld radio system:

- Perform a radio frequency survey to select a clear, dependable frequency for communication with the central.
- For golf courses that presently use radios for voice communication, order handheld radios with one of the voice communication channels utilizing the existing frequency.
- Install the radio antenna so anticipated paths of communication are unobstructed.
- Install lightning/surge protection at antennas and connect to earth ground.
- Follow the manufacturer's installation recommendations.

Weather Station

Another common accessory integrated with central controller/computer systems is a weather station. The function of the weather station will vary according to manufacturer and the preference of the superintendent.

Selection of the site for a weather station is critical for obtaining accurate meteorological data. Manufacturers have detailed guidelines to follow for site selection. There are a number of factors important to the location of a weather station site. The site should be:

- Representative of typical areas of the course
- An open area free from obstructions such as trees, tall shrubs, and buildings (defined by minimum distances from obstructions)

- Relatively level and covered by turfgrass
- Away from bodies of water that may influence ambient temperature
- In an irrigated area where the sensors will not be hit by sprinkler heads

Sometimes it is not possible to locate a weather station in an area that will be free from potential damage by vandalism or traffic. In these instances, the weather station can be located inside a 6 ft high security fence with a lockable access gate. The fence is typically installed 8 ft out from the weather station in all directions, and it should not interfere with the accuracy of the sensors. On golf courses that encompass extraordinarily large parcels of land or that have areas with different microclimates, more than one weather station may be required to provide accurate meteorological data.

Weather stations are typically installed on poured-in-place concrete pads. The procedure for construction of the concrete pad is similar to that for construction of a field controller pad. The dimensions of a weather station pad usually differ from those of a typical field controller pad. The size of the exposed surface area of the weather station pad is kept to a minimum to reduce the influence of the concrete pad on solar radiation and temperature. The weather station pad is also typically poured substantially deeper in order to support the weather station and stabilize it in windy conditions. Ample cure time is required prior to mounting and assembling the weather station. To provide accurate wind direction, the weather station must be properly oriented to true north. True north differs from magnetic north by a number of degrees, which vary according to the area of the country. True north can be found by reading a magnetic compass and applying the correction for magnetic declination between true north and magnetic north. Magnetic declination for a specific area can be obtained from a local airport, found on magnetic charts on the United States Geological Survey (USGS) website, or determined with a GeoMag Calculator, available on the National Geophysical Data Center (NGDC) website.

The manufacturer's instructions should be carefully followed during assembly and wiring of the weather station. Particular attention should be paid to grounding and lightning protection. Auxiliary surge/lightning protection equipment must be installed where the weather station is wired directly to the central computer.

INITIAL START-UP

In an ideal situation, a new irrigation system is flushed, adjusted, and activated as it is installed. This requires that a water source be on-line, a portion of the mainline completed, and power available to the field controllers. Such is rarely the case. Frequently, a substantial portion or even all of the irrigation system is in place when water and power become available.

Flushing Pipes

Certainly, every attempt should be made to keep dirt and debris from entering the pipe system during installation. However, every pipe system requires flushing prior to use. Proper system flushing often requires a compromise of one basic design principle under controlled conditions. Flushing effectiveness is directly related to flow velocity. At low velocities the only particles to be removed during flushing are those that are easily suspended in water. Generally, the larger the particle, the higher the velocity required to flush it. Ideally, the best way to flush a 2 in. PVC pipe is to allow it to run full bore for a period of time related to the length of the pipe. The optimum method of flushing a 6 in. PVC pipe is also to allow it to run full bore for a period of time. In reality, larger-diameter pipes are often flushed by discharging water through a smaller-diameter pipe. For example, a 6 in. mainline pipe may be flushed through a 2 in. lateral pipe. If the flow through the 2 in. diameter pipe at open discharge was 150 gpm, it would produce a velocity of 13.5 fps. That flow through the 6 in. mainline pipe produces a velocity of only 1.7 fps. The velocity through the 2 in. pipe is sufficient to flush most debris from the pipe. However, the 1.7 fps is probably too slow to be effective. Debris that remains in the piping system after flushing will eventually work its way down the piping system and become lodged in a smaller-diameter pipe, fitting, valve, or sprinkler head.

Flushing can be facilitated by the inclusion of one or more larger-diameter flush valves in the piping system. A flush valve is installed off one of the larger-sized mainlines and is piped to a location where it can discharge a substantial quantity of water without creating a problem. Preferably, the flush valve is sized to provide sufficient velocity to purge the larger pipes in the system of debris. The flush valve(s) can be used not only during initial start-up but also as part of normal maintenance or to flush debris should a major break occur that allows debris to enter the pipe.

Flushing of the pipe system should start with the mainline distribution pipe, beginning at the water source and progressing out in a logical sequence. Lateral isolation valves feeding greens, tees, and fairways should remain closed during mainline flushing. After a segment of mainline has been flushed, the lateral pipes feeding greens, tees, and fairway and serviced by that mainline can be flushed (Figure 7.57). On loop style piping systems, the lateral piping should be flushed from the high end of the fairway to the low end of the fairway. Preferably, flushing should occur through one or more open pipe ends. Installation of one or more sprinkler heads can wait until after the lateral pipe has been flushed. Some irrigation contractors prefer to leave just the sprinkler head off and flush through the swing joint. There is, however, always the risk of a rock or other debris becoming lodged in the swing joint. Several sprinkler head manufacturers produce valve-in-head sprinklers with removable valves and screens. By removing the internal drive assembly, the valve assembly, and the screen, flushing can be done with the sprinkler head installed. Again, there is a risk of debris becoming lodged in the swing joint or sprinkler head. On block style lateral piping systems, flushing can be done through the lateral end or swing joint. Lateral pipes can also be flushed through quick coupling valves. Here again, there is the risk of stones or other debris becoming lodged in a swing joint or quick coupling valve.

As lateral flushing is completed, the sprinkler heads should be checked for proper setting and height. A final adjustment of the arc should be made in all part-circle sprinklers. Exactly how far the arc of a part-circle sprinkler travels is largely a matter of personal choice.

FIGURE 7.57
Lateral piping being flushed prior to installation of end sprinkler heads.

Preferably, the golf course irrigation tech or an assistant superintendent responsible for irrigation should be an integral part of adjusting all the part-circle sprinkler heads. Having course personnel involved helps to ensure that the heads will be adjusted to everyone's satisfaction.

Typically, the bayonet cavities of many quick coupling valves accumulate debris during installation. Each quick coupling valve should be checked, the cavity cleared, and the valve flushed.

Each combination air release/vacuum release valve should be checked to make sure it is functioning properly. If equipped with a wye strainer, the strainer should be purged of debris.

The initial start-up, flushing, and adjustments provide an opportunity to fine-tune and correct many conditions that would otherwise show up on the punch list.

RECORD DRAWINGS

Long after the irrigation system installation has been completed, the memories have faded, and staff has changed, all that will remain to assist in the maintenance, repair, and troubleshooting of the irrigation system will be the installation documentation provided at the completion of the job. Installation documentation should include more than just Record Drawings.

A minimum of three binders should be assembled, each containing installation instructions, parts breakdowns, and maintenance and troubleshooting manuals for all components of the irrigation system. A page should be included that lists the major supplier of the irrigation equipment and the sources for all the ancillary products. Prefabricated pump stations generally come with their own maintenance manuals.

Photo documentation of major connections and fittings can prove invaluable should excavation or repair be needed in the future. Among the key elements that should be documented and photographed are wet well and intake structure, Z-pipe and connection to pump station, major (large) mainline tee and valve groups, bridge and road crossings, and a typical earth ground grid assembly. Copies of the photographs, as well as copies of the sprinkler head, valve, controller, and other construction details, should be included in the installation manuals.

Data Collection

For years the as-built drawings or Record Drawings were manually drafted from field notes taken during installation. The accuracy of the drawings was directly related to the thoroughness and correctness of the field notes and the quality of the base map. The ability to locate a lost gate valve or quick coupling valve using a drawing depended on precise measurements having been taken from the lost object to two fixed points. With the advent of CAD, computer-generated drawings are replacing hand-drafted ones, but the quality and accuracy of the finished product is still reliant on the thoroughness and correctness of the field notes.

The majority of Record Drawings are now generated utilizing GPS technology. Although GPS is capable of accurate collection of data, the thoroughness and quality of the finished drawing is largely dependent on timely collection of field data. Accuracy is dependent on the data collector being able to precisely follow pipe and wire routes and locate all sprinkler heads, valves, quick coupling valves, fittings, and other irrigation hardware. The data collector should be able to see and follow the trench or vibratory plow lines. Delays in the collection of data allow vibratory plow lines to heal over and trench lines on new construction to disappear, thus hindering the accurate collection of data. The key to obtaining accurate data is to collect the data shortly after installation.

Collecting data by means of GPS does not eliminate the necessity of taking and maintaining accurate field notes. The GPS data collector can only follow a trench or vibratory plow mark. Without accurate field notes, what is installed in that trench or vibratory plow mark is a mystery. Other information that should be recorded in the field notes to assist the GPS data collector includes the following (see Figure 7.58):

- Sprinkler head type and nozzle size
- Field controller station assignment
- Pipe type, size, and pressure rating
- Transition locations where pipe types change
- Wire type and size
- Wire splice locations
- Contents of each valve box
- Fitting configuration and location for every tee and elbow

HOLE #3
AS INSTALLED
MAY 19, XXXX

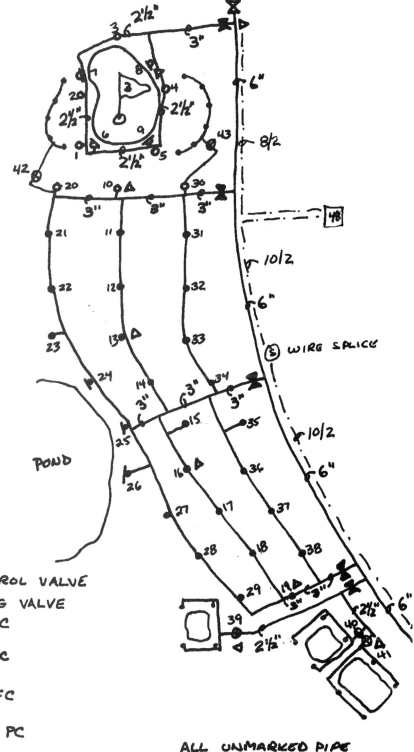

ELECTRIC CONTROL VALVE

QUICK COUPLING VALVE

75' SPACING FC
NOZZLE XX

75' SPACING PC
NOZZLE XX

70' SPACING FC
NOZZLE XX

70' SPACING PC
NOZZLE XX

40' SPACING FC
NOZZLE XX

POND

WIRE SPLICE

ALL UNMARKED PIPE
IS 2" PVC

FIGURE 7.58
Typical field notes.

401

A GPS Record Drawing should be considered a work in progress from the time the first foot of pipe goes in the ground until the irrigation installation is complete and the finished drawing is printed. The amount of time required for the collection of data varies according to the size and complexity of the system. Even a basic double-row 18-hole irrigation system typically takes several days of data collection. Multiple collection trips will be required at varying intervals. After each collection trip, a progress drawing should be produced and forwarded to the irrigation contractor, consultant, and superintendent for review. This allows an opportunity to critique the drawing and to provide the data collector with a list of missed items and corrections. These items can then be corrected on the next trip. Memories fade and details are forgotten if the first review of the collected data occurs after the system is completed. After the final collection trip has been made, a preliminary drawing should be produced with all the collected data. The irrigation contractor, superintendent, and irrigation consultant/designer should all review one common copy. Corrections and omissions should be redlined and comments noted. Required corrections should be made, a revised drawing produced, and a final review made.

Even after the final GPS Record Drawing is approved and printed, the drawing should still be considered a work in progress. One of the benefits of utilizing GPS technology is the ease with which changes or additional information may be incorporated. Tee or green reconstruction, bunker irrigation, and rough irrigation are only a few examples of additions to a system which require modifications to Record Drawings.

Nonirrigation Data

GPS Record Drawings frequently include additional data unrelated to the irrigation system. This data is usually recorded on dedicated layers, allowing it to be printed independently of the irrigation system data. The following are examples of additional data frequently collected and archived with GPS technology:

- Yardage from sprinkler heads and other fixed objects
- New and existing drainage
- Electric services, water lines, telephone cables, gas pipes, and other utilities.
- Tree and shrub inventory, including plant age and condition
- Signage and routing for tournaments

GPS technology can also be utilized for selective control of disease and insect infestation. Problem areas can be defined by GPS and preventative treatment applied to those areas.

Non-GPS Record Drawing

Not all new irrigation systems have Record Drawings that are produced with GPS technology. Budgetary restraints may dictate the Record Drawings be produced the old-fashioned way, hand drawn. The following considerations apply in producing Record Drawings by methods other than GPS:

- A drawing will only be as accurate as the base map on which it is produced.
- Any and all items that require accurate location should be measured and triangulated.
- Items that may require locating in the field, such as isolation valves, quick coupling valves, air release valves, electric control valves, and wire splices, should be measured from two fixed objects and the measurements depicted on the drawings.
- Record Drawings are most frequently produced at a scale of 1 in. = 100 ft. A larger scale, such as 1 in. = 50 ft, may be required to properly portray pipe and sprinkler head detail in such features as greens, tees, and bunkers.

PUNCH LIST

After the system installation is finished, initial start-up has been completed, the Record Drawings and supporting documents and manuals have been submitted, and the system is determined to be complete and fully operational, the irrigation consultant/designer, contractor, golf course superintendent, and other relevant persons should meet and walk through the entire system. A detailed punch list should be developed and distributed to all. All items should be checked against the specifications and construction details to ensure that they were properly installed. The following are specific items that should be checked on the punch list:

Sprinkler Heads
- Installed per details in specifications

- Correct nozzle installed
- Performs properly, no clogged nozzles
- Part-circle heads properly adjusted
- Operates automatically from the intended field controller

Quick Coupling Valves

- Uniform model number throughout the system
- Stabilized on swing joint according to specifications
- Operates properly
- If installed in a valve box, there is clearance between the quick coupling lid and the valve box top. The quick coupling valve lid can open freely and allow the quick coupling key to be inserted and fully opened.

Electric Control Valves

- Correct model number and size per application
- Proper pressure regulation set
- Centered in valve box to facilitate servicing

Isolation Valves

- Centered on valve box and sleeve
- Operation key can easily fit over cross top or operating nut
- Opens fully and closes completely

Air Release/Vacuum Relief Valves

- Perform a simple test to verify valve is operational.
  - Close isolation valve under air release/vacuum valve.
  - Open purge valve on wye strainer and allow water to drain.
  - Close purge valve and open isolation valve. A small quantity of air should discharge from the vent on the top of the air release/vacuum valve, then stop.
- Make sure that street elbows are installed in the vent on the top of air release/vacuum valve and that there is clearance between the street elbows and the valve box lid.
- Check for vent holes in the valve box lid to allow air to freely enter and exit.

Valve Boxes

- Proper model number per application
- Installed at proper height, plumb, and level
- Supported with gravel and/or block as per specifications

Field Satellites

- Correct model number installed per location

- Ground grid connected, tested, and recorded
- Power wire polarity maintained
- Station wiring sequence as desired and consistent throughout
- All stations operate from both the face plate and manual switches
- Communication wire connected and communicating with the central

Central Controller/Computer
- Dedicated electric circuit from building distribution panel
- Ground grid connected, tested, and recorded
- Central communicating with all field controllers
- Programming complete as per specifications
- Remote control operates correctly

The irrigation consultant/designer and/or superintendent should check all punch list items after they have been corrected.

GUARANTEE PERIOD

Typically, golf course irrigation systems are guaranteed for a period of one year from the date of acceptance by the owners. During this period it is usually expected that the golf course personnel will perform the routine maintenance on the system. Such maintenance commonly includes cleaning an occasional clogged nozzle, readjusting a sporadic part-circle sprinkler head, and sometimes cleaning a weeping sprinkler head or electric control valve. If there is an excessive amount of problems of this nature, the contractor should correct them. Trench settling, leaks, and nonfunctioning heads and valves should be the sole responsibility of the contractor. Manufacturers frequently provide extended warranties on various components of an irrigation system. The extended warranties relate only to the irrigation equipment and, unless otherwise defined in the specifications, do not concern the irrigation contractor.

IRRIGATION SYSTEM WINTERIZATION

In colder climates irrigation systems must be winterized to prevent damage from freezing temperatures. The irrigation contractor is typically responsible for winterizing a new system in the fall, following completion, and then activating the system the following spring.

The most common method of winterizing an irrigation system involves purging the water from the system with compressed air. Extreme caution must be exercised during this process. Excessive air pressure can damage many components of an irrigation system, particularly the sprinkler heads. There is a general misconception that high pressure is required to blow out a golf course irrigation system. The volume of air is important, not the pressure.

Diesel-powered turbine type compressors are generally used to blow out systems. Most compressors are rented from a construction equipment supplier. Because these compressors are normally used to power pneumatic construction tools and accessories, the set discharge pressure is usually high, often 150 psi or more. Often the discharge pressure on the compressor can be lowered to an acceptable setting. Another option is to purchase a pneumatic pressure-regulating valve from an industrial supply company. These pressure-regulating valves usually come equipped with a pressure gauge that registers the discharge pressure. The valves are adjustable, allowing for easy control of the air pressure entering the system. The regulating valve on the compressor does not have to be adjusted.

The size of compressor required to blow out a system will vary according to the size of the system and the time allotted for winterization. A 250 to 300 cfm (cubic feet per minute) compressor is probably the minimum size that is suitable. Smaller compressors can be used, but the amount of time required for the winterization process is increased. The air-carrying capacity of the hose is as important as the compressor size. One larger or multiple smaller hoses are usually required to provide adequate airflow. Where multiple hoses are used, a manifold is needed where the hoses connect to the irrigation system. The manifold can also incorporate the pressure-regulating valve.

Opinions vary as to where the pressure-regulating valve should be set. The pressure setting should certainly not exceed 80 psi. The procedure for winterizing a system will also vary from course to course. The following exemplifies a typical procedure:

1. A day or two before winterizing, shut off the main isolation valve(s) at the water source(s) and open any mainline drain valves to predrain the system.

2. Connect the compressor and pressure-regulating valve to the blow-out point. Opinions vary as to where the point of con-

nection should be. A common point of connection is on the "Z" drop pipe off the pump station or water source. A very important factor in determining a point of connection is the temperature of the air produced by the compressor. Air temperatures can be in the 100°F to 150°F range or higher. The connection point should not be directly located on PVC pipe. Extended exposure to the warm temperatures can weaken or damage the PVC pipe. If the connection is to the steel "Z" drop, the air temperature can moderate before prolonged exposure to the PVC pipe.

3. Evacuate the water from sections of the mainline first. The water can be blown through mainline drain valves and quick coupling valves. Progress in a preplanned, logical sequence. Leaving one or more mainline drain valves slightly open during the blow-out procedure acts as a safety against high pressure building up in the system. If too much air is being lost, the valves can always be closed.

4. As sections of the mainline are completed, green, tee, and fairway laterals can be blown out. The sprinkler heads can be activated from the field controller, manually from the pilot valve, or via remote handheld radio. Each head should be activated long enough to evacuate the water from the pipe that services it. Heads should not be operated for extended periods when only air is being discharged because the drive assembly could be damaged. Proper winterization does not require that the sprinkler heads be blown completely dry.

5. Each quick coupling valve should be blown out. On green, tee, and fairway loops, quick coupling valves can be used to evacuate most of the water from the loop before blowing through the sprinkler heads. Special attention should be paid to quick coupling valves installed on dedicated pipe. The only way to evacuate the water from the pipe is through the quick coupling valve. If the quick coupling valve is overlooked, there can be freeze damage to the pipe.

6. High holes on the course are typically winterized first, and low holes last.

7. Drain valves and other points where water can reenter the system should be closed. Take air release valves into the shop, clean all internal parts, and verify correct operation.

Pump Station Winterization

Pump stations should also be winterized. The procedure will vary, depending on the type of pump station and how it is installed. Manufacturers' recommendations for winterization of the pump station and accessories should be followed. Among the procedures to be considered are the following:

- Compressed air can be used to evacuate the water from the pump station piping.
- Drains should be opened on filters, strainers, and centrifugal pumps.
- Small pilot and sensing tubing should be disconnected and blown out. The tubing should remain disconnected to prevent condensation from building up in the tubing and freezing.
- Ball valves should be left half open to prevent water from being trapped between the ball and seals in the valve.
- Suction lines should be disconnected and drained.
- If the pump house is heated, the thermostat should be set to maintain temperatures above freezing.

Backflow protection devices require special attention. Procedures vary, depending on the type of device and installation. Manufacturers' recommendations should always be followed.

Wells, water meters, pressure-reducing valves, check valves, main control valves, and drinking fountains are among the other items that may require special procedures for winterization. Manufacturers' recommendations should always be followed.

SYSTEM ACTIVATION

Certain procedures should also be followed in activating a system. The following are typical:

- The pump station should be reassembled and activated. Motors should be lubricated and the packing checked and adjusted.
- Backflow devices should be reassembled and tested.
- Mainlines should be filled slowly. Many VFD pump stations have an auto-fill feature that controls the rate at which the piping system is filled. Before starting to fill the mainline, lateral isolation valves should be closed, drain valves opened,

and quick coupling keys installed in valves at high points. Mainlines should be filled from the pump station out to the most distant holes. Mainline isolation valves should be opened slowly, allowing water to flow gradually from one section of mainline into the next. As mainlines are filled, the drain valves can be closed and quick coupling keys removed. Mainlines on the lower elevations should be filled first, progressing up to the higher elevations. When all of the mainlines are completely filled, flush valves and drain valves should be opened and the entire mainline distribution system flushed for a period of time.

- Once mainlines have been filled and flushed, lateral and submain pipes to the greens, tees, and fairways can be filled and flushed. For greens and tees, a quick coupling key should be inserted in the piping and the isolation valve slowly opened until the pipes are completely filled and flushed. On loop style fairway piping, a quick coupling key should be inserted at the high end of the fairway. The isolation valve at the low or opposite end of the fairway is then opened slowly, filling and flushing the loop system. With block or herringbone style lateral systems, quick coupling keys should be placed in each lateral and the lateral valve gradually opened, filling and flushing the lateral pipe. The last head in the lateral should then be activated to purge the remaining air from the lateral.

- The wye strainer at each air/vacuum relief valve should be purged and the valve tested to ensure that it is operating properly

- Each field controller should be checked to make sure that all the sprinkler heads and valves it controls operate automatically.

- The central controller should be checked to ensure that it is communicating with every field controller.

When a system is being activated for the first time following completion, trenches should be checked for settling. Sprinkler heads, quick coupling valves, and valve boxes should also be checked to ensure that they are set to the proper height and that no settling has occurred.

IRRIGATION SYSTEM MAINTENANCE

Most components of an irrigation system require a degree of maintenance to ensure that the quality and integrity of the system are maintained. The following are some maintenance procedures recommended for the various components of the system:

- **Piping system**—Flush the distribution system at least once a year. Coatings on exposed steel piping should be maintained. Hangers and clamps on bridge crossings should be inspected annually.

- **Isolation valves**—Packing nuts should be inspected for leakage. The proper procedure should be used to open and close gate valves. The valves should be opened fully and then closed one turn, removing the pressure on the valve stem. Likewise, when a valve is closed, the stem should be backed off, relieving pressure on the stem. All valves should be exercised at least once a year. Valve boxes and access sleeves should be maintained to allow easy operation of the valves. Any accumulated debris should be removed.

- **Drain valves**—Maintain an obstruction-free discharge pipe. Open the drain valve at least once a year.

- **Quick coupling valves**—Trim around quick coupling valves on a regularly scheduled basis to facilitate locating and operation.

- **Air release/vacuum relief valve**—Test periodically for proper operation. Maintain valve box and exhaust ports free of obstructions. Disassemble and clean annually.

- **Valve boxes**—Valve boxes should be trimmed and cleaned on a regularly scheduled basis. Valve boxes should be leveled and reset if settling occurs or if turf builds up around them.

- **Sprinkler heads**—The areas around the heads should be trimmed periodically to prevent roots from penetrating into the internal assemblies. Heads should also be checked for plumb and level and proper grade setting. Low or crooked heads should be excavated and reset. Heads should be inspected on a regularly scheduled basis for clogged nozzles and performance. After the system has been installed for a number of years, the sprinkler heads should be checked for nozzle wear, and worn nozzles should be replaced.

- **Field controllers**—The earth ground grid should be tested on a regularly scheduled basis.

- **Backflow devices**—Backflow preventers with test ports should be inspected and tested according to local and/or state codes. When no applicable code exists, the backflow preventer should be tested at least once a year, preferably at the start of the irrigation season.

- **Record Drawings**—The Record Drawings should be updated whenever alterations or additions are made to the system.

8 Conservation

Water is not a renewable resource. There is a finite quantity on the planet, and the amount has not changed for eons. Approximately 97 percent of the water on earth is salt water. The remaining 3 percent is fresh water, but two-thirds of that is tied up in glaciers and polar ice caps. Only 1 percent of all water on the planet is available to meet the needs of the world's population, including direct human use, manufacturing, mining, agricultural irrigation, and turf irrigation, which includes golf courses.

GOLF COURSE STATISTICS

According to the preliminary results of a survey done by the Golf Course Superintendents Association of America in 2000, the median annual golf course water use in the United States is 13.5 inches over an average area of 77.7 irrigated acres, or 28.5 million gallons. Of course, there are regional differences. For example, average annual water use among respondents in the Southwest was 88 million gallons; for those in the Mid-Atlantic States it was 10 million.

The Irrigation Association, using data from several federal government sources, has computed that, of all the fresh water consumed in the United States for irrigation, agriculture accounts for 79.6 percent, landscape 2.9 percent, and golf course use 1.5 percent.

As the world population grows and puts a continually increasing strain on the fresh water supply, it is ever more important that all water users improve the efficiency of water and power usage. For a golf course (or any other) irrigation system, this requires an efficient system, based on proven design principles, proper installation, and responsible operation and maintenance of the system. Fortunately, the achievement of these goals dovetails neatly with the superintendent's main objective, which is to produce firm and consistent playing conditions throughout the course. Overwatering wastes water and energy. It also produces undesirable playing conditions, poor agronomic conditions for healthy turfgrass, and leads to environmental degradation through runoff and deep percolation.

DESIGN CONSIDERATIONS

Uniform coverage and application and precise control are the cornerstones of efficient design and water management. Informed selection of head/nozzle combinations, spacing, and system pressure will produce uniform application coverage. Application rates should not exceed soil infiltration rates, thus avoiding losses due to runoff.

Correct pressure at the pump station, proper pipe sizing and routing, and pressure regulation at the valve-in-head sprinklers and control valves will ensure optimum operation. In conjunction with well-thought-out pipe design, pressure regulation of the heads means that all similar sprinklers will operate identically throughout the course, regardless of elevation differences. The use of sprinklers designed for lower operating pressures will result in reduced horsepower requirements at the pump station (when properly designed), and therefore lower electric bills. Lower system pressure helps reduce strain on pipe and fittings and can help components last longer. Low-pressure heads also fight the wind better and, in combination with advanced nozzle design, produce good uniformity.

Precise control is based primarily on discrete control of areas with different water use requirements. The smaller the area that can be watered separately from surrounding areas, the more control over the system. The ultimate objective is individual head control throughout the course. However, two (or more) heads can be effectively combined on one control station, provided that the entire area they cover has uniform site conditions and irrigation requirements.

Precise control also requires the proper selection and location of sprinkler heads. Part-circle heads are often needed to achieve precise borders between adjacent areas. The use of shorter radius heads improves irrigation precision and accuracy. For high-wind areas, lower-angle nozzles operated at lower pressures typically provide greater water application uniformity.

Sophistication and flexibility in the control system are important for efficient management. They provide the system operator with the tools to respond accurately to any change in the variables (climatic, agronomic, and golf) that affect the soil/water status. Features like solid-state timing, water budget, cycle and soak, and flow management are definite necessities. Central flow management keeps the entire system operating at the point of optimum pump efficiency, and thus maintains correct system pressure, minimizes cycle time, and reduces electric power consumption. With a properly set up hydraulic tree (a database that assigns every sprinkler head to a pipe), flow management will also limit flow to the designer's intended velocities, ensuring that pressure at the nozzles will be correct. Limiting the flow in all pipes also minimizes the damage caused by water hammer.

Other important control elements include remote control devices like handheld radios and Pocket PCs. They allow for precise local control of irrigation in areas that need special attention. The operator can syringe or irrigate during hours of play without disrupting golfers because of inivdual control and the line of sight to the area being watered. Heads can also be activated to check for proper operation.

For accurate estimates of water use, the control system should include an on-site weather station. The station should be capable of reading and recording temperature, wind speed and direction, relative humidity, solar radiation, and precipitation. The data is fed to the central controller, where software computes on-site evapotranspiration (*ET*) values, which form the basis for establishing station run times. The control system should allow the operator to adjust automatically the calculated run times. On courses with severe variations in climatic conditions, two or more weather stations, each controlling a portion of the system, have sometimes been used.

Accuracy (and therefore efficiency) is further enhanced by the use of sensors throughout the system. Wind sensors in the exposed areas of a course can transmit wind speed data to the central controller. When the speed exceeds a preset value, the central software uses if/then logic to pause irrigation (only in the windy part of the course) until the wind speed diminishes to an acceptable level. At that time, the central resumes irrigation in the affected area. During the entire procedure, irrigation in the rest of the course continues unchanged. Rain gauges are used in a similar fashion. If a preset rainfall threshold is exceeded in a portion of the course, irrigation events in the affected part of the system will be terminated. Temperature sensors can be used to modify *ET* values in microclimates different from that at the weather station location.

Soil moisture sensors have not been used successfully in golf irrigation systems, partly because of the wide range of variables found across most courses. The problem includes difficulty in locating the point where soil moisture should be measured and determining its relationship to the rest of the irrigated area.

To improve irrigation efficiency, a sufficient number of quick coupling valves should be included in the design. Regardless of the sophistication and extent of the automatic irrigation, hand-watering is the only way certain areas can be properly covered. Greens and tees obviously need quick couplers, as do other typical problem areas such as bunker framing mounds, steep slopes, sharp ridges, south-facing (in the Northern Hemisphere) slopes, and known dry spots caused by hydrophobic soils or shallow soil over rock. At greens, quick couplers should be located on both sides of the putting surface to minimize disruption of play, especially in climates where syringing is a frequent requirement.

The pump station should be designed to operate at maximum efficiency. Variable frequency drive for the main pumps should be utilized. Pump and motor selection must properly match system operating parameters. Premium efficiency motors should be considered. Accurate pressure sensors, and flow meters that read flow and total the usage, are other important management tools.

SYSTEM MANAGEMENT AND MAINTENANCE

The irrigation system is the single most important tool available to the superintendent. However, sound design is worth little if it is not complemented by responsible and conscientious scheduling, operation, and maintenance. When properly maintained and managed for high efficiency, the irrigation system will be a major contributor in reaching each of the following objectives:

- Maintaining uniformity of playing conditions
- Minimizing water and electrical consumption
- Minimizing water loss to runoff and deep percolation
- Reducing the potential for turfgrass disease
- Reducing fertilizer and chemical usage
- Minimizing course maintenance requirements

Well-thought-out scheduling, derived from on-site water use measurements, high application uniformity, and precise site adjustment will provide the turfgrass with the precise amount of needed moisture.

System maintenance personnel must check all components on a regular basis. Conditions like nozzle wear, incorrect rotation time, low (or high) pressure, and improper arc adjustment in part-circle heads can seriously degrade the performance of a system. Heads set too low or at an angle distort the pattern and reduce application uniformity. Closed or partially closed mainline isolation valves adversely affect flow and pressure. Dirty or clogged screens in valve-in-head or remote control valve pilot valves will reduce operational efficiency. An established routine for checking the condition and operation of all components, including the pump station, should be performed on a regular basis.

Supplemental hand-watering of small problem areas can be better than operating the sprinkler system longer. It saves water and power, because water is being applied only to the area that needs it. The adjacent areas do not get overwatered, as they would when sprinklers are operated to apply the needed water. The playing conditions also remain more consistent.

In addition to the benefits of intelligent scheduling, water conservation in an existing system can be enhanced by a process known as auditing. An auditor first checks the material and operating condition of the system and identifies components that should be repaired or adjusted to put the system back in design condition. Data is also collected on soil types, root depth, local ET, distribution uniformity, and precipitation rates. The collected data is used to calculate irrigation requirements and run times.

The Irrigation Association and the Golf Course Superintendents Association of America have jointly produced an education and certification program titled "Golf Course Irrigation Auditor." The program covers field audit procedures and then explains how to derive an accurate irrigation schedule based on the audit results. Certification is available upon taking the course and successfully passing an examination. Auditing is further addressed in Chapter 6.

RELATED CULTURAL PRACTICES

Other methods of conserving irrigation water come under the heading of nonirrigation cultural practices. These include regular aerification and thatch control and the use of wetting agents and turf growth regulators.

Compaction reduces infiltration rates and ultimately wastes water and power through poor irrigation efficiency. Rerouting cart traffic on a regular basis can minimize compaction. If the traffic pattern cannot be changed, paving should be considered in areas of high compaction.

To summarize the philosophy of an efficient golf course irrigation system:

1. Apply the water as uniformly as possible.
2. Apply only the amount needed by the turfgrass.

SOURCES

The Irrigation Association. 2000. *Golf Course Legislative Brochure*. Falls Church, VA.

Golf Course Superintendents Association of America. 2000. *1999–2000 performance measurement survey*. Lawrence, KS: GCSAA.

Glossary

24-volt wire   Low-voltage wires from field controller to VIH or remote control valve.

ABS   Acrylonitrile-butadiene-styrene (pipe and fittings).

ACME thread   Straight threads used in PVC fittings to prevent problems associated with over tightening of taper thread fittings.

Adhesion   Attraction of water molecules for solid surfaces (IA).

Air release valve   Device that releases air from pipeline automatically without permitting loss of water (IA).

Air release/vacuum relief valve   Device that releases air from pipeline automatically without permitting loss of water or admits air automatically if internal pressure becomes less than atmospheric (IA).

Ampere   Unit of electrical current produced in a circuit by 1 volt acting through a resistance of 1 ohm.

Notes:

Terms defined in the text are not included in this glossary. Check the index for terms not listed here.

(IA) indicates definitions from the Irrigation Association glossary of irrigation terms.

Angle valve   Valve configured with outlet oriented 90 degrees from inlet.

Atmospheric pressure   Absolute pressure measured at any location—14.7 PSI at sea level.

Audit   Procedure to collect and present information about the uniformity and efficiency of an irrigation system and its operation(IA).

AWG   American Wire Gauge—U.S. numbering system designating conductor size.

AZMET   Arizona Meteorological Network—Weather station network in Arizona.

Backflow preventer   Safety device which prevents the flow of water from the water distribution system back to the water source (IA).

BSP   British standard pipe.

CAD   Computer-aided design.

Capillary water   Water held in the capillary, or small, pores of the soil, usually with soil water pressure (tension) greater than $\frac{1}{3}$ bar. Capillary water can move in any direction.

C Factor   Pipe wall roughness factor for Hazen-Williams formula.

cfm   Cubic feet per minute.

Check valve   Valve that allows flow in one direction only.

CIC Certified Irrigation Contractor—Irrigation Association.

CID Certified Irrigation Designer—Irrigation Association.

CIMIS (California Irrigation Management Information System). Weather station network in California.

Circuit breaker Device designed to open and close a circuit by nonautomatic means and to open the circuit automatically on a predetermined overcurrent without damage to itself when properly applied within its rating.[1]

Cohesion In soils, the attraction of water molecules to one another.

Combination air release valve See *air release/ vacuum relief valve.*

Common wire Low-voltage wire from field controller to all VIHs and/or remote control valves connected in series.

Conduit Tubular raceway for protection of cables or wires.

Constant voltage transformer Power line conditioner with voltage regulation.

Consumptive use Total amount of water taken up by vegetation for transpiration or building of plant tissue, plus the unavoidable evaporation of soil moisture, snow, and intercepted precipitation associated with vegetal growth.

Cross connection Any actual or potential connection or structural arrangement between a private or public potable water system and any other source or system through which it is possible to introduce into any part of the potable system any used water, industrial fluids, gas, or substance other than the intended potable water with which the potable system is supplied.

CSA Canadian Standards Association.

Current The flow of electrons in a conductor (IA).

Decoder A resin-encapsulated printed circuit board that acts as a switching device.

Deleterous materials Excavated material unsuitable for use as bedding or backfill.

Detectable lid A valve box lid equipped with a metal part so it can be located with a metal detector.

Dimension ratio Ratio of the average pipe diameter to the minimum wall thickness.

Distribution uniformity Measure of the uniformity of irrigation water over an area (IA).

Dowser One who seeks to locate groundwater through nonscientific means.

Drawdown The amount, usually expressed in inches or feet, the water level in a pond or well is lowered by an irrigation cycle.

Dredging Removal of accumulated silt and organic debris from pond bottom.

Dual system Irrigation system with parallel but separate piping networks and sources—one for potable water and one for nonpotable water.

Dynamic pressure Pressure when water is moving in a piping network.

Eccentric reducer Reducing fitting with one flat side, used to prevent the entrapment of air in pump suction piping.

Effluent Wastewater.

FCC Federal Communications Commission.

Fertigation Application of liquid fertilizer and other chemicals through an irrigation system.

Field capacity Amount of water remaining in a soil when the downward water flow due to gravity becomes negligible (IA).

Friction loss Pressure loss in pipe, fittings, and valves due to friction of moving water in contact with walls of pipe, fitting, or valve.

Gasket joint Joints in PVC pipe that are sealed by elastomeric gaskets.

Georeferencing The attachment of a coordinate system to a photograph or other data form.

Hertz Cycles per second.

Hydrogeologist Geologist specializing in groundwater.

---

1. Reprinted with permission from NFPA 70-2002, National Electric Code®, Copyright ©2001, National Fire Protection Association, Quincy, MA 02269. This reprinted material is not the complete and official position of the NFPA on the referenced subject, which is represented only by the standard in its entirety.

Hygroscopic water Water that is bound tightly by the soil solids at potential values lower than minus 31 bars.

ID Inside diameter.

Impedance The total opposition offered by an electric current to the flow of an alternating current of a single frequency; it is a combination of resistance and reactance and is measured in ohms.

Impeller Rotating element in a pump that imparts velocity and thus pressure to the water.

Impermeable layer Layer of soil or rock that does not allow water to pass through.

Inductance The capacity of an electric circuit for producing a counter electromotive force when the current changes.

Injection The process of introducing liquid material (fertilizer, chemicals) into irrigation water.

Insulated wire connector Electrical spring connector with insulation.

Insulation displacement connector Water-resistant connector for low-voltage and communication wires requiring no stripping of insulation.

Intake rate Rate at which water infiltrates a bare soil at a specific time during the water application period (IA).

MAD Management allowed depletion (IA).

Megger Test instrument for measuring the resistance of ground electrodes to earth ground. A registered trademark of the James Biddle Company.

Mercoid switch Bourdon tube pressure switch. Mercoid is a registered trademark of Dwyer Instruments, Inc.

Microclimate Atmospheric conditions within or near a crop canopy (IA).

MSDS Material Safety Data Sheet.

Nonpotable water Water not safe for human consumption.

Nonpressurized A pipe or vessel open to atmospheric pressure.

NPSHA Net positive suction head available.

NPSHR Net positive suction head required.

NPT National (American) Standard Pipe-Taper. Designator for common U.S. pipe thread. In common usage, "National Pipe Thread," or "Nominal Pipe Thread." Also comparable to IPT, used to mean the same thing.

OD Outside diameter.

ohm A measure of electrical resistance.

OSHA Occupational Safety and Health Administration.

Permanent wilting point Moisture content, on a dry weight basis, at which plants can no longer obtain sufficient moisture from the soil to satisfy water requirements (IA).

pH Measure of acidity or alkalinity.

PLC Programmable logic controller.

Pore space The portion of soil volume occupied by air or water.

Precipitation rate Rate at which a sprinkler system applies water to a given area.

Pressure transducer Device that converts pressure to an electronic signal.

Punch list List of items remaining to be completed or corrected to complete a project.

Recharge The filling of a pond or reservoir.

Resilient-seated valve A gate valve whose seat is coated with an elastomeric compound.

rpm Revolutions per minute.

Scheduling coefficient A number which relates to uniformity of coverage and which indicates the amount of extra watering time needed to irrigate the driest areas (IA).

SIDR Standard inside dimension ratio (PE pipe only).

Sprinkler profile Graph showing application rate versus distance of throw for a sprinkler head.

Static pressure Pressure in a piping system with no water moving.

Step-down transformer Device that reduces incoming power to a lower output voltage.

Surge arrestor Device that eliminates damage from surges.

Syringing Applying a light amount of water to cool the turf microclimate.

TBE (nipple) Threaded on both ends.

Thatch Build-up of clippings and organic matter on the soil surface.

TOE (nipple)   Threaded on one end (other end is plain).

UF   Underground feeder (NEC wire designation).

UL listed   Listed by Underwriters Laboratories, Inc.

UPS   Uninterruptible power supply.

UV   Ultraviolet.

Vapor pressure   Pressure at which a liquid will vaporize or boil at a given temperature.

VFD   Variable frequency drive.

VIH   Valve-in-head sprinkler.

Voltage   Electromotive force, expressed in volts.

Volute   Curved funnel increasing in area from the pump impeller to the discharge port. As the area of the cross section increases, the volute reduces the velocity of the water and increases the pressure.

Water hammer   Phenomenon that occurs when the velocity of water flowing in pipelines is rapidly changed, usually by a rapid or sudden gate or valve closure, starting or stopping of a pump, or sudden release of air (IA).

Water-holding capacity   The portion of water in a soil that can be readily absorbed by plant roots (IA).

Wetting agent   Chemical used to reduce the surface tension of a liquid, causing it to make better contact with the intended target.

WOG   Water, oil, gas.

Wye strainer   In-line screen device to remove debris from water flowing in a pipe.

Appendix: Tables and Charts

Friction loss charts were derived from the Hazen-Williams formula:

For C = 150:

$$H_f = .0425654\left(\frac{Q^{1.852}}{d^{4.866}}\right)$$

where

H_f = head loss due to friction, in psi per 100 ft
Q = flow in gpm
d = internal diameter of pipe, in inches
.0425654 = constant

Velocity charts were derived from the following formula:

$$V = \frac{.408 \times Q}{d^2}$$

where

V = velocity, in feet per second
.408 = constant
Q = flow, in gpm
d = internal diameter of pipe, in inches

SDR 26 (Class 160) PVC Pipe
Friction Loss in psi per 100 Feet (*C* = 150)
Velocity in Feet per Second

Nominal Size (ID)	1 in. (1.195)		1¼ in. (1.532)		1½ in. (1.754)		2 in. (2.193)		2½ in. (2.655)		3 in. (3.230)		4 in. (4.154)	
Flow—gpm	Vel	Loss	Vel	Loss	Vel	Loss	Vel	Loss	Vel	Loss	Vel	Loss	Vel	Loss
2	0.57	0.06	0.35	0.02	0.27	0.01	0.17	0.00	0.12	0.00	0.08	0.00	0.05	0.00
4	1.14	0.23	0.70	0.07	0.53	0.04	0.34	0.01	0.23	0.00	0.16	0.00	0.09	0.00
6	1.71	0.49	1.04	0.15	0.80	0.08	0.51	0.03	0.35	0.01	0.23	0.00	0.14	0.00
8	2.29	0.84	1.39	0.25	1.06	0.13	0.68	0.04	0.46	0.02	0.31	0.01	0.19	0.00
10	2.86	1.27	1.74	0.38	1.33	0.20	0.85	0.07	0.58	0.03	0.39	0.01	0.24	0.00
12	3.43	1.78	2.09	0.53	1.59	0.28	1.02	0.09	0.69	0.04	0.47	0.01	0.28	0.00
14	4.00	2.37	2.43	0.71	1.86	0.37	1.19	0.12	0.81	0.05	0.55	0.02	0.33	0.01
16	4.57	3.04	2.78	0.91	2.12	0.47	1.36	0.16	0.93	0.06	0.63	0.02	0.38	0.01
18	5.14	3.78	3.13	1.13	2.39	0.58	1.53	0.20	1.04	0.08	0.70	0.03	0.43	0.01
20	5.71	4.59	3.48	1.37	2.65	0.71	1.70	0.24	1.16	0.09	0.78	0.04	0.47	0.01
22	6.29	5.48	3.82	1.64	2.92	0.85	1.87	0.29	1.27	0.11	0.86	0.04	0.52	0.01
24	6.86	6.44	4.17	1.92	3.18	0.99	2.04	0.34	1.39	0.13	0.94	0.05	0.57	0.01
26	7.43	7.47	4.52	2.23	3.45	1.15	2.21	0.39	1.50	0.15	1.02	0.06	0.61	0.02
28	8.00	8.56	4.87	2.56	3.71	1.32	2.38	0.45	1.62	0.18	1.09	0.07	0.66	0.02
30	8.57	9.73	5.22	2.91	3.98	1.50	2.55	0.51	1.74	0.20	1.17	0.08	0.71	0.02
35	10.00	12.95	6.08	3.87	4.64	2.00	2.97	0.67	2.03	0.27	1.37	0.10	0.83	0.03
40	11.43	16.58	6.95	4.95	5.30	2.56	3.39	0.86	2.32	0.34	1.56	0.13	0.95	0.04
45			7.82	6.16	5.97	3.19	3.82	1.07	2.60	0.42	1.76	0.16	1.06	0.05
50			8.69	7.48	6.63	3.87	4.24	1.31	2.89	0.52	1.96	0.20	1.18	0.06
55			9.56	8.93	7.29	4.62	4.67	1.56	3.18	0.61	2.15	0.24	1.30	0.07
60			10.43	10.49	7.96	5.43	5.09	1.83	3.47	0.72	2.35	0.28	1.42	0.08
65			11.30	12.16	8.62	6.30	5.51	2.12	3.76	0.84	2.54	0.32	1.54	0.09
70					9.28	7.22	5.94	2.44	4.05	0.96	2.74	0.37	1.66	0.11
75					9.95	8.21	6.36	2.77	4.34	1.09	2.93	0.42	1.77	0.12
80					10.61	9.25	6.79	3.12	4.63	1.23	3.13	0.47	1.89	0.14
85					11.27	10.35	7.21	3.49	4.92	1.38	3.32	0.53	2.01	0.16
90							7.64	3.88	5.21	1.53	3.52	0.59	2.13	0.17

Use caution at velocities below **bold line.**

SDR 26 (Class 160) PVC Pipe
Friction Loss in psi per 100 Feet ($C = 150$)
Velocity in Feet per Second

Nominal Size (ID)	3 in. (3.230)		4 in. (4.154)		6 in. (6.115)		8 in. (7.961)		10 in. (9.924)		12 in. (11.77)	
Flow—gpm	Vel	Loss	Vel	Loss	Vel	Loss	Vel	Loss	Vel	Loss	Vel	Loss
100	3.91	0.72	2.36	0.21	1.09	0.03	0.64	0.01	0.41	0.00	0.29	0.00
110	4.30	0.85	2.60	0.25	1.20	0.04	0.71	0.01	0.46	0.00	0.32	0.00
120	4.69	1.00	2.84	0.30	1.31	0.04	0.77	0.01	0.50	0.00	0.35	0.00
130	5.08	1.16	3.07	0.34	1.42	0.05	0.84	0.01	0.54	0.00	0.38	0.00
140	5.47	1.34	3.31	0.39	1.53	0.06	0.90	0.02	0.58	0.01	0.41	0.00
150	5.87	1.52	3.55	0.45	1.64	0.07	0.97	0.02	0.62	0.01	0.44	0.00
160	6.26	1.71	3.78	0.50	1.75	0.08	1.03	0.02	0.66	0.01	0.47	0.00
170	6.65	1.91	4.02	0.56	1.85	0.09	1.09	0.02	0.70	0.01	0.50	0.00
180	7.04	2.13	4.26	0.63	1.96	0.10	1.16	0.03	0.75	0.01	0.53	0.00
190	7.43	2.35	4.49	0.69	2.07	0.11	1.22	0.03	0.79	0.01	0.56	0.00
200	7.82	2.59	4.73	0.76	2.18	0.12	1.29	0.03	0.83	0.01	0.59	0.00
225	8.80	3.22	5.32	0.95	2.45	0.14	1.45	0.04	0.93	0.01	0.66	0.01
250	9.78	3.91	5.91	1.15	2.73	0.18	1.61	0.05	1.04	0.02	0.74	0.01
275	10.75	4.67	6.50	1.37	3.00	0.21	1.77	0.06	1.14	0.02	0.81	0.01
300	11.73	5.48	7.09	1.61	3.27	0.25	1.93	0.07	1.24	0.02	0.88	0.01
325	12.71	6.36	7.68	1.87	3.55	0.28	2.09	0.08	1.35	0.03	0.96	0.01
350	13.69	7.29	8.28	2.14	3.82	0.33	2.25	0.09	1.45	0.03	1.03	0.01
375		8.29	8.87	2.44	4.09	0.37	2.41	0.10	1.55	0.04	1.10	0.02
400		9.34	9.46	2.75	4.36	0.42	2.58	0.12	1.66	0.04	1.18	0.02
425		10.45	10.05	3.07	4.64	0.47	2.74	0.13	1.76	0.04	1.25	0.02
450		11.62	10.64	3.41	4.91	0.52	2.90	0.14	1.86	0.05	1.33	0.02
475		12.84	11.23	3.77	5.18	0.58	3.06	0.16	1.97	0.05	1.40	0.02
500			11.82	4.15	5.46	0.63	3.22	0.18	2.07	0.06	1.47	0.03
550			13.00	4.95	6.00	0.75	3.54	0.21	2.28	0.07	1.62	0.03
600			14.19	5.82	6.55	0.89	3.86	0.25	2.49	0.08	1.77	0.04
650			15.37	6.75	7.09	1.03	4.18	0.28	2.69	0.10	1.91	0.04
700			16.55	7.74	7.64	1.18	4.51	0.33	2.90	0.11	2.06	0.05
750			17.73	8.79	8.18	1.34	4.83	0.37	3.11	0.13	2.21	0.06

Use caution at velocities below **bold line.**

SDR 26 (Class 160) PVC Pipe | DR 25 C905 PVC Pipe (CI OD)
Friction Loss in psi per 100 Feet (C = 150)
Velocity in Feet per Second

Nominal Size (ID)	8 in. (7.961)		10 in. (9.924)		12 in. (11.77)		14 in. (14.076)		16 in. (16.008)		18 in. (17.94)	
Flow—gpm	Vel	Loss	Vel	Loss	Vel	Loss	Vel	Loss	Vel	Loss	Vel	Loss
800	5.15	0.42	3.31	0.14	2.36	0.06	1.65	0.03	1.27	0.01	1.01	0.01
850	5.47	0.47	3.52	0.16	2.50	0.07	1.75	0.03	1.35	0.02	1.08	0.01
900	5.79	0.52	3.73	0.18	2.65	0.08	1.85	0.03	1.43	0.02	1.14	0.01
950	6.12	0.58	3.94	0.20	2.80	0.09	1.96	0.04	1.51	0.02	1.20	0.01
1000	6.44	0.63	4.14	0.22	2.95	0.09	2.06	0.04	1.59	0.02	1.27	0.01
1050	6.76	0.69	4.35	0.24	3.09	0.10	2.16	0.04	1.67	0.02	1.33	0.02
1100	7.08	0.75	4.56	0.26	3.24	0.11	2.27	0.05	1.75	0.03	1.39	0.02
1150	7.40	0.82	4.76	0.28	3.39	0.12	2.37	0.05	1.83	0.03	1.46	0.02
1200	7.73	0.89	4.97	0.30	3.53	0.13	2.47	0.06	1.91	0.03	1.52	0.02
1250	8.05	0.96	5.18	0.33	3.68	0.14	2.57	0.06	1.99	0.03	1.58	0.02
1300	8.37	1.03	5.39	0.35	3.83	0.15	2.68	0.06	2.07	0.03	1.65	0.02
1350	8.69	1.10	5.59	0.38	3.98	0.16	2.78	0.07	2.15	0.04	1.71	0.03
1400	9.01	1.18	5.80	0.40	4.12	0.18	2.88	0.07	2.23	0.04	1.77	0.03
1450	9.33	1.26	6.01	0.43	4.27	0.19	2.99	0.08	2.31	0.04	1.84	0.03
1500	9.66	1.34	6.21	0.46	4.42	0.20	3.09	0.08	2.39	0.04	1.90	0.03
1550			6.42	0.49	4.56	0.21	3.19	0.09	2.47	0.05	1.96	0.03
1600			6.63	0.52	4.71	0.23	3.29	0.09	2.55	0.05	2.03	0.03
1650			6.84	0.55	4.86	0.24	3.40	0.10	2.63	0.05	2.09	0.04
1700			7.04	0.58	5.01	0.25	3.50	0.11	2.71	0.06	2.16	0.04
1750			7.25	0.61	5.15	0.27	3.60	0.11	2.79	0.06	2.22	0.04
1800			7.46	0.64	5.30	0.28	3.71	0.12	2.87	0.06	2.28	0.04
1900			7.87	0.71	5.60	0.31	3.91	0.13	3.03	0.07	2.41	0.05
2000			8.29	0.78	5.89	0.34	4.12	0.14	3.18	0.08	2.54	0.05
2100			8.70	0.85	6.18	0.37	4.32	0.16	3.34	0.08	2.66	0.06
2200			9.11	0.93	6.48	0.41	4.53	0.17	3.50	0.09	2.79	0.06
2300			9.53	1.01	6.77	0.44	4.74	0.18	3.66	0.10	2.92	0.07
2400			9.94	1.09	7.07	0.48	4.94	0.20	3.82	0.11	3.04	0.07
2500			10.36	1.18	7.36	0.51	5.15	0.22	3.98	0.12	3.17	0.08

Use caution at velocities below **bold line.**

SDR 21 (Class 200) PVC Pipe
Friction Loss in psi per 100 Feet ($C = 150$)
Velocity in Feet per Second

Nominal Size (ID)	1 in. (1.189)		1¼ in. (1.502)		1½ in. (1.720)		2 in. (2.149)		2½ in. (2.601)		3 in. (3.166)		4 in. (4.072)	
Flow—gpm	Vel	Loss	Vel	Loss	Vel	Loss	Vel	Loss	Vel	Loss	Vel	Loss	Vel	Loss
2	0.58	0.07	0.36	0.02	0.28	0.01	0.18	0.00	0.12	0.00	0.08		0.05	
4	1.15	0.24	0.72	0.08	0.55	0.04	0.35	0.01	0.24	0.01	0.16		0.10	
6	1.73	0.51	1.09	0.16	0.83	0.08	0.53	0.03	0.36	0.01	0.24	0.00	0.15	
8	2.31	0.86	1.45	0.28	1.10	0.14	0.71	0.05	0.48	0.02	0.33	0.01	0.20	
10	2.89	1.30	1.81	0.42	1.38	0.22	0.88	0.07	0.60	0.03	0.41	0.01	0.25	
12	3.46	1.83	2.17	0.59	1.65	0.30	1.06	0.10	0.72	0.04	0.49	0.02	0.30	0.00
14	4.04	2.43	2.53	0.78	1.93	0.40	1.24	0.14	0.84	0.05	0.57	0.02	0.34	0.01
16	4.62	3.11	2.89	1.00	2.21	0.52	1.41	0.17	0.96	0.07	0.65	0.03	0.39	0.01
18	5.19	3.87	3.26	1.24	2.48	0.64	1.59	0.22	1.09	0.09	0.73	0.03	0.44	0.01
20	5.77	4.71	3.62	1.51	2.76	0.78	1.77	0.26	1.21	0.10	0.81	0.04	0.49	0.01
22	6.35	5.62	3.98	1.80	3.03	0.93	1.94	0.32	1.33	0.12	0.90	0.05	0.54	0.01
24	6.93	6.60	4.34	2.12	3.31	1.09	2.12	0.37	1.45	0.15	0.98	0.06	0.59	0.02
26	7.50	7.65	4.70	2.45	3.59	1.27	2.30	0.43	1.57	0.17	1.06	0.07	0.64	0.02
28	8.08	8.78	5.06	2.82	3.86	1.46	2.47	0.49	1.69	0.19	1.14	0.07	0.69	0.02
30	8.66	9.97	5.43	3.20	4.14	1.65	2.65	0.56	1.81	0.22	1.22	0.08	0.74	0.02
35	10.10	13.27	6.33	4.26	4.83	2.20	3.09	0.74	2.11	0.29	1.42	0.11	0.86	0.03
40	11.54	16.99	7.23	5.45	5.52	2.82	3.53	0.95	2.41	0.38	1.63	0.14	0.98	0.04
45			8.14	6.78	6.21	3.51	3.98	1.19	2.71	0.47	1.83	0.18	1.11	0.05
50			9.04	8.24	6.90	4.26	4.42	1.44	3.02	0.57	2.04	0.22	1.23	0.06
55			9.95	9.83	7.59	5.08	4.86	1.72	3.32	0.68	2.24	0.26	1.35	0.08
60			10.85	11.55	8.27	5.97	5.30	2.02	3.62	0.80	2.44	0.31	1.48	0.09
65			11.76	13.39	8.96	6.93	5.74	2.34	3.92	0.93	2.65	0.36	1.60	0.10
70					9.65	7.95	6.18	2.69	4.22	1.06	2.85	0.41	1.72	0.12
75					10.34	9.03	6.63	3.05	4.52	1.21	3.05	0.46	1.85	0.14
80					11.03	10.17	7.07	3.44	4.82	1.36	3.26	0.52	1.97	0.15
85					11.72	11.38	7.51	3.85	5.13	1.52	3.46	0.58	2.09	0.17
90							7.95	4.28	5.43	1.69	3.66	0.65	2.21	0.19

Use caution at velocities below **bold line.**

SDR 21 (Class 200) PVC Pipe
Friction Loss in psi per 100 Feet (C = 150)
Velocity in Feet per Second

Nominal Size (ID)	3 in. (3.166)		4 in. (4.072)		6 in. (5.993)		8 in. (7.805)		10 in. (9.728)		12 in. (11.538)	
Flow—gpm	Vel	Loss	Vel	Loss	Vel	Loss	Vel	Loss	Vel	Loss	Vel	Loss
100	4.07	0.79	2.46	0.23	1.14	0.04	0.67	0.01	0.43	0.00	0.31	0.00
110	4.48	0.94	2.71	0.28	1.25	0.04	0.74	0.01	0.47	0.00	0.34	0.00
120	4.88	1.11	2.95	0.33	1.36	0.05	0.80	0.01	0.52	0.00	0.37	0.00
130	5.29	1.28	3.20	0.38	1.48	0.06	0.87	0.02	0.56	0.01	0.40	0.00
140	5.70	1.47	3.44	0.43	1.59	0.07	0.94	0.02	0.60	0.01	0.43	0.00
150	6.11	1.67	3.69	0.49	1.70	0.08	1.00	0.02	0.65	0.01	0.46	0.00
160	6.51	1.89	3.94	0.55	1.82	0.08	1.07	0.02	0.69	0.01	0.49	0.00
170	6.92	2.11	4.18	0.62	1.93	0.09	1.14	0.03	0.73	0.01	0.52	0.00
180	7.33	2.35	4.43	0.69	2.04	0.11	1.21	0.03	0.78	0.01	0.55	0.00
190	7.73	2.59	4.68	0.76	2.16	0.12	1.27	0.03	0.82	0.01	0.58	0.00
200	8.14	2.85	4.92	0.84	2.27	0.13	1.34	0.04	0.86	0.01	0.61	0.01
225	9.16	3.55	5.54	1.04	2.56	0.16	1.51	0.04	0.97	0.02	0.69	0.01
250	10.18	4.31	6.15	1.27	2.84	0.19	1.67	0.05	1.08	0.02	0.77	0.01
275	11.19	5.14	6.77	1.51	3.12	0.23	1.84	0.06	1.19	0.02	0.84	0.01
300	12.21	6.04	7.38	1.78	3.41	0.27	2.01	0.07	1.29	0.03	0.92	0.01
325	13.23	7.01	8.00	2.06	3.69	0.31	2.18	0.09	1.40	0.03	1.00	0.01
350	14.25	8.04	8.61	2.36	3.98	0.36	2.34	0.10	1.51	0.03	1.07	0.01
375		9.13	9.23	2.68	4.26	0.41	2.51	0.11	1.62	0.04	1.15	0.02
400		10.29	9.84	3.03	4.54	0.46	2.68	0.13	1.72	0.04	1.23	0.02
425		11.52	10.46	3.38	4.83	0.52	2.85	0.14	1.83	0.05	1.30	0.02
450		12.80	11.07	3.76	5.11	0.57	3.01	0.16	1.94	0.05	1.38	0.02
475		14.15	11.69	4.16	5.40	0.63	3.18	0.18	2.05	0.06	1.46	0.03
500			12.30	4.57	5.68	0.70	3.35	0.19	2.16	0.07	1.53	0.03
550			13.53	5.46	6.25	0.83	3.68	0.23	2.37	0.08	1.69	0.03
600			14.76	6.41	6.82	0.98	4.02	0.27	2.59	0.09	1.84	0.04
650			15.99	7.43	7.38	1.13	4.35	0.31	2.80	0.11	1.99	0.05
700			17.22	8.53	7.95	1.30	4.69	0.36	3.02	0.12	2.15	0.05
750			18.45	9.69	8.52	1.48	5.02	0.41	3.23	0.14	2.30	0.06

Use caution at velocities below **bold line.**

SDR 21 (Class 200) PVC Pipe | DR 18 C905 PVC Pipe (CI OD)
Friction Loss in psi per 100 Feet (C = 150)
Velocity in Feet per Second

Nominal Size (ID)	8 in. (7.805)		10 in. (9.728)		12 in. (11.538)		14 in. (13.600)		16 in. (15.466)		18 in. (17.334)	
Flow—gpm	Vel	Loss	Vel	Loss	Vel	Loss	Vel	Loss	Vel	Loss	Vel	Loss
800	5.36	0.46	3.45	0.16	2.45	0.07	1.76	0.03	1.36	0.02	1.09	0.01
850	5.69	0.52	3.66	0.18	2.61	0.08	1.88	0.03	1.45	0.02	1.15	0.01
900	6.03	0.57	3.88	0.20	2.76	0.09	1.99	0.04	1.54	0.02	1.22	0.01
950	6.36	0.63	4.10	0.22	2.91	0.09	2.10	0.04	1.62	0.02	1.29	0.01
1000	6.70	0.70	4.31	0.24	3.06	0.10	2.21	0.05	1.71	0.02	1.36	0.01
1050	7.03	0.76	4.53	0.26	3.22	0.11	2.32	0.05	1.79	0.03	1.43	0.02
1100	7.37	0.83	4.74	0.28	3.37	0.12	2.43	0.06	1.88	0.03	1.49	0.02
1150	7.70	0.90	<u>4.96</u>	0.31	3.52	0.13	2.54	0.06	1.96	0.03	1.56	0.02
1200	8.04	0.98	5.17	0.33	3.68	0.15	2.65	0.07	2.05	0.04	1.63	0.02
1250	8.37	1.05	5.39	0.36	3.83	0.16	2.76	0.07	2.13	0.04	1.70	0.02
1300	8.71	1.13	5.60	0.39	3.98	0.17	2.87	0.08	2.22	0.04	1.77	0.02
1350	9.04	1.21	5.82	0.42	4.14	0.18	2.98	0.08	2.30	0.04	1.83	0.03
1400	9.38	1.30	6.04	0.44	4.29	0.19	3.09	0.09	2.39	0.05	1.90	0.03
1450	9.71	1.39	6.25	0.47	4.44	0.21	3.20	0.09	2.47	0.05	1.97	0.03
1500	10.05	1.48	6.47	0.51	4.60	0.22	3.31	0.10	2.56	0.05	2.04	0.03
1550			6.68	0.54	4.75	0.23	3.42	0.11	2.64	0.06	2.10	0.03
1600			6.90	0.57	<u>4.90</u>	0.25	3.53	0.11	2.73	0.06	2.17	0.03
1650			7.11	0.60	5.06	0.26	3.64	0.12	2.81	0.06	2.24	0.04
1700			7.33	0.64	5.21	0.28	3.75	0.12	2.90	0.07	2.31	0.04
1750			7.54	0.67	5.36	0.29	3.86	0.13	2.98	0.07	2.38	0.04
1800			7.76	0.71	5.52	0.31	3.97	0.14	3.07	0.07	2.44	0.04
1900			8.19	0.78	5.82	0.34	4.19	0.15	3.24	0.08	2.58	0.05
2000			8.62	0.86	6.13	0.38	4.41	0.17	3.41	0.09	2.72	0.05
2100			9.05	0.94	6.44	0.41	4.63	0.18	3.58	0.10	2.85	0.06
2200			9.48	1.03	6.74	0.45	<u>4.85</u>	0.20	3.75	0.11	2.99	0.06
2300			9.92	1.11	7.05	0.49	5.07	0.22	3.92	0.12	3.12	0.07
2400			10.35	1.21	7.36	0.53	5.29	0.24	4.09	0.13	3.26	0.07
2500			10.78	1.30	7.66	0.57	5.51	0.25	4.26	0.14	3.39	0.08

Use caution at velocities below **bold line.**

SDR 13.5 (Class 315) PVC Pipe
Friction Loss in psi per 100 Feet (*C* = 150)
Velocity in Feet per Second

Nominal Size (ID)	1 in. (1.121)		1¼ in. (1.414)		1½ in. (1.618)		2 in. (2.023)		2½ in. (2.449)		3 in. (2.982)		4 in. (3.834)	
Flow—gpm	Vel	Loss	Vel	Loss	Vel	Loss	Vel	Loss	Vel	Loss	Vel	Loss	Vel	Loss
2	0.65	0.09	0.41	0.03	0.31	0.01	0.20	0.00	0.14	0.00	0.09	0.00	0.06	0.00
4	1.30	0.32	0.82	0.10	0.62	0.05	0.40	0.02	0.27	0.01	0.18	0.00	0.11	0.00
6	1.95	0.67	1.22	0.22	0.94	0.11	0.60	0.04	0.41	0.02	0.28	0.01	0.17	0.00
8	2.60	1.15	1.63	0.37	1.25	0.19	0.80	0.06	0.54	0.03	0.37	0.01	0.22	0.00
10	3.25	1.74	2.04	0.56	1.56	0.29	1.00	0.10	0.68	0.04	0.46	0.01	0.28	0.00
12	3.90	2.43	2.45	0.79	1.87	0.41	1.20	0.14	0.82	0.05	0.55	0.02	0.33	0.01
14	<u>4.55</u>	3.24	2.86	1.05	2.18	0.54	1.40	0.18	0.95	0.07	0.64	0.03	0.39	0.01
16	5.19	4.15	3.26	1.34	2.49	0.70	1.60	0.23	1.09	0.09	0.73	0.04	0.44	0.01
18	5.84	5.16	3.67	1.67	2.81	0.86	1.79	0.29	1.22	0.12	0.83	0.04	0.50	0.01
20	6.49	6.27	4.08	2.03	3.12	1.05	1.99	0.35	1.36	0.14	0.92	0.05	0.56	0.02
22	7.14	7.48	4.49	2.42	3.43	1.25	2.19	0.42	1.50	0.17	1.01	0.06	0.61	0.02
24	7.79	8.79	<u>4.90</u>	2.84	3.74	1.47	2.39	0.50	1.63	0.20	1.10	0.08	0.67	0.02
26	8.44	10.19	5.31	3.29	4.05	1.71	2.59	0.58	1.77	0.23	1.19	0.09	0.72	0.03
28	9.09	11.69	5.71	3.78	4.36	1.96	2.79	0.66	1.90	0.26	1.28	0.10	0.78	0.03
30	9.74	13.28	6.12	4.29	<u>4.68</u>	2.23	2.99	0.75	2.04	0.30	1.38	0.11	0.83	0.03
35	11.36	17.67	7.14	5.71	5.45	2.96	3.49	1.00	2.38	0.39	1.61	0.15	0.97	0.04
40	12.99	22.63	8.16	7.31	6.23	3.79	3.99	1.28	2.72	0.50	1.84	0.19	1.11	0.06
45			9.18	9.09	7.01	4.72	4.49	1.59	3.06	0.63	2.06	0.24	1.25	0.07
50			10.20	11.05	7.79	5.74	<u>4.98</u>	1.93	3.40	0.76	2.29	0.29	1.39	0.09
55			11.22	13.19	8.57	6.84	5.48	2.31	3.74	0.91	2.52	0.35	1.53	0.10
60			12.24	15.49	9.35	8.04	5.98	2.71	4.08	1.07	2.75	0.41	1.67	0.12
65			13.26	17.97	10.13	9.33	6.48	3.14	4.42	1.24	2.98	0.48	1.80	0.14
70					10.91	10.70	6.98	3.61	<u>4.76</u>	1.42	3.21	0.55	1.94	0.16
75					11.69	12.16	7.48	4.10	5.10	1.62	3.44	0.62	2.08	0.18
80					12.47	13.70	7.98	4.62	5.44	1.82	3.67	0.70	2.22	0.21
85					13.25	15.33	8.47	5.17	5.78	2.04	3.90	0.78	2.36	0.23
90							8.97	5.75	6.12	2.27	4.13	0.87	2.50	0.26

Use caution at velocities below **bold line.**

Schedule 40 PVC Pipe
Friction Loss in psi per 100 Feet ($C = 150$)
Velocity in Feet per Second

Nominal Size (ID)	1 in. (1.049)		1¼ in. (1.380)		1½ in. (1.610)		2 in. (2.067)		2½ in. (2.469)		3 in. (3.068)		4 in. (4.026)	
Flow—gpm	Vel	Loss	Vel	Loss	Vel	Loss	Vel	Loss	Vel	Loss	Vel	Loss	Vel	Loss
2	0.74	0.12	0.43	0.03	0.31	0.02	0.19	0.00	0.13	0.00	0.09	0.00	0.05	0.00
4	1.48	0.44	0.86	0.12	0.63	0.05	0.38	0.02	0.27	0.01	0.17	0.00	0.10	0.00
6	2.22	0.93	1.29	0.25	0.94	0.12	0.57	0.03	0.40	0.01	0.26	0.01	0.15	0.00
8	2.97	1.59	1.71	0.42	1.26	0.20	0.76	0.06	0.54	0.02	0.35	0.01	0.20	0.00
10	3.71	2.40	2.14	0.63	1.57	0.30	0.95	0.09	0.67	0.04	0.43	0.01	0.25	0.00
12	4.45	3.36	2.57	0.89	1.89	0.42	1.15	0.12	0.80	0.05	0.52	0.02	0.30	0.00
14	5.19	4.47	3.00	1.18	2.20	0.56	1.34	0.16	0.94	0.07	0.61	0.02	0.35	0.01
16	5.93	5.73	3.43	1.51	2.52	0.71	1.53	0.21	1.07	0.09	0.69	0.03	0.40	0.01
18	6.67	7.12	3.86	1.88	2.83	0.89	1.72	0.26	1.20	0.11	0.78	0.04	0.45	0.01
20	7.42	8.66	4.28	2.28	3.15	1.08	1.91	0.32	1.34	0.13	0.87	0.05	0.50	0.01
22	8.16	10.33	4.71	2.72	3.46	1.28	2.10	0.38	1.47	0.16	0.95	0.06	0.55	0.01
24	8.90	12.14	5.14	3.20	3.78	1.51	2.29	0.45	1.61	0.19	1.04	0.07	0.60	0.02
26	9.64	14.08	5.57	3.71	4.09	1.75	2.48	0.52	1.74	0.22	1.13	0.08	0.65	0.02
28	10.38	16.15	6.00	4.25	4.41	2.01	2.67	0.60	1.87	0.25	1.21	0.09	0.70	0.02
30	11.12	18.35	6.43	4.83	4.72	2.28	2.86	0.68	2.01	0.28	1.30	0.10	0.76	0.03
35	12.98	24.41	7.50	6.43	5.51	3.04	3.34	0.90	2.34	0.38	1.52	0.13	0.88	0.04
40	14.83	31.26	8.57	8.23	6.30	3.89	3.82	1.15	2.68	0.49	1.73	0.17	1.01	0.04
45			9.64	10.24	7.08	4.83	4.30	1.43	3.01	0.60	1.95	0.21	1.13	0.06
50			10.71	12.44	7.87	5.88	4.77	1.74	3.35	0.73	2.17	0.25	1.26	0.07
55			11.78	14.84	8.66	7.01	5.25	2.08	3.68	0.88	2.38	0.30	1.38	0.08
60			12.85	17.44	9.44	8.24	5.73	2.44	4.02	1.03	2.60	0.36	1.51	0.10
65			13.93	20.23	10.23	9.55	6.21	2.83	4.35	1.19	2.82	0.41	1.64	0.11
70					11.02	10.96	6.68	3.25	4.69	1.37	3.03	0.48	1.76	0.13
75					11.81	12.45	7.16	3.69	5.02	1.55	3.25	0.54	1.89	0.14
80					12.59	14.03	7.64	4.16	5.35	1.75	3.47	0.61	2.01	0.16
85					13.38	15.70	8.12	4.65	5.69	1.96	3.68	0.68	2.14	0.18
90							8.59	5.17	6.02	2.18	3.90	0.76	2.27	0.20

Use caution at velocities below **bold line.**

SDR 11 HDPE Pipe
Friction Loss in psi per 100 Feet ($C = 150$)
Velocity in Feet per Second

Nominal Size (ID)	3 in. (2.864)		4 in. (3.682)		6 in. (5.421)		8 in. (7.057)		10 in. (8.796)		12 in. (10.432)	
Flow—gpm	Vel	Loss	Vel	Loss	Vel	Loss	Vel	Loss	Vel	Loss	Vel	Loss
100	<u>4.97</u>	0.79	3.01	0.23	1.39	0.04	0.82	0.01	0.53	0.00	0.37	0.00
110	5.47	0.94	3.31	0.28	1.53	0.04	0.90	0.01	0.58	0.00	0.41	0.00
120	5.97	1.11	3.61	0.33	1.67	0.05	0.98	0.01	0.63	0.00	0.45	0.00
130	6.47	1.28	3.91	0.38	1.80	0.06	1.07	0.02	0.69	0.01	0.49	0.00
140	6.96	1.47	4.21	0.43	1.94	0.07	1.15	0.02	0.74	0.01	0.52	0.00
150	7.46	1.67	4.51	0.49	2.08	0.08	1.23	0.02	0.79	0.01	0.56	0.00
160	7.96	1.89	<u>4.82</u>	0.55	2.22	0.08	1.31	0.02	0.84	0.01	0.60	0.00
170	8.46	2.11	5.12	0.62	2.36	0.09	1.39	0.03	0.90	0.01	0.64	0.00
180	8.95	2.35	5.42	0.69	2.50	0.11	1.47	0.03	0.95	0.01	0.67	0.00
190	9.45	2.59	5.72	0.76	2.64	0.12	1.56	0.03	1.00	0.01	0.71	0.00
200	9.95	2.85	6.02	0.84	2.78	0.13	1.64	0.04	1.05	0.01	0.75	0.01
225	11.19	3.55	6.77	1.04	3.12	0.16	1.84	0.04	1.19	0.02	0.84	0.01
250	12.44	4.31	7.52	1.27	3.47	0.19	2.05	0.05	1.32	0.02	0.94	0.01
275	13.68	5.14	8.28	1.51	3.82	0.23	2.25	0.06	1.45	0.02	1.03	0.01
300	14.92	6.04	9.03	1.78	4.17	0.27	2.46	0.07	1.58	0.03	1.12	0.01
325	16.17	7.01	9.78	2.06	4.51	0.31	2.66	0.09	1.71	0.03	1.22	0.01
350	17.41	8.04	10.53	2.36	<u>4.86</u>	0.36	2.87	0.10	1.85	0.03	1.31	0.01
375		9.13	11.29	2.68	5.21	0.41	3.07	0.11	1.98	0.04	1.41	0.02
400		10.29	12.04	3.03	5.55	0.46	3.28	0.13	2.11	0.04	1.50	0.02
425		11.52	12.79	3.38	5.90	0.52	3.48	0.14	2.24	0.05	1.59	0.02
450		12.80	13.54	3.76	6.25	0.57	3.69	0.16	2.37	0.05	1.69	0.02
475		14.15	14.30	4.16	6.59	0.63	3.89	0.18	2.50	0.06	1.78	0.03
500			15.05	4.57	6.94	0.70	4.10	0.19	2.64	0.07	1.87	0.03
550			16.55	5.46	7.64	0.83	4.51	0.23	2.90	0.08	2.06	0.03
600			18.06	6.41	8.33	0.98	<u>4.92</u>	0.27	3.16	0.09	2.25	0.04
650			19.56	7.43	9.02	1.13	5.33	0.31	3.43	0.11	2.44	0.05
700			21.07	8.53	9.72	1.30	5.73	0.36	3.69	0.12	2.62	0.05
750			22.57	9.69	10.41	1.48	6.14	0.41	3.96	0.14	2.81	0.06

Use caution at velocities below **bold line.**

SDR 11 HDPE Pipe
Friction Loss in psi per 100 Feet ($C = 150$)
Velocity in Feet per Second

Nominal Size (ID)	8 in. (7.057)		10 in. (8.796)		12 in. (10.432)		14 in. (11.454)		16 in. (13.090)		18 in. (14.728)	
Flow—gpm	Vel	Loss	Vel	Loss	Vel	Loss	Vel	Loss	Vel	Loss	Vel	Loss
800	6.55	0.75	4.22	0.26	3.00	0.11	2.49	0.07	1.90	0.04	1.50	0.02
850	6.96	0.84	4.48	0.29	3.19	0.13	2.64	0.08	2.02	0.04	1.60	0.02
900	7.37	0.94	<u>4.75</u>	0.32	3.37	0.14	2.80	0.09	2.14	0.05	1.69	0.03
950	7.78	1.03	5.01	0.35	3.56	0.15	2.95	0.10	2.26	0.05	1.79	0.03
1000	8.19	1.14	5.27	0.39	3.75	0.17	3.11	0.11	2.38	0.06	1.88	0.03
1050	8.60	1.24	5.54	0.43	3.94	0.19	3.27	0.12	2.50	0.06	1.97	0.03
1100	9.01	1.36	5.80	0.46	4.12	0.20	3.42	0.13	2.62	0.07	2.07	0.04
1150	9.42	1.47	6.06	0.50	4.31	0.22	3.58	0.14	2.74	0.07	2.16	0.04
1200	9.83	1.59	6.33	0.55	4.50	0.24	3.73	0.15	2.86	0.08	2.26	0.04
1250	10.24	1.72	6.59	0.59	4.69	0.26	3.89	0.16	2.98	0.09	2.35	0.05
1300	10.65	1.85	6.86	0.63	<u>4.87</u>	0.28	4.04	0.18	3.10	0.09	2.45	0.05
1350	11.06	1.98	7.12	0.68	5.06	0.30	4.20	0.19	3.21	0.10	2.54	0.06
1400	11.47	2.12	7.38	0.73	5.25	0.32	4.35	0.20	3.33	0.10	2.63	0.06
1450	11.88	2.26	7.65	0.77	5.44	0.34	4.51	0.21	3.45	0.11	2.73	0.06
1500	12.29	2.41	7.91	0.82	5.62	0.36	4.66	0.23	3.57	0.12	2.82	0.07
1550			8.17	0.88	5.81	0.38	4.82	0.24	3.69	0.13	2.92	0.07
1600			8.44	0.93	6.00	0.41	<u>4.98</u>	0.26	3.81	0.13	3.01	0.08
1650			8.70	0.98	6.19	0.43	5.13	0.27	3.93	0.14	3.10	0.08
1700			8.96	1.04	6.37	0.45	5.29	0.29	4.05	0.15	3.20	0.08
1750			9.23	1.10	6.56	0.48	5.44	0.30	4.17	0.16	3.29	0.09
1800			9.49	1.16	6.75	0.50	5.60	0.32	4.29	0.17	3.39	0.09
1900			10.02	1.28	7.12	0.56	5.91	0.35	4.52	0.18	3.57	0.10
2000					7.50	0.61	6.22	0.39	<u>4.76</u>	0.20	3.76	0.11
2100					7.87	0.67	6.53	0.43	5.00	0.22	3.95	0.13
2200					8.25	0.73	6.84	0.46	5.24	0.24	4.14	0.14
2300					8.62	0.79	7.15	0.50	5.48	0.26	4.33	0.15
2400					9.00	0.86	7.46	0.54	5.71	0.28	4.51	0.16
2500					9.37	0.93	7.77	0.59	5.95	0.31	4.70	0.17

Use caution at velocities below **bold line.**

SDR 9 HDPE Pipe
Friction Loss in psi per 100 Feet (*C* = 150)
Velocity in Feet per Second

Nominal Size (ID)	3 in. (2.722)		4 in. (3.500)		6 in. (5.153)		8 in. (6.709)		10 in. (8.362)		12 in. (9.916)	
Flow—gpm	Vel	Loss	Vel	Loss	Vel	Loss	Vel	Loss	Vel	Loss	Vel	Loss
100	5.51	1.65	3.33	0.48	1.54	0.07	0.91	0.02	0.58	0.01	0.41	0.00
110	6.06	1.97	3.66	0.58	1.69	0.09	1.00	0.02	0.64	0.01	0.46	0.00
120	6.61	2.31	4.00	0.68	1.84	0.10	1.09	0.03	0.70	0.01	0.50	0.00
130	7.16	2.68	4.33	0.79	2.00	0.12	1.18	0.03	0.76	0.01	0.54	0.00
140	7.71	3.07	<u>4.66</u>	0.90	2.15	0.14	1.27	0.04	0.82	0.01	0.58	0.01
150	8.26	3.49	5.00	1.03	2.30	0.16	1.36	0.04	0.88	0.01	0.62	0.01
160	8.81	3.93	5.33	1.16	2.46	0.18	1.45	0.05	0.93	0.02	0.66	0.01
170	9.36	4.40	5.66	1.30	2.61	0.20	1.54	0.05	0.99	0.02	0.71	0.01
180	9.91	4.89	6.00	1.44	2.77	0.22	1.63	0.06	1.05	0.02	0.75	0.01
190	10.46	5.41	6.33	1.59	2.92	0.24	1.72	0.07	1.11	0.02	0.79	0.01
200	11.01	5.95	6.66	1.75	3.07	0.27	1.81	0.07	1.17	0.03	0.83	0.01
225	12.39	7.40	7.49	2.18	3.46	0.33	2.04	0.09	1.31	0.03	0.93	0.01
250	13.77	8.99	8.33	2.65	3.84	0.40	2.27	0.11	1.46	0.04	1.04	0.02
275	15.14	10.73	9.16	3.16	4.23	0.48	2.49	0.13	1.60	0.05	1.14	0.02
300	16.52	12.60	9.99	3.71	4.61	0.56	2.72	0.16	1.75	0.05	1.24	0.02
325	17.90	14.62	10.82	4.30	<u>4.99</u>	0.65	2.95	0.18	1.90	0.06	1.35	0.03
350	19.27	16.77	11.66	4.93	5.38	0.75	3.17	0.21	2.04	0.07	1.45	0.03
375		19.05	12.49	5.61	5.76	0.85	3.40	0.24	2.19	0.08	1.56	0.04
400		21.47	13.32	6.32	6.15	0.96	3.63	0.27	2.33	0.09	1.66	0.04
425		24.03	14.16	7.07	6.53	1.08	3.85	0.30	2.48	0.10	1.76	0.04
450		26.71	14.99	7.86	6.91	1.20	4.08	0.33	2.63	0.11	1.87	0.05
475		29.52	15.82	8.69	7.30	1.32	4.31	0.37	2.77	0.13	1.97	0.05
500			16.65	9.55	7.68	1.45	4.53	0.40	2.92	0.14	2.07	0.06
550			18.32	11.40	8.45	1.74	<u>4.99</u>	0.48	3.21	0.16	2.28	0.07
600			19.98	13.39	9.22	2.04	5.44	0.56	3.50	0.19	2.49	0.08
650			21.65	15.53	9.99	2.36	5.89	0.65	3.79	0.22	2.70	0.10
700			23.31	17.81	10.76	2.71	6.35	0.75	4.08	0.26	2.90	0.11
750			24.98	20.24	11.52	3.08	6.80	0.85	4.38	0.29	3.11	0.13

Use caution at velocities below **bold line.**

SDR 9 HDPE Pipe
Friction Loss in psi per 100 Feet (*C* = 150)
Velocity in Feet per Second

Nominal Size (ID)	8 in. (6.709)		10 in. (8.362)		12 in. (9.916)		14 in. (10.888)		16 in. (12.444)		18 in. (14.000)	
Flow—gpm	Vel	Loss	Vel	Loss	Vel	Loss	Vel	Loss	Vel	Loss	Vel	Loss
800	7.25	0.96	4.67	0.33	3.32	0.14	2.75	0.09	2.11	0.05	1.67	0.03
850	7.70	1.08	4.96	0.37	3.53	0.16	2.93	0.10	2.24	0.05	1.77	0.03
900	8.16	1.20	5.25	0.41	3.73	0.18	3.10	0.11	2.37	0.06	1.87	0.03
950	8.61	1.32	5.54	0.45	3.94	0.20	3.27	0.13	2.50	0.07	1.98	0.04
1000	9.06	1.45	5.83	0.50	4.15	0.22	3.44	0.14	2.63	0.07	2.08	0.04
1050	9.52	1.59	6.13	0.54	4.36	0.24	3.61	0.15	2.77	0.08	2.19	0.04
1100	9.97	1.73	6.42	0.59	4.56	0.26	3.79	0.16	2.90	0.09	2.29	0.05
1150	10.42	1.88	6.71	0.64	4.77	0.28	3.96	0.18	3.03	0.09	2.39	0.05
1200	10.88	2.04	7.00	0.70	4.98	0.30	4.13	0.19	3.16	0.10	2.50	0.06
1250	11.33	2.20	7.29	0.75	5.19	0.33	4.30	0.21	3.29	0.11	2.60	0.06
1300	11.78	2.36	7.59	0.81	5.39	0.35	4.47	0.22	3.43	0.12	2.71	0.07
1350	12.24	2.53	7.88	0.87	5.60	0.38	4.65	0.24	3.56	0.13	2.81	0.07
1400	12.69	2.71	8.17	0.93	5.81	0.41	4.82	0.26	3.69	0.13	2.91	0.08
1450	13.14	2.89	8.46	0.99	6.02	0.43	4.99	0.27	3.82	0.14	3.02	0.08
1500	13.60	3.08	8.75	1.05	6.22	0.46	5.16	0.29	3.95	0.15	3.12	0.09
1550			9.04	1.12	6.43	0.49	5.33	0.31	4.08	0.16	3.23	0.09
1600			9.34	1.19	6.64	0.52	5.51	0.33	4.22	0.17	3.33	0.10
1650			9.63	1.26	6.85	0.55	5.68	0.35	4.35	0.18	3.43	0.10
1700			9.92	1.33	7.05	0.58	5.85	0.37	4.48	0.19	3.54	0.11
1750			10.21	1.40	7.26	0.61	6.02	0.39	4.61	0.20	3.64	0.11
1800			10.50	1.48	7.47	0.65	6.19	0.41	4.74	0.21	3.75	0.12
1900			11.09	1.63	7.88	0.71	6.54	0.45	5.01	0.24	3.96	0.13
2000					8.30	0.78	6.88	0.50	5.27	0.26	4.16	0.15
2100					8.71	0.86	7.23	0.54	5.53	0.28	4.37	0.16
2200					9.13	0.94	7.57	0.59	5.80	0.31	4.58	0.17
2300					9.54	1.02	7.92	0.64	6.06	0.34	4.79	0.19
2400					9.96	1.10	8.26	0.70	6.32	0.36	5.00	0.21
2500					10.37	1.19	8.60	0.75	6.59	0.39	5.20	0.22

Use caution at velocities below **bold line.**

Conductor Properties for Insulated Annealed Copper Direct Current Resistance—Ohms per 1000 Feet

Copper AWG	Temperature (°F)				Cross-Sectional Area (Circular Mils)
	167	149	77	68	
	Temperature (°C)				
	75	65	25	20	
18 Solid	7.77	7.519	6.515	6.390	1,620
18 Stranded	7.95	7.693	6.666	6.538	1,620
16 Solid	4.89	4.732	4.100	4.021	2,580
16 Stranded	4.99	4.829	4.184	4.104	2,580
14 Solid	3.07	2.971	2.574	2.525	4,110
14 Stranded	3.14	3.039	2.633	2.582	4,110
12 Solid	1.93	1.868	1.618	1.587	6,530
12 Stranded	1.98	1.916	1.660	1.628	6,530
10 Solid	1.21	1.171	1.015	0.995	10,380
10 Stranded	1.24	1.200	1.040	1.020	10,380
8 Solid	0.764	0.739	0.641	0.628	16,510
8 Stranded	0.778	0.753	0.652	0.640	16,510
6 Stranded	0.491	0.475	0.412	0.404	26,240
4 Stranded	0.308	0.298	0.258	0.253	41,740
2 Stranded	0.194	0.188	0.163	0.160	66,360
1/0 Stranded	0.122	0.118	0.102	0.100	105,600
2/0 Stranded	0.0967	0.094	0.081	0.080	133,100

Note: System designer must use resistance values that correlate to temperatures and applications for each specific project.

Source: 2002 edition of National Electric Code (NFPA 70), Chapter 9, Table 8. Reprinted with permission from NFPA 70-2002, National Electric Code®, Copyright ©2001, National Fire Protection Association, Quincy, MA 02269. This reprinted material is not the complete and offical position of the NFPA on the referenced subject, which is represented only by the standard in its entirety.

National Electrical Code ® and NEC® are registered trademarks of the National Fire Protection Association, Quincy, MA.

Estimated Average Monthly Effective Precipitation (Inches) as Related to Mean Monthly Precipitation and Average Monthly Crop Evapotranspiration

Monthly Mean Precipitation (Inches)	Average Monthly Crop Evapotranspiration, ET_C										
	0.00	1.00	2.00	3.00	4.00	5.00	6.00	7.00	8.00	9.00	10.00
0.0	0.00	0.00	0.00	0.00	0.00	0.00	0.00	0.00	0.00	0.00	0.00
0.5	0.28	0.30	0.32	0.34	0.36	0.38	0.40	0.42	0.45	0.47	0.50
1.0	0.59	0.63	0.66	0.70	0.74	0.78	0.83	0.88	0.93	0.98	1.00
1.5	0.87	0.93	0.98	1.03	1.09	1.16	1.22	1.29	1.37	1.45	1.50
2.0	1.14	1.21	1.27	1.35	1.43	1.51	1.59	1.69	1.78	1.88	1.99
2.5	1.39	1.47	1.56	1.65	1.74	1.84	1.95	2.06	2.18	2.30	2.44
3.0		1.73	1.83	1.94	2.05	2.17	2.29	2.42	2.56	2.71	2.86
3.5		1.98	2.10	2.22	2.35	2.48	2.62	2.77	2.93	3.10	3.28
4.0		2.23	2.36	2.49	2.63	2.79	2.95	3.12	3.29	3.48	3.68
4.5			2.61	2.76	2.92	3.09	3.26	3.45	3.65	3.85	4.08
5.0			2.86	3.02	3.20	3.28	3.57	3.78	4.00	4.23	4.47
5.5			3.10	3.28	3.47	3.67	3.88	4.10	4.34	4.59	4.85
6.0				3.53	3.74	3.95	4.18	4.42	4.67	4.94	5.23
6.5				3.79	4.00	4.23	4.48	4.73	5.00	5.29	5.60
7.0				4.03	4.26	4.51	4.77	5.04	5.33	5.64	5.96
7.5					4.52	4.78	5.06	5.35	5.65	5.98	6.32
8.0					4.78	5.05	5.34	5.65	5.97	6.32	6.68

Note: Based on 3 in. soil water storage. For other values of soil water storage, multiply by the following factors:

Storage (inches)	0.75	1.0	1.5	2.0	2.5	3.0	4.0	5.0	6.0	7.0
Factor	0.72	0.77	0.86	0.93	0.97	1.00	1.02	1.04	1.06	1.07

Source: National Engineering Handbook, Part 623, Chapter 2, Table 2-43 (NRCS-USDA).

Pressure Loss in Valves and Fittings*

Nominal Pipe Size (Inches)	Angle Globe Valve (Feet)	Gate Valve (Feet)	Run of Straight Tee (Feet)	Branch of Straight Tee (Feet)	90° Elbow (Feet)	45° Elbow (Feet)	Reducing Bushing One Size (Feet)	Reducing Bushing Two Sizes (Feet)
Equivalent Footage of SDR-26 PVC Pipe								
1½″	31.8	2.8	4.4	13.2	6.5	3.6	2.8	12.7
2″	36.3	3.2	5.1	14.9	7.5	4.1	5.1	12.9
2½″	46.5	4.2	6.4	19.3	9.7	5.1	2.7	19.3
3″	52.7	4.7	7.2	21.7	10.9	5.8	5.7	19.3
4″	62.8	5.7	8.6	25.9	13.0	7.0	10.4	41.9
6″	84.3	7.6	11.6	34.8	17.5	9.3	36.9	141.7
8″	106.0	9.5	14.6	43.9	22.0	11.7	21.8	192.7
10″	128.4	11.6	17.7	53.1	26.6	14.2	16.1	108.2
12″	150.1	13.4	20.7	62.1	31.1	16.5	10.8	71.0
Equivalent Footage of SDR-21 PVC Pipe								
1½″	28.9	2.5	4.0	12.0	5.9	3.3	2.5	11.5
2″	32.8	2.9	4.6	13.5	6.8	3.7	4.6	11.7
2½″	42.0	3.8	5.8	17.5	8.7	4.7	2.4	17.5
3″	47.5	4.2	6.5	19.6	9.9	5.2	5.1	17.4
4″	56.5	5.1	7.8	23.3	11.7	6.3	9.4	37.7
6″	76.2	6.9	10.5	31.5	15.8	8.4	33.4	128.1
8″	95.4	8.5	13.2	39.5	19.8	10.5	19.6	173.4
10″	115.0	10.4	15.9	47.6	23.8	12.7	14.4	97.0
12″	134.2	12.0	18.5	55.5	27.8	14.8	9.7	63.5
Equivalent Footage of Schedule 40 Galvanized Steel Pipe								
1½″	10.5	0.9	2.7	8.1	4.0	2.2	1.7	7.8
2″	13.5	1.2	3.5	10.3	5.2	2.8	3.5	8.9
2½″	16.1	1.5	4.1	12.4	6.2	3.3	1.7	12.4
3″	20.0	1.8	5.1	15.3	7.7	4.1	4.0	13.6
4″	26.3	2.4	6.7	20.1	10.1	5.4	8.1	32.5
6″	39.6	3.6	10.1	30.3	15.2	8.1	32.1	123.2
8″	52.1	4.6	13.3	39.9	20.0	10.6	19.8	175.2
10″	65.4	5.9	16.7	50.1	25.1	13.4	15.2	102.1
12″	77.9	7.0	19.9	59.7	29.9	15.9	10.4	68.3

*Note: This chart is to be used with pressure loss tables included in this book.

Standards

Note: Most Standard designations have two parts separated by a hyphen (C509-94). Before the hyphen is the Standard Number, and after it is a two-digit number indicating the year the standard was approved or last revised (some standard organizations give a year and a month). Contact the organization which developed a given standard to determine the current version.

1. Pipe, Fittings

A. PVC

Construction Procedures for Buried Plastic Pipe **ASTM F 1668**

Design, Installation and Performance of Underground, Thermoplastic Irrigation Pipelines **ASAE S376.2**

Elastomeric Seals (Gaskets) for Joining Plastic Pipe **ASTM F 477**

Joint Restraint Products for Use with PVC Pipe **ASTM F 1764**

Joints for IPS PVC Pipe Using Solvent Cement **ASTM D 2672**

Joints for Plastic Pressure Pipes Using Flexible Elastomeric Seals **ASTM D3139**

Primers for Use in Solvent-Cement Joints with PVC Pipe and Fittings **ASTM F656**

PVC Plastic Pipe, Schedules 40, 80, 120 **ASTM D1785**

PVC Plastic Pipe Fittings, Schedule 40 **ASTM D2466**

PVC Pressure Fittings for Water **AWWA C907**

PVC Pressure-Rated Pipe (SDR Series) **ASTM D2241**

Recommended Practice For the Installation of PVC Pressure Pipe **UNI-B-3**

Recommended Standard Specification for Thermoplastic Pipe Joints, Pressure and Non-Pressure Applications **UNI-B-1**

Safe Handling of Solvent Cements, Primers and Cleaners Used for Joining Thermoplastic Pipe and Fittings **ASTM F402**

Selection, Design, and Installation of Thermoplastic Water Pressure Piping Systems **ASTM F645**

Short Term Hydraulic Failure Pressure of Plastic Pipe and Fittings **ASTM D1599**

Socket Type PVC Plastic Fittings, Schedule 80 **ASTM D2467**

Solvent Cements for PVC Plastic Piping Systems **ASTM D2564**

Solvent Cement Joints with PVC Pipe and Fittings **ASTM2855**

Taper Pipe Threads (60°) for Thermoplastic Pipe and Fittings **ASTM F1498**

Terminology Relating to Plastic Piping Systems **ASTM F412**

Thermoplastic Pressure Piping Compendium **CSA B137 Series**

Thermoplastic Expansion and Contraction in Plastics Piping Systems **PPI TR-18**

Threaded PVC Plastic Pipe Fittings, Schedule 80 **ASTM D2464**

Time-To-Failure of Plastic Pipe Under Constant Internal Pressure **ASTM D1598**

Underground Installation of PVC Pressure Pipe and Fittings for Water **AWWA C605**

Underground Installation of Thermoplastic Pressure Piping **ASTM D2774**

B. PE

Butt Heat Fusion PE Plastic Fittings for PE Plastic Pipe **ASTM D3261**

Canadian Electric Code **CSA C22.1**

PE Plastic Pipe (DR-PR) Based on Controlled Outside Diameter **ASTM D3035**

PE Pressure Pipe and Fittings 4″ Through 63″ for Water Distribution **AWWA C906**

PE Plastic Pipe (SDR-PR) Based on Outside Diameter **ASTM F714**

2. Miscellaneous

Air Release, Air/Vacuum and Combination Air Valves for Waterworks Service **AWWA C512**

Backflow Prevention **CSA B64 Series**

Disinfecting Water Mains **AWWA C651**

Design and Fabrication of Pressure Vessels **ASME Boiler and Pressure Vessel Code, Section VIII, Division 1**

Drinking Water System Components—Health Effects **NSF No. 61**

Double Check Valve Backflow-Prevention Assembly **AWWA C510**

Guideline for Earth Grounding Electronic Equipment in Irrigation Systems **ASIC Guideline 100-2002**

National Electric Code (NEC) **NFPA 70**

National Standard Plumbing Code **PHCC**

Pipe Threads—General Purpose **ANSI/ASME B1.20.1**

Plastic Piping System Components and Related Materials **NSF No.14**

Polyethylene Encasement for Ductile Iron Pipe Systems **AWWA C105**

Precast Reinforced Concrete Manholes **ASTM C478**

Procedure for Sprinkler Testing and Performance Reporting **ASAE S398.1**

PVC Pressure Pipe, 4″ Through 12″ **AWWA C900**

PVC Water Transmission Pipe, 14″ Through 36″ **AWWA C905**

Reduced Pressure Principle Backflow Preventers **ASSE 1013**

Reduced-Pressure Principle Backflow Prevention Assembly **AWWA C511**

Resilient Connectors Between Reinforced Concrete Manhole Structures, Pipes and Laterals **ASTM C923**

Resilient-Seated Gate valves for Water Supply **AWWA C509**

Safety Devices for chemigation **ASAE EP409.1**

Schedule 40 and 80 Rigid PVC Conduit **UL 651**

Steel Welded Wire Reinforcement, Plain, for Concrete **ASTM A185**

Welded and Seamless Wrought Steel Pipe **ASME B36.10M**

Index